'so excellent a...'

The Charity School in the Royal Liberty
and
the Education of the English Lower Orders

Charity School at Romford, 1800

1710-1834

Giles Drew

Published by New Generation Publishing in 2023

Copyright © Giles Drew 2023

First Edition

The author asserts the moral right under the Copyright, Designs and Patents Act 1988 to be identified as the author of this work.

All Rights reserved. No part of this publication may be reproduced, stored in a retrieval system or transmitted, in any form or by any means without the prior consent of the author, nor be otherwise circulated in any form of binding or cover other than that which it is published and without a similar condition being imposed on the subsequent purchaser.

ISBN
    Paperback -978-1-80369-884-7
    Hardback – 978-1-80369-885-4
    eBook –   978-1-80369-886-1

www.newgeneration-publishing.com

New Generation Publishing

www.gilesdrewauthor.com
giles@gilesdrewauthor.com

*Queen Anne, reigned 1702-1714, from a painting
by Sir Godfrey Kneller*

'For as much as the pious Instruction and Education of Children is the Surest Way of Preserving and Propagating Knowledge and Practice of True Religion, it hath been very acceptable for Us to hear that for the attaining these Good Ends many Charity Schools are now created throughout this Kingdom by the Liberal Contributions of our Good Subjects; We do therefore earnestly recommend it to you, by all Proper Ways to encourage and promote **so excellent a Work**, and to Countenance and assist the Persons principally concerned in it as they shall always be sure of our Protection and Favour.'

Extract from a letter which Queen Anne wrote to the Archbishops of Canterbury and York, 20 August 1711.

*

The 'Parliamentary Committee on **the Education of the Lower Orders**' was set up in 1816 with Henry Brougham MP as Chairman.

For my wife, Jane,
whose marriage vows made no commitment to an unacceptable burden of proof-reading
and
whose half a century of support for my commitment to public education
might reasonably have been expected to have ended with our retirement.

Contents

		Page
Illustrations, with sources and acknowledgements		viii
Preface, with Introduction		xi
Preliminary notes		xvi
Chapter 1	Place and time: the Royal Liberty of Havering 1710	1
Chapter 2	Religious belief and the 18th century Charity School Movement 1699 - 1711	18
Chapter 3	'So Excellent a Work': the founding of the Charity School at Romford 1710 - 1718	34
Chapter 4	A new treasurer and the first substantial legacy 1718 - 1722	53
Chapter 5	Building the School House 1723 - 1729	70
Chapter 6	The Mary Hide Charity and the death of James Hotchkis 1731 - 1734	87
Chapter 7	Joseph Bosworth, the unintentional benefactor 1735 - 1739	100
Chapter 8	Financial malaise and the Archbishop's intervention 1734 - 1753	111

Chapter 9	Stagnation 1739 - 1760	120
Chapter 10	Reform 1761 - 1762	128
Chapter 11	The school and society during the early years of George III 1762 - 1771	139
Chapter 12	The early years of Thomas Graves, treasurer 1771 - 1786	157
Chapter 13	Absent clergy in a time of political revolution 1786 - 1797	169
Chapter 14	Sectarian Strife 1796 - 1807	180
Chapter 15	A story of two brewers and two schoolmasters 1807 - 1817	197
Chapter 16	The National Society, expansion and reform 1811 - 1817	215
Chapter 17	A Brougham to sweep old charities clean 1818 - 1821	227
Chapter 18	Sarah Bourne and Oswald Adams 1814 - 1823	240
Chapter 19	The scandal of the Methodist banker 1823 - 1826	251
Chapter 20	A Case in Chancery 1826 - 1832	268
Chapter 21	Acrimony and a finely balanced decision 1833	285

Chapter 22	A debate in Parliament and a new Scheme to regulate the Charity 1833	295
Chapter 23	'An honour and ornament to the Liberty' 1833 - 1834	306
Epilogue	Christmas 1834	324

Appendices

Appendix I	Treasurers of the Charity School, Chaplains of Romford, Vicars of Hornchurch, and Masters and Mistresses of the Charity School	328
Appendix II	Early supporters of the School and the first trustees	331
Appendix III	Pre-decimal coinage and the changing value of money	336
Appendix IV	Ready Reckoner: the changing value of money, 1700 - 1840	340
Appendix V	Index to places of interest marked on Chapman and Andre's Map of Essex, 1777	343

The Royal Liberty of Havering and part of Chafford Hundred: Chapman and Andre's *Map of Essex* of 1777 — 345

Part of the 1805 Ordinance Survey map of Essex which includes the Royal Liberty (Havering Libraries-Local Studies) — 350

Acknowledgements	351
Bibliography	354
Notes	359
Index	374

Illustrations

with sources and acknowledgements

The images on the cover and on page 99 are of the statues carved by Thomas Staynor in 1732 of the boy and girl in their charity school clothes. They originally stood above the entrance to the Charity School at Romford and are now preserved at St Edward's C of E Primary School, Romford. (Author's photographs)

Page	Illustration
i	Charity School at Romford, 1800 Lithograph from a copy of an original drawing in the Guildhall Library by Bennett Bamford (Havering Libraries-Local Studies)
iii	Queen Anne From a painting by Sir Godfrey Kneller (National Portrait Gallery) (Wikimedia Commons)
5	'The Horned Church' at Hornchurch, from an engraving of 1828. (Havering Libraries-Local Studies)
16	The entry in the Vestry Book for St Edward's Chapel, Romford, recording the meeting of 5 September 1710. (Reproduced by courtesy of the Essex Record Office)
37	The first entry in the Trustees first volume of *Accounts*. (Reproduced by courtesy of the Essex Record Office)
61	The copy in the Charity School trustees' *Accounts* of the extract from Mary Hide's will recording her bequest. (Reproduced by courtesy of the Essex Record Office)
67	Rev'd Dr William Derham DD, FRS, Rector of Upminster. (Havering Libraries-Local Studies)
69	Dagnams, engraved by T. Hawksworth from a sketch by J. Greig. (Havering Libraries-Local Studies)

79	The Court House in Romford Market Place, with the gaol on the lower right-hand side, in 1800. (Havering Libraries-Local Studies)
83	The minutes of the meeting of the Trustees on 27 July 1728 formalising the purchase of the land on which the school would be erected. (Reproduced by courtesy of the Essex Record Office)
86	Entries in the *Accounts* relating to the building of the School House. (Reproduced by courtesy of the Essex Record Office)
89	The School House and the Master's House in 1905, unchanged from when they were built in 1728 and 1734. (Havering Libraries-Local Studies)
117	Dr Thomas Herring, Archbishop of Canterbury from 1747 to 1757, a print from an engraving and etching by Bernard Baron from a painting by William Hogarth,1750. Copyright, the Trustees of the British Museum. (Wikimedia Commons)
153	Engraving of Hare Hall, the Seat of John Arnold Wallinger Esqr. (Havering Libraries-Local Studies)
156	Rumford and the part of the Royal Liberty to the north of the town showing Rumford Market Place with the Charity School and turnpike, from Chapman and Andre's 1777 map of Essex. (Havering Libraries-Local Studies)
182	Dr Andrew Bell in later life, from a mezzotint by C. Turner, 1825, after W. Owen. (Wikimedia Commons)
186	Two images from *Méthode britannique d'éducation lancastérienne* (1816), a French edition of Joseph Lancaster's *Improvements in Education (1803).* (Wikimedia Commons)
192	Title page of the Trustees' third volume of *Accounts and Transactions,* 'Commencing June 14th 1803'. (Reproduced by courtesy of the Essex Record Office)
197	Samuel Whitbread MP, stipple engraving by W. Holl, c. 1815. (Wellcome images) (Wikimedia Commons)

209	Romford Chapel looking south, from an engraving published in 1809. (Havering Libraries-Local Studies)
211	'W. Adams Junr Script': the entry in *The Romford Ringers' Book* recording the peal rung on 10 February 1811. (Reproduced by courtesy of the Essex Record Office)
214	Edward Ind, taken from a portrait, now lost. (Havering Libraries-Local Studies)
237	Henry Brougham MP in 1820, from an image published in the *London Magazine* after a portrait by J R West. (A portrait from the Welsh Portrait Collection at the National Library of Wales.) (Wikimedia Commons)
241	Joseph Lancaster, from a portrait by John Hazlitt (died 1837), given to the National Portrait Gallery in 1860. (Wikimedia Commons)
258	Sir Richard Digby Neave of Dagnams, from a portrait by John Constable. (Digital image courtesy of the Paul Mellon Centre Photograph Archive [PA-F06823-0035])
270	An extract from Hornchurch Parish Map, 1812, showing the position of the Charity School in the Market Place and Joseph Bosworth's property in Hornchurch Lane. (Havering Libraries-Local Studies)
284	The record in *The Romford Ringers Book* of the muffled peal rung for William Adams on Thursday 21 August 1828. (Reproduced by courtesy of the Essex Record Office)
293	Rev'd Dr George Croly, from a photograph. (Wikimedia Commons)
326	An engraving of Romford Market Place in 1831. (Havering Libraries-Local Studies)
345	An extract from Chapman and Andre's 1777 map of Essex showing the Royal Liberty of Havering and part of Chafford Hundred. (Internet)
346	Part of the 1805 Ordinance Survey map of Essex which includes the Royal Liberty. (Havering Libraries-Local Studies)

Preface, with Introduction

How many parents, anxious to secure a place for their child at the school of their choice, understand how the system which educates 93% of us has evolved? Contrary to other countries, why is it that a quarter of state-funded primary schools and 6% of secondary schools in England are still controlled by the protestant church? What causes the annual miracle of an intense (if temporary) religious conversion amongst so many of those with four year old children who live in the vicinity of a popular Church of England primary school? The evolution of our system of public education is, indeed, as mysterious to most of these people as their new-found 'faith'.

Many shelves could be filled with books about individual public and independent schools, voluminously turning past events and personalities into legend. They are of little interest to the general reader, except perhaps when the institution has contributed a significant number of prominent actors to the national pageant and we wish to understand the eccentricities and privileges of the education these men have shared. Conversely - and this is perhaps an interesting reflection on our national culture - few of our thousands of state schools can boast a published history, their anonymous contribution to the education of nine out of ten of us recorded only in general histories of state education, often dry and academic volumes.

This book attempts to bring together these two strands by integrating and illustrating the important story of the development of our public system of education with that of an individual Foundation which was set up in 1710 in a market town in a unique English polity, the Royal Liberty of Havering. It is the interrelationship between national and local settings and events, together with a cast of rich personalities, which propels the narrative. A few of the actors in this drama - the politicians and educational reformers - were national figures who played the same significant role in the development of schools across the country; others were influencial only within the confines of the Liberty of Havering, but these local clergy and worthies had their counterparts wherever a school was founded and flourished. William and Oswald Adams and their wives Jemima and Sarah have never enjoyed the fame or notoriety of two of their contemporaries, Dr Arnold at Rugby and Dr 'Flogger' Keate at Eton, but they are more representative of the schoolmasters and mistresses of the early 19th century. It was the commitment of men and women such as these and the many others who gave financial support to each successful school which ensured that it survived in the worst of times and flourished in the best of times.

*

Despite the COVID pandemic and the subsequent 'working from home' movement having greatly reduced their numbers, every workday morning thousands of cramped, dozing Essex commuters still speed to Liverpool Street Station and the beginning of their day's work. Leaving Romford they pass on their right the corrugated 'architecture' of the Brewery Centre, the spire of St Andrew's Church, the backs of some Victorian or 'thirty-something' houses, and then Romford Stadium (or, colloquially, 'the dog track'). The backs of more houses are then followed by a broad belt of uncultivated and unimproved waste ground - ironically named 'Nonsuch Park' by the locals - behind which stands the square outline of a four story tower-block built in the distinctive style of a 1960's secondary school. When first erected this building was lauded for its modernity, but now such architecture appears utilitarian, perhaps even unlovely and cheap.

This is St Edward's Church of England Academy, and probably only those amongst these somnolent travellers who were themselves educated there will know that it is the successor to 'The Charity School for Hornchurch Romford and Havering'. Against the odds, it is a rare survivor of the first great initiative to create a nationwide system of schools for the poor, the Charity School Movement of the late 17th and early 18th centuries, financed by public subscriptions and donations. There are state schools which are older, such as those individual grammar schools founded by a local benefactor or trade guild (often in the Tudor period) and funded for posterity with an endowment. St Edward's is not the only Church of England secondary school which has developed from a former charity school: in London there are the Grey Coat Hospital (1698/1701) and St Martin-in-the-Fields High School for Girls (1699), and outside the capital, to give just one example, there is the Nottingham Bluecoat Academy. This was established in 1706, and like St Edward's is unusual in having developed into a secondary and a primary school. (St Edward's Church of England Primary School is now situated half a mile north of the church of St Edward the Confessor in Romford's historic Market Place, where the schools began in

1710.) The St Edward's Schools are not alone in never having left the town in which they were founded, some miles beyond the edge of the capital, yet having now been London schools for over half a century. In none of these ways are these two schools unique, yet they are highly unusual in that for three hundred years they have mirrored every major movement and change in the development of English public education.

*

In August 2008 I retired, having spent the final 17 years of my working life as Headteacher of what was then St Edward's Church of England Comprehensive School. Two years earlier the Rev'd Stephen Waine, the Vicar of Romford and Chair of Governors of both schools, had called a meeting to begin planning for the celebrations which would mark the schools' 300th anniversary in 2010. An early suggestion was to republish the 32 page monograph on the history of the schools which had been written in 1950 by Dr Frederick Davis, headmaster of the Secondary School between 1946 and 1958, adding a postscript to cover the intervening sixty years. Many of the ideas which were suggested at this and subsequent meetings were never developed, the intensity of school life leaving little time for the necessary work. When I retired in 2008 the task of updating the history had not been started, and I agreed to take this on.

Dr Davis clearly had a very great knowledge of the school's history from its earliest days, and his booklet, with its Preface by the Bishop of Chelmsford, is a scholarly work. However, as he says in his Foreword, 'this abbreviated account of St Edward's Schools omits, with great regret, much of the story'. As I began work I found it very difficult to write anything meaningful in the few pages I would have if the 1950 - 2010 supplement was not to dwarf the original 1710 - 1950 narrative. Over these 60 years both the primary and secondary schools had moved away from their original site in the Market Place, both had more than doubled in size, and the secondary modern had become a comprehensive. How could I explain these developments without providing the necessary local and national background?

Re-reading Dr Davis's book I wondered what had been omitted, and I became increasingly frustrated by the lack of context. I started to look deeper into the early history of the Foundation and discovered how bound up it was with the life of the Royal Liberty of Havering at that time, and an examination of its later history confirmed how closely it had reflected every major change in the national story of public education. I concluded that a contextualised history of the school, set in the Royal Liberty and enlivened with the personalities of those who had contributed to its story over the years, would be more dramatic and, perhaps, more entertaining than many of the general histories of the development of English state education.

I therefore decided to ignore the 2010 deadline and attempt to write a history worthy of its subject, aware that I had great advantages which Dr Davis had lacked. Having retired, I could give the project the time it required, and the outcome need not be limited to a bare few pages. Living in Shenfield, I had relatively easy access to the principle places which held the sources I needed to study: Cambridge University Library (where the SPCK papers are held), the National Archives (for relevant government and legal records), Lambeth Palace (where the National Society Papers are accessed), and the Essex Record Office (for the *Accounts and Transactions* of the Charity from 1710, school Log Books, and much other information). The final advantage was beyond the imagination of those writing in the 1950's: access at home to an increasing number of digital resources, including Hansard, the British Newspaper Archive, and various family history websites. With regard to the latter, I was to become a serial stalker of the long dead and largely forgotten, allowing me to give the semblance of an independent identity to some of those who served the school from its earliest days. (These sources also enabled me to correct Dr Davis's list of Masters and Mistresses, reinstating one Mrs Adams and reuniting another with her correct husband.)

Research, whether in an archive or on the internet, can be as frustrating and as rewarding as one imagines prospecting for gold must be: hours sifting dross will often be wasted, but occasionally they will end with the sight of a bright speck which will then be followed by others, amounting to a gram or two of new and valuable information. Both the book and the time it was taking to write lengthened as this information slowly accumulated and the context needed to explain it grew. Then COVID struck. Research was limited to the confines of my study and the reach of my computer, and I returned to the earlier chapters and began to prepare them for publication. It was this exercise which forced me to acknowledge that when finished the work would be far too long for a single volume. This first part of the history ends in 1834, the year after Parliament had voted its first ever grant to augment the charitable endeavours which up until then had funded public education and the year before 'The Charity School for Hornchurch, Romford and Havering' would be transformed into 'The National School for Hornchurch, Romford and Havering'.

Preliminary notes

Romford or Rumford?
A recent search for 'Rumford' in the British Newspaper Archive for the period 1700 to 1749 produced 92 results. This compared with just 8 for 'Romford', of which only 1 referred to the town of Romford, Essex. The search engine sometimes confuses the two spellings so such analysis is at best only approximate, but with this proviso it seems that it was over the next half century, between 1750 and 1799, that Romford became the preferred spelling. In this period 'Romford' was used about twice as often as Rumford, and between 1800 and 1850 it was used four times as frequently. For the sake of uniformity, the modern spelling, Romford, is used throughout this text except when 'Rumford' is used in quotations.

One school or two (or three)?
From its/their opening in 1710/11, the Charity School for Boys and Girls has sometimes been referred to as a single entity and sometimes as two. No consistency is maintained in this text except in referring to the one Foundation and the one Charity, the school(s) being referred to in the singular or plural depending on what seems appropriate in each particular context.

Pre-decimal coinage and the changing value of money
Many monetary figures are quoted throughout this book, such as the minimum of twenty shillings a year which in February 1721 the trustees agreed they would each subscribe to the Charity School. What would be the equivalent sum three hundred years later? The answer is about £153.

Rather than have numerous footnotes giving spurious modern equivalents, in Appendix III an attempt has been made to decode the mystery of pre-decimal coinage (for those who became financially literate after 15 February 1971) and then to explain why making comparisons of changing monetary values over time can be problematic. With this guidance and use of the two Ready Reckoners provided in Appendix IV, it is hoped that an informed guess can be made as to the relative value today of those figures cited in the text. From time to time, as a reminder of these changing values, an approximate modern equivalent will be given after a figure in the text. These will be in{brackets}, will be taken from the first (RPI) table in Appendix IV or the www.measuringworth.com/ukcompare website from which the figures in Appendix IV have been calculated, and will always refer to the value in 2020. They will also, inevitably, be inexact approximations.

Sources

I have endeavoured to acknowledge all the sources I have used either in the end notes to each chapter or in the bibliography. I apologise if I have inadvertently omitted or incorrectly attributed any references or sources.

Much of the information about the school is taken from the Trustees' Account Books and, after 1833, a little from the trustee's correspondence with the National Society and the Committee of the Privy Council on Education. Details of these sources are listed in the bibliography, but as each reference, including the date, is clear from the text or can be easily worked out separate references in footnotes have been omitted.

Chapter 1

Place and time: the Royal Liberty of Havering in 1710

1710

3 February 2010: Westminster Abbey
On Wednesday 3 February 2010 pupils, staff, governors, parents and other supporters of the two St Edward's Church of England Schools in Romford gathered in Westminster Abbey to celebrate the schools' 300th anniversary. The 250th and the 275th anniversaries had been marked by services at St Paul's Cathedral, but the Abbey was considered by many to be a more fitting venue because it had been founded by Edward the Confessor, after whom the schools and their mother church were named. Cost was also a consideration: the fee for hiring the Abbey for the duration of the service was about £5,000, less than half that of hiring the Cathedral, so on this occasion historical sentiment and financial prudence were in happy alignment. In 1960 the service had been attended by every pupil in both schools and in 1985 over 1000 pupils had travelled from Romford to St Paul's in a fleet of 26 double-decker buses, but those pupils who travelled to the Abbey in 2010 arrived by public transport, chaperoned by a parent, and were self-selecting representatives of the 2,000 pupils who then attended the schools.

The service was led by the Dean, the Very Reverend Doctor John Hall, who prior to his appointment at the Abbey had been General Secretary of the Church of England Board of Education, in which post he had acquired a deep knowledge and regard for the family of Church of England schools. Happily, therefore, the service of thanksgiving was conducted by the most appropriate clergyman in the most appropriate building; happily, too, one of the Abbey vergers on duty that day was James Prior, who had been a St Edward's pupil in the 1990's. The central act in the service was the processing of a large, time-worn volume from the back of the nave, through the choir and chancel, to the Shrine of St Edward the Confessor. This was carried with great solemnity by the Reverend Stephen Waine, Vicar of the

Church of St Edward the Confessor in the Market Place, Romford, and Chair of Governors of both schools. He was flanked by the two headteachers, the head boy and girl of the Secondary School, and a boy and girl from Year 6 representing the Primary School. This tome was the parish Vestry Book which contained the record of a meeting held on Tuesday 5 September 1710, and it is this record which the schools accord the status of their 'foundation document'. If this description perhaps stretches our usual understanding of the term too far, it is more accurate than 'Trust Deed', which is how it was described in the service sheet. Whatever gloss we give it, the meeting it records is certainly the starting point for this history.

The lost Liberty of 1710
Today the two St Edward's Schools are situated in Romford in the most easterly of the London Boroughs. For over four hundred years the greater part of this area was a distinct, independent polity designated the Royal Liberty of Havering. By the end of the 19th century this had been completely absorbed into Essex, but in 1965 its independence was resurrected, the ancient communities of Upminster, Cranham and Rainham which lay to the south were added to the former Royal Liberty, and it was incorporated into Greater London as the Borough of Havering.

Havering takes its name from the village of Havering-atte-Bower, which lies in the north of the present London borough, where its history began. It is still surrounded by countryside, and this has allowed it to retain its identity as a separate community from the other main centres in the borough, Romford, Hornchurch and Upminster, which have now expanded and coalesced to become a unified urban sprawl with a population of a quarter of a million.[1] It requires imagination to strip away this concretion of buildings, roads and railways in order to envisage the landscape of field, wood, heath, and sparse habitation which was the Royal Liberty of Havering in 1710. It was an agricultural area, its crops and livestock helping to feed London. Brewing, which in the 19th and 20th centuries would make Romford famous around the world, had been a significant industry since the 15th century, and both Romford and Hornchurch were early centres for the manufacture of leather goods, with its odiously odorous accompanying trade, tanning - indeed, the making of leather breeches was by the 18th century proverbially associated with Romford.[2] The population of the Liberty at this time was perhaps 5,000 people living in the farms, hamlets and manors, and in the three larger communities of Havering-atte-Bower to the north, Hornchurch to the south, and Romford between the two. These three settlements were linked by the principal north-south track in the Liberty, which at the west end of the Market Place in Romford crossed the important east-west highway which for centuries had taken travellers between the port of Harwich and the city of London, a journey which took them through the ancient Roman capital of Colchester. If the terms 'track' and 'highway' are perhaps too pejorative, the word 'road' would be a misnomer at this time.

Buildings are usually our most tangible link with the past, but apart from the churches of St Laurence in Upminster and St Andrew in Hornchurch, both dating back to the 12th century, few in this landscape today were there in 1710. Church House in Romford Market Place dates from the 15th century and is a rare survivor[3], urban 'improvements' in the town over the last sixty years having destroyed almost all of the older buildings which had survived up to the second world war. The four oldest, surviving institutions in the town are the church, first represented by a chapel of about 1177 but now by a building of 1849; the market of 1247 which is now held in a market place two-thirds of its original size; the Roger Reede almshouses of 1483, now reincarnated in 1961 buildings; and the St Edward's Schools, whose original 1723 school-house was destroyed in the 1970's and which are now housed in buildings dating from 1965 and 1976. It must be regretted that today the rich and fascinating history of this unique part of 'Essex in London' exists for most of its inhabitants only in the names of places, roads and schools whose derivation is a mystery to them, but a knowledge of the outlines of this history is essential for an understanding of the community which supported and funded the schools from their earliest years.

The Royal Liberty of Havering from the tenth century to 1710
'Unique' is an often misused word, but not when used to describe the Royal Liberty of Havering. Its history began in the present village of Havering where, in the 10th century, Edward the Confessor built a hunting lodge. After the Norman conquest this royal demesne passed into the ownership of William I and his successors, and in 1086 it is recorded in the Domesday Book as 'Haueringas', a name which covered an area of 12,550 acres and which was coterminous with an ancient parish. By the 1150's the village of Havering in the north of the parish was evolving around the royal residence set in its hunting park, whilst five miles south a well-established community was settled around the parish church. The palace was a favourite of Henry

II who visited it on a number of occasions and carried out notable improvements, including adding the luxury of glass windows to the Queen's chamber in 1151 (undoubtedly in preparation for his marriage to the hot-blooded Eleanor of Aquitaine the following year) and rebuilding the chapel in 1163.[4] His interest in the area led to two gifts which were to profoundly change the church, the community of Havering, and their subsequent development.[5]

Henry II held extensive lands and interests in France, and in the winter of 1158-9 he sent envoys to the Holy Roman Emperor, Frederick Barbarossa. This journey required them to take the ancient St Nicholas Pass over the Alps between what are now Switzerland and Italy. A hundred years earlier Saint Bernard had been archdeacon of Aosta on the Italian side of the pass and had regularly seen distressed travellers arriving there, terrorised by the mountain brigands. To overcome this problem he had founded a hospice at the summit of the pass, which was subsequently renamed the Great St Bernard Pass in his memory. The King's envoys undoubtedly took advantage of the safety and hospitality offered by the hospice and its monks, and, in gratitude for their safe return, Henry II gave 1,500 acres in the area of the church in Havering to this hospice of St Nicholas and St Bernard, Mountjoux. By 1163 he had, in addition, given them the church itself, beside which the Augustinian monks of the hospice built a priory. Although the exact date of these gifts is uncertain, they were confirmed by a bull of Pope Alexander III in 1177 in which there is mention of a chapel at *Romfort*, the first recorded reference to this place.

The name Romford means 'wide or spacious ford', and here a community had developed where the River Beam[6] was crossed by the ancient road connecting London with the port of Harwich. It was situated midway between the royal palace and village at Havering to the north and the community around the priory, with its church, to the south. At about this time the church acquired the bovine decoration which was to give this community its modern name of Hornchurch, for in 1222 we find the first record referring to 'the Horned Church'. It was also in the 13th century that the suffix '-atte-Bower', meaning 'at the royal residence', was added to the name of the village of Havering, and from this period the community living within the wider demesne enjoyed a special status and accrued various benefits, of which the charter granted by King Henry III in 1247 authorising a market at Romford would prove the most important for its future identity and prosperity. This stipulated that no other market was permitted to be set up within a day's sheep drive, a distance of six and two-thirds miles, and the town jealously guarded this privilege which would enable it to develop and maintain its position as the commercial centre of the surrounding agricultural area.

'The Horned Church', Hornchurch, with the horned head above the East window

Hornchurch priory prospered, and in 1323 the monks built a new chapel dedicated to St Andrew to the south-west of Romford town centre and on the other side of the river, in the area now known as 'Oldchurch'. However, within thirty years the Black Death had overturned the existing social and economic systems in Europe, and not least those of the Catholic church. By the end of the 14th century England had become embroiled in a long struggle to stem the flow of its wealth to the papacy, particularly the transfer of land and property held by churchmen and of money the church received in rents and tithes. In 1390, in consequence of a new law which banned foreign ownership of land, the priory at Hornchurch and the extensive lands it owned in Havering, Kent and London were confiscated by the king, Richard II, and the monks were forced out. The following year William of Wykeham, the Lord Chancellor, was permitted to buy all of this land which he then granted to New College, Oxford, which he had founded twelve years earlier for the education of priests. Following the Black Death there was a shortage of properly educated clergy, but use of the considerable resources of the original priory to promote the work of the church in this way was no doubt of little comfort to the evicted monks. The transfer of this property and the appropriation of the church and chapels in Havering to New College were confirmed by a bull of Pope Boniface IX in 1392, and from that date the appointments of the Vicar of Hornchurch and the Chaplain of the Chapel in Romford passed to New College, which has remained the patron of the parishes to this day. Many of those who were appointed to the livings of Romford and Hornchurch after 1710 will feature in this history, and most of them had previously been fellows of New College.

In 1410 a new chapel was built in Romford, replacing the 'old church' of 1323 and dedicated to St Edward the Confessor. It was set in its own graveyard on the north side of the Market Place, and was confirmation of the increasing size and status of this commercial centre between the two older communities of Havering and Hornchurch. Then, in 1465, the various privileges which over the years had been granted to the residents of the royal manor of Havering were consolidated in a charter in which the demesne was granted the status of a Royal Liberty. This freed the residents from taxation and gave them their own local magistrates and gaol. The Liberty also had its own gibbet, although there is no record of an execution since the mid-17th century. It was sited to the north of the commemoratively named flyover and roundabout to the East of Romford, Gallows Corner. The Manor and Liberty of Havering were owned by the crown, but within its demesne there were some 22 subservient manors. From the earliest records in the 12th century these were a feature of the area, and some of their wealthy owners in the 18th century will impinge on this history. At the end of the 19th century and in the early 20th century they were sold off one-by-one for the urban development which would transform the area and have major consequences for its few schools.

Despite the considerable religious, political and social turbulence during the 250 years of the Tudor and Stuart dynasties, the civic and social framework of the Royal Liberty of Havering remained essentially unchanged. However, over this period the relative importance of the three main communities altered dramatically. Up to the middle of the 16th century Hornchurch and Romford had been of a comparable size and wealth, but over the following hundred years Romford greatly outgrew its neighbour. In 1670 there were 364 houses in 'Romford side', that is the five parish wards in the north of the Liberty, but only 185 in the three wards 'Hornchurch side'. Both were far larger than Havering-atte-Bower, where the ancient royal palace was vacant and falling into ruin, although one of its two Chapels was maintained for the use of the villagers. In 1638 Charles I became the last monarch to stay there, and few of those who might have caught a fleeting glimpse of that unhappy king were still alive in 1710.

The unique arrangements which characterised the governance of the Royal Liberty would continue until eroded by the local government reforms of the Victorian periods, with the final vestige being swept away in 1892. The parochial structure was similarly resistant to change. Under an agreement dating from the opening of the new chapel in 1410 the people of Romford were bound to contribute as before to the repair of the parish church in Hornchurch, as well as maintaining their own chapel. This had been a cause of dispute since at least the 1520's according to one history,[7] although a letter in the *Chelmsford Chronicle* on 4 May 1849, the year Romford finally became an independent parish, gives a different account. The writer, a Romford man, maintained that for 200 years there had been no issue over this matter because the two parties had made an arrangement for the income from a certain piece of land owned by Romford to be paid to Hornchurch in lieu of church rates. Then, at some point in the past (the writer is vague about dates), 'an unlucky schoolmaster' found amongst the Hornchurch church papers the original document of about 1410 specifying the obligation on Romford to pay Hornchurch 'an equal moiety' for the support of the mother church, but no subsequent agreement regarding the income from the land. It is possible, he says, this agreement, which would have nullified the first, had been lost or destroyed, 'for about the same time the parish church had been, it is said, broken open, and its papers therein thrown and scattered about the open field adjoining the church'. Despite Hornchurch 'having received for a great many years £20 or £25 for some land, to which it acknowledged it had no right', it went to the courts, 'and after many heavy law suits, remonstrances, &c. &c. succeeded in forcing the yearly payment of an equal moiety, and intends to continue it as long as the law remains unaltered.' The uneasy relationship between Romford and Hornchurch will be another theme of this history.

Romford chapel felt aggrieved, but whilst resenting its own lack of independence from Hornchurch it had, over the centuries, successfully gained control over the four northern wards of the parish: Collier Row, Harold Wood, Noak Hill, and the original settlement of Havering-atte-Bower. By 1700 Romford had been levying chapel-rates on the inhabitants of these wards for at least the same 200 year period. Yet Havering-atte-Bower had the same arguments for its strong opposition to this arrangement as Romford had in opposing its financial commitments to Hornchurch: it had its own chapel, like Romford, and by 1700 its own graveyard too. There had been an initiative to sort out this confusion in 1650, at the beginning of the Commonwealth, when it had been proposed that two new parishes be carved out of Hornchurch Parish, one to include Romford Town, Harold Wood and Collier Row, and the other Havering and Noak Hill, but sixty years later the situation remained unchanged. It is a complex story. Havering would eventually gain independence from Romford in 1750 but not from Hornchurch until 1784, and Romford would continue to pay church-rates to Hornchurch until 1814, but would still be under its control when the nakedly partisan letter was written to the *Chelmsford Chronicle* in 1849. But we must return to 1710.

The 'new chapel' built in the Market Place in 1410 had developed over the years to accommodate the expanding population, and in addition to the original nave and chancel it now possessed a north aisle, two chapels, and a west tower which for at least 150 years had housed a set of six bells and been adorned with a clock. This was the building in which the meeting of 5 September 1710 took place. Since the end of the 15th century the appointment of its chaplain had been delegated by New College to the Vicar of Hornchurch, and under a longstanding, voluntary arrangement the chaplain's income came mainly from the 'small tithes' of Romford levied on items such as kitchen herbs, fruit, vegetables and small farm animals, whereas the Vicar's income derived from the 'great tithes' administered on grain and large farm animals. For this arrangement to work harmoniously it was important that the two clergymen were on good terms, and Thomas Roberts, Vicar since 1696, and James Hotchkis, Chaplain of Romford since 1706, were on very good terms. If this had not been the case, if they had not shared a common vision and worked together to achieve it, it is quite possible there would never have been a charity school in the Royal Liberty.

1710: the road to London

Romford's position on the 80 mile Essex Road has ensured it has always orientated itself towards London. Harwich, at the other end of this highway, was a principal port of entry for many returning Englishmen and women and for foreign merchants, diplomats and tourists. London was close enough to be an important market for the agricultural produce of the region, yet far enough away for the inns in the Market Place to provide a final staging post or bed for these travellers. So it was that this otherwise self-contained, traditional market town accommodated a regular flow of passing travellers from both the distant Essex hundreds[8] and from the continent.

Only 45 years before our story begins London had been the epicentre of the plague. Daniel Defoe tells us that many terrified refugees fled east through Hainault Forest towards Rumford and Brentwood, camping in the woods and fields in that area and surviving by robbing, plundering and killing cattle, or by 'building huts and hovels by the roadside, [and begging], and that with an importunity next door to demanding relief; so that the county was very uneasy, and had been obliged to take some of them up.'[9] Then the following year the City had been largely destroyed by the Great Fire. However, its recovery from what many saw as God's punishment for the wickedness of its inhabitants and the licentiousness of its court had been remarkable. By 1700 its population numbered 550,000 and it had overtaken Paris to become the second largest city in Europe, surpassed only by Constantinople. The most easterly tentacle of this great octopus of human endeavour and enterprise (of both the loftiest and the basest kind) reached out as far as Whitechapel, only fifteen miles distant from Romford. It was this wonderfully rebuilt city that the foreign tourists passing through Romford had come to see, and in particular Wren's magnificent new cathedral, finally completed in this year of 1710.

A map of Romford drawn in 1696 includes a perspective view of the town with the buildings spread out along the only clearly marked road, which widens in the centre of the town to accommodate the market. The Chapel of St Edward the Confessor, with its square tower, is shown set back from the Market Place, the heart of the town. Here the old Court House had stood for at least 225 years, alongside the ancient gaol and those survivors of medieval justice, the cage, stocks, and ducking stool. In 1695 an Act of Parliament had been passed allowing the county justices to establish turnpikes on parts of the Essex Road, and the same year the first of these had been set up at Mountnessing, 10 miles to the east, but fifteen years later it would still be another eleven years before the section of this road running through Romford would benefit from the improvements this legislation had been enacted to achieve.

Travellers bound for London in 1710 would have set out from the 'Swan', 'Cock and Bell', or another of Romford's numerous inns in the Market Place and High Street. Many would have been on business, like the carters with their wagons of produce, or the bewigged merchants and gentlemen on their horses or in their coaches. At the western end of the Market Place they would have crossed the lane between Hornchurch, 2½ miles to the south, and Havering-atte-Bower on the higher ground three miles to the north. At the end of the High Street, beyond this intersection, the travellers would have crossed the bridge over the river, where a hundred years later Edward Ind would establish the brewery on which the prosperity of the town in the 19th and 20th centuries was to depend, and whose owners would so generously support the Charity School.

The journey to London was not without risk, and two miles beyond Romford was Chadwell Heath, the most dangerous place on this dangerous journey. Now just part of the East London suburban sprawl, in 1710 the Heath was a barren, deserted region where the road was crossed by the lane running north from Dagenham in the south to Marks Gate and Hainault Forest. This junction was made more sinister by the great ribs from a whale which had reputedly died in the Thames in 1658 and been set up here to mark the death of Oliver Cromwell that year.[10] The number of robberies on this stretch of the road had led in 1643 to 'a stronge watch neere the Whalebone in the great roade neere Romford by reason of sundry greate robberies there lately committed',[11] but these robberies were still being committed a century later. Given that the earliest newspaper reference to 'Rumford' in the British Newspaper Archive dates from 1716[12] and the nearest newspapers were in Ipswich, Stamford and Derby, any reference to an incident at 'the Whalebone' is significant, and there were a surprising number. To mention just four, in February 1730 a weaver from Lavenham was stopped there, but he had only a half crown on him which his assailant generously refused to take, although he did relieve his travelling companion of three guineas before riding off towards the Forest; in September that year a Mr Mitchell of Rumford was robbed 'near the Whalebone'; in June 1733 Mr Mears, a Rumford farmer, was attacked 'by the Whalebone'; and on 1 January 1741 Mr Selwin and two other gentlemen were waylaid 'near the Whalebone' on their way to Harwich. If the victim was on horseback, the horse would be turned loose. At least one of these men was beaten 'in a barbarous manner', and although on occasions shots were fired, no one was hit. The haul from these few examples were two silver watches, a tobacco box, and gold and silver coins. The great period for highway robbery is said to have been from the end of the civil war in the early 1650's to the end of Queen Anne's reign, so we may assume that as all the reports we have come after this date there were many incidents before these. 'The Whalebone' was a classic haunt for such crimes, situated where a major route out of London crossed an isolated heath, with an easy escape route to 'the Forest'.

Beyond the Heath lay Chadwell Street where there were inns and refreshments for travellers and their horses. This was exactly nine miles from Whitechapel church, from which Essex highways were measured. Next came Ilford, then Stratford. As Defoe noted on his travels in 1722, all the villages in proximity to London had prodigiously increased in size over the previous 20 or 30 years, and he believed Stratford had more than doubled over this period. Two miles further on lay what would become, over the next few years, the Mile End Turnpike Gate. The road now improved for the last two miles before the first buildings in London were reached at Whitechapel, but Charing Cross was then still three miles distant.

Having reached London, the traveller was not out of danger. On Saturday 10 May 1718 a 'Country Man' from Romford who had come to London to be married on the Monday was set upon by four footpads in Moor Fields. It was 10.00 pm, and they cut his throat and robbed him of £18. Fortunately they missed his windpipe and he was found alive and taken to 'The Five Bells'. Unusually, two of the 'Rogues' were also found, but they were taken to Newgate. When our travellers finally reached their accommodation they no doubt felt safer than they had done since leaving Romford that morning.

The vestry meeting of 5 September 1710

This was the local world occupied by the nine men who met in the Chapel of St Edward the Confessor in the Market Place in Romford on Tuesday 5 September 1710. The universe in which it nestled had recently behaved in a very strange way, with the winter of 1708/1709 being the coldest for five hundred years. The Rector of Upminster, the parish adjoining Hornchurch to the south-east, was William Derham. He was to become a great supporter of the Charity School at Romford, but he is remembered today as a great scientist. He had recorded a low of minus 12° centigrade on the night of 5 January 1709 and had written in the *Philosophical Transactions* of the Royal Society: 'I believe the Frost was greater (if not more universal also) than any other within the Memory of Man.' Across Europe livestock froze to death and crops failed, causing widespread starvation, death, and economic disaster. So many Swedish troops froze to death - 2,000 in a single night - that the outcome of the Great Northern War was tipped in Russia's favour.[13]

In England it was politics, rather than the weather, which caused a sudden change in the course of the war with France and her allies. Over the last six years the Duke of Marlborough and his armies had enjoyed stunning successes at the Battles of Blenheim, Ramillies, Oudenaard and Malplaquet, but on 8 August, the month before the gathering in the Chapel at Romford, Queen Anne had dismissed her Chief Minister, Godolphin. The Whig-Tory coalition ministry which he had led with the Duke and which had prosecuted the war had finally fallen, and with Harley and the Tories now in power and wanting peace and with a general election called for October, who knew what the future held?

Today a vestry meeting is narrowly concerned with the affairs of the church and is of interest only to the congregation, but at that time it had far more significance for the whole community. It was not just that the role of the church was so much more central to the life of the whole parish 300 years ago, but until the 1830's the ecclesiastical parish vestries, of which there were more than 15,600 across the country, were the most important element in the system of local government. As the vestry will feature significantly in the course of this narrative some background is necessary.

The secular role of the church began in Tudor times, when the old manorial system of local administration was in decline and communities increasingly turned to the ancient parish system to meet their social and economic needs. Meetings were held in the church vestry, hence they came to be called vestry meetings, and were supervised by the parish priest as he was usually the best educated member of the community. These vestry committees developed through custom and practice without any formal, legal foundation, and their existence and ubiquity provided a ready-made structure for the administration of the systems of poor relief set up under Edward VI. The Act for the Provision and Relief of the Poor of 1552 required the appointment of two overseers from each parish to collect voluntary donations to support the poor of the parish. As these donations were often unforthcoming, even after the final sanction of a meeting with the local bishop had been applied, other Acts followed. These culminated in the Elizabethan Poor Law of 1601 which made each parish responsible for taxing its wealthier citizens in order to provide basic shelter, food and clothing for the needy in their community. This greatly increased the legal powers of the parish vestry and would remain in force until replaced by the Poor Law Amendment Act of 1834. Over these 233 years further civil responsibilities were delegated to the parish vestries in the country, which came to be responsible for their own

> churches and burial grounds, parish cottages and workhouses, endowed charities, market crosses, pumps, pounds, whipping posts, stocks, cages, watch houses, weights and scales, clocks and fire engines. Or to put it another way: the maintenance of the church and its services, the keeping of the peace, the repression of vagrancy, the relief of destitution, the mending of roads, the suppression of nuisances, the destruction of vermin, the furnishing of soldiers and sailors, even to some extent the enforcement of religious and moral discipline. These were among the multitudinous duties imposed on the parish and its officers, that is to say the vestry and its organisation, by the law of the land, and by local custom and practice as the situation demanded.[14]

The churchwardens were important and powerful local dignitaries, and the parish clerk who implemented the decisions and managed the accounts of the vestry committee was a key appointment. As its portfolio of responsibilities increased the parish vestry had to appoint a variety of other parish officials to administer these, including 'the overseers of the poor, sextons and scavengers, constables and nightwatchmen'. By the 1830's, when their powers and influence peaked, the church vestries would be responsible for the expenditure of about a fifth of the national government budget.

The secular nature of these vestry meetings is well illustrated by the fact that a meeting of the Romford vestry held on 6 June 1710 had unanimously agreed 'to endeavour a redress of Grievance' on account of an illegal market which had been set up at Ingatestone and which infringed the ancient privilege enjoyed by Romford. Amongst those who had attended that meeting were four men who would play a crucial role in the early history of the school and who now, thirteen weeks later, again made their way to the Chapel in the Market Place: James Hotchkis (Chaplain), William Sandford (a wool stapler and Chapel Warden), and Thomas Gilman and Christopher Bayley (both described as mercers, they were also working partners and related by marriage). The others present that Tuesday were John Jermin, John Carter, Thomas Taylor, John Youngs and Thomas Kneaton, the vestry clerk. When these men came to sign the record of the meeting in the Vestry Book, Thomas Kneaton left a respectful space between his signature and those of the others, and it was probably he who wrote 'Ye mark of Tho. Taylor' around the tremulous T which was all the illiterate Thomas Taylor could write.

The sole purpose of this vestry meeting was to discuss the possible use of the room over the vestry in the church as a school room. The minutes of their meeting, duly recorded in the Vestry Book, succinctly summarised the situation: a decision had been made to set up, as soon as possible, a charity school in Romford to teach poor children to read and write and to instruct them in the Christian religion; several people, both locals and others living outside the parish, had subscribed money for this purpose and agreed to make further contributions; a representation had been made that a school room, or school rooms, could be made out of the room over the vestry if a new floor was laid and extended to the partition between this space and the back of the gallery. The entry concludes with the unanimous decision of those present that they wished to 'promote and encourage' such a charitable undertaking and they therefore 'cheerfully consent[ed]' to this space being made convenient for use as a Charity School (or Schools) and being used for this purpose 'for ever'. The record of the meeting is somewhat clumsy in both its wording and its execution, but is enlivened by the obvious enthusiasm for the project and the addition of all their signatures. It is this document which is recognised as the 'foundation document' of the present schools and had been carried with such reverence to the Shrine of St Edward the Confessor that February morning three centuries later. The Vestry Book records no earlier discussions leading up to this decision and there are no later entries recording the progress of the school.

The context for this discussion and for the ideas which had so enthused these men lay beyond Romford, principally in events which had taken place over the previous fifteen years in London. Before travelling there, however, we must briefly examine the existing state of public education in England.

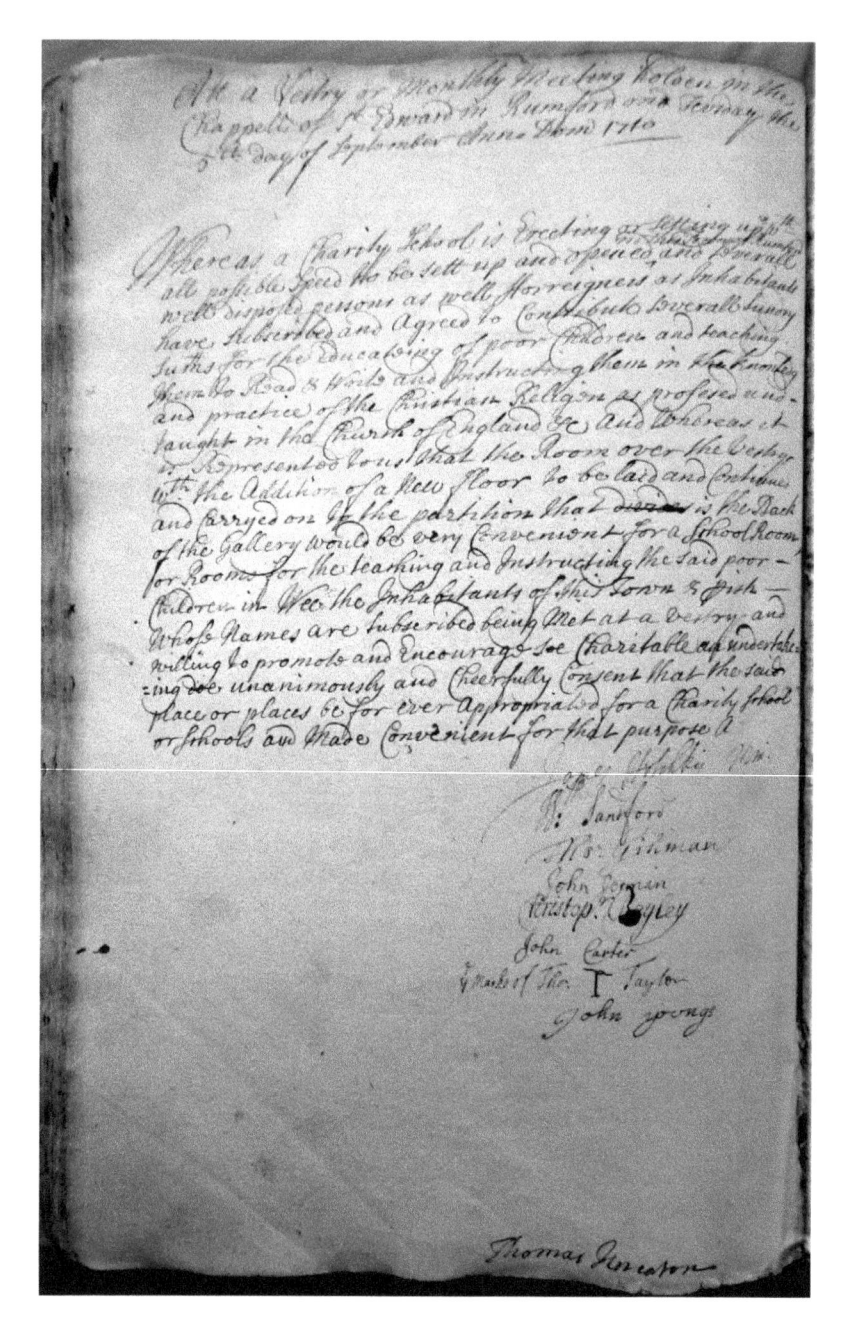

The entry in the Vestry Book for St Edward's Chapel, Romford, recording the meeting of 5 September 1710

Att a Vestry or Monthly Meeting holden in the Chappell
of St Edward in Rumford ond Teusday the
5th day of September Anno Dom 1710

Whereas a Charity School is Erecting or setting up w^th
all possible Speed to be sett up and opened in this Town of Rumford and Severall
well disposed persons as well fforreigners as Inhabitants
have subscribed and Agreed to Contribute severall sundry
sums for the Education of poor Children and teaching
them to Read & Write and Instructing them in the knowledg
and practice of the Christian Religion as professed and
Taught in the Church of England & and whereas it
Is Represented to us that the Room over the Vestry
wth the Addition of a New floor to be laid and Continued
and carryed on to the partition that divides is the Back
of the Gallery would be very convenient for a School Room
or Rooms for the teaching and Instructing the said poor
Children in. Wee the Inhabitants of this Town & p[ar]ish
Whose names are subscribed being met at a vestry and
Willing to promote and Encourage soe Charitable an undertake=
=ing doe unanimously and Cheerfully Consent that the said
Place or places be for ever appropriated for a Charity School
Or Schools and made Convenient for that purpose

       James Hotchkis   Min
       W^m: Sandford
       Ths: Gillman
       John Jermin
       Christop.^r Bayley
       John Carter
       Y^e mark of Tho. T Taylor
       John youngs

       Thomas Kneaton

Chapter 2

Religious belief and the 18th century Charity School Movement

1699 - 1711

Schools before 1700
There is little evidence of education in the Royal Liberty before 1710. Records suggest that in 1548 some poor children were taught by a priest in Hornchurch, and that in the 1620's boys there were taught grammar by a curate in the church. Perhaps more significantly, there is mention of a free school in Romford which had been kept by Thomas Horrocks in the 1640's,[15] and of a grammar school in the town run by a Mr Stonehouse in 1674.[16] Fortunately this was not representative of the country as a whole. Today there are some two hundred schools which were founded before 1640, and these fall into three broad categories: the ancient, charitable foundations; church foundations, including the choir schools; and the remaining endowed grammar schools, most originating in Tudor times, of which there had originally been more than 500. These had provided a classical education to the sons of both the wealthier and the poorer members of the community, although there were undoubtedly more of the former than the latter. Some are now state schools, but many remain independent. By 1640 there were also some early 'dame' schools, institutions existing randomly across the country in which the proverbial 'dame' charged a proverbial 'penny a week', for which fee she attempted to pass on her own basic education to those in her care. These would become a ubiquitous part of the national schooling system, and there were a number of these schools in Romford in the 19th century. After 1872, tackling the low standard of education they offered (and, indeed, their very existence) would provide an early challenge for the first Romford Board of Education, elected that year.

Important changes to this haphazard provision of national education took place during the turbulent period of the Civil War and the Commonwealth in response to the changes in politics, religion, and society. First, there were legislative changes which marked the faltering beginnings of a national commitment to spreading 'popular' education to a wider social group. In 1641, early in the Long Parliament, the House of Commons authorised the use of Church revenues 'to the advancement of piety and learning'. In 1649, the year of the King's execution, there were three Education Acts: the first resulted in the setting up and financing of 60 free schools in Wales with funds which became available as a result of the disestablishment and partial disendowment of the Church in Wales; the second Act redirected certain taxes which had previously accrued to the Crown to augment the salaries, stipends and allowances of preaching ministers and schoolmasters; and the third Act made provision for the propagation of religion and education in the New England colonies and, in what would later be seen as a prototype for the funding of the 18th century charity schools, authorised the collection of voluntary contributions throughout England and Wales to finance this work.

This legislation was supported by a growing enthusiasm for education and its reform, championed by a number of distinguished and forward thinking Englishmen (including the poet John Milton). An essential element in these reforms was a move away from the classically dominated curriculum and a gradual change in the language of the classroom from Latin to English. This change was both heard in the words of the masters and their students and read in the text-books they studied. The commitment to this change was underlined by a stipulation made by some of those who endowed new schools at this time expressly forbidding the teaching of Latin.

The growth in the number of people literate in their native language during this period was additionally stimulated by the increasing output of pamphlets and newssheets during the Civil War. If the Common Man at the beginning of the century had revelled in the sound of the words heard in the Elizabethan and Jacobean playhouses, the political turmoil of the mid-century turned him into a reader. For the Common Woman, the change came much later. According to Coleridge, it was during this period that 'A learned body as such gradually disappeared and literature in general began to be addressed to the common miscellaneous public'.[17]

In contrast to the classical instruction provided in the grammar schools and public schools, these 'English' or 'elementary' schools taught religion and the '3 R's': reading, writing and arithmetic. Despite the growing influence as the century progressed in the thoughts and writings of men such as Sir Isaac Newton, Robert Boyle and John Locke, and despite the founding of such symbolic structures as the Greenwich Observatory and the Royal

Society, the efforts of some of those progressive reformers behind the new schools to include mathematics and the natural sciences in the curriculum were unsuccessful. These subjects were taken up by some of the Dissenting academies in the course of the next century, but they did not generally feature in the curriculum of other schools until very much later.[18] However, even if these new and exciting scientific ideas did not penetrate the classroom, the new economic and social forces of the 17th century were to change the perception of the need for wider education and to structure the provision of that education. It was Coleridge's 'common miscellaneous public', open to the new ideas they were reading and hearing, whose commitment would ensure the embedding and growth of popular education over the coming century.

By the end of the 17th century there were over 460 of these elementary schools using English as the language of instruction. Yet despite the addition of all these new English schools to the ancient grammar schools the bulk of the people were still without access to schooling at this time, and those who could afford to educate their children sent them to the increasing number of fee paying schools. There were many ordinary people who wished to participate in these increased learning opportunities but who lacked the means to do so, and it was this pent up demand which was partially met for the poorer members of society by the charity school movement which had begun to develop by 1700 and was to transform the provision of education, if not its curriculum, over the 18th century.

Many poor parents wanted their children to have the opportunity to broaden their knowledge and skills and thereby to increase their social and economic independence. However, many of those who already possessed such advantages were afraid that extending them to the working classes, and particularly the poor, would be socially disruptive and politically dangerous and therefore opposed the benevolence of those who provided the money required for the setting up and maintenance of the Charity Schools. Indeed, the motivation of the benefactors themselves often had more to do with the social control of the poor and the saving of their souls than with a desire for universal, basic education. Such a confusion of motives for and against the equality of opportunity offered by universal education would continue into the 20th century, but at the end of the 17th century the debate centred on the problem of the poor.

The problem of the poor at the end of the 17th century

Until the Civil War in the 1640's the problem of pauperism in England had been managed with varying degrees of efficiency under the arrangements set up by the Tudor poor laws, but by the second half of the 17th century this system had broken down. Poverty had had one advantage in that it provided cheap labour and thus increased overall wealth, but by this time the poor had become too heavy a charge on national income. The poor tended to have large families, their children often became the responsibility of their parish, and the parish then maintained them in idleness until they were apprenticed or put out to work or service, probably at the age of 12. Not only were the poor therefore an economic cost to society, they were also seen as a threat to the stability of that society owing to their 'moral delinquencies'. The condition many of these children lived in was appalling, particularly in the cities where they 'swarmed like locusts in the streets', at best neglected, at worst abandoned. The majority of abandoned babies died, there being no obvious inducement to encourage them to live to become a burden on the parish. According to one contemporary commentator, Gregory King, in 1688 up to half the population were dependent or semi-dependent on the local community, and pauperism was to become 'the leading domestic problem' of the 18th century.

It was the children of the poor who raised most compassion and whose welfare and salvation was at the forefront of public concern, and by the end of the 17th century two methods to achieve their rescue were being debated. The first was to build workhouses and working schools, as they were doing in Holland, to provide moral, religious and physical sustenance through manual work, church on Sundays, and bread. The opening of the London Workhouse in 1698 was a manifestation of this approach, which numbered amongst its advocates the rationalist philosopher John Locke.

The second method was being championed by those who thought the answer lay in religion, and particularly in reinstating and reinvigorating the discipline of catechising children. This practice involved the use of questions, asked by the priest or schoolmaster, to elicit formulaic answers which summarised church docterine and which the children had learnt by heart. For example:

Question:	How many Sacraments hath Christ ordained in his Church?
Answer:	Two only, as generally necessary to salvation; that is to say, Baptism, and the Supper of the Lord.
Question:	What meanest thou by this word Sacrament?

Answer:	I mean an outward and visible sign of an inward and spiritual grace given unto us, ordained by Christ himself, as a means whereby we receive the same, and a pledge to assure us thereof.
Question:	How many parts are there in a Sacrament?
Answer:	Two: the outward visible sign, and the inward spiritual grace.[19]

The Prayer Book required the clergy to catechise the children of the parish during evening service each week, but by the end of the 17th century this was rarely done. The neglect of this duty, it was argued, meant that the poor lacked the means of religious salvation and moral improvement enjoyed by the rich. The problem was not just one of clerical negligence, however, because even when the clergy were conscientious in their attempts to catechise, the inability of the children and their parents to read meant that the lesson was forgotten by the following week. Education was needed if the poor were to benefit from the teaching in church, but they were unable to access whatever advantages a school might have to offer because even if the town or village had a dame school, and many did not, the poor could not afford either the 'weekly pence' or the opportunity for the children to earn it though begging or casual work.

The first of these alternative solutions to the problem, the workhouse system, was not new to England, having evolved in the 17th century. It would develop in the second quarter of the 18th century, when over 600 parish workhouses would be built in England and Wales, and would find its ultimate expression in the large and expensive 'union' workhouses which were the bleak, utilitarian consequence of the Poor Law Amendment Act of 1834. However, 140 year before this those with influence favoured catechetical instruction rather than the workhouse as the way to discipline the infant poor. It was a variant of an old system these people understood, there being many charities already existing for educating, clothing, and apprenticing poor scholars in the old grammar and English schools. It was also much cheaper than building workhouses, requiring only an unoccupied house or room, some benches and slates, a uniform for each child costing about 16s, and a Master whose salary would amount to perhaps £35 a year. In many places it was possible to raise these minimal funds from the local community because at the turn of the 17th and 18th centuries the upper and middle orders of society were experiencing a period of comparative affluence and could be motivated to subscribe to this cause by the prevailing religious thought.

Two other factors supported religious instruction over the workhouse as the preferred means of tackling child poverty. The first was that during the reigns of Anne and George I trade grew much faster than population in many parts of the country, and in these favourable economic conditions labour was in demand and so, it was argued, workhouses were unnecessary. [20] The second was that both Anglicans and Nonconformists supported charity schools over workhouses because they saw such schools, with the religious instruction they would provide, as a bulwark against Roman Catholicism. This was not just a doctrinal issue; Rome presented a real threat to the Protestant Succession. The Glorious Revolution of 1688 had deposed the Catholic James II, but the Jacobite invasions of 1715 and 1745 would prove the protestant majority's continuing fear of Catholicism to have been justified.

For a mixture of religious, social, economic and educational reasons, therefore, and despite strong opposition for a similar mix of reasons, at the very end of the 17th century public opinion came to support the setting up of charity schools for the poor. The aim, in the words of a modern historian, was 'to create a dutiful and subordinate working class, with just enough education to turn the children of the poor from pagan savages into obedient and Christian apprentices or servants'.[21]

But what kind of people led the movement which turned general ideas and sympathies into the reality of functioning schools, and what were their specific religious beliefs?

The Charity School Movement and religious belief at the end of the 17th century

From the outset the leadership in setting up and then managing the new charity schools came from the clergy, with support from the middle classes. These people were austere and devout men and women who were puritan in their attitudes and behaviour, if not in their religious beliefs. They endeavoured to live their lives according to the teachings of the Christian church, and this inculcated in them a sense of pity and responsibility for these poor children. The political and religious upheavals of the 17th century had left them with a zeal to overcome the pernicious effects of the irreligion and pauperism which they saw as characteristic of the lower classes, and they thought that instructing children from their youngest years in the teachings of the Bible and in the catechism would produce God-fearing adults cured of their parents' idleness, debauchery and beggary.

They believed that the prosperity of the country and the happiness of the individual were dependant on each person doing their duty according to the station to which they were called. This idea was perhaps summed up most memorably 150 years later in Mrs Cecil Frances Alexander's 1848 hymn 'All things bright and beautiful', with its (now notorious) lines in the third verse:

> The rich man in his castle,
> The poor man at his gate,
> God made them, high or lowly,
> And ordered their estate.

The idea that economic and social inequalities were the will of God and part of His great design lasted a very long time, and although universal sentiment now ensures this verse is omitted, as late as 1982 the Inner London Education Authority believed it necessary to actively ban it from being sung in any London school.[22]

If the devout middle classes at the end of 17th century accepted that God had decreed their estate, they had to accept also that their prosperity came with responsibilities; if it was the duty of the poor to accept their lot in life as 'hewers of wood and drawers of water' (Joshua 9:23), it was the duty of those with means to use their wealth to promote the greater glory of God by helping these ignorant 'hewers' and 'drawers' who all too often deprived God of his glory by their idle and debauched behaviour. Scripture could be cited to justify these beliefs. The existence of poverty was timeless, ubiquitous and inevitable, for as Jesus said, 'You have the poor among you always' (Matthew 26:11)[23], and God is the giver of all things, for in his Epistle James had stressed how 'All good giving and every perfect gift comes from above, from the Father' (James 1:17). James also said that 'a man is justified by deeds and not by faith in itself' (James 2:24), and these works included a true Christian response to the needs of the poor: 'The kind of religion which is without stain or fault in the sight of God our Father is this: to go to the help of orphans and widows in their distress and keep oneself untarnished from the world' (James 1:27). Scripture also provided the solution to the problems of the irreligious poor: 'Start a boy on the right road, and even in old age he will not leave it.' (Proverbs 22:6) By following the 'right road', the virtuous Christian path, in this world, the poor would receive their spiritual rewards in the next. This truth, little questioned at the end of the 17th century, was the ultimate argument for leading a blameless, God fearing life in whatever station you had been cast for your allotted time on earth.

Looking back from the vantage point of the 21st century, with 150 years of research into the social causes of poverty to enlighten our thinking, the belief that God deliberately condemns some to a life of deprivation and want seems, at best, quaint and archaic. A pioneer in that research was the great social reformer Charles Booth, who shortly after Mrs Alexander wrote her famous hymn had a very different response when he first encountered extreme poverty whilst canvassing in the slums of Toxteth, Liverpool, as a candidate in the 1865 parliamentary elections: rather than accepting the condition of the poor as the will of God, this experience led him to question and ultimately abandon his religious faith as he pursued his great campaigns for social justice.

The charity school movement was, then, very much a product of its time, and it is essential to understand contemporary thinking if we are to understand both the rise of the charity schools and the curriculum which they taught: in the words of the pioneering historian of the movement, M G Jones, 'The charity schools came into being chiefly . . . to condition the children for their primary duty in life as hewers of wood and drawers of water'.[24] The curriculum the children followed was therefore based around knowing their catechism and their Bibles, which required the ability to read. After this, for the boys, came writing and possibly casting accounts. For the girls, sewing took precedence over accounts, and possibly over learning how to write.

1699 to 1710: the Society for Promoting Christian Knowledge (SPCK) and the first decade of the movement

There was by now a solution to the problem of child poverty, as it was then understood, which a large group of the influential, educated and compassionate could support: it attuned with their religious beliefs and met the essential economic criterion of providing value for money. All that was now needed was a catalyst for action. This was provided in 1699 with the formation of the Society for Promoting Christian Knowledge (SPCK). For this reason 1699 is arguably the first important date in the development of popular, national education in the British Isles. Previously, individual schools had been founded randomly by individual acts of charity, but this date marks the first organised movement with the aim of setting up schools in towns and villages across the country according to a published blueprint. At first sight the entry in the Romford Vestry Book for 5 September 1710 might appear to record an entirely local initiative, but the inspiration behind that initiative, and even some of the wording used in the record, came directly from the SPCK.

The SPCK was founded by five pious and public spirited men with two original aims: to carry the Gospel to the plantations abroad, and to establish catechetical schools at home. Their inspiration for this second aim had come from Germany, and particularly the work of the Lutheran Hermann Francke at Halle. Francke balanced Luther's doctrine of justification by faith with an emphasis on good works. God's will could be done, he believed, by rescuing neglected and godless children and placing the means of salvation in their hands. In the schools which he established more than half of the seven hour school day was devoted to the Bible, catechism, worship and religious discipline, and part of the rest was given to the godly discipline of labour. Here was a clear model which the SPCK wished to replicate on these shores.

In 1699 the Society sent its first circular letter to the clergy in England and Wales inviting them to become corresponding members of the society and to forward its aims by setting up schools in their parishes. The earliest practical response was, unsurprisingly, in London and Westminster. Indeed, the first charity schools here predated the formation of the Society. Very soon parishes in the capital were competing with each other to set up schools. Compared to those elsewhere, London schools benefitted from a greater supply of 'qualified' and experienced teachers, greater access to financial support, and greater opportunities for the children to find suitable work after they left the schools. Progress was swift, and on 8 June 1704, the Thursday in Whitsun-Week, those gentleman concerned in promoting the charity schools in and around the cities of London and Westminster arranged a celebratory meeting and service at St Andrew's Church, Holborn. This was attended by around two thousand people, including the Masters and Mistresses from many of these schools who were accompanied by the poor children in their care.

The Sermon preached on this occasion was subsequently published in a volume which also contained *An Account of the Methods Whereby the Charity Schools have been Erected and Managed, And of the Encouragement given to them Together with A Proposal of Enlarging their Number, and Adding some Work to the Children's Learning, thereby to render their Education more Useful to the Publick*. The first pages in this *Account* give details of 54 schools in and about London and Westminster 'and within Ten Miles thereof', 12 parishes having two or more schools. Two of these schools had been set up 11 or 12 years previously, allowing us to date the start of the movement to 1692, and all the others within the last 8 years. Together, these school were educating over 2000 children and had attracted annual subscriptions of £2,164. There then followed *A short Account of some Charities of the like Nature in other Parts of the Kingdom*. Thirty-three places were listed with brief details of their Charity Schools, which numbered about 50 in total educating about 5,000 children. None of these schools was in Essex, although the reader is advised that the published list is not comprehensive: there are many others, 'but of these we can give no certain account'. This 1704 report indicated that the SPCK's first circular letter of 1699 had met with a very positive response and that the Society had successfully launched a co-ordinated, popular mass movement which was gradually spreading across the country.

On the Thursday in Whitsun-Week 1705 a similar meeting was held, but on this occasion in St Sepulchre's, Holborn, and again the Sermon (delivered by a different but equally eminent Divine) and *The Account of the Charity Schools* were published together. This became the annual format: the St Sepuchre's gathering on the Thursday in Whitsun week, followed by the publication of the Sermon and the *Account* of the London and Westminster schools, to which was added a list with brief details of the schools which the Society had been informed had been set up in places outside London.

The SPCK blueprint for setting up and running a charity school

The SPCK did not manage schools itself and only rarely helped finance them, but through its publications, public meetings and private correspondence the Society gave advice on fund-raising and the management of schools, notably through the annual publication of the *Account of Charity-Schools*. This included a blue print for how new schools might be set up and run, based on successful practice in London and Westminster. This document would have been read in parishes up and down the country, and from it we can reconstruct the early life of a typical charity school such as the one soon to be established in Romford.

The publication[25] begins with a statement of principle which neatly links the needs of the poor with the needs of the wider society:

> It is manifest, That a Christian and Useful Education of the children of the POOR, is very necessary to their Piety, Virtue, and honest Livelihood.

These are necessary not only for their happiness 'both Here and Hereafter', but also for the 'Ease and Security of all other People' who may need their help or be liable 'to receive Injuries from them'. It continues by reminding the 'private individual' that the beginning and end of Christian charity is the glory of God and the good of mankind, and that he cannot achieve these ends better than by contributing to the Christian education and useful bringing up of the poor. It is for this purpose that some Charity Schools have recently been set up 'For the education of Poor children in the Knowledge and Practice of the Christian Religion, as professed and Taught in the Church of England'. These final words are repeated again and again in the SPCK literature, and their echo is clearly heard in the foundation document of the Romford school, indicating the influence of the SPCK literature on its founders.

The statement of principle is followed by practical advice. The usual process for setting up a school begins with the parish priest (or some other person) gathering a group of 4 or 5 supporters of the project, and this group then publicises their intentions and seeks other subscribers. The *Account* states that it usually takes about 7 or 8 months to raise the funds necessary to open the school, and during this time rules must be agreed for the governing and managing of the school. It then specifies the qualities required of the schoolmaster, how he should run the school, the curriculum to be followed, how trustees should be appointed and how they should conduct their business. It is a template which the Society hoped would be followed up and down the country as each town set up its own school.

The *Account* is very clear about the children to be admitted to these schools, stating that they 'shall be real Objects of the Charity' living in or near the Parish and 'be of the full Age of Seven Years, and not above the Age of Twelve Years.' They are to be selected by the subscribers, perhaps in turn, and the subscriber presenting the child should check that they are genuine 'objects of charity' and this should be verified by the treasurer and trustees also. Such 'real Objects of the Charity' would certainly have been from very poor families living on the margins of existence, probably idling away undisciplined lives, possibly adding to the family income by casual work or begging, perhaps even resorting to petty theft. (For those found guilty of straying into such criminality society was unforgiving: between 1710 and 1720 there are records of teenagers being hanged at Tyburn for burglary and theft, and from 1717 convicted criminals began to be transported to America.) This was the type of child whose life would be transformed by the Charity School, having been forced into a strict daily regime, force fed a wholesome diet of religious learning, and probably also forced into an unwonted coat, cap and pair of shoes. To ensure that more prosperous families did not take advantage of an apparent opportunity for an education at the expense of the subscribers, the *Account* states that the master must teach only the poor children of the school and that he shall not receive any money at any time for any child's education 'but shall content himself with his Salary, upon Pain of forfeiting his place'.[26]

Such a system would work only with the co-operation of the parents, and the *Account* notes in detail the 'Orders' which were to be read and given to the parents on the admittance of their child. Indeed, the Society had these printed on a half sheet for schools to purchase and give to parents. These 'Orders' state that parents must ensure they send their children to school during school hours, 'clean wash'd and comb'd', sickness being the only acceptable reason for keeping them at home. To ensure consistent discipline, they must set their children good examples and keep them in good order at home, correcting them for their faults or informing the Master, 'Whereby the whole Behaviour of their Children may be the better ordered'. They must also accept without complaint whatever discipline the Master shall inflict on their child:

> That in Regard the Subscribers to this School will take due care that the Children shall suffer no Injuries by their Master's Correction, which is only designed for their Good; the Parents shall freely submit their Children to undergo the Discipline of the School, when guilty of any Faults, and forbear coming thither on such Occasions. So that the Children may not be countenanced in their Faults, nor the Master discouraged in the Performance of his Duty.

Supporting the school in disciplining the child was not the only responsibility of parents; they had also to test them on their work. The Society acknowledged that this was to be done for the benefit of the parent as well as the child, thereby disseminating discipline, religion and learning amongst the adult poor:

> And that this School may not only serve for the Instruction and Benefit of the Children, but also of their Parents, particularly of such who cannot Read; they for their own Sakes, as well as their Childrens, are frequently to call on them at Home to repeat their Catechism, and to Read the holy Scriptures, especially on the Lord's-Day, and to use Prayers Morning and Evening in their Families; so that all may the better be informed of their Duty, and by a constant and sincere Practice thereof, procure the Blessing of God upon them.

And not just the Blessings of God, but also the approbation of the school which, if the parents did not observe these orders, would be withdrawn, the children being dismissed from the school and forfeiting their school-clothes.[27]

These clothes were one of the three elements the ideal and well financed charity school provided for each child: learning, clothing whilst at school, and an apprenticeship upon leaving. For the parent, the provision of a good suit of clothes and a pair of shoes for their raggedly-dressed and barefoot child was undoubtedly a keen incentive to send them to school. For the school governors and subscribers, having the children clothed was not simply a source of pride, it also made them conspicuous in the community so any aberrant behaviour was more likely to be detected:

> The children shall wear their Caps, Bands,[28] Cloaths, and other marks of Distinction, every Day; whereby the Trustees and Benefactors may know them, and see what their Behaviour is abroad.

However, the cost of clothing all the children in a school made this an ideal which many trustees could not afford.

Then as now, to ensure attendance, whether clothed, partially clothed or unclothed, the roll was to be called every morning and afternoon and the names of those who were 'Tardy' or 'Absent' noted down. It was also recommended that the Master keep a chart where 'Great Faults' such as swearing and stealing were to be noted and laid before the subscribers or trustees at their next meeting so the offender might be corrected or expelled.

It would seem that those championing the system believed that for it to be successful the child should have as little time as possible in which to be tempted away from the prescribed path. The Master was permitted to allow the children to break-up up to three times a year at the 'usual Festivals', but not oftener, and they were specifically not to be allowed to be off school during Bartholomew Fair[29] 'for fair of any Harm by the ill Examples and Opportunities of Corruption'. A marginal note adds that children in Cambridge should not be off school during Stourbridge Fair[30] for the same reason. (If the attractions of Romford Market were more prosaic, the position of the Charity School in the Market Place inevitably provided regular and far more frequent opportunities for temptation which over two and a half centuries many scholars failed to resist.)

Finally, the *Account* addressed the issue of the cost of setting up such a school, which in London was typically about £75 per year for 50 boys cloathed, 'for which a School-Room, Books and Firing are provided, and a Master paid, and to each Boy is given Yearly 3 Bands, 1 Cap, 1 Coat, 1 Pair of Stockings, and 1 Pair of Shoes'. The equivalent cost for a school in London for 50 girls was about £60 a year, her annual clothing consisting of '2 Coifs, 2 Bands, 1 Gown and Petticoat, 1 Pair of knit Gloves, 1 Pair of Stockings, and 2 Pair of Shoes'. Acknowledging that for some schools the subscriptions would not meet the sum required to teach and clothe the proposed number of children, the Society suggested that in this case the minister, or someone else, might preach a yearly (or quarterly or monthly) sermon or lecture to promote the charity and attract funding at the church door. There was a greater likelihood of success in this if the public were able to observe the visible improvement of the children in answering their catechism and joining in the church services. The next best way of raising support and funding, it advised, was through the examination of the children in their schools in order to highlight their improvement in spelling, reading, and particularly in their knowledge of Church doctrine and scriptural references and their knowledge of the importance of practising their Christianity. Other schools, the *Account* continued, would be in the fortunate situation where the monies subscribed would be more than sufficient for their requirements, and in such cases the 'overplus' had sometimes been used to increase the number of schools in the town or to increase the number of scholars in the school; sometimes it was used to put out children in apprenticeships or to purchase land to endow apprenticeships; sometimes to build school houses or work houses; and sometimes to find work and employment for the children.

1707 to 1711: the early impact of the charity school movement in Essex
In 1707 Malden and Woodhamwater[31] were the first two places in Essex to appear on the SPCK list of towns with Charity Schools, with Colchester added in 1709 and Bradfield in 1710. When the *Account* appeared in May 1711 it detailed 112 schools in and around London and Westminster, and listed over 345 places outside London with schools, some having more than one. (Oxford, for example, had five schools.) In just seven years the number of schools in the London and Westminster area had doubled, and the number in the rest of the country had increased tenfold. To keep down the cost of the publication the descriptions of these provincial schools were kept short, but a comparison of the entries for the eight places in Essex listed that year indicates the variation in provision in the schools which had already opened in the county.

> **Bradfield**: 'A School for 20 Children, Subscriptions £10 *per Annum,* where is also a School-House and Accommodation for a Master built by a private Person.'
> **Chigwell**: '10 poor Girls taught, to each of which are given Caps, Bands, and Aprons at the Charge of a private Person.'
> **Colchester** [A longer entry, summarised here]: 2 schools, 1 for 70 Boys and the other for 50 Girls &Boys. Partly clothed; rest distinguished by caps and bands. 2 schools and 3 dwellings for masters and mistresses provided at cost of £232 5s 3d. (including cost of repairs). Income last year £164 18s 6d.
> **Malden**: '£6 *per Annum* for ever bequeathed for teaching 6 poor children here. And 40s by the same person to each of them towards their Cloathing.'
> **Rumford**: 'A School for 40 Boys and 20 Girls they are taught, and in part cloathed. Subscription about £60 *per Annum.* The Master and Mistress have £35 a Year.'
> **Stansted Mount Fitchet**: '10 Children taught at the Expence of a private Person.'
> **Withersfield**: 'Mr Fitch deceased has given £20 a Year for ever, for the teaching 20 Boys and has given more to cloath them as they leave the School. He has also given £5 a Year towards teaching 20 other poor Children here.'
> **Woodhamwater**: 'The Minister keeps some of the poorest Children at School at his own Charge.'

Some of these schools were financed by subscriptions, some by an endowment, some by the generosity of a single benefactor; some children were clothed, others not; only at Bradfield and Colchester were there school houses and, additionally, accommodation provided for the Master or Mistress; no school is able to provide apprenticeships when their scholars leave school. Clearly Romford was second only to Colchester in the size of the subscriptions to fund its school and the number of children the town could therefore educate.

The extent to which the charity school movement had taken root by the time the Charity School at Romford admitted its first pupils is highlighted in this extract from a letter which Queen Anne wrote to the Archbishops of Canterbury and York six months later, on 20 August 1711:

> For as much as the pious Instruction and Education of Children is the Surest Way of Preserving and Propagating Knowledge and Practice of True Religion, it hath been very acceptable for Us to hear that for the attaining these Good Ends many Charity Schools are now created throughout this Kingdom by the Liberal Contributions of our Good Subjects; We do therefore earnestly recommend it to you, by all Proper Ways to encourage and promote so excellent a Work, and to Countenance and assist the Persons principally concerned in it as they shall always be sure of our Protection and Favour.

Six months after this, on 6 February 1712, Sir Richard Steele was to write in the most popular periodical of the time, *The Spectator*:

> The Charity-Schools which have been erected of late Years, are the greatest Instances of publick Spirit the Age has produced.

However, he immediately quashed any suggestion there might be that the financial support for these institutions was widespread:

> But indeed when we consider how long this Sort of Beneficence has been on Foot, it is rather from the good Management of those Institutions, than from the Number or Value of the Benefactions to them, that they make so great a Figure.[32]

As the century advanced, his words were to prove prescient.

Chapter 3

'so excellent a Work': the founding of the Charity School at Romford

1710 - 1718

1710/11: The opening of the Charity School

The SPCK had two types of membership: Subscribing Members, the great and the good whose subscriptions sustained the work of the Society and some of whom were actively involved in deciding its policies and strategies, and Corresponding Members. Corresponding Members were

> such Persons in Great Britain and Ireland, and other Protestant Countries, as are chosen to correspond with the Society, on purpose to acquaint them, from time to time, with the State of Religion in their Neighbourhood; to suggest such Methods of doing Good as occur to them; to distribute Bibles, and several useful Tracts recommended by the Society; and to remit occasional Benefactions, which they themselves are pleased to contribute, or collect from well disposed Christians.[33]

These were the Christian foot soldiers, mainly clergymen, who pushed forward the work of the Society in every part of the Kingdom (and beyond), particularly in championing the setting up of charity schools in their localities and in securing the subscriptions to fund these schools. The Society sent out regular circular letters and packets of Bibles, tracts and other printed material for distribution, and if the individual correspondent did not write to the Society for any other reason he frequently wrote a letter of thanks acknowledging receipt of this material, perhaps adding a sentence or two on developments in his locality. Each of these letters was meticulously summarised in the Society's Abstract Letter Book, and it is from these entries that we find the earliest references to the Charity School at Romford.

The first person to inform the Society of the intention to set up a school in the town had, as far as we know, no contact with it. His name was Robert

Watts, he was a fellow of St John's College, Oxford, and he was nominated as a Corresponding member in the spring of 1708 when he was 24 or 25 years old. Watts was to prove exceptional in his commitment to the Society, actively promoting the setting up of schools, passing on information gleaned on his travels, and offering practical suggestions for improving the administration of the society and its publications (suggestions which were not always accepted and were sometimes, perhaps, unwelcome). Watts also promoted the Society internationally through his correspondence with sympathisers abroad and through his translations of relevant German texts for the Society.

On 3 October 1708 he wrote to the Society to thank them for a parcel he had received and reported that several members of the University were 'great encouragers of the Society's excellent Designs, and had not a little contributed to promote the Noble Charity School at Oxford, the Subscriptions for which were now at about £150 per annum'. At the end of December that year he travelled to London and attended the SPCK meeting on 13 January 1709. The fact his name, followed by 'Correspond.', is in brackets suggests he was a guest visitor at this regular meeting, but he did make one contribution which was recorded in the minutes: 'Mr Watts acquainted the Society that there was a design of erecting a School at Rumford in Essex.' At the back of the 1708 – 1711 Volume of the Minutes of the SPCK are several Appendices, one of which is headed 'Charity Schools reported to be erecting'. Mr Watt's information was duly recorded in this list, but with no additional detail.

How did this young man pick up this information? There is no evidence that his travels took him into Essex, nor that he mentioned Romford or its school again in his correspondence with the Society. A possible explanation is that he heard about the plans from a contact at New College, the Patron of the Living and almost certainly the *Alma Mater* of the Vicar of Hornchurch, Thomas Roberts.[34] Had Roberts written to the College to ask for financial support for the proposed school? Whatever its source, this information stands alone, being (as far as we know) the only reference to the proposed school prior to the minute of the Vestry meeting of 5 September 1710, twenty months later. It does, however, modify our reading of the opening of that minute: 'Whereas a Charity School is Erecting or setting up wth all possible Speed' suggests the urgency of a new project, but we now know that the gestation period was rather longer than this might suggest.

Following the Vestry meeting the SPCK received fresh information on activity in Romford from two sources. John Brett was from a Romford family and was Minister at Dagenham when he became a Corresponding Member in July 1710. He wrote on 31 October to thank the Committee for a packet of literature they had sent, adding 'that there is a Church School erecting at Rumford, and that several [people] thereabouts privately put poor children to school at their own charge.' On 9 November the Society received further information when 'Mr Skeate . . . reported that at Rumford in Essex the subscriptions amount to £70 per annum for 30 Boys and 20 Girls, to be taught in 2 Schools and that they have likewise had a promise of [a further £5].' We do not know the identity of Mr Skeate nor the source of his information, but a further letter from John Brett, written on 29 January 1711 confirmed what he had reported:

> That ye 2 Church Schools [in Rumford] were opened ye Monday after 12th Day, one consisting of 40 Boys and the other of 20 Girls, taught & cloathed. That ye Subscriptions are about 60 pounds per annum, of which the Master and Mistress are allowed £35 a year. They come to Church on Holydays & Sundays & have Common Prayer books, Bibles & Testaments given 'em, according as they are taught.

Even in the paraphrase in the Abstract Letter Book one can sense his excitement.

The school has traditionally dated its origin from the entry in the Vestry Book on 5 September 1710, but this records only the agreement of the Vestry for the room over the vestry in the church to be used to accommodate the schools. The school in fact received its first students on 8 January 1711, the Monday after Twelfth Night. However, as England then used a calendar which started on March 25th (Lady Day), January fell in the last quarter of 1710. This anachronism supports the truth of the claim that 1710 was indeed the year when the school was founded, although for the sake of clarity throughout this history January, February and March will be treated as falling at the beginning of the new year rather than at the end of the old year, although this change did not take place until 1751.

The early management and financing of the school

Did the school open with 30 or 40 boys? Had John Brett visited the school in its first three weeks or was he reporting what he had heard? A few months later the first entry for the schools in the 1711 SPCK *Accounts of the Charity Schools* agreed that '40 Boys and 20 Girls' were taught, but states they are only 'in part cloathed'. Furthermore, when we turn to the first volume of *Accounts* we see that both he and Mr Skeate had exaggerated the school's resources.

The first page of this volume commences:

> The Book of Accounts for the Charity School at Romford Commencing at Christmas 1710
>
> At which time Samuel Hopkinson was Elected Master of the said School by
>
> | Mr Thomas Roberts | } |
> | Mr James Hotchkis | } |
> | Mr Thomas Gilman[35] | } Trustees – of which Mr William |
> | Mr William Sandford | } Sandford is Treasurer |
> | Mr John Milligan | } |
> | Mr Christopher Bayley | } |

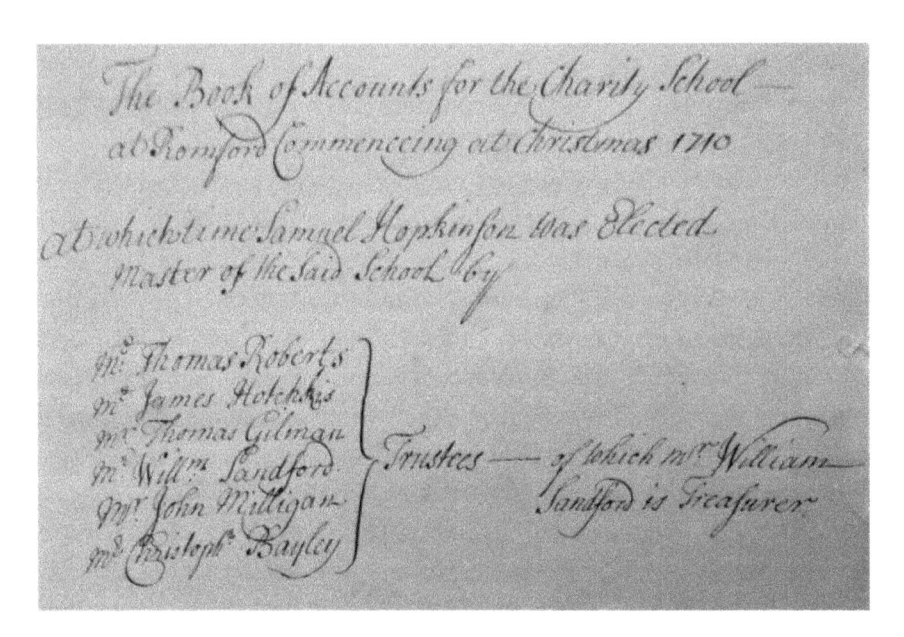

The first entry in the Trustees' first volume of *Accounts*

It then states that the money which had been raised between Michaelmas and Christmas 1710 amounted to £34 16s 7½d (approximately equivalent to £5,225 in 2020).[36] This money had come from three sources: £17 08s 7½d was collected from 'severall contributors' (the first subscribers); £16 02s was a gift from Thomas Roberts, the Vicar of Hornchurch; and another £1 06s was raised by private charity.

The distinction between subscribed money and unsubscribed gifts will remain important, and we should note that when these first contributions are added together the school opened with the bare minimum of funds. Mr Hopkinson was paid 13s 6d a week for his services and those of his wife, which amounted to £35 02s a year (as correctly reported by Brett), and it is possible that Mr Roberts' very generous gift was made to ensure that the school would open with sufficient funds to cover the salary of the schoolmaster for the first year, if nothing more. Was the twenty months or more between the idea of setting up the school and its opening because the first trustees had difficulty at first in attracting subscribers? Was it necessary to secure the use of the room above the vestry because by September 1710 there were sufficient subscriptions promised to pay for the schoolmaster but not enough for alternative accommodation? Perhaps they hoped that with the school in operation the sight of the children cloathed (or 'part cloathed') would elicit the necessary further subscriptions. If so, in this they would be proved correct.

The Vestry Minutes of 5th September 1710 refer to 'Severall well disposed persons' from both within and outside the parish [of Hornchurch] having 'subscribed and Agreed to Contribute severall sundry Sums'. In the *Annual Account* the SPCK gave very precise instructions for how a charity school should be managed, and to ensure these orders were known and observed it required that they be displayed in the school. The subscribers were expected to play an important role, meeting on the first Wednesday after every quarter day with the orders being read aloud in public before the business of the meeting commenced. Rules specified that the decision of the majority at these meetings was to be binding, that a treasurer and six trustees were to be chosen each year from the subscribers at a meeting on Wednesday in Easter Week, and that with the minister (who was always to be a trustee) these people were to have the immediate care and government of the school and were to report its state and condition to the subscribers at each quarterly meeting. The subscribers were also to play an important role in the management of the funds of the school: they were to decide how any spare money was to be invested; the treasurer had to give his Bond to four or more subscribers so that if he should die in office the money would not be lost to the school; and the treasurer had to keep accounts of all income and expenditure which was to be open to the inspection of the subscribers and others and which was to be examined by the subscribers at least twice a year at their quarterly meetings.

This was the theory, but practice in Romford was, from the start, very different. Six elected trustees, a treasurer and the minister suggests an executive of eight, but there were only six in total when the school opened in Romford. There would be times when the trustees would number many more than eight, and although they were in theory all subscribers some at times fell seriously into arrears with their subscriptions. There would also be subscribers to the Romford School who never seem to have played any role in its management, which never seems to have been as transparent as the SPCK intended it to be. From the beginning it was the trustees, not the subscribers, who appointed replacement or additional trustees, and it was the trustees, not the subscribers, who inspected the accounts (irregularly) and then countersigned them. Because the early minutes do not start with a list of those present, it is only from the signatures under the accounts that we know which trustees were in attendance at any meeting. Assuming that William Sandford was usually present, which we do not know for certain because he did not countersign his own accounts at first, most of the early meetings appear to have been attended by five or all six of the trustees, but no other name is noted until later when additional trustees were agreed by these men.

The accounts never refer specifically to meetings of subscribers, although the meeting on 27 October 1718 is described as a 'Yearly Meeting', and there is reference at a meeting held in August 1723 to the dinner at the Yearly Meeting. On 2 February 1723 there is reference to the Michaelmas General Meeting, and the meeting on 3 June 1727 is described as a General Meeting. Was a General Meeting the same as the Yearly Meeting, or were there quarterly General Meetings of subscribers, at one of which a dinner was held? Or was the dinner just for the trustees? We do not know. Even on those rare occasions when the minutes refer to a General or a Yearly Meeting we never have a list of attendees nor a list of subscribers, nor is there ever a record of the amount each subscribed.

There is, however, one group of subscribers who escape from this anonymity: those who defaulted on their subscriptions. We know these men because the accounting method of the first treasurer, William Sandford, was to include all promised subscriptions under Receipts, and then if any of this money did not materialise to record the sum as 'lost money' or 'deficiencies' on the disbursement side. For example, the accounts signed in February 1714 contain the figure of 7s 6d described as 'Lost Money by Mr John Petchy 3 quarters' and also 2s 6d 'lost' by John Allibond for 1 quarter, indicating that both of these people had subscribed 2s 6d a quarter. Over the next four years there were to be at least another sixteen such entries recording 'lost' money, these indicating that John Jermyn, one of those present at the vestry meeting on 5 September 1710, had subscribed 5s a quarter and that by October 1716 he was six quarters behind with payments, and that John Locksmith, who as we shall see performed various services for the school and succeeded Thomas Kneaton as the parish clerk, had promised 1s a quarter and was two years behind by September 1717. John Brett, the Vicar of Dagenham and SPCK correspondent, was noted in August 1715 as being behind with two instalments of his 2s 6d a quarter subscription, money which would never be recovered because he had joined his forebears in the Romford churchyard the previous month. If these subscriptions were typical, most of the subscribers had pledged 2s {equivalent to about £15 in 2020} or 2s 6d a quarter, occasionally 1s or 5s. Two of the more generous were also noted as 'behind' because they had died: Thomas Gilman, one of the original trustees, had pledged 7s 6d but had died by October 1716, and Madam Mildmay was dead by the following September, depriving the charity of her quarterly 10s. To put these sums into perspective, at this time the Master was being paid 13s 6d a week and in April 1714 a total of £2 12s was 'lost', the equivalent of his salary for a month.

We should not necessarily be sanctimoniously critical of those who fell behind with their promised subscriptions. In those days, before modern banking, cheque books and direct debits, physically collecting the money was time consuming, and we would therefore expect some subscribers to be six or nine months behind with payment. Much of this 'lost' money was subsequently 'found' when arrears in subscriptions were received, and these sums were then added to the 'Receipts' side of the accounts. However, there were those such as John Newbold who by April 1714 had not paid his subscription for nine quarters, and Thomas Freckleton of Brinks Place, Hornchurch, who in October 1716 was eleven quarters in arrears and owed £2 15s. Whether he caught up we do not know, but in February 1722 he was 'aged and very infirm' and wrote his will in which the first two items (after the payment of his funeral expenses) were bequests of £5, the first to the Charity School and the second 'to my loving friend' James Hotchkis, the Chaplain of Romford.

We do not know the names of many of these first subscribers, but can we work out how many there might have been? The first entry in the account book gives an opening figure of £17 8s 7½d having been collected from 'severall contributors' between Michaelmas and Christmas, the quarter year before the school opened (or approximately between the vestry meeting on 5 September 1710 and the end of the year). Assuming the average subscription was indeed 2s or 2s 6d a quarter, we have a very approximate figure of between 140 and 175, but this may be very inaccurate. It seems a high figure, but the list of those who were behind with their subscriptions added to the six trustees comes to nearly twenty-five, to which we have to add all those unnamed subscribers who never defaulted.

Setting up schools in country parishes was much more difficult than in London, from where the SPCK drew its exemplars, and depended to a much greater extent on the commitment and the ability of the local clergyman. History frequently records the 18th century clergy as idle and apathetic, but many were hardworking men who accepted responsibility for the poor and were keen to improve their lot. Romford and Hornchurch were blessed at this time with two such men, and with both Roberts and Hotchkis exhorting their congregations to support the venture 150 subscribers is perhaps not unrealistically high. Although comparatively close to London, and at this time a parish in the Diocese of London, Romford and Hornchurch were essentially of a similar size with comparatively large and diverse populations, and the evidence suggests that the enthusiasm for the new school and the desire to support it was quite widespread both socially and economically. The few names we do have suggest early support from both the local nobility and gentry and the middle class traders and manufacturers. Whether the important farming middle-class contributed we do not know: they were often hostile to the education of the poor because it deprived them of cheap child labour.

In addition to subscriptions, the school also received legacies and gifts from people who may or may not have been subscribers: in 1712 'a person unknown' donated £10 15s {perhaps equivalent to £1,400 in 2020}[37], and in May 1717 two legacies were received, one of £1 1s 6d and the other of 10s 9d. All of these sums, large or small, indicate good will and support for the new school.

On 27 March 1718 William Sandford balanced his accounts with two last entries on the 'Disburstments' (or debit) side. The first recorded that the subscriptions owed by 'Severall persons' and due at Michaelmas amounted to £21 1s 7½p; the second noted: 'More of Mr Grafton £01 05s'. The following day he resigned the treasurership and this source of information about the early subscribers closes. In future there would be no presumption that subscriptions would be paid: the money collected was entered under 'Receipts', with a not infrequent separate heading for payments in arrears, and the entries for 'Lost Money' with the names of the defaulters disappear from the debit side.

The first six trustees
What do we know about the first six trustees, the small, self-perpetuating group of men who appear to have been answerable only to themselves? The two clergy head the list in the Account Book, followed by the four laymen. Thomas Roberts was probably in his early 50's in 1710. A bachelor, he had been the Vicar[38] of Hornchurch since 1696 and was a comparatively wealthy man. Without his initial gift of £16 2s the Charity School might not have opened when it did. His housekeeper was probably his niece, Dorothy, who predeceased him: we know she was a spinster who lived in Hornchurch, and when she made her will in September 1718, the year before she died, she asked that her body be 'decently buried at the discretion of my honored uncle Thomas Roberts, Vicar of Hornch., whom with the advice and assistance of my loving friend Mrs Elizabeth Hotchkis of Rumford I desire to order my funeral'.

Elizabeth's husband, James Hotchkis, was the Chaplain of Romford and undoubtedly the man who had the greatest influence on the early history of the schools. His entry in the Oxford University Alumni states:

> Hotchkis, James, s[on of] J[ohn], of North Okington, Essex, pp. ALL SOULS' COLL., matric. 26 March, 1686, aged 16; B.A. 1689.

We should note the dates. The phrase 'the 18th century Charity School movement' suggests rationality and enlightenment, but those responsible for the creation of these schools had experienced the final drama in the religious conflicts which had divided the country for the previous 170 years. In 1688, during Hotchkis's second year at Oxford, the 'Glorious Revolution' had forced the Catholic James II to flee the country, surrendering the throne to his protestant daughter Mary and her husband, William of Orange. Unlike Roberts, a probable Welshman, Hotchkis was from Essex, having been born and brought up in North Ockendon, seven miles south-east of Romford. He was 41 in 1710, having been baptised on 20 November 1669. His father's first wife had died in November 1660 leaving him with at least three surviving children, and James was the fifth of seven children born to the second wife, Mary Staploo, who came from East Horndon, twenty miles south of North Ockendon. John Hotchkis seems to have been a prosperous country gentleman of independent means and the family were well connected locally.[39] Their neighbours and friends included Sir Thomas Littleton, 3rd Baronet of North Ockenden, Essex, and Stoke St Milborough, Shropshire, and his wife Lady Anne. Between 1689 and his death in December 1709 Sir Thomas sat in the House of Commons, serving as Speaker from 1698 to 1700.[40]

On 10 May 1704 James married Elizabeth Thickness at St Antholin Budge Row in London,[41] a City church with Hotchkis connections, the rector between September 1679 and May 1696 having been one Joshua Hotchkis. Elizabeth came from Kelveden Hatch, eleven miles north of North Ockendon, and her family appears to have been more affluent than James's. In 1706 the couple moved to Romford where, unusually and perhaps eccentrically, James chose the burial register to document his arrival, writing that 'Mr Roberts Vicar of Hornch was pleased to appoint me J. Hotchkis to succeed him and yt I entered upon ye curacy ye 14 Day of October 1706' after he had recorded that his predecessor, Samuel Keckwich, Curate of Romford and Vicar of Boreham, had died on 18 September 1706 and been buried at Boreham. Boreham is 4 miles north-east of Chelmsford, which is 18 miles north-east of Romford, a total distance which suggests that Keckwich held the Curacy of Romford as a sinecure. Such an accusation would not be levelled at Hotchkis, who does not seem to have held any other position and was very much part of the local community. Indeed, as an All Souls man his appointment was unusual because for the next 150 years all the Hornchurch and Romford clergymen would be, like Thomas Roberts, graduates of New College. Hotchkis had noted in the burial register that it had been Roberts who had appointed him, Roberts having the delegated authority from New College to do so.

James and Elizabeth's contacts in North Ockendon would prove beneficial to the school. They seem to have been particularly close to Lady Anne Littleton: when she died in 1714 she left £100 {£14,400} to the Charity School and a silver coffee pot to Elizabeth. He was probably the last of the six founding trustees to arrive in Romford, and the fact that there is no evidence of a move to set up a school before he became chaplain suggests that he may well have been the motivating spirit behind the initiative. Thomas Roberts and his niece Dorothy and James and Elizabeth Hotchkis were very close friends. When she died in 1719 Dorothy's bequests included £10 to her 'loving friend' Elizabeth Hotchkis, a guinea to James Hotchkis, and £10 to the Charity School.

William Sandford is a shadowy figure. He was a wool stapler by trade, buying the wool from the producers and sorting and grading it prior to selling it on to the manufacturers, and there is evidence that he was possibly born in March 1679 at Blackmore, Ingatestone, ten miles north-east of Romford on the Colchester Road. He was sufficiently prosperous to be listed with those Gentlemen and '40 shilling freeholders' in Romford entitled to vote in the 1715 parliamentary election. John Milligan was a linen draper who had been Churchwarden in 1696,[42] and his will mentions both his 'household goods' and his 'shop goods'. He was certainly much more prosperous than this might suggest, owning a farm called 'Archers' in Upminster and other 'real estate' in Romford, Hornchurch and High Ongar, as well as items of silver and plate which are itemised in his will. Like the other three lay trustees he had been (or was) a Churchwarden at St Edward's Chapel in Romford.

The final two trustees were brothers-in-law and business partners. It is probable that the Thomas Gilman in whom we are interested was the man of that name born in Navestock, six miles north-east of Romford, in 1639. He was therefore aged about 71 in 1710. He married Elizabeth Bayley, who came from Mountnessing, a village nine miles north-east of Romford on the Essex Road to Colchester. Her younger brother, Christopher, later went into partnership with Gilman, who was about twelve years older than him. There is evidence that these men were both members of the Worshipful Company of Founders and therefore enjoyed the benefits of being Freemen of the City of London, but this did not mean they were 'founders' by trade. They are also referred to as 'mercers', suggesting a more general trading activity. Whatever their business, their wills confirm that they were successful and prosperous. Confusingly both men had eldest sons who bore the same name as themselves and followed their fathers as trustees of the school and business partners: when the elder Christopher Bayley wrote his Will in April 1714 he referred to 'my loving Nephew and partner Thomas Gilman', this being the younger Thomas Gilman.[43]

The partial and fragmented information which has survived about these first six trustees indicates that they all came from a narrow band of wealthy and educated men at the top of the local society. They were influential in the small world encompassed within a twelve mile radius of Romford, the principal town in the area, and they knew each other well. The witnesses to Bayley's will in 1714 were the other five trustees of the Charity School, and in March 1725 John Milligan was to 'request my good friends Mr James Hotchkis and Mr Christopher Bayly to be Trustees of this my last Will'. This small group of men were moved by the spirit of the times, and their close friendships and relationships undoubtedly contributed to the success of the great enterprise they undertook together in setting up the school.

The first schoolmaster and schoolmistress and the curriculum they taught

Between 1715 and 1718 one of the appendices at the back of the SPCK's annual *Account of Charity-Schools* was headed 'A list of the Charity-School Masters and Mistresses, who have been sent from London into the Country; and who will be ready to inform any Persons that shall apply to them, in the Methods used in the London Schools'. This short list includes 'Mr and Mrs Hopkins at Rumford'. We know from this that they had previously taught in London, and we can assume that they were considered to be good role models who approached the SPCK's ideal schoolmaster and mistress both in character and in the manner in which they conducted their school. Fortunately the Society outlined in the *Account* the type of person who should be appointed schoolmaster, and this undoubtedly reflects a faint but not too distorted image of Mr Hopkins (or Hopkinson).

The schoolmaster, the Society advised, should be a communicant member of the Church of England, 'of a sober life and conversation', and at least 25 years old; he should be meek, humble, and self-controlled; he must understand the Christian Religion; he must 'write a good hand' and 'understand the Grounds of Arithmetick'; he must 'keep good Order in his Family'; and he should be approved by the Minister of the parish. As to his duties, he should be present during the appointed hours for teaching which are specified as 7 to 11 in the morning and 1 to 5 in the evening in the summer half-year, and 8 to 11 and 1 to 4 in the winter half-year. By being present, the advice continues, he will 'prevent the Disorders that frequently happen for want of the Master's Presence and Care'. The inclusion of this apparently self-evident statement shines a light on the practices and conditions which then prevailed in some schools. (That schoolmasters were not always valued as paragons of learning and character is evidenced by a reply from the Society on 6 March 1712 to a clergyman in Embeldon, Northumberland, 'about the pressing [i.e pressganging] of several Schoolmasters in your neighbourhood as vagabonds'.)

Having described the ideal Master, the Society prescribed what he should teach and how he should go about it. The main purpose of the school was 'the Education of Poor Children in the Knowledge and Practice of the Christian Religion, as Profess'd and Taught in the Church of England' - words we find echoed in the 5 September 1710 Vestry minute - and the Master's first duty was to instruct the children in these principles as they are laid down in the Church Catechism. Twice a week without fail he had to teach them to pronounce this clearly and then explain its meaning, so that even the child with the least capacity for learning would be able to repeat and understand it perfectly. In religious matters, the SPCK stressed that the master should follow the direction of the minister, informing him when a group of children were able say their catechism so that they could then be catechised in Church. Once this was achieved, the Master, using *The Whole Duty of Man*[44] as an aid in his instruction, was to develop the children's understanding of their duty as Christians. He was to take particular care of their manners and behaviour, and by all 'proper methods ... discourage and correct the Beginnings of Vice, and particularly Lying, Swearing, Cursing, taking God's name in vain, and the Prophanation of the Lord's Day, &c', reminding them when necessary of those places in the Bible and the catechism where these things are forbidden by God. In this way they would understand the use of the Holy Scriptures and the catechism and learn to govern their lives by these.

After these detailed pronouncements on the children's religious instruction, the *Account* devotes just seven lines to the secular curriculum: the Master shall teach the children 'the true spelling of Words and Distinction of Syllables, with the Points and Stops, which is necessary to true and good Reading'. Once the boys can read 'competently well', they are to be taught 'to Write a fair legible Hand, with the Grounds of Arithmetick, to fit them for Services or Apprenticeships'. A marginal note, possibly appended since the previous edition and reflecting information the Society had gained about practice in some London schools, adds: 'Note the Girls learn to read &c. and generally to knit their Stockings and Gloves; to Mark, Sew, Make and Mend their Cloaths; and several learn to Write, and some to spin their Cloaths.' Girls were expected to learn to read and to knit and sew, therefore, and although some might learn to write none appeared to learn arithmetic.

The Master's responsibilities did not end on Friday night, because he had to bring the children to Church twice every Sunday and Holy Day and teach them how to behave appropriately and join in the service. For this purpose they always had their *Bible* bound with the *Common Prayer*. (The *Account* notes after this that 'In many places the Masters and Mistresses bring the Children to Church every Day', suggesting this as an ideal.) On school days, the Master had to say prayers in the mornings and evenings, and teach the children to pray at home both when they rose and when they went to bed, and to say grace both before and after meals. These prayers and graces were to be from the public prayers of the church or as approved by the Minister.

That the Romford Charity School followed closely this recommended curriculum is indicated in the entry for the school in the 1714 edition of the *Annual Account*, which reads: 'A Sch[ool] for 40 B[oys] and 20 G[irls] partly cl[othed]. The B[oys] are taught to read, write, and cast Accompts, and the Girls, beside this, to knit and sew. *Sub.* about [£]70, *per Ann.* The Master and Mistress conduct the Ch[ildren] every *Sunday* to and from Church, and have [£]35 a Year allowed to them.' (This is ambiguously phrased: it would have been very unusual for the girls to learn elementary number work, as this implies.) This was to be the last full entry on the school because from 1715 the Society published just a simple list of schools in each county with details of the numbers of children. Only those towns appearing in these lists for the first time were accorded a more detailed entry.

The significance of the girls being taught to knit and sew lies only in the date of this entry, 1714. From the beginning of the charity school movement there had been those who believed that educating the poor was a waste of time at best, and at worst it inculcated them with idleness and pride. Mindful of this criticism, in 1712 the Society published a letter saying they 'recommend it to your consideration, whether the bringing up the Children to Husbandry, or putting them out to Services in sober Families, may not be more useful to the Publick, and no less beneficial to themselves.' There were examples of charity school children being 'usefully employed' prior to this: the minutes of the SPCK Standing Committee for 13 February 1710 record how the children in St Margaret's Westminster were employed in spinning, weaving, sewing, knitting, and making and mending shoes, and how 'At Wapping and other places near the sea' they pick Oakum. However, there is no record of a discussion about the respective merits and value of these two types of occupation, one teaching skills (as at St Margaret's) and the other providing cheap, unskilled child labour which earned the school a small income.

In 1719, five years after Rumford had recorded that it taught the girls knitting and sewing, the Society had hardened its opinion in favour of children being instructed in useful work. In an impassioned letter to its correspondents it stressed how this prepared them for the discipline of work, gave them the skills needed in their local industries, and countered a common criticism of charity schools:

> Next to improving the Minds of the Poor in all necessary Christian Knowledge, the Society have desired, and do again earnestly intreat all their Correspondents, to use their utmost endeavours to get some kind of Labour added to the Instruction given to Children in the Charity-Schools; as Husbandry in any of its Branches, Spinning, Sewing, Knitting, and any other useful Employment, to which the particular Manufactures of their respective Countries may lead them: This will bring them to an Habit of Industry, as well as prepare them for the Business by which they are afterwards to subsist in the World, and effectually obviate an Objection against the Charity-Schools, that they tend to take poor Children off from those servile Offices which are necessary in all Communities, and for which the wise Governor of the World has by his Providence designed them.

Here again is reference to the belief that charity schools upset the natural order of things by educating children above their God given station in life, to carry out the menial jobs in society.

The 1720 *Annual Account* contained an even stronger exhortation, stressing that country children could undertake 'Gardening, Plowing, Harrowing, or other servile Labour, every other Day for their Parents, [without] Prejudice to their Progress in Learning.' Nine years later, in a sentence resonant with the extreme hardship of rural life at the end of that decade, the Society went yet further in pressing the case for agricultural employment:

> The general Usefulness of Husbandry to this Nation, the real Want there has been of Persons to be imployed in it, and the Mortality

that has lately happen'd in many Countries, especially among the lower and more laborious sort of People, are in the Opinion of the Society all of them very good Reasons to engage their Members to use their utmost Endeavours, that poor Children may be bound out Apprentices to that Business.

There is no evidence that the Romford Charity School responded to this or to the similar pleas which were published in 1733 and in later *Annual Accounts*, possibly because the town's proximity to London ensured it did not suffer the extremes of rural hardship experienced elsewhere.

The school accounts in its early years

If the qualities of the schoolmaster and the nature of the curriculum must be inferred from the general advice published by the SPCK, the first account book provides specific details which help to individualise the school at this time.

Following the custom which the 18th century had inherited from the Middle Ages, the accounts of the school were based, sometimes flexibly, round the quarter days. These were the four dates in each year on which servants were hired, rents were due, and other financial transactions took place: 25 March (Lady Day), 24 June (Midsummer Day), 29 September (Michaelmas) and 25 December (Christmas). Thus we read in the Account Book that between Christmas 1710 and Lady Day 1711 a further £20 6s 10½d was raised, and on 22 June 1711 the collection at the first charity sermon raised £3 9s 4¼d. It is of note that the SPCK suggested an annual sermon as a means of raising money if the subscriptions failed to meet the sum required to teach and clothe the proposed number of children, and in Romford the tradition of a Charity School Sermon started in the school's first year. When the accounts were examined by Thomas Roberts, Thomas Gilman, John Milligan and Christopher Bayley on 26 June 1711 it was recorded that a total of £58 12s 10¼d {£8,000} had been raised, from which £41 3s 10d had been 'disburst', leaving £17 9s 0¼d 'in Mr Sandfords hand'. These disbursements are not detailed, but were noted with the words 'as appears by severall Receipts in particular'. Between midsummer and Michaelmas a further 'disburstment' of £17 18s 1d was recorded in a similar way.

However, from the beginning of the next quarter at Michaelmas 1711 we are given details of the expenditure. The main item was of course the teachers' remuneration, and Mr Hopkinson was paid every 2 or 3 weeks at 13s 6d a week, and on 22 December he was paid '4 weeks salary & Bounty Money', the latter amounting to one guinea {£140}. We do not know why this was paid. It might have been simply a bonus at the end of a successful first year, but possibly 'Bounty Money' was used in the particular sense of Queen Anne's Bounty. This was paid for the 'Augmentation of the Maintenance of Poor Clergy', but the funds from which this derived, the First Fruits, had been used to fund schoolmasters during the Long Parliament, as we noted in Chapter 1. In fact at that time many poor clergy actually became schoolmasters to make ends meet. We cannot be sure, but it is possible that a little of this Bounty made its way to Mr Hopkinson. Although we know that Mrs Hopkinson taught the girls, she is never mentioned in the accounts: all the payments are recorded as being made to her husband, to whom they legally belonged. It was to be another 160 years before the Married Women's Property Act of 1870 would change the law and recognise the wages earned by a wife as being her own, separate property.

From other itemised payments in this period from Michaelmas to Christmas 1711 we begin, dimly, to picture the needs of the school and to learn the names of those in the local community who served it: on 24 November £1 19s 6d was paid for 'a Chaldron Coles & Carriage'; on 27 December two payments were made for shoes, £1 17s to Mr Stampro and £3 15s 10d to Richard Haynes; Mr Locksmith was paid 2s 6d for 'makeing a drawer'; and a ream of paper was purchased for 10s 6d. All of the payments over this period totalled £18 13s 4d, and on 5 February 1712 the third examination of the accounts confirmed a surplus of £20 13s 4d 'in Mr Sandfords hand'. The accounts for the following quarter give us further details: on 1 March 1712 2s was paid for 'four hundred quills & 3 dozen of book covers', and on 29 March 5s was paid for '12 Lewis's Expositions', the first recorded book purchase. Mr Hopkinson received £1 bounty money on 22 March, and a further four reams of paper were purchased for £2 8s.

When the SPCK published the 1713 edition of the *Accounts of the Charity Schools*, the entry for Rumford showed the subscriptions had risen to 'about' £70 {£10,000} a year (up from 'about' £60 in 1711), and we are told 'The Master and Mistress conduct the Ch[ildren] every Sunday to and from Church'. No doubt the fact that the children and the Master and Mistress were a visible presence in church every Sunday encouraged the rise in subscriptions, and that no doubt enabled the trustees to increase the number of boys in the school. One of the great difficulties facing the trustees of a new school was appointing a competent schoolmaster, and that the school had so successfully established itself in its first two years was undoubtedly due to the qualities of Mr and Mrs Hopkinson. On 16 October 1713, after the Accounts had been examined and approved, 'it [was] agreed that Sam'l Hopkinson Schoolmaster shall have sixteen shilling a week salary from Michaelmas last'. (Michaelmas now falls on 29 September, but under the Julian calendar it then fell on 10 October.) The Master's quarterly salary therefore rose by 22% from £9 2s to £11 2s; however, the 'Bounty Money' of £1 or a guinea which he had received in December 1711, May and September 1712 and April 1713 now ceased. This salary of 16 shillings a week for the Master and Mistress would now remain fixed until April 1731, dropping in value by 12% over these years owing to inflation.

One entry in the accounts for the period from Michaelmas to Christmas 1711 is particularly intriguing: a Mr Pricklove received a Quarters Rent of £1 5s for what a later entry refers to as 'the Charity School House'. This rent was probably paid from January 1711 although it had not been itemised before now, and it raises the question of where the schoolrooms were located in these early years. An entry in the accounts for March 1712 itemises 1s paid for 'half a years Window Tax due at Ladyday' but does not specify to which property this applied, but as it was not the church it was probably this 'Charity School House'. Although the Vestry meeting of 5 September 1710 had agreed the room above the vestry could be used as a schoolroom, there is no evidence that it was in fact ever used for this purpose. Was the new floor which was required ever laid? Unfortunately we do not know because of the lack of itemised expenditure in that first year. Was this space used to begin with but proved inadequate and so the house was rented? Was new accommodation acquired to separate the girls and boys? Whatever the reason, two years later, in the autumn of 1713, a new payment appears: 'Richard Hayns for a Quarters Rent due at Michaelmas last for an additional Room to the School: 7s 6d.' (Mr Haynes, one of those who provided the school with shoes, presumably lived in or near to the Market Place.) We know that by the end of March 1714 the number of boys had risen to 50 from the 30 or 40 in January 1711, and perhaps these extra pupils either necessitated the additional room or this new space enabled the school to expand. From now on this is a regular payment, alongside the £1 5s rent to Mr Pricklove, suggesting if the room above the vestry had not been vacated by all the pupils at the end of the first year, it was most probably not in use two years later. The difference in the payment suggests Mr Pricklove provided the greater accommodation: did Mr and Mrs Hopkinson live in 'the Charity School House' and also teach some of the pupils there, or all of them until the additional room was rented?

Other entries in the accounts in these early years show that between Christmas 1715 and Lady Day 1716 a second pair of Charity Sermons was preached, this time by a Dr Clark, and that £16 11s 7d was raised, to which the preacher added a further guinea donation. This was five times the sum raised in 1711. The Charity also received 10s from the SPCK on this occasion. However, there was an outlay: Joseph Swaffield was paid 12s for the printing of Hymns prior to Dr Clark's visit and Sermon. The importance of these charity sermons and the need to present the schools in the most favourable light (and sound) is hinted at in the payment on 28 February 1718 of £2 10s for two bills submitted by Robert Magnus, 'Singing Master'. On 28 May he is paid a further £1 5s, and again on 2 September, after which these payments stop. He was undoubtedly preparing the children for the next Charity Sermon service which took place on 12 October that year.

Chapter 4

A new treasurer and the first substantial legacy

1718 - 1722

1718: a change of treasurer and trustees
The first change of trustee took place at a meeting on 13 April 1716 when Thomas Gilman, described as a mercer, was invited to take the place of his father, who had been buried on 8 March 1715/16. Having accepted, he duly signed his name under the appropriate minute. Christopher Bayley joined his brother-in-law in the burial ground on 31 December 1717, and on 28 March 1718 William Sandford, having balanced the accounts, stepped down as both trustee and treasurer and passed the money to the temporary care of Thomas Gilman Junior. At a meeting held three days later in the 'King's Head', a 40 year old pub in the Market Place, Alexander Weller, Peter Sykes and John Searle were signed up as trustees, raising the number to seven. Alexander Weller was then appointed treasurer until Michaelmas 1719 (a position which would be renewed annually until December 1723) and received the balance of £55 19s 3½d from Thomas Gilman. Three resolutions were then passed, indicating the intention to be more businesslike in their management of the Charity in future: the accounts would be audited quarterly; the treasurer would 'order the Charity School master to give to the Trustees timely notice of Every Quarterly Meeting'; and a quorum of trustees would be five, providing one of the two ministers was present.

One imagines Alexander Weller had been invited to become a trustee and take on the treasurership because he had expertise in these matters, and he certainly brought a greater clarity to the accounts. His first entry makes the source of funding clearer: the subscriptions from Michaelmas 1717 to Michaelmas 1718 'in cash' came to £57 14s, in addition to which Mr Mildmay (the father of the future trustee of that name) gave a guinea 'on the death of his Lady', Christopher Bayley had left a legacy of £3, Mrs Sarah Greenway had left £2, and £5 8s 9d was 'Received by old arrears'. The collection at a Charity Sermon preached by the Rev'd Dr Bennet on 12 October 1718 amounted to £26 17s 1¼d.

On 27 October 1718 a meeting was held which is described as a 'Yearly' meeting, although there is no record of the subscribers present. Apart from the accounts, up until now 'The Book of Accounts' has recorded only memoranda of changes of trustees and of the treasurer and extracts from Wills; now, for the first time, we have an entry which records a meeting. Above the signatures of all seven trustees are recorded the two resolutions which were agreed - perhaps by them, perhaps by the majority of subscribers present. The first, to which we will return, was a policy decision on the funding of apprenticeships; the second was a decision regarding uniform:

> It is further ordered at this Meeting the Treasurer doe provide sixty suits of Cloaths for boys and Girles by Christmas next to be distributed as the major part of the Trustees shall see convenient.

It is significant that it is the treasurer who has to action this decision. Although the two clergymen were trustees, throughout its period as a Charity School the lay treasurer was also effectively the Executive Chairman of the Foundation. Only in 1839, following the 'scandals' of the 1820's and 1830's, would the two roles be separated with the treasurer's responsibilities limited to the finances and the executive and leadership role passing to Archdeacon Grant and his successors as Vicars of Romford.

Uniform

The SPCK *Account* specified three elements the ideal and well financed charity school provided for each child: learning, clothing whilst at school, and an apprenticeship upon leaving. The entry for Rumford in May 1711 states that the children were 'in part cloathed'. Did this mean that only some children were fully clothed or that they all had only part of a uniform?

The first itemised list of expenditure covers the period from Michaelmas to Christmas 1711, and this expenditure falls under six 'headings': the Master's salary, coals, rent, paper, the making of a drawer, and shoes. Out of a total spend of £18 3s 4d {approximately equivalent to £2,430 in 2020}[45] the largest sum after the Master's salary was the £5 12s 10d {£750} paid to John Stampro and Richard Haynes for shoes. At a cost of 2s {£13} a pair, this sum would have bought about 56 pairs for the 60 children then in the school, implying that few (if any) of the children would have had these, and this was therefore the first and most important item with which to provide them.

Did being well shod justify the description of 'part cloathed', or had any money been spent on uniform prior to this? When the first, unitemised audit took place on 26 June 1711 £41 3s 10d had been 'disburst'. Approximately £18 {£2,400} of this sum would have been the salary paid to the Master, Mr Hopkinson, and probably £2 10s {£270} on two quarters rent to Mr Pricklove. We know from John Brett's letter of 29 January that when the school opened the children each had 'Common Prayer books, Bibles & Testaments', which would have cost at least £10 {£1,338}, leaving perhaps £11 for coals, paper, quills and other sundries. How much of this was available for shoes and clothes? With the cost of clothing a charity school girl or boy at this time being about 16s {£107}, including shoes, it is possible a dozen or so children may have had a full uniform, but it seems more likely a greater number had a partial uniform such as a cap and bands. Indeed, the first itemised entry for the purchase of uniform other than shoes was made on 16 July 1712 when Richard Parker was paid £4 6s 8p for such 'capps and bands'. Then, sometime between Michaelmas 1712 and March 1713, an entry records the receipt of £10 15s {£1,438} 'Charity money gave by a person (who desires to be unknown) towards cloathing some of the poor Children ten guineas', and it was no doubt this money that was used to pay Richard Parker £12 17s {£1,615} on the 22nd January 1713 for 'Cloths for the Children'. However, fourteen months later not all the children had the benefit of a uniform as recorded in two letters to the SPCK. The first, dated 25 March 1714, was from William Derham, Rector of Upminster, who said that the '... Romford Schools are advanced to 48 Boys & 20 Girls partly cloath'd...' and the second, written by James Hotchkis less than two weeks later, states that '50 B's and 20 Girls are taught and partly cloath'd.' These two letters also provide evidence that the number of boys in the school had increased from the original 30 (Mr Skeate) or 40 (John Brett) in January 1711.

It is not until January 1717, when Mr Parker is paid £37 8s 6d, that we find the first substantial payment for uniform, sufficient perhaps to clothe 45 children. This was followed by a decision in October 1718 to provide sixty suits of clothes 'by Christmas next' for which Mr Parker was paid £51 15s {£6,600} on 10 December (with a further 10s 6d being expended for bags in which to put the boys' clothes). It would seem then that the Christmas services in 1718 were the first occasions the 70 Charity School children paraded together in church all dressed in their distinctive uniforms.

From then on uniform became the major item of expenditure after the salaries of the Master and Mistress. Between 1719 and 1733 the treasurer is ordered on nine occasions to order suits of clothes, usually 40 suits for the boys and 15 or 20 for the girls, but the number varies and it is not clear how frequently a child might expect a new suit of clothes nor whether those which were outgrown but not worn out were passed on to a younger child. Possibly some or all the children were allowed to keep their charity uniforms after they left school, as certainly happened in some other places. Statements that the new clothes were 'to be distributed as usual' or 'to be distributed as the trustees shall see convenient' are no longer self-explanatory. These records show that orders were not placed for delivery at the same time each year, although phrases such as 'for Easter Sunday', 'against Whitsontide', 'against midsummer next' and 'when they come to school again after the Harvest Month is expired' suggest a religious festival or a secular date by when the trustees wanted the children to look their best. One fact is certain, however, and that is that Mr Parker benefitted greatly from these payments which were usually in excess of £43. When both the order and the payment are noted, as on 2 February 1725 when he is paid £43 13s {£6,700} for 40 boys suits and 12 gowns and petticoats, we can work out that it was costing about 16s 9d to clothe each child.

There are few references now to shoes, because from 1712 it seems Mr Hopkinson paid for these when required and was then reimbursed. That year he was repaid exactly £7, which at 2s 6d a pair would equate to fifty-six pairs. In June 1727 an order was placed for 40 suits for the boys and 16 suits for the girls, and in the autumn Mr Marshall and Mr Webber were contracted to provide a corresponding number of shoes at a cost of £5 18s 8d. This equates to a fraction under 2s 1½d a pair.

The next payment for clothes was made in 1732/33 and was split between Mr Meakins, who was paid £40 10s 4d for 'cloaths', and Henry Gillum, who received £4 7s 6d for breeches, separately itemised for the first time. These were undoubtedly the proverbial Romford leather breeches, perhaps made by Mr Gillum himself.

Book purchases
The expenditure on books in these early years requires a little analysis. We do not have the spending in the school's first 9 months itemised, but we

know from John Brett's letter of 29 January 1711 that the 60 children already had Common Prayer Books, Bibles & Testaments. The first recorded expenditure on books was for 12 copies of *Lewis's Expositions* (on the scriptures) which cost 5s on 29 March 1712; the second, in January 1713, was £3 0s 4d paid to Mr Runnington, the school's regular book supplier, for 18 Bibles and their carriage; and the third, in October 1714, was £1 14s for 6 Bibles and 6 *Whole Duty of Man*, and 12s for 12 Testaments.

From 1712 an Appendix to the SPCK's annual *Account* contains two lists of books: 'A Catalogue of Books fit to be put into the Hands Of the Masters of Charity Schools' and 'Books proper to be used in Charity-Schools'. The first of these contains about fifty titles, mainly of a religious nature and including sermons, Bible commentaries, *Expositions of the Church-Catechism, The Whole Duty of Man*, Bishop Taylor's *Holy Living and Dying*, and *Sermons at the Anniversary Meeting of the Charity-Schools in London*. Only about a quarter of the books on this list are to do with education, and these include Professor Franck's Account of the Hospital at Halle, Dr Talbot's *Christian School-Master, The Christian Education of Children*, Ayer's *Youth's Introduction to Trade*, a dictionary, and books on spelling, grammar, copying, and arithmetic.

The list of 'Books proper to be used in Charity-Schools' is weighted even more to religion, emphasising the motives of those encouraging the setting up of these schools and indicating the curriculum they offered. The list includes *A Bible, Testament, and Common-Prayer Book, The Church-Catechism* and six other titles expounding the catechism, *The first Principles of practical Christianity, Prayers for Charity Schools, The Christian Scholar, An Exercise for Charity-Schools upon Confirmation, The Whole Duty of Man by Way of Dialogue*, and the *Abridgement of the History of the Bible*. For the pupil suffering from over-indoctrination there was just one non-religious title, although it was unlikely to have provoked euphoria: *The Anatomy of Orthography: Or, a practical Introduction to the Art of Spelling and Reading English*.

The evidence we have suggests that the Charity School in Romford was very conservative in its choice of texts. The various entries for book purchases record only *Bibles* (at 3s each), *Testament* (1s), *Lewis's Expositions* (5d), and *The Whole Duty of Man* (2s 3d). This last was an English protestant devotional work published anonymously in 1658 which, partly perhaps as a result of its use in charity schools, would be a popular and influential volume amongst members of the Anglican church for over two centuries. It would be found alongside *The Bible*, *Pilgrim's Progress* and *Fox's Lives of the Martyrs* in many otherwise bookless English homes. It took its title from Ecclesiastes 12:13: 'Let us hear the conclusion of the whole matter: Fear God, and keep his commandments: for this is the whole duty of man.' One can see why it was recommended reading in the Charity Schools: this one sentence is a summary of the message the sponsors were trying to impart to the children in their charge. One must hope the charity school children gained more from it than the God fearing and grammar school educated Samuel Johnson, who later in the century would tell James Boswell that his mother made him read it but 'from a great part of [it] I could derive no instruction.'[46]

After 1719/20 book purchases are not an infrequent entry in the accounts, but the actual items purchased are not recorded. That year £4 19s 3d was paid in total for two orders from a Mr Edmond Parker. The following year he was paid £1 12s 6d, but significantly £7 was spent on books from the SPCK. Over the next few years this is where the trustees bought books for the school, spending £3 9s 6d in 1723/24 and £2 1s 9d in 1725/26 (which averages just 1s 07d {£11} per child over these two years).

The Hide family and the first substantial legacy

Of the three benefits the ideal charity school provided for its pupils, free instruction was in place from January 1711 when the school opened, and by 1718 all the children were clothed. It was also in 1718 that money became available to provide the third benefit, if only to three boys: the opportunity of an apprenticeship. Tracing this money from its source illustrates the circumstances of one of the local, wealthy families, two of whose members were to play an important part in the history of the school.

Richard Hide[47] had been born in Silchester, Southampton, and by the 1690's had taken possession of the 99 year lease on an estate at Sutton Courtney, Berkshire, which his father had signed, perhaps not coincidentally, two days after the fire of London had ended. He therefore had no connections with the area when he acquired the Manor of Nelmes, a mile north-east of Hornchurch, possibly in January 1688.[48] The manor dated back to the 1200's, but the timber-framed house he moved into had been built in the 16th century and had been greatly extended and improved by 1650, not least by the addition of a kitchen wing. In 1670 it had 15 hearths, a figure which indicates the size of the house and the wealth of its owner.[49]

The extent of Richard Hide's wealth is manifest in the Will he wrote on 4 February 1695, when 'sick of body but of sound and perfect mind and memory'. In this he instructed that his manor and lands in Essex and the lease of the estate in Berkshire be sold in order to liquidate his debts and honour all the financial agreements he had entered into, after which his remaining estate would make handsome provision for his wife and children. He appears to have had nine sons and two daughters aged between 23 (Richard) and 2 (Humphrey) at the time of his death, and his remaining estate included four houses in St Giles-in-the-Fields, six in Fleet Street (which he had recently acquired at a cost of £1,610), and unidentified land he had purchased in 1684 for £2,000. Apart from Humphrey, for some unexplained reason, he stipulated that all his younger children (that is all except the eldest, Richard, his main beneficiary) were to receive equal shares of the available money when they reached twenty-one or when they married. This lack of financial discrimination against his two daughters, Frisweed and Mary, is reinforced in the phrase he used more than once: the money was to be divided 'amongst all my younger children share and share alike'. Being a man who understood business, land and property, Richard's final request in his Will was that his executrix (his wife Mary) and the two guardians of his estate should wisely invest the money he had left to his younger children 'at interest or in the purchase of lands of inheritance or of leases or otherwise ... for the good of my children and increase of their portions'. Within two months he was dead, but the provisions he had made ensured that at the age of twenty-one his two daughters became wealthy and independent women.

Almost exactly twenty years later, on 28 February 1715, daughter Mary wrote her will. She was still living at Hornchurch, probably with her mother. After various itemised bequests the residue of her estate was to be divided between her two executors, her brother William and her sister Frisweed, but before this there is, for us, her most important lagacy:

> I doe hereby devise the summe of Two hundred pounds to the Charitie School belonging to the said Parish of Hornchurch and the Town of Rumford And doe hereby expressly, Order direct and appoint the same to be laid out by my Executors herin after named in the purchase of some freehold Estate of the yearly value of Twelve pounds as soone after my decease as conveniently may be, and in the meane time they to keep the mony and pay interest for it from six months after my decease after the purchase of such estate[.] I doe desire my said Executors to settle the same on such

Trustees and in such manner and form as by Councill learned in the Law shall be advised To the use and intent that there may be forever yearly Three Boyes of the said Parishes whereof Two to be of Hornchurch and one of Rumford put out Apprentice to some honest imployment, and each of them to have the summe of fouer pounds towards his putting out, for as the said parishes give respectivelie due Securite for the performance of this my Will Item I give devise and bequeath to the poor of the parish of Hornchurch aforesaid the sum of Ten pounds of like mony to be paid in Three Months after my decease.

Mary was probably one of the early, anonymous subscribers to the charity, and may have been privy to discussions about the desirability of funding apprenticeships. On 13 August 1715 there is the first reference to such an arrangement with £5 being paid to Mrs Sarah Slator, whose trade we do not know, for taking on Stephen Handcomb, but no other apprenticeships are recorded before Mary's death.

On 2 March 1716 Frisweed wrote her will. She was then 33 and living independently in Greenwich, but asked to be buried in Hornchurch 'where my father now lyeth'. She left £270 in varying amounts to her 'loving brother[s]', but most to her sister Mary and the executor of her will, her brother William. Ann Drayton, her servant, received £100. What is of most interest to us, however, is her commitment to her local charity school: 'I give devise and bequeath to the use of the Blue Coat Girls Charity School at Greenwich aforesaid for and towards its better support and Maintenance the sume of one hundred and fifty pounds' {£21,500}. At this time the rich frequently left a comparatively small sum to the poor of their parish, and Frisweed duly left £10 {£1,400} to the poor of Hornchurch, as her sister had done.

It is impossible to believe that the two sisters did not discuss their intentions of leaving money to their local charity schools. They both seem to have been caught up in the popular enthusiasm generated by the SPCK which was easily directed in their parishes towards their new schools, and both responded with a generosity which, in Romford, would not be matched for another ninety years.

Neither charity would have to wait long for its legacy. Mary was buried in Hornchurch on 28 December 1717, a few days short of her twenty-eighth birthday.[50] Her will was proved in the Prerogative Court of Canterbury on 7 February 1718, nine months before the first recorded 'yearly meeting' of

The copy in the Charity School Trustees' Accounts of the extract from Mary Hide's will recording her bequest. (The spelling of certain words differs from that in the transcript of her will on the previous page.)

trustees and subscribers was held on 27 October. Two important decisions were taken on this occasion: the first, as we have seen, was to provide sixty suits of clothes 'by Christmas next'; the second was a resolution concerning apprenticeships:

> Resolved at this Yearly meeting that it shall be a standing rule that the Trustees doe Never give or allow above four pounds towards puting out of an Apprentice of a boy or Girl out of the said school And it is further Order'd that there shall not more than three children be put out in a year Exclusive of Mrs Mary Hide's charity and that the Treasurer for the time being doe pay the money upon shewing the Indenture of Apprenticeship by the said Master And persuant to this Order Wee doe allow five pounds towards puting out Henry Clements and five pounds to John Jefferson and five pounds to Samuel Hanscom Apprentices out of this Charity.

This implies that somehow the trustees had committed themselves to paying £5 to fund each of these three boys, but in future the sum for each apprenticeship would be limited to a maximum of £4, in line with the sum to be received by those benefitting from the Mary Hide Charity. This might suggest that the subscribers present were unhappy with the more generous allowance to which the trustees had committed themselves. There is no commitment to fund a minimum number of children in addition to the three boys benefiting each year from the Mary Hide Charity, only to limit the number to (a further) three. It is notable that whereas Mary Hide's will had specified 'boyes', both boys and girls are included as potential beneficiaries of the school's provision. However, there is no evidence that any girl ever benefited from the charity in this way.

A total of six apprenticeships a year does not sound a great number for the size of the school, but on the assumption that there were 50 boys in the school aged between 7 and 12 at this time and that they were equally distributed across the age range, there would have been a maximum of 10 who might have wished to move on to an apprenticeship in any year. Of course it is extremely unlikely the school was structured so neatly, but the general point is that in principle Mary Hide's legacy would have provided apprenticeships for a third of the boys and the school could have doubled this number. As some would not have wished to progress in this way or possibly would have been prevented from doing so by their fathers, the provision of six might well have been sufficient for the needs of the boys in the school at this time.

Frisweed, executrix with William of Mary's will, died early in 1717 (to be followed within a year by her mother, who left £20 to the poor of the parish of Hornchurch). William alone now had responsibility for ensuring the terms of Mary's will were implemented. Her wishes were straightforward: within six months he had to purchase a freehold which would bring in £12 a year; this income was to be divided equally to pay for the apprenticeships of three chosen scholars; and trustees were to be appointed to manage this. What in fact happened?

It was not until Michaelmas 1720 that William Hide made the first payment to the trustees of £22 10s, covering the first period of 2¼ years since his sister's will was proved, and it was two months after this that the first boy was apprenticed through the Hide Charity, to be followed by three more in 1721. Over this period a further three boys are mentioned as receiving funding for their apprenticeships through the funds of the trustees of the school. The first was John Harwood, whose master, a Mr Jones, was given £4 with which to buy him clothes on 6 July 1720. Then, over the next two years, John Hughs, a Barber, was given £3 to take on James Jefferson, and John Stampro, one of the shoemakers who supplied the school, £4 for taking on Edward Harris.

On 14 April 1722 a meeting was held at which, by a Deed dated the same day, William Hide settled 9 acres of land near Gore House at the west end of Romford on Stephen Collier, who was to pay an annual rent-charge to the Mary Hide Charity of £10 p.a. 'in leiw and full compensation' of the £200 Mary had left to the school to fund the three apprenticeships each year. On the same day William Hide was elected the fifteenth trustee of the Charity School, and it was probably at this time that the first trustees were appointed to run the Mary Hide Charity, William Hide being one and the Vicar of Hornchurch and the Chaplain of Romford (by virtue of their offices) two others. Excepting the fact that her £200 would now raise only £10, not the £12 she had intended, Mary's wishes had now been fulfilled.[51]

1720: The appointment of additional trustees
On 13 February 1720 it was agreed that two more should be appointed because 'the Business of the Trust reposed in us is and has been Obst[ructed] for want of a greater number of Trustees'. The school had been founded to serve the whole of the Royal Liberty of Havering, and it is significant that

on this occasion they appointed one from Hornchurch, Thomas Clark, about whom we know little, and one from Romford, John Coleman. Coleman must have been well known to the original trustees having been one of the witnesses to Thomas Gilman's will (with James Hotchkis) and also a witness to the Codicil to Christopher Bayley's will. He was a Barber, a very different profession from today, and a very wealthy man who owned houses, land and farms in Romford, Hornchurch and Noak Hill. Two months later, on 25 April, the Account Book records that because Thomas Roberts was too infirm to attend the meetings and because 'the Number of the Trustees in Hornchurch side ought to bear proportion to the subscriptions on that side' it was agreed to appoint two new trustees, so John Evererd of Hornchurch and William Grafton of Romford brought the total up to ten.

From this time on a dated memorandum was inserted in the Account Book: 'That Mr [e.g. William Grafton] appearing this Day personally at [e.g. the 'Swan'] in Romford doth Accept to be a Trustee of the Charity School in Romford to Act & perform all such matters as relate to that Trust'. This was followed by the signature of the new trustee, the entry being made on the day of his election or within two or three months.

At a meeting the following February, 1721, the trustees recorded that 'Whereas there was from the first setting up of the Charity School of Romford a Verbal or Tacit agreement . . . . every Trustee should be a Subscriber of Twenty Shillings p. annum to the said School' and that this had always been conformed with, 'for the better Establishing and perpetuating of . . . [this] agreement, and to prevent all deviations from the same for the future [it was agreed] that no person be nominated or elected a Trustee [unless] he subscribe and pay annually Twenty Shillings or upwards to the said Charity School.' One assumes this minute was necessary because one or more of the trustees was in breach of this 'tacit' agreement. Having clarified this, they unanimously agreed that it would be of 'great use and service' to enlarge the number of trustees with others 'who are known to be well affected to the said school', and then appointed Carew Hervey *alias* Mildmay, William Russell, and the Rev'd Mr Thomas Whetham.

These three trustees are of particular interest. Mr Thomas Whetham, the Rector of North Ockendon, and William Russell, who owned the estate of Stubbers, were the first trustees from outside the Royal Liberty and both were gentry from the parish where James Hotchkis had been born and raised and were undoubtedly well known to him. This gives an indication of the circles in which he and his family moved and the social elite he was able to call upon to support the school. Apart from Stubbers, Russell also owned 'estates' in Leytonstone, Kelvedon, and Fetter Lane in London, travelling between these properties in his coach and four, an equipage of which he seems to have been very proud because it is the first item mentioned in his will, left to his wife.

If Russell was wealthy, the third new trustee, Carew Hervey *alias* Mildmay, was financially and socially in a different league from all the other trustees. In 1596 a George Hervey purchased the Manor of Marks from the great Elizabethan politician and polymath, Francis Bacon. This property, with its moated manor house, was in the north-west corner of the Royal Liberty, now part of Dagenham. In 1622 his son, Sir Gawen Hervey, adopted as his heir Carew Mildmay, directing him to take the name of Hervey before Mildmay, which explains why his great-grandson, the newly appointed trustee, is referred to as Carew Hervey *alias* Mildmay. He was born at Marks in 1691, his mother being the daughter of Richard Barrett Lennard of Belhus, so he was related to two important Essex families. He spent the earlier part of his life at the court of Hanover and returned to England with a reputation for brilliance. Here he mixed with some of the great men of the age including Alexander Pope, Joseph Addison and Lord Bolingbroke. He was elected as Tory MP for Harwich in 1714 in controversial circumstances, but he was now on the wrong side of history. Queen Anne died that year and the crown passed to the elector of Hanover, George I, and in January 1715 two Whigs were returned for his constituency. The Whig ascendency which would see the Tories out of power for fifty years had begun, and at the age of 24 his active political career was over. Thereafter, although he would maintain a keen interest in politics and write for a number of periodicals, he refused to accept any of the great civil offices he would be offered, preferring to remain an untainted, independent country gentleman. As a country gentleman he had immense estates to occupy him, for in addition to the Manor of Marks[52] he inherited Hazlegrove House in Somerset which he remodelled in the fashionable Palladian style. He was also to inherit extensive estates in Dorset from his first wife, Dorothy Eastmont of Sherborne. (He married well: his second wife was Edith, the daughter and co-heir of Sir Edward Phelips of Montacute in Somerset, now owned by the National Trust.) He was a man who loved life and would live long to enjoy it, continuing to hold large social gatherings at his house well into old age and dying in January 1784 at the age of 93 in full possession of his faculties. Now, in February 1721, he was just 30, and six years after the end of his brief parliamentary career he had become a trustee of the Charity School in his native Romford.

The year 1721 also saw the death of Thomas Roberts, who was buried on 15 September in Hornchurch. He left an estate of £500 in the will he had written in October 1719. Amongst his smaller legacies were a guinea to Elizabeth Hotchkis, and to his 'loving friend James Hotchkis the Reverend Dr Barrow's[53] works and any other Books out of my Study besides not exceeding the number of Six More'. The following January his successor, the Rev'd Henry Levett, became a trustee by virtue of his office. Levett was 32 and, like his predecessor, a graduate of New College, Oxford.

These were the men now responsible for the Charity.

November 1722: the death of Samuel Hopkinson

The school had now been open for eleven years and had become a model charity school: it was full, the children were all provided with uniforms, the new treasurer's accounts showed a healthy surplus, arrangements were now in place to provide up to six apprenticeships a year, and the school enjoyed an excellent reputation. Evidence for this early success comes mainly from one learned and acute observer whom we have already met, the scientist William Derham, who was Rector of Upminster from 1689 until his death in 1735. In 1709 he had produced the earliest, reasonably accurate estimate of the speed of sound. He did this by using a telescope from the tower of his church in Upminster to observe the flash of shotguns fired from a number of local landmarks a known distance away and then measuring the time until he heard the report. One of these land marks was the church in North Ockendon. Although Upminster lay outside the Royal Liberty, Derham undoubtedly knew his fellow clergymen James Hotchkis and Thomas Roberts, and he followed the fortunes of the Charity School closely.

On 7 November 1715 Derham wrote to the SPCK from Upminster to say 'That their Charity School at Rumford flourisheth & not only ministers to the good of that neighbourhood, but is exemplary to other parishes who have set up some lesser Schools after its pattern.' (Perhaps one of the parishes he had in mind was South Ockendon, two and a half miles from North Ockendon, where a charity school for 14 boys had opened in 1714.[54]) On 21 December 1716 he reported that 'Ye Charity School at Rumford is in a thriving condition', and on 30 September 1717 he wrote to say 'That the Charity School at Rumford is in great prosperity & does good Service in the

Engrav'd by Jos.ʰ Baker.

Rev'd Dr William Derham DD, FRS, Rector of Upminster

neighbourhood.' In 1716 he became a Canon of Windsor in addition to being Rector of Upminster, and the vestry minutes show that from this date he divided his time between those two places. This explains the observation in his letter of 11 October 1718 'That the school at Rumford in Essex is in a flourishing Condition, and he wishes he could say the same of the school at Windsor, which hath a large Income enough, but he fears wanteth management answerable thereto.' On 9 January 1722 Derham wrote again from Windsor Castle to say 'That the Charity-School at Rumford in Essex is in a flourishing Condition, notwithstanding some of its principal Benefactors are dead, But the Ch[arity] School at Windsor as well as can be expected, considering it is under the worst Management of any, and would infallibly sink was it not for the ample Contributions of the College there.'[55]

The clause 'notwithstanding some of its principal Benefactors are dead' refers to Thomas Gilman, Christopher Bayley and Thomas Roberts, and the word 'notwithstanding' is significant: raising the funds to open a school was only the first challenge; the second was to ensure its continuance. Many schools were set up with the same enthusiasm as the one in Romford but closed after a few years for want of sponsors, sound management, or a competent schoolmaster. (The school in South Ockendon would disappear from history after 1724.) In May 1722, four months after Derham wrote this letter, the Honourable Anne Rider made her will. She was a wealthy lady who had inherited the ancient Manor of Dagnams and Cockerels which stood in what is now known as Harold Hill. She supported the school and wished it to prosper, but at this time, despite its success, entertained the possibility that it would not do so. After itemising the bequests to her family she wrote:

> I give and bequeath to the Charity School at Rumford *if there be one at my decease* the sum of one hundred pounds or else the said sum to be disposed as my executor shall approve to the poor of Rumford and Noke Hill. [Author's italics]

In 1731 the school duly received the £100.

There can be little doubt that the greatest contribution to the school's success in its first decade was the good fortune of acquiring Samuel Hopkinson as schoolmaster; if in 1722 there was a single reason to doubt that the school would not continue to thrive it would have lain in concern for his continuing good health. He had done sterling work for over eleven years, but in the course of 1722 he became unwell and by the end of October he was too ill to continue on his own. Mrs Hopkinson engaged Mr Daniel Marshall to assist him, but an entry in the register of St Edward's Church records that on 11 November 1722 the burial of 'Sam'l Hopkinson Charity Sch. Mr' took place. We know little more about him than his name, but from William Derham letters we know that he was a man who distinguished his profession.

Dagnams, engraved by T. Hawksworth from a sketch by J. Greig for the 'Excursions through Essex'.

Dagnams was the home of the Honourable Anne Rider and one of the ancient Manors of Havering whose owners supported the Charity School over the 18th and 19th centuries. It later passed into the possession of the Neave family: Sir Thomas Neave, 2nd Baronet, was born there in November 1761, and his son Sir Richard Loi Digby Neave was elected a trustee of the Charity School on 27 April 1824.

Chapter 5

Building the School House

1723 - 1729

1723: a new Master
Daniel Marshall continued to teach the boys until this temporary situation was resolved at a meeting of the trustees to appoint Mr Hopkinson's successor on 2 February 1723. The importance of this meeting ensured a high attendance: of the fifteen trustees, only Carew Hervey Mildmay and Alexander Weller were absent. First, it was agreed that the two weeks that Daniel Marshall assisted Mr Hopkinson before his death 'The widow is to pay him according to her own agreement', but that for the twelve weeks which had elapsed since his death the allowance of 16s a week was to be divided equally between the two of them. Secondly, William Stracy[56] was elected 'by a majority of the Trustees' as schoolmaster until next Michaelmas and 'Widow Hopkinson' was elected School Mistress for the same period, he to receive 9s {£70} a week and she 7s {£54}. It can be assumed that Daniel Marshall wished to continue as schoolmaster, and the fact that William Stracy was elected 'by a majority' would suggest that there was a minority who supported Marshall's application. It was also recorded here that 'At the Michaelmas General Meeting it is agreed and determined that a schoolmaster and mistres shall be annually chosen.' Why this is recorded here, four months after the meeting, and why the present tense is used is unclear, but the temporary nature of their appointments must have been only too clear to William Stracey and 'Widow Hopkinson'.

Peter Earle has some interesting comments on the salary and the social position of teachers at this time.[57] Having said that in general 'an annual income of about £50 . . . provide[s] a lower bound for the middle station', he later says of schoolmasters that

> a salary of £20 or £30 seems to have been quite normal for masters in the smaller grammar schools, despite their graduate status; this was no more than was being paid to charity school masters, who needed to have very little formal education, just a 'good character

and religious knowledge', and were averaging £30 per annum in the early eighteenth century. The low salaries of schoolteachers were often cushioned by free houses, free coals and other perks.

Like the 'lesser clergy', their 'low incomes but genteel pretensions' placed these 'reasonably well educated and usually salaried people . . . firmly in the lowest and most shabbily genteel rank of the rapidly expanding educated lower middle class . . . on incomes well below what could be earned by many skilled artisans.'

The finances of the school, 1718 to 1727

From Alexander Weller's appointment as treasurer in April 1718 the accounts have a greater clarity. Between Michaelmas 1718 and June 1727 the average annual income from subscriptions (including those collected in arrears) was approximately £66 10s, and the average expenditure approximately £70 12s. The small difference between these figures was more than made up for by the exceptional income the school received each year. In 1719 there was no charity sermon, but the accounts show that £35 was received from James Hotchkis by a 'Collection from the Monthly Communion'. This collection never seems to have been repeated, but the occasional Charity Sermons delivered by 'celebrity' preachers continued to contribute the greatest sums to this additional income. The first of these was on 21 May 1721 when £76 17s 1d was raised following Charity Sermons preached by Hugh, Lord Bishop of Bristol, and the Rev'd Joseph Watson DD, Rector of St Stephen's Walbrook; the second was three years later, on 5 July 1724, when the preachers were the Bishop of Sodor and Man[58] and the Rev'd Mr Middleton, Lecturer at St Brides, whose sermons produced a collection of £47 7s 9¾d.

There were costs associated with these events, but they were trifling compared with the sums raised. In 1721 19s was paid for printing Hymns and £2 2s 6d was recorded for the Bishop's expenses. In 1724 it cost £1 4s for the hire of the coach to bring the two preachers from London, 6s was spent advertising twice in the *Post Boys*, and John Locksmith was paid £1 for printing 840 hymn sheets (including the paper) and a further £2 2s 6d for the hire of horses so that he and his son could ride to London in order to deliver 'the Hymns with the Circular Letters to the Gentlemen when the two Charity Sermons were preached' in Romford. This entry suggests that having obtained the services of their eminent preachers the trustees made every effort to boost the attendance (and the collections) by exploiting Romford's proximity to London, the heart of the charity school movement and the home of most of its wealthy patrons. One wonders whether having a trustee with the social cachet of Carew Hervey Mildmay enabled them to tempt more of the fashionable elite to hazard the journey to Romford Market Place. Highway robberies on this road to the capital would continue to be reported for at least another three decades, despite its improved maintenance following the erection of turnpikes at Whitechapel Church, Stratford, and half a mile outside Rumford, with the first tolls being taken at the end of March 1722.[59] (These improvements led to another activity which was reported from time to time, such as this item in the *Derby Mercury* of 7 April 1737:

> Last Sunday Morning, at Half an Hour after Five, Mr Burgess, of East Ham in Essex, started his Grey Horse, and ran from Whitechapple Church to Rumford Turnpike in thirty Minutes, for 100l. which he performed so near the Time, that 'tis undetermin'd whether he won or lost: The Ground measures 11 Miles and a Half, and 364 Yards.)

Occasional legacies also contributed to the school's funds. In the financial year ending in Michaelmas 1720 two legacies of £5 were received, one from the Reverend Symonds, Rector of the nearby parish of Stapleford Abbotts, and the other from a perhaps less typical supporter, Mr William Higgens, late servant to the Honourable Madam Rider of the Manor of Dagnams. On 25 April 1726 John Milligan, one of the founding trustees, was buried at St Edward's Church, leaving the school a £2 legacy. One or two legacies were much larger, such as the £50 which on 16 February 1725 the then treasurer, Thomas Gilman, reported had been left to the school by his late brother Samuel.

Alexander Weller's accounts distinguish between back payments of smaller subscriptions, which are consolidated under 'Arrears', and arrears in subscriptions for larger sums, often built up over several years, which are listed separately. One example of the latter is worth noting. On 15 January 1725 John Locksmith was paid 9s for two journeys and the necessary horse hire to attend on 'the Honourable Dacre Barrett Esq at Bellows' - or Belhus, to give the estate, one of the largest in Essex, its correct name. This man was Carew Hervey Mildmay's uncle, his mother's brother, who had inherited the estate from their father, so again we find a connection between these local wealthy and influential supporters of the school. Since at least 1719 Barrett had undertaken to subscribe a very generous £4 a year, but by Michaelmas 1723 he was four years in arrears, money which the trustees did not wish to lose. Locksmith's journey took him south through Upminster to Aveley, riding on a road which had been improved over the last twelve years since an agreement had been made between the two parishes to share the cost of its maintenance. Just before reaching Aveley he would have turned into the great deer park which for over a century had surrounded Belhus, a Tudor house which was fifty years old when Queen Elizabeth had stayed there in 1578. We do not know when Locksmith made this journey, but it seems to have been an urgent mission because two days before he was paid for this work the 71 year old Dacre Barrett had been laid to rest. The 9s {£68} outlay the trustees had made was handsomely offset by the £16 {£2,450} they had recovered.

A guinea was the usual subscription, sometimes a half guinea, and in order to encourage gifts in excess of this the trustees resolved on 4 May 1723 'that for perpetuating the memory of facts and persons and for promoting of Donations and Legacies to the Charity School' the names of those who gave or bequeathed 'forty shillings' should be written on the front of the gallery in the south 'Isle' in the Chapel. This was done by a Mr Faris, who on June 3rd 1723 was paid £4 11s for his work. This record was backdated, so the first donation recorded was the £16 which the Revd Thomas Roberts made in 1711 which guaranteed the Master's salary for the first year. It is fortunate that before this information was lost with the destruction and rebuilding of the church in 1849 someone copied out this list of subscriptions, which shows that between the opening of the school in 1711 and the end of 1724 these more generous legacies and donations amounted to £161 2s. (This figure clearly does not include the £200 left by Mary Hide for apprenticeships, which was recorded separately.)

This additional funding from donations, legacies and the charity sermons enabled the school to build up considerable surpluses most years, which it invested in two £100 East India Bonds. The first of these was purchased on 27 January 1722 at a cost of £101 6s 3d, and the second on 30 July 1725 at a cost of £103 19s 6d. Each of these bonds brought in £5 interest a year to further augment the school's income.

On 3 August 1723 a decision was made which reflects the varying commitment of the trustees: it was 'Fully agreed' that if either the Minister or the Treasurer was absent from a quarterly meeting they should forfeit, on each occasion, 2/6d, and if any other member was absent they should forfeit 1s, the forfeits to go towards paying for the dinner at the Yearly Meeting. The decision was taken to compel attendance rather than to raise money, of course, and was no doubt prompted by there being only 9 of 15 trustees present at that meeting. One absentee was the Rev'd Henry Levett of Hornchurch who had also missed the previous meeting, and Carew Hervey Mildmay had last attended on 30 October 1721. Although sickness was allowed as the only exception to this rule, the raised sense of obligation to attend must have played on the mind of Alexander Weller who had been 'continued' as treasurer at the meeting on 1 November. On 24 December, 'being very much Indisposed, & advis'd to goe to the Bath for the recovery of his health', he passed the Account Books, cash and treasurer's responsibilities to Thomas Gilman Junior, in the presence of James Hotchkis. Whether the resolution to fine absentees was ever enforced we do not know: there are no records of such payments, but then there are no records of the annual dinners which undoubtedly did take place.

1720 to 1726: the early years of the Mary Hide Charity

In November 1720, three years after Mary Hide's death, the first boy had been apprenticed under her Charity, but even though the trustees of the school were now receiving regular payments of £10 a year from this source they were very tardy in their duty to arrange the apprenticeships of the three boys specified in her bequest. Mr Weller's accounts show that only five grants of £4 were made in his time, although he received £52 10s from the Charity. He therefore passed a surplus of £32 10s to Thomas Gilman in December 1723, and although six further awards were made in his time, the balance in the fund had risen to £38 10s. when he stepped down in June 1727.

The records rarely name individual children before the second half of the 19th century,[60] and the details we have of those who received apprenticeships, although often incomplete, are therefore a valuable source of information. We can compile a list of the first eleven scholars to be apprenticed through the Mary Hide Charity from the Trustees *Accounts*, and this illustrates the variety of trades they moved into and the geographical spread of their destinations.

Date	Boy's Name	R or H	Apprenticed to:	Trade
30/11/20	Peter Harris	R	James Moory of the City of London	Patten Maker

24/04/21	Robert Clark	H	John Patrick of Herongate, Essex	Blacksmith
11/06/21	Wm Waterman	H	John Whiting of Hornchurch	Cooper
19/10/21	Henry Turner	R	Thomas Marshall of Romford	Shoemaker
26/10/22	James Cove	H	James May of Dagenham	Glover & Fellmonger
18/03/23	John Whales	H	Henry Lucas of Billericay	Wheelwright
09/10/24	Nathaniel Skinner	R	Mary Langdon of Ratcliff Highway	Cane chair maker
20/05/25	John Skinner	R	Richard Shadling of Barking	Fisherman
19/08/26	Wm Ealestone	R	Henry Gillum of Romford	Breaches maker
20/08/26	James Prentice Vail	H	John Prentice of Barking	House Carpenter
13/09/26	Francis Barr	H	Thomas Harris of Plaistow	Gardener

Although Mary Hide had stipulated that two boys should come from Hornchurch (H) and one from Romford (R), this was strictly observed only until 1723.

Peter Harris would seem to have been fortunate in gaining a London apprenticeship, which offered the opportunity of becoming a Freeman of the City with the status, privileges, and financial advantages which went with this. Other boys would follow him there, including Samuel Skinner, whose brother Nathaniel is listed above. However, we should note that at this time the value of apprenticeships, both in London and more generally, was in decline. One reason for this was the growing practice of purchasing membership of a Livery Company (with its concomitant benefits) rather than gaining it through the traditional route of an apprenticeship. In London another contributing factor was the relative decline in the hegemony of the City as an increasing amount of trade and business was conducted outside its limits and jurisdiction.

In his study of the rise of the English middle class between 1660 and 1730, Peter Earle[61] has noted how the background of those who became apprentices over the previous two hundred years had changed: in the 16th century London apprentices not infrequently came from poor families, but this had become increasingly unusual by the beginning of the 18th century. In the earlier period their fathers might possibly have been husbandmen;

now they were more likely to be the sons of yeomen or such 'middling' members of rural society as innkeepers, clothiers, and millers. Clearly the charity school boy did not enjoy such social and economic status.

The rise in the father's social status was reflected in the costs he had to pay for his son's placement. Writing of the 1670's, Earle cites figures of £30 for a boy to be apprenticed to a milliner, £10 - £35 to a cooper or a cutler, and £20 - £50 to a goldsmith. The apprentice also needed clothes, which even for a less exalted trade might cost between £5 and £10. With prices having risen over the ensuing years, these figures lead one to question the status and the quality of training which would be provided by a master who in the 1720's would take on an apprentice for the meagre £3 or £4 offered by the Mary Hide Charity. The answer might lie in the reasons Earle quotes Benjamin Clement, a wire-drawer, as having given for accepting an apprentice with a premium of £7 10s instead of the usual £20 or £30: the boy would not be trained for the first two or three years, he said, but would be employed running errands. Such a statement would support the argument of those critics at the time who claimed that few trades required the full term of seven years to learn their 'mysteries', that for some a few months was quite sufficient, and that in general the arrangement simply offered the unscrupulous master a source of cheap labour.

In conclusion, although an apprenticeship was seen as the best next step for a boy from a poor family after he left a charity school, this ideal was fast becoming an anachronism. Samuel Skinner was undoubtedly not the only boy whose apprenticeship under the Mary Hide trust enabled him, as we shall see, to gain wealth and a position in society far above that which could have been expected from his comparatively lowly birth; however, we should not believe, sentimentally, that his 'rags to riches' story was a universal experience.

1726: the accommodation crisis - temporary solutions

The school might have continued for many years in its existing accommodation if the landlord, John Pricklove, had not died. He was buried at St Edward's Church on 28 July 1719 and ownership of the property passed to Mr Rowland Nicholls. We do not know whether Nicholls acquired it by inheritance or purchase, but we do know that the rent rose from £5 a year in 1719 to £8 a year by 1721. Perhaps motivated by this steep rent rise alone, perhaps by Mr Nicholls having intimated that he had other plans for his property, three years later the trustees made an historic decision: on 1 February 1724 it was resolved to prepare 'a Parchment Roll with a proper

Preamble seting forth the nature and designe thereof . . . to take Subscriptions for Erecting and Building of a Charity School in the Town of Romford'.

How actively they followed up this resolution and how many subscriptions they obtained over the following twenty-one months we do not know, but at a meeting in November 1725 it was reported that Nichols 'has warned us out of the Charity School House; He purposing to Build upon the Premises'. Forced to act with urgency, it was agreed that James Hochkis, John Milligan (the last two of the original trustees) and Thomas Gilman Junior should endeavour, before Christmas, to provide a suitable house or rooms for the reception of the children, and that they should discuss with Nicholls whether he would be willing to sell them a piece of ground on which to build a school or, alternatively, whether he would build one for them.

At this critical time for the school, it is perhaps indicative of the commitment of the more recently elected trustees that when these three reported back on 5 February 1726 only three others were present. They were told that Mr Nichols having been unwilling to negotiate, it was proposed that at the next quarter sessions for the Liberty an application would be made to the Justices of the Peace to obtain a grant for a piece of waste ground on which to build the Charity School. They were also told that a house had not yet been found in which to teach the children in the interim, although Hotchkis, Milligan and Gilman said they had one in view which they believed would be 'commodious' for that purpose.

It must have been shortly after this that the school had to vacate its original accommodation, because by the next meeting on 6 August 1726 the girls were being taught in William Stracy's House, where Mary Hopkinson had also been accommodated. This suggests that previously she and her husband had been living in Mr Pricklove's house where either the girls or the boys were taught. At this meeting the trustees resolved to allow Mr Stracy twenty shillings 'for the last quarter due at midsummer' in consideration of this, and then addressed the vacancy for a school mistress, Mary Hopkinson having resigned and moved out of Stracy's house on account of her marriage to Dennis Spooner, a Romford widower. This ceremony had taken place on 25 July, and one can imagine an excited gathering of charity school girls outside St Edward's Church that day. The trustees agreed that her position should be filled by Mary Stracy for the coming quarter year, although her employment was subsequently extended. Husband and wife were to be paid 16s a week.

Thomas Gilman Junior had now been treasurer for three and a half years, during which period the uncertainty regarding the schools' future accommodation had become a crisis. Having presented his accounts at the General Meeting on 13 June 1727 he, in turn, 'did (being often Indispos'd and Infirm) resign up His Trust as Treasurer to us the Trustees'. He was succeeded by Thomas Pratt, who had been elected a trustee on 4 June 1726 at the same time as Christopher Bayley Junior and two others. Their appointments seem to have brought the total number of trustees to about 23, and another 17 would be elected before December 1734. These numbers indicate the difficulty of distinguishing between subscribers and trustees in the context of the Romford School, because it is so at variance with the SPCK model of an annual meeting of subscribers on Wednesday in Easter Week to elect from their number a treasurer and six trustees who, with the minister, would have the immediate care of the charity. How many subscribers were there who were not counted as trustees? Were all those who paid an annual subscription of £1 or more considered to be trustees? Who, and how many others, attended the 'General' meetings and the 'Yearly' meetings (and dinners)? None of this is clear from the existing records, and from now on it will only be possible to name those trustees who made a significant contribution to the schools' history.

The arrangement whereby the girls were taught in William Stracy's house would continue for at least the next two years at a cost of £1 a quarter. They may well have been there until 1729 when the new School House was completed. Meanwhile, new accommodation had been found for the boys who had moved into the Court House, as can be inferred from the order given to the treasurer at a meeting on Saturday 21 October 1727 that he should 'as soon as maybe' partition off the Court House 'with deales up to ye main Beam and... to make ye School Room for ye Boys warmer during the winter season', work which Mr Hills had completed by 2nd December when he was paid £2 8s. This Court House was probably the 'court hall' mentioned in 1484 as sited in 'Romford Street', which meant the Market Place. Like its accompanying gaol, we can picture a very old, draughty building beyond the end of its useful life. Whether it was still in use for judicial work we do not know. The Charter of 1465 establishing the Royal Liberty had created a court of quarter sessions, the functions of which overlapped with those of the older manor courts, but by the 18th century the functions of Havering quarter sessions would have been minimal: the area was still largely rural, there was little crime, and serious offences were normally sent to the assizes. The justices also had important administrative duties, of course, including the issuing of various licenses, the regulation of the highways, apprentices, and Romford market, and the supervision of parish government. However, these would not necessarily have required the use of the Court House.[62]

Two conclusions may perhaps be drawn from these temporary arrangements. First, the fact that the room above the vestry, 'for ever appropriated for a Charity School', was not used at this critical time suggests it had never been adapted or used for this purpose; second, at some point the agreement to rent a room from Richard Haynes must have been terminated. We should also note that the Court House was being prepared for the boys' occupation in winter, but they may well have already been resident there for some months. Had they moved out in 1726 as the girls had done, and already suffered one draughty spring in the Court House? Was this the temporary, 'commodious' house James Hochkis, John Milligan and Thomas Gilman had in mind when they reported back to the trustees on 5 February 1726?

The Court House, Romford Market Place, in 1800. It was rebuilt 1737 - 1740, shortly after the boys had used it as a schoolroom. The gaol is on the lower right-hand side.

1727/1728: the accommodation crisis - towards a permanent solution

Clearly it was now urgent that permanent accommodation should be found. There is no further reference to the suggestion made at the February 1726 meeting that the JP's should be approached for the grant of a piece of wasteland, so presumably if this was followed up the request had been unsuccessful. Almost two years passed before a solution was found. At a meeting held at the 'Cock and Bell' in Romford on Saturday 9 December 1727 Mr Pratt, the treasurer, told the other six trustees present that he had received a letter from Mr Hide notifying him that he had contracted with Mr Alex Weller for 2 tenements and a barn near the turnpike, and that if the trustees wished he would sell this property to them for £126. The turnpike, or toll gate, had been erected in 1721 and stood at the east end of the Market Place, marking the end of that section of the Harwich - Colchester - Chelmsford toll road leading into Romford. Once through the town travellers would reach the next section of toll road on their journey to London. It was these toll roads with their improved surfaces which ushered in the age of the stage-coach, faster travel, and the coaching inns which were to be a feature of Romford life for a century and a half.

Both Mr Hide and Mr Weller were trustees, but both were absent from this meeting. Those who were present agreed to accept this offer, and the treasurer was asked to conclude this bargain as soon as possible and to pay for the premises before Christmas Day. Christmas Eve being a quarter day, this would allow three months notice to be given to the present occupiers to quit so that building could start as soon as possible after Lady Day. To forward the work with all possible speed three further decisions were taken at this meeting: five of the trustees (including the clergy, the treasurer and Mr Ffinch) were tasked with circulating the subscription rolls which had been prepared nearly four years earlier; the treasurer was instructed to sell one of the East India Bonds to pay for the purchase of the land and to consult with a lawyer to ensure the title of the land was good; and a committee was appointed to supervise the removal of the present buildings on the premises and to oversee the planning and building of the school. This committee consisted of the Rev'd Pyle (who in 1725 had succeeded Henry Levett as Vicar of Hornchurch), the Rev'd Hotchkis, and Messrs Ffinch, Weller, Gilman, Clark, and Pratt, the treasurer. They were to report back to the trustees at the next meeting in January. The work, it was agreed, should 'be done frugally after a decent mannor'. The minutes of this important meeting end: 'Resolved Nomine Contradicente that every Trustee will in his several station and to the best of his skill and power promote and advance this work and endeavour to engage as many as he can to contribute to and further the same', followed by the signatures of the seven trustees present. However, despite their committed urgency, the legal formalities for the purchase of the land were not to be completed until the middle of August.

One hundred and six years after this meeting a case was heard in the Court of Chancery relating to the governance of the school, and the court records give further information on this land purchase. This was undoubtedly taken from the title deeds to the land, kept in the 'Charity Chest' belonging to the trustees. According to these records, the land is described as lying 'on the South side of Romford Town at the East End thereof in the Parish of Hornchurch'. It measured 59 feet in front, where it abutted the road, and extended back 140 feet. The sale included the two old timber dwellings and accompanying outbuildings and barns which stood on the site. This document reveals that the original 'Indenture of Bargain and Sale' took place on 26 June 1727 between Mr Weller and Mr Hide, and was confirmed 'on or about' 26 January 1728, exactly seven weeks after it had been authorised at the meeting on 9 December. In this second indenture William Hide declared that the Sum of £150 (not the £126 mentioned in his letter) paid for the purchase of the property was not his money, but the money belonging to the Charity Children of Hornchurch and Romford. On 27 July 1728 it was agreed that the draft deed for the purchase of the buildings and ground from Alexander Weller was in order and should be executed, and that John Ward, lawyer, should be engaged for this purpose. Finally, on 16 August 1728 an indenture of bargain and sale was made between William Hide and the trustees, in which Hide stated that 'in pursuance and performance of the Trust in him' he had sold the property to the trustees of the Charity School and again declared that the £150 paid for the property by the agreement of the 26th January 1728 was not his money but had been paid by the trustees.

The explanation for this very confusing method of purchasing the property is that the 'Trustees' had no legal, corporate status at that point and so the purchase had first to be made privately by one of their number. It had been agreed that William Hide's name was to be used in the original Indenture of Bargain and Sale and in all other conveyances made by the vendor, Alexander Weller. The indenture of 16th August 1728 conferred the ownership of the land to 18 named trustees, giving them for the first time a legal status. It is for this reason that it was this document which would be the starting point for the case in the Court of Chancery 103 years later. On 21st August 1728 ten trustees were present to 'Sign, Seal and Deliver ' the deed which confirmed the purchase.

Lawyers have always profited handsomely from the sale and purchase of land, and in due course a Humphrey Brent was paid £20 13s {£3,100}, a very high percentage of the selling price, 'for the Deeds and Charges relating to the said Charity School'. It was no doubt such practise which envenomed the MP, soldier and philanthropist James Oglethorpe against lawyers. He was to spend his final years five miles from Romford at Cranham Hall, where he died in 1785, but in this year of 1728 he chaired the Parliamentary committee on prison reform which would lead him to set up the Colony of Georgia in America, from which he would ban slavery, alcohol and - eccentrically but touchingly - all lawyers.

January 1728 to January 1729: the building of the Charity School

At meetings in January and February 1728 the treasurer had been ordered to calculate the cost of the materials which would be needed for the building, including everything from the bricks, tiles, glazing, and the stone for coping and steps, down to the iron work for nails and hinges. He was also tasked with preparing 'Articles to bind the Bricklayer for the meet performance of his contract and to sign it.' It appears there was no equivalent to an architect's drawing, but instead a General Meeting was held at the 'Crown Inn', Romford, on Tuesday 6 February 1728 'to receive proposals from the carpenters for the building of the Charity School and to contract with them.'

On 27 February articles were drawn up with James Hills and Thomas Molton, carpenters, and Clement Hambleton, bricklayer, confirming the arrangements 'for Completing and perfecting' the building, and the treasurer was empowered to act for the trustees to ensure the execution of this contract. In April alterations to the plans were approved which reduced the cost, and one assumes work started as soon as possible after the deed for the sale of land was signed in August. In December the treasurer was ordered to appoint a 'measurer' to 'measure all the work done at ye Charity School', presumably to check the trustees were not being cheated, and the Carpenters were ordered to make a fence of 4 foot pail at the bottom next to Mr Grafton's yard. One can assume that by now the main building was nearing completion, and this is confirmed by the decision on 31 January 1729 that the treasurer should sell the second East India Bond and pay Mr James Hills and Mr Thomas Molton £60. At 'A Yearly Meeting at ye Crown Inn' on 25 April, attended by just six trustees, the treasurer was ordered to pay the remainder of the workmen's bills, presumably all the work having by then been satisfactorily completed.

The minutes of the meeting of the Trustees on 27 July 1728 formalising the purchase of the land on which the School House would be erected. This meeting also agreed the apprenticeship of Samuel Skinner to a gingerbread maker and the purchase of a 20 gallon brewing copper for the use of the Schoolmaster. Samuel Skinner would prosper and later become a trustee of the school.

The Charity School building was finished. It was accessed by four or five shallow steps leading to a door which was flanked by circular columns, the capitals of which supported an elaborate cornice. Above this a plaque was set into the wall referencing the conclusion of the parable of the Good Samaritan in Chapter 10, verse 37 of St Luke's Gospel:

> **THE CHARITY SCHOOL FOR HORN CHURCH ROMFORD AND HAVERING.**
> **ANNO DOMINI MDCCXXVIII.**
> Goe and doe thou likewise
> St Luke ye 10th & 37th verse

The date on this plaque, 1728, was to give rise to the myth that this was the date not just of the building but also of the foundation of the school. This amnesia regarding the school's first eighteen years was to become so institutionalised over the following 200 years that at the ceremony to mark the laying of the Foundation Stone for a new school building in 1935 the following statement was printed in the service sheet and read out to the assembled dignitaries:

> In the year 1728, John Bosworth, Merchant of this town, with other like-minded citizens, founded a School where children might be taught free of all charge and from which they should proceed, endowed with apprenticeships, to their calling in this world. Succeeding generations have added to the School of Bosworth . . .

Not only is the date wrong, but who, you will be asking, is this John Bosworth? In fact his name was not John but Joseph, and eighteen years after the actual date of the school's foundation by James Hotchkis *et al* he has yet to make his appearance in this story. This is a perfect example of how time sublimates solid history into airy myth, changing fact into fiction.

On 22 May a General Meeting was held at the 'White Hart' in the High Street, an old inn dating back to at least the 1480's. It was here the accounts for the previous year were presented and those relating to the building of the school house were examined. From these we learn that £148 3s 6d {£23,000} was raised from the Subscription Roll for building the school, £7 7s from the sale of Mr Weller's Old Barn, and 10 guineas from Sir Nathaniel Mead for 'Incroachin'.[63] This additional income of £166 and 6d helped offset the total cost, excluding the cost of the land, which came to £420 4s 9d for a building which, with various modifications and enlargement, was destined to house the school for the next 197 years and, as the town library, to serve the Romford public for a further 40.[64]

The accounts for the building work show that £4 19s was paid for some unspecified work to Captain Harle, who at this meeting was elected a trustee. Captain John Harle had been born into a seafaring family in South Shields in 1688, and by the 1720's he was master of the *Mary* trading in the Baltic and Mediterranean. In 1728 he settled near Rainham Creek, where the River Ingrebourne, tidal at this point, joined the Thames. Sailing barges connected this agricultural area with the markets in London, and Harle's business interests also included shipping coal from his native South Shields, one of his customers for this being the new school. Harle's principal legacy to posterity is the splendid Rainham Hall, now in the care of the National Trust, which he had built that same year of 1729. It survives as one of the very few buildings in Havering capable of taking us back to the early 18th century, and several of its occupants were to have links with the Charity School at Romford.

	£	s	d
Contra			
To Labourers Digging y.e Cellar	1	=	=
To Daniel Pain for Bricks	26	16	=
To Wid.o Skingly for Bricks & Tyles	21	10	=
To Clem.t Hambleton for Brick Work	27	8	6
To Ditto for Plaistering	7	9	5
To Ditto for Dayes work Lime Bricks & Mortar	5	17	=
To Tho.s Steyner	10	=	=
To Rich.d Davis	23	18	7
To John Davis	10	1	=
To John Gibson	10	=	=
To Mr Walker	9	19	=
To Mr Martin	10	8	5
To Mr Ransfield	8	4	=
To James Childress	9	19	2
To James Hills for Laths	3	2	6
To Rob.t Dumbleton	15	=	=
To Step Stones & Other Charges	4	2	8
To Kiln Stocks	1	11	=
To 17 Bushells of Hair	17	=	
To Allen Burnley	15	=	
To y.e Several Men that bro.t y.e Bricks	2	17	=
To y.e Turnpike			
To Jn.o Tracy Surveyo.r	3	4	=
To y.e Labourers	14	6	
To a Millstone	1	11	6
To Mr Jones	1	6	=
To James Hills & Tho.s Molton	154	4	=
To Humphrey Brent Attorney	20	13	=
To Mr Hyde	16	10	=
To Capt.a Harle	4	19	=
To Mr Rowe	1	9	=
Carried Over	£421	2	2

Entries in the *Accounts* relating to the building of the School House

Chapter 6

The Mary Hide Charity and the death of James Hotchkis

1731 - 1734

1731 to 1734: a change of Mistress, a change of Master, and the Master acquires a House
From August 1726, when Mary Stracy replaced 'the Widow Hopkinson', a second husband and wife team had been paid their 16s a week, Mary teaching the 20 girls in her own house and William teaching the 50 boys in the Market Hall. By the late spring of 1729 it would seem the school building was finished and boys and girls were united under their new roof. The trustees had appointed Mrs Stracy even though there was evidence that her health was not good: in July 1725 they had agreed that as the schoolmaster's wife had been 'much indisposed' and a great cost to him during her illness he was to have an additional allowance of 1s a week 'for his better support and subsistence; and this to be during pleasure', a decision which reflects their loyalty, their humanity, and the value they placed on his services. We do not know the degree to which she continued to suffer from ill health over the next few years, but on 30th March 1731 the burial of 'Mary Wife of Wm Strace' took place in St Edward's Church. At a trustees' meeting just four days later it was agreed that 'the School Master be allowed the full salary of Master & Mistress to this day', but again we do not know how long she had been unable to carry out her duties. At that same meeting the trustees reappointed him as schoolmaster until Lady Day 1732 and appointed Elizabeth Aliss, a widow, as school mistress for the same period. She was to be paid 7s a week, as Mrs Hopkinson had been, but his salary was raised by 1s to 10s a week. Whether the decision in 1725 to give him an additional shilling in consequence of his wife's illness had ever been rescinded we do not know: having granted an increase in salary, albeit temporarily, it may have been hard to take it away again, and perhaps this decision in March

1731 simply made permanent the existing practice. Whatever the explanation, it is yet another indication that the trustees valued his service.

However, he was to serve them for only another nineteen months, because on 1 October 1732 'William Strace Master of Charity School Romford' was buried in St Edward's Church. On 21 October sixteen trustees were present at a meeting at which 'Daniel Marshall was elected by a majority of the Trustees Schoolmaster . . . at 10s a week; Eliz Alliss widow continues at 7s a week.' A decade after having taught the boys following Samuel Hopkinson's death and then been passed over in favour of William Stracy, Daniel Marshall had finally been appointed schoolmaster, although the wording suggests it was not a unanimous decision.

William probably lived just long enough to see the addition of the new school building's most distinctive features. The accounts for 1731/32 record under income the receipt of six guineas 'For the statues', but do not state the source of this money. Subsequently, on 7 June 1732, Thomas Staynor was paid £6 'for statues'. The gates or facades of charity schools up and down the country were embellished with twin statues of a charity school boy and girl dressed in their distinctive uniforms, and the Romford school had been built with two niches above the door to receive these figures. They now stand outside the head teacher's office in the primary school, the last remaining vestige of that original school building apart from the foundation stone. The boy is dressed in a knee length blue coat, neck bands, blue stockings and black shoes; the girl wears a long-sleeved blue dress laced up the front, a white apron, and a blue and white bonnet. He clutches a black hat to his chest and she holds a Bible, and in their other hands they each carry a scroll.[65] The accounts for the building of the school record an earlier payment to Thomas Staynor of £10 for some unspecified work, so he was probably a general stonemason. This might explain the grotesque appearance of the two children, seen in all their horror now they stand at ground level. We must hope and believe that their physical distortions and repellent faces are the crude and inaccurate work of a clumsy carver rather than an accurate and skilful depiction of two of the most hideous children ever to have stalked the Market Place.

The school building did not take up the whole road frontage which the trustees had purchased, and after its completion they began to plan the building of an adjoining house. In 1734 they carried out this project, for which Thomas Moulton was paid £183, with a possible further unknown payment to Thomas Green, the mason.[66] The house appears to have been finished that summer, because at a meeting on 23 April the trustees agreed to let the house to the schoolmaster, Daniel Marshall, for the sum of £10 a year with entry at Michaelmas.

Where was Elizabeth Allis then living? We cannot be certain, but she was almost certainly living above the schoolrooms. We have no plans of the Charity School, although we know the appearance of the front of the building, facing the Market Place, from surviving drawings and photographs. These show two long windows to each schoolroom either side of the door, and two smaller, higher windows each side of the statues. The proportions of the facade suggest that these would have provided light to an upper story which probably provided accommodation. There is no record of this, but it can perhaps be inferred from later entries in the log.

This picture of the School House and adjoining Master's House was taken in 1905, but the facades of these two building had not changed since they were built.

1727 to 1735: the Mary Hide Charity

It would appear that the arrangement set up in April 1722 whereby the land settled on Stephen Collier was to pay the annual £10 to the school from the Mary Hide Charity did not last long. In 1728 William Hide did not pay the £10, but the following year he paid £25 as a further two years' annuity, and from then on £10 was paid each year. From July 1733 this money was paid by John Merttins, who had been a trustee of the school since that April. Whether he made the payment because he was the successor chairman of the Hide charity trustees or whether he had bought the annuity and so was making the annual payments himself we do not know,[67] but payments were now being received regularly, and over the next nine years a further seventeen boys were apprenticed.

Date	Boy's Name	R or H	Apprenticed to:	Trade
1727	John Turner	R	Thomas Marshall of Romford	Shoemaker
1728	Samuel Skinner	R	[Israel Hammond] of London	Gingerbread maker
1729	Bartholomew Watton	H	His father of Hornchurch	Town sawyer
1729	James Godfry	R	John Sturton of Collier Row	Butcher
1730	Thomas Staines	R	Wm Sheppard of Romford	Butcher
1730	Wm Whalesby	H	John Steward of Hornchurch	Farrier
1731	James Sammis	R	Robert Spurling of Romford	Blacksmith
1731	John Lee	H	His father (Local)	Barber
1731	?? Watton	H	Jon Badgard of Hornchurch	Carpenter
1731	John Allen	R	John Hibble of Romford	Butcher
1732	Caleb Franklin	R	Israel Hammond of London	Gingerbread maker
1732	Peter Ward	H	His father (Local)	Glover
1733	William Crooks	R	James Burrows of Chadwell	Wheelwright
1734	William Small	R	George Hart of ?	Perukemaker & Barber
1734	Robert Stains	R	Thomas Haggaday of Bungy, Suffolk	Cooper
1735	John Godfrey	R	John Betts of ?	Glover
1735	John Letch	R	Phillip Easton of ?	Barber

A total of twenty-eight boys had now been apprenticed, and from the records we know the occupations of some of their fathers. This, in turn, gives a glimpse of the background from which they came: Peter Harris's father was a broom maker and William Small was the son of a tailor; Nathaniel, John and Samuel Skinner (assuming they were brothers), James Sammis and John Godfrey were sons of husbandmen, or small tenant farmers; and the father of John Letch was a fellmonger and dealt in the very smelly and unpleasant trade of buying hides and skins which he would then prepare for tanning, an important local industry in the Liberty at this time. Three were apprenticed to their fathers, who probably therefore had secure employment in their trades. Significantly, five of the others lived with their widowed mothers, another probably with his aunt, and in the two years which elapsed between 1729 when Bartholomew Watton was apprenticed to his father and 1731 when his brother was apprenticed, the father had died. On this limited evidence it would appear that the socio-economic background from which these boys came was, at best, one of lower middle-class and small scale enterprise. Only with difficulty could those who fell into this category be defined (in the SPCK's words) as 'real Objects of the Charity', although in this pre-Welfare State society a widow and her family could find themselves living on the margins of existence very soon after the death of the bread-winning husband, and a quarter of these boys were fatherless. Furthermore, as it was probably the boys with the most reliability, application and initiative whom the trustees would have selected to benefit from an apprenticeship, it is not unreasonable to assume that the background of the other children was likely to have been more impoverished than this.

The details of these apprentices are taken from the trustees' *Account Book*. For those apprenticed in London it is sometimes possible to corroborate, augment or correct these details by referring to their Freedom of the City Admission Papers. From these we learn that Caleb Franklin was apprenticed to Israel Hammond on 29 February 1731/2 for the usual term of 7 years. He was the son of Henry Franklin of Rumford, Husbandman, deceased. The only difference in the two records is that Hammond is described in the 'City' papers as a Fruiterer and not a Gingerbread maker. In the space following the words 'in Consideration of the sum of . . . .' no figure has been filled in, which is usually the case. From this source we also discover that two years earlier on 1 October 1729 'Samuel Skinner son of Nathaniel Skinner of Rumford in the County of Essex Husbandman' had also been apprenticed to Israel Hammond, Fruiterer of London, 'to learn his Art'.

According to the Trustee's accounts Samuel's brother Nathaniel had been apprenticed to Mary Langdon, a Cane chair maker of Ratcliff Highway, East London, on 9 October 1724.[68] However, his apprenticeship document records his Master as William Thompson, Draper of London, with the date of 13 October 1725 and again no sum recorded. Had he spent a year with Mary Langdon and having proved his capability been passed on to William Thompson to begin his formal apprenticeship? The name of his father and the town of Rumford on the form leave little doubt that this is the same person, and there is no contradiction in the trade to which he was apprenticed: 25 years later in the Poll Book for 1750 he is listed under the Drapers Company as a 'chairmaker' in St Paul's Churchyard. There may be a similar explanation for the entry in 1734 relating to Robert Stains, which seems to imply that he was apprenticed to a Cooper in Bungay, Suffolk, called Thomas Haggaday. In fact Thomas Haggaday was a cooper in Romford, and although there are several references in the records to him paying duty for the indentures of the apprentices he took between 1732 and 1776, there is no reference to Robert Stains. Did Robert subsequently move to a different Master in Bungay, or was there some confusion when the entry was made in the *Account Book*?

Did the trustees record in their accounts some of their decisions as to who was to benefit from the Mary Hide Charity but not others? In other words, is this a complete list? We have no reason to believe that it is not. That being so, it would appear that over the eight year period between 1727 and 1735 only seventeen children were apprenticed, and not the twenty-four Mary Hide had provided for. Furthermore, twelve of these were from Romford and only five from Hornchurch, the reverse of the proportion she had stipulated. Up to 1735 the trustees of the school had probably received £147 10s from the Mary Hide Charity, yet in total they seem to have dispensed only about two-thirds of this sum. Furthermore, in the course of this period only one child is recorded as having received funding for his apprenticeship from the trustees themselves. This was John Summers, whose widowed mother was awarded £2 on his apprenticeship to Benjamin Rutland of Plaistow (in what trade we do not know) in July 1729. The trustees had now funded eight boys, but John was to be the last. The resolution at the yearly meeting on 27 October 1718 had been to limit the number of additional apprentices to three and to limit the grant to each of these to £4, it had not been a resolution to fund three at this cost every year. The fact was that the funds of the Charity had been so depleted by the cost of building the school and the Master's house that they were unable to continue the programme, such as it had been.

1730 to 1733: school attendance and discipline

The little we know of life in the schoolroom at this time has to be deduced from the occasional comment in the minutes of the trustees' meetings. These, although few in number, most frequently refer to behaviour and attendance. The first such entry was made on Saturday 21 February 1730: 'Resolved at this Meeting that Wm Stracy doth signify to the parents of ye Charity Children that if they doe not keep them constantly to school they shall be discharg'd at the next meeting & forfeit their school cloths.' The provision of clothes was a strong inducement for parents to send their children to charity schools, and removal of these was therefore the greatest threat the trustees could make to encourage compliance with their rules. Entries such as this are a salutary reminder that rather than rushing to the Market Place each day eager to learn, these children probably bore a closer similarity to Shakespeare's 'whining schoolboy . . . creeping like snail / Unwillingly to school'.

The following April this threat was repeated with a time limit.

> Resolv'd at this meeting that every Hornchurch Boy or Girl that shall be absent from ye Charity School Six Kalender Months in one year shall be Discharg'd out of ye said School and likewise every Romford Boy or Girl that shall be absent three Kalender months in one year shall be discharg'd as aforesaidd and not have ye benefit of their cloths.

This entry reveals the fact that children could be absent for as long as 6 months and, up to this time, still be considered part of the school. The fact that Hornchurch children could be absent for twice as long as those from Romford before suffering the ultimate penalty was no doubt an acknowledgement of the considerable distance the Hornchurch children had to walk to school, and in the winter, with the shorter days and the bad weather, there may have been many who were absent for much of the time. This entry also provides evidence that perhaps fewer Hornchurch boys were awarded apprenticeships because fewer of them were in school. Another problem was addressed at this meeting in April 1731: 'Resolved that Every

Boy or Girl that will not be subsirvent to ye Orders of ye Charity School & ye School Master' [and, added above the line as an afterthought, '& Mistress'] 'upon Complaint made to Mr Treasurer if he think proper shall be suspended till the next Quarterly Meeting.'

On 21 October 1732 sixteen trustees were present when the decision was made that Mr Pyles and Mr Hotchkis, the two clergy, 'do inspect into the methods of the school until the next quarterly meeting'. We do not know how actively concerned any of the trustees were in the day-to-day life of the school before this time as this is the first entry to provide evidence of an involvement extending beyond financial and building matters, but the high turnout at this meeting and the introduction of more formal inspection arrangements shows a positive response to the awareness they must now have had that all was not well in the school room. At a meeting the following month Richard Meakins and Simon Hillatt were chosen as the Inspectors for that quarter, to be followed by two others in an informal rota for each quarter.

On 17 December 1732 nine trustees met to discuss a particular incident which was to result in the first recorded exclusion from the school.

> Danl Marshall the Schoolmaster having complained of several of the Parents of the Children in the School had on Friday the 15th Instant Insulted and abused him very grossly viz. In particular the Wido Harvey the Wife of Wil'm Willson & the Wife of Richard Barker the Trustees present having maturely weighed the Offence came Unanimously to this Resolution That the said three persons were blameworthy and that unless they did begg pardon of the Trustees & of the School M[aste]r & Promise to behave better for the future their several Children should be Dismissed When this was notified to the Delinquents Willson & Barker submitted but Harvey behaved perversely & refused to comply upon which the M[aste]r was ordered to [remove] her Childs name out of the List & to Expell her.

It is typical of the random nature of the information (other than the accounts) which is recorded in these books that we have no further reference to the appointment of two Trustees as inspectors each quarter nor, if the system continued, what observations the inspectors made. At a meeting in October 1733 they ordered that in future no children were to be admitted under the age of 7 or to be allowed to continue at the school beyond the age of 14. The 1711 edition of the SPCK guidance on setting up a Charity School stated that children should 'be of the full Age of Seven Years, and not above the Age of Twelve Years.' How many children were there in the Romford school outside this age range? Had this variation been agreed, or had it just happened? Who decided which children were to be admitted at this time? It is significant that a formal decision had now been made to extend the upper age limit by two years, and maybe this was done to keep the school full: the Trustees' leniency with long term absentees suggest they were not overwhelmed with demand for the places they had to offer.

1734: the death of James Hotchkis and the end of the beginning

The burial of the Reverend Mr James Hotchkis on 21 October 1734 marks the end of the first stage of the school's history. He was a month short of his sixty-fifth birthday and the last survivor of the original six trustees. Thomas Roberts had been buried in Hornchurch in 1721, and the other four in the cemetery adjoining the Chapel in Romford: Thomas Gilman in 1715, Christopher Bailey in 1717, John Milligan in 1726, and William Sandford in December 1729 or January 1730. On 4 May 1730 Thomas Gilman Junior, the seventh trustee, had been buried at the age of 57. In his will he had referred to Christopher Bayley Junior as his 'cousin' and a Partner Trustee of the Charity School in Romford, reminding us of the relationship of these two families and their support for the school over two generations. This second Thomas Gilman had three brothers (two of whom were priests) and a sister, all of whom would in due course bequeath money to the Charity School.

Twenty-four years had now passed since the September vestry meeting at which those present had unanimously agreed to 'promote and encourage' a Charity School in Romford, and in his final years James could contemplate with great satisfaction his work in the town, and particularly the success of the Charity School, housed for the past five years in its new building with the Master now in the adjoining house. Looking back over three hundred years we might, mistakenly, assume that there was an inevitability that the school would prosper, but this was far from certain in its earliest years. That it did so was due in no small measure to the personal qualities of James Hotchkis. He was a 'dear and loving friend' to a number of those who predeceased him and remembered him in their wills, and Elizabeth seems to have been equally valued. His commitment to the Charity School was second to none, and he had faithfully attended nearly every recorded meeting of the Trustees.

In his will, written four years before his death, James first commends his soul 'into the hands of Almighty God my Creator hoping through the merits of Our Redeemer the Lord Jesus Christ to have the full pardon and forgiveness of all my sins and to inherit everlasting life', sentiments echoed at the beginning of almost every will at this time but, one senses, repeated on this occasion with a genuine fervour. He then directed that his body should be buried in the porch of the chapel with a Latin inscription cut in the stones above recording that he had been the curate there and noting his age and the month and year of his passing. Regarding his earthly goods, he left just eight individual bequests. The very close friendship he and Elizabeth had had with Thomas Roberts was continued with his successor, and James left 'to my very good friend the Reverend Mr Pyle, Vicar of Hornchurch, a guinea {£160} to buy him a ring in testimony of the great esteem I have for him and in acknowledgement of his many favours he has vouchsafed to me'. His final individual bequest, and the largest, was to the treasurer of the Charity School of Hornchurch and Rumford: 'the sum of five pounds and five shillings {£800} in trust for the use and benefit of the said Charity School to be paid within six months after my decease[.] I am sorry I am not able to doe more for it and I earnestly conjure all the Trustees of the said Charity School to exert their best skill and management and application for the support and continuance of it till the final confirmation of all things . . .'

The residue of his estate he left to 'my dear and loving wife Elizabeth'. She was his sole executrix, but she herself was to be buried only four months later, on 14 February 1735. They had no children, but she seems to have had a favourite nephew, James, and niece, Elizabeth. James received £10 and 'a silver teapot which was left me by my cozen Thorowgood' and her 'very good friend the Reverend Francis Pyle a silver coffee pott left me by my Lady Littleton'. She also mirrored the bequest of Thomas Roberts to her husband, expressing the desire that her husband's successor, the Reverend Mr Phillip Fletcher, might choose six books out of the study 'which he shall use best (excepting the Great Bible)'.

These two wills are the most personal documents which have come down to us from James and Elizabeth Hotchkis, and they testify to a loved and loving couple who lived a good and decent life in the semi-obscurity of early 18th century Romford.

Christmas 1734

Many of the good people of Romford crossing the Market Place to the church on Christmas morning 1734 would have walked past the Charity School at the end of the Market Place, now five years old. As for the charity school children, they had long been part of the local scene, and entering the church the congregation would have seen them sitting in their uniforms with Mr Marshall and Mrs Allis. It was no doubt a joyful but also a poignant occasion, the first Christmas without James Hotchkis who had ministered to them for so long and been buried so recently.

One member of that congregation would have been Simon Hillatt, the treasurer of the school for the past seven months. As he sat in his pew reflecting on the past year his mind might well have been distracted. When the accounts had been audited on 5 May 1734, the day he had taken over as treasurer from Thomas Pratt, a surplus of £151 2s 6½d had been confirmed. However, the finances over the previous seven years had been complex, and with the building of the house adjoining the school to be paid for this balance was worryingly small.

He no doubt knew well the events and the figures of the last seven years. When the accounts had been audited on 13 June 1727 the Trustees had £112 13s 0d in hand and were in possession of two £100 East India Bonds; however, two years later there had been an expenditure of £468 9s 9d following the purchase of the land and the building of the school. This figure was about six times the usual annual expenditure and had been covered by selling the two East India Bonds and utilising the £148 3s 6d raised from the Subscription Roll. The costs had all been covered, but the money left in the treasurer's hand had been reduced to just £6 11s 2p. Over the following five years a healthy financial balance had been restored. Leaving aside the £148 3s 6d raised from the special Subscription Roll for the building, the average annual sum collected from ordinary subscriptions between 1728 and 1735 was £76 14s (including arrears, amongst which was £25 14s 3d paid in 1728 by the then treasurer, Mr Thomas Gilman). This figure was 15% higher than for the previous decade, which would have given the trustees a comfortable surplus if it had not been for the building costs. Fortunately savings had been built up again, principally through the collections at two Charity Sermons (£36 15s 6d in 1729/30 and £41 16s in 32/33) and from the £100 legacy from Mrs Anne Rider which had been received in 1731. Simon would have been only too aware that but for these last three sums the finances of the charity would already have been in deficit.

If he had read the *Account Book* which was now in his possession from the very beginning he would have come across an early entry which illustrated how fortune rode with life itself in the precarious world of the 18th century. Sometime during the final quarter in 1713 the school received a legacy of £2 from Lawrence Walker, whose will contained a clause which promised more and which William Sandford and John Millington, his executors and also Trustees of the Charity School, were punctilious in recording:

> But in case the said Susanna White happens to dye before her day of marriage and without issue then I give devise and bequeath one of my said Houses now in the Tennure or occupation of the said Mr John Tomlins situate lying & being in Collier Row lane in Romford aforesaid; unto [the Trustees of the Charity School] that they apply the Rents and proffits thereof to and for the use and towards the cloathing & warning [presumably this is a mis-copying of 'warming'] of the poor boyes and poor Girles of the said Charity School.

Eighteenth and nineteenth century fiction is full of sudden deaths which divert fortunes to remote and (often) poverty stricken distant cousins. In this it reflected a not unknown reality, medical science then having limited success in curtailing the frequency with which capricious Death could remove even the strongest and most healthy without the courtesy of allowing a period of preparation on a sick bed. There is no reason to doubt, therefore, that even if Messrs Sandford and Millington knew the lady whose mortal presence lay between the school and this inheritance to be of robust health and a strong constitution, when they copied out these words they must have considered it an even chance that the school would take possession of this property.

That Christmas of 1734, twenty-one years later, any such possibility must have long passed. Perhaps Simon could see Susanna and her husband in the congregation that Christmas morning surrounded by their happy 'issue'. What he could not foresee was that another conditional clause in another will which had been written only four years before might have a different outcome for the school. In this case it would not be dependent on a death, but a death was needed to start the process. Had he known this, and that the death would take place in just over a year, Simon Hillatt would have had a more hopeful and a lighter heart as he greeted friends with a 'Merry

Christmas' in the churchyard after the service, perhaps standing close to the vault which, four years earlier, had been reopened to receive the body of Joseph Bosworth.

The statues of the girl and boy in their charity school clothes, carved by Thomas Staynor, which stood above the entrance to the Charity School at Romford

Chapter 7

Joseph Bosworth, the unintentional benefactor

1735 - 1739

1736: The beginning of the end of the growth in the charity school movement
If October 1734 marks the end of the first phase of development of the Romford Charity School, by then the passionate enthusiasm across the country for the setting up of such schools had also ended. From about 1725 the interest of the SPCK transferred from the charity schools at home to missionary work overseas and to the establishment of its great publishing business. The value of the support that it gave to the charity school movement between 1699 and 1730 can be measured by the decline in the number of schools which were established each year after this period: in those first 3 decades of the century the figure had averaged 19 or 20 a year, between 1730 and 1740 it fell to 11 or 12, and for the remainder of the century it was just 7. The information collected and published by the SPCK also reflected this shift of interest: from 1725 this was reduced to abbreviated tables of schools by counties, and even this ceased in 1736. Only the London and Westminster charity schools continued to be reported on in any detail: in 1729 there were 132 of these teaching over 5,000 pupils at a cost of £3 per head per year.[69]

In Essex, the expansion in the number of charity schools after 1710 was impressive, and the 1715 *Account* lists 24 schools in 18 places, Colchester having three schools and Chelmsford, Chipping Ongar, Romford, and Withersfield two each. Romford educated more boys and girls than anywhere else in the county except Colchester. Over the next 11 years a further 13 schools were established, the most unusual being that in Tilbury Fort, opened in 1721: 'A School for 8 Children, taught by one of the Corporals of the 2 Companies of Invalids in Garrison there.' The most pertinent to our story, however, was the foundation at Havering-atte-Bower by Lady Anne Tipping of Pyrgo Park.

The Manor of Pyrgo lay north-east of Havering-atte-Bower, on the northern boundary of the Royal Liberty. The estate had been acquired by Sir Thomas Cheeke in 1621 and after his death passed down the family until in 1723 it came into the possession of his great grand-daughter Anne, who was married to Sir Thomas Tipping. The following year she built a free school on the Havering village green to accommodate twenty poor children, endowing it with an annuity of £10 to be paid by the Pyrgo Park estate. Was she inspired to do this by the example of the school in Romford, founded to serve the whole Royal Liberty but too distant for the children of Havering-atte-Bower to attend? She died four years later, but her school survives to this day, albeit in a different location and having experienced difficult times in its long history. The existence of Dame Tipping School (as it is now called) explains why the village will make few appearances in this history of 'The Charity School for Hornchurch, Romford and Havering'.

National figures (including London and Northern Ireland) published by the SPCK in 1726 indicated there were 1,612 schools educating 26,146 boys and 6,842 girls. One has to be careful about the relative numbers of boys and girls because if the gender make up of a particular school was not clear the Society noted all the pupils in the boys' column, but with this proviso it would seem that the national averages were just over 16 boys and 4 girls in each school. That year the SPCK recorded 37 schools in Essex, most of which were very small: Great Oakley, for instance, had only 3 children, taught at the expense of the minister. Together they educated 498 boys and 178 girls, which averaged 13 or 14 boys and 5 girls in each school, or about a quarter of the numbers in the Romford schools. By 1736 a further one hundred and thirty-five schools had opened across the country, although the average number of scholars in each remained virtually unchanged. However, over those ten years no further schools had opened in Essex and the number of pupils was the same as in 1726. Across the country charity schools would continue to open throughout the century, but that initial period of explosive growth was now over. Religious sentiment and political and economic interest had moved on, and they would not again coalesce behind a renewed drive for popular education until the beginning of the next century.

1739: The Foundling Hospital
There was to be one final, glittering and grandiose manifestation of the benevolent spirit of the early eighteenth century towards its deprived

children: the Foundling Hospital. Foundling Hospitals had been set up by the government in Dublin in 1704 and in Cork in 1737, but the one in London was pioneered by a private citizen, Thomas Coram, a retired sea captain who was so appalled by the sight of abandoned babies and destitute, dying and dead young children in London that he petitioned George II for the grant of a Royal Charter to establish a hospital to receive abandoned babies. With the instinct of a modern public relations executive, he organised that his first petition in 1735 displayed the signatures of twenty-one women from prominent, aristocratic families, women who 'as a class [were] no strangers to the complications of bastardy', as Jerry White sardonically commented.[70] This made the project both respectable and fashionable. In 1737 he presented two further petitions with male signatories from the nobility and gentry and from the professions and judiciary. Eventually in 1739 he was presented with the Royal Founding Charter, signed by the king and containing a long list of founding Governors and Guardians which included over fifty members of the aristocracy as well as the Lord Mayor of London. The first children were admitted to a temporary house in Hatton Garden in March 1741 before the building of the permanent Hospital in Bloomsbury, which was later to be described as 'the most imposing single monument erected by eighteenth century benevolence'.[71]

The Hospital offered education, but its main priorities were providing the children with simple clothing and food, and protecting them from the many dangers and diseases which killed so many so prematurely. When a baby was taken in it was sent to a wet nurse in the country for four or five years at a cost of 2s 6d {£18.40} per week. The records show that a number of these children were fostered in the healthy surroundings of Romford and Hornchurch. To ensure the welfare of these children the Hospital maintained a network of voluntary inspectors who were often local clergy or gentry, so it is possible this oversight was carried out by one or two of those who were also trustees of the Charity School at Romford. When they were old enough the children returned to London and an education and future probably not unlike their contemporaries in the charity schools, with the boys being apprenticed for (usually) seven years and the girls becoming servants.

One of the founding governors was William Hogarth, and he and his wife Jane fostered foundling children. Hogarth designed the children's uniforms and the Hospital's coat of arms. He also persuaded Sir Joshua Reynolds, Thomas Gainsborough and other celebrity artists of the time to contribute works to the permanent art exhibition he opened in the new buildings, and in doing so created what was arguably Britain's first public art gallery. This turned the Hospital into one of London's most fashionable attractions and popular charities, with visitors flocking to view works of art and make donations. In 1749 Handel would hold a benefit concert in the Hospital chapel for which he composed and performed the *Foundling Hospital Anthem* which included the 'Hallelujah' chorus from his *Messiah*, premiered seven years earlier. On 1 May 1750 he directed a performance of the oratorio, and this became an annual event which not only benefited the Hospital but helped to establish the lasting popularity of the work with the British public.

Because the Foundling Hospital is such an icon in the history of British philanthropy we can be blinded to the difficulties experienced by those working to maintain the many other, less prestigious charitable enterprises at that time, including those 1,747 charity schools being maintained by local communities across the country in 1736.[72]

1730: the Quinta De Villar d'Allen at Oporto, the Charity School at Romford, and Joseph Bosworth

There were probably few of the great and the good who supported the Foundling Hospital who did not support their vintner to a far greater extent, and much of the wine they drank was shipped from the city of Oporto. Amongst the popular tourist destinations in Oporto today is the Quinta De Villar d'Allen, the family home of the Allen family since 1739, the year the Foundling Hospital in London received its Royal Founding Charter. An important attraction of the property is its five gardens, Portugal's first Romantic gardens, built between 1780 and 1839 and famous for their collection of camellias.[73] The Allen family are important and successful wine merchants and producers today, as they have been for ten generations, and the connection between their famous gardens and the Charity School in Romford is that they have both flourished for over two hundred years on the wealth created early in the 18th century by two Englishmen involved in the wine trade: John Stevenson of Oporto, wine exporter, and Joseph Bosworth of London, wine importer.

To understand their story we must go back another sixty years. In 1654 a treaty had conceded important privileges to British merchants, after which trade steadily grew, boosted by the marriage of Charles II to Catherine of Bragança in 1662 and the outbreak of war with France in 1689. By the end of the century it had become patriotic to drink port if you supported the

Protestant Accession, leaving claret to the Catholics who supported the 'King over the Water' in France.[74] Over these years a colony of English, Scottish and Dutch wine traders grew up around Oporto and its twin city of Gaia across the Douro, men who began to explore the hot, inland vineyards upstream. If the grapes from here were better, the wine they produced still tended to be weak and rustic, and if the merchants had started to stabilise it by adding brandy, it was far from being the fortified wine we prize today.

One of these men was a London merchant called John Stevenson. His sister Elizabeth was married to Thomas Allen and living in the Strand when in November 1698 she gave birth to a son, George. We do not know when Thomas started to work with his brother-in-law, but he was certainly doing so by 1701. Two years later the 1703 Treaty of Methuen between Portugal and England cut the duty on Portuguese wine to a fraction of that on French wine and turned Oporto into an eldorado. Exports soared, and Stevenson and Allen were well placed to profit from the bonanza. Thomas Allen was probably based in London, but by 1718 his son George, now twenty, had arrived in Portugal to work as a forwarding-agent in his uncle's office, and at some point the company became known as 'Messrs Stevenson and Allen'. So successful was this enterprise that when John Stevenson died in 1734 it had become one of the three largest exporters of port.

Joseph Bosworth was born about 1675, the son of another Joseph Bosworth, a citizen and Member of the Salters' Company of London. On 12 November 1689 he was bound apprentice to Stephen Hulse, a London Cooper, and on 2 February 1697 he finished his apprenticeship and became 'free of the Coopers' Company'. We do not know what he did for the next few years, but his father had died in about 1692 and perhaps he had received an inheritance. By 1706 he seems to have acquired a property portfolio in London,[75] and sometime prior to 1715 he began shipping wine from Oporto and entered into a business relationship with Stevenson and Allen. The development of the Portuguese wine trade in the 18th century was accompanied by a systematic cultivation of the great Iberian cork forests to provide stoppers, and Bosworth was also importing cork from a Robert Dodd. His transactions with 'Messrs Stevenson and Allen' and Robert Dodd were recorded in his Account Book[76] which runs from 1715/16 to 1722, when it seems certain payments due to him were left pending. What his business interests were after 1722 we do not know.

What we do know is that when he wrote his last Will and Testament on 26 July 1730 he left over £1,000 and a house he owned in Romford as specified legacies, with the residue of his estate to go to his sister Hester Mansell and then to her daughter Susanna. The Romford house was in Hornchurch Lane, not very far south of the Market Place, and this, together with his household goods, he left to Mary Stanniland during her life. We do not know the details of his relationship with Mary, but it was obviously very close:

> My body I commit to the Earth . . . to be buryed . . . in my vault in the churchyard att Rumford . . . in which vault the coffin that now lies therein and alsoe my owne coffin I order and appoint shall be both wrapped upp in Lead and so[l]dered and that the corpse of Mary Staniland hereafter named shall be buryed in the said vault upon the coffin that is now therein and afterwards that the said vault shall be closed upp and that no other persons corpse shall afterwards be buryed there . . .

Bosworth instructed that after Mary's death the house in Hornchurch Lane was to pass to the Charity School of Romford 'so long as it shall be continued to be endowed with charity', unless an outstanding debt which was owed to him by John Stevenson and Company of Oporto, Portugal, came to £1,000, in which case this money and the house in Hornchurch Lane were both to be given to the Worshipful Company of Coopers in London.

It is strange that he places the two possible outcomes in this order, as elsewhere in his will he states that 'there is now due and owing unto me from John Stevenson and Company . . . the sum of One thousand pounds Sterling and upwards', suggesting that he did not believe the house in Hornchurch Lane would, in fact, pass to the Charity School. This is supported by his very specific directions about how the money and the property were to be used by the Company of Coopers: the interest and profits from the thousand pounds were to be used to build and endow four almshouses in or near Romford, two for two poor men from Romford and two for two poor members of the Company of Coopers, all these men to be at least sixty years of age and 'of good life and conversation'; the rents and profits from the house in Hornchurch Lane were to be distributed amongst the Alms people belonging to the Almshouses at Ratcliffe, 'over and above what is now allowed them by the Donor of the said Almshouses'. It is also significant that he left no instructions as to what was to happen to the money owed to him in Oporto if it did not amount to the £1,000 'and upwards' which he expected. This lack of clarity suggests that the will was dictated at speed during his final illness, and indeed just nine days later, on 4 August, he was interred in the vault at Romford as he had directed.

There are many mysteries about Joseph Bosworth. Whose body was already in the vault? What was his relationship with Mary Stanniland? Having probably been born and then lived and died in the City of London, what were his ties with Romford? Most of the little we do know about him derives from his Will. To ensure his wishes were carried out he named four people to act as joint executors: his sister Hester Mansell, his 'beloved kinsman' Stephen Monteage the Elder (to whom he left £200), John Montford the Elder, and Abraham Culver. Of these, we can only be sure of the identity of Abraham Culver (a contraction of the original family name of Culverhouse). [77]

Bosworth bequeathed Culver £50, with an additional 30s for a ring and £5 for a ring for his wife. He was a generation younger, having been born in Reading in 1696. In February 1712 he was apprenticed to a cooper in London, and this coincidence of profession may have been what brought them together. On 1 January 1717 Culver made a financially advantageous marriage, and in the later 1720's he and Bosworth were near neighbours in the Seething Lane precinct of the City. Perhaps it was Bosworth's influence which brought Culver to Romford. When his death was briefly announced in the *Ipswich Journal* of 28 February 1756, presumably because he was then a prominent and wealthy man, he was described as 'Abraham Culver Esq. of Rumford'. His will shows that he lived on an estate in Hornchurch and owned two houses in Rumford, as well as farmland and premises in South Weald, Great Burstead, Tatsfield in Surrey, Westerham in Kent, and the leaseholds of various properties in London. This is relevant in that it helps us to know a man if we know something of his close friends, and because on 12 June 1745 Abraham Culver would become a trustee of the Charity School.

These four executors had the Will proved in the Prerogative Court of Canterbury on 3 September and then took upon themselves its Execution. Mary Stanniland was now secure in the house in Hornchurch Lane, but what would happen after her death? It seems that it took three years to resolve Bosworth's account with Stevenson and Company, because the note confirming the final settlement in his account book is dated 1733. This confirmed that the company owed him only £365 17s 7d, just over a third of the £1,000 minimum which would have been necessary for the Worshipful Company of Coopers to inherit the property on Mary's death.

The death of Mary Stanniland and the case in Chancery, 27 January 1739

We do not know how much Simon Hillatt and his fellow trustees knew of the contents of Bosworth's will when Mary Stanniland died in January 1736. The first reference we have to this is an entry in the *Accounts* for 26 April 1736:

> Ordered that Revd Mr Phillip Fletcher & Capt John Harle, Mr William Hyde and Mr Richard Meakins be appointed to wait on Council learned in the law with such a case as they shall think proper in relation to a legacy left by the late Mr John [sic] Bosworth to the Charity School and that they wait on the Coopers Company at London in order to treat with them on all such matters as shall bear relation thereto and that the said Gentlemen shall report to the Trustees at their next meeting all such their Transactions.

The will was now being contested in the Court of Chancery by 'The Master Wardens or Keepers of the Commonalty of Freemen of the mystery of Coopers in the City of London and the Suburb of the said City', to give the plaintiffs their full, grandiloquent title.

The law worked slowly, and three years were to pass before the next reference to this matter on Saturday 27 January 1739. At this meeting it was ordered that Richard Meakins (then Treasurer), the Rev'ds Francis Pyle and Phillip Fletcher, and Messrs William Hide, Thomas Pratt and Simon Hillatt ('or one or more of them'), were to attend the trial between the Trustees and the Coopers Company in London in relation to the late Mr Bosworth's House in Romford 'given and bequeathed to the said Charity School of Romford', and to speak and act on behalf of the Trustees. They clearly believed they had a right to the property and were confident of the outcome of the Court hearing because they had already taken possession of it, as shown by another entry under the same date:

> Memorandum . . . .Trustees then present have agreed and let the late Mr Bosworth's House to the Rev'd Mr Phillip Fletcher for the sum of twelve pounds a year to commence from Christmas last.

This suggests that the minister of Romford had moved into the vacant property the previous month. Indeed, four months earlier, on 26 September

1738, Mr John Walker of Romford, a 'sworn appraiser', had made an inventory and valuation of the goods left in the house. These items (principally curtains and hangings, fire grates, fire irons, a table, a copper in the Brewhouse and, incongruously, a map) were valued at £11 8s 6d and were sold to Mr Fletcher on 7 February 1739, three weeks before the case came before the Lord Chancellor on 27 February.

The defendants in court that day were Stephen Monteage and Abraham Culver, the two surviving Executors of Joseph Bosworth's Will; Benjamin Lewis, a tailor in Dukes Place, St James', London and his wife Susannah, who was the only child and heir of the deceased Hester Mansel and therefore the residuary legatee of her uncle's estate; the trustees of the Charity School; and Thomas Clarke, Churchwarden, and Richard Meock and John Stacey, Overseers of the Poor, in the Parish of Romford.

Lord Hardwicke, the Lord Chancellor, subsequently wrote an account of the case and the reasons for his judgement. In brief, there was no dispute that the money owed by John Stevenson and Company at the time of Joseph Bosworth's death did not amount to £1,000, and that the rents and profits from the house in Romford therefore ought to be applied to the benefit of the Charity School at Romford. He decreed that Benjamin Lewis and his wife were to convey the house to the trustees of the Charity School, the costs of this to come out of the rents and profits of the property. This decision was straight forward, but a more difficult decision arose from Joseph Bosworth having omitted to say what should happen to the money recovered from John Stevenson and Company in Oporto if it did not amount to £1000: what should happen to the £365 17s 7d? Benjamin and Susannah Lewis argued that this was a lapsed legacy which should pass to them as the residual legatees, but this argument was overruled. The Churchwarden and the two overseers of the poor from Romford then argued that the money should go where the £1,000 would have gone, to build the almshouses in the town. They argued that the almshouses in Ratcliffe were not intended to have any benefit from the £1,000. However, the case for the Coopers Company was that the £365 17s 7d ought to go to the same charity as the house would have gone in the event that the whole £1,000 had been paid, that being to the almshouses at Ratcliffe. Having heard these arguments the Lord Chancellor ruled that because these alms houses could not possibly have the benefits of the rents accruing from the house in Romford, 'equity would that they should have the consideration which was to have been given for it'. This money was therefore to be invested, with the interest being distributed amongst the alms-people belonging to the almshouses at Ratcliffe.

In the event, then, Benjamin and Susannah Lewis gained nothing from the judgement, and if Romford did not acquire the hoped for new almshouses it did benefit in having a financially more robust Charity School. Indeed, as we shall see, the ownership of Joseph Bosworth's property, now confirmed in law, was to augment the charity's annual income for 180 years, after which time the capital raised from its sale would contribute to the rebuilding of the school.[78]

Tenants and Rents: 1734 to 1750

The trustees were now in possession of two houses, but their tenants were often irregular in their rent payments and maintenance of Bosworth's property in the early years was to prove expensive. It is never stated that the house adjoining the school was built for the use of the schoolmaster (and mistress), and it does not appear to have been a foregone conclusion that Daniel Marshall would move into it when it was completed. However, he was the first leaseholder (from Michaelmas 1734) at a rent of £10 a year. Daniel received 10s a week payment for his work as the schoolmaster, so this rent represented a very large proportion of his salary of £26 a year. He does not seem to have been very assiduous in paying this money, however, because the trustees accounts show that on 26 June 1736 he paid eighteen months rent arrears which had been 'due at Misummer last'. Perhaps it was for this reason that on 2 April 1737 the trustees reappointed him as School Master at a salary of 6s a week 'with the use of the Charity house adjoining to the School'. The 4s now deducted each week made the annual rent for the house £10 8s {£1,450}. This was a marginal increase on the £10 which he had paid previously, but maybe the trustees still had some money to recoup from him. Certainly this arrangement was a foolproof way of ensuring they obtained their rent.

From now on, and in effect from the time it was built, this house was the schoolmaster's house, and it remained the schoolmaster's house until Alfred Jex vacated it on his retirement in September 1932. Many other charity schools provided accommodation for the master and mistress so it did not make these posts in Romford uniquely attractive, but it would no doubt have been more difficult to find a suitable teacher had the house not been available.

The house in Hornchurch Lane was let to the Reverend Phillip Fletcher for £12 a year, but he was no more prompt in paying his rent than was Daniel Marshall. Fletcher moved out at Lady Day 1744 owing eighteen month's rent which he paid over the following year, and the property passed to Edward Robinson on a seven year lease at £14 a year. However, in his first year of occupation the trustees had to pay £20 12s 8d to a carpenter, bricklayer, plumber and smith for necessary work. Robinson also fell behind with his rent, and by 30 March 1749 he had been replaced by a Mr Horncastle. There were still two years of Robinson's seven year lease to run, and an enigmatic entry on 30 April recording 12s 'Expences about Robinsons affair & letting of House' suggests that Mr Robinson's departure may not have been straightforward. He owed £28 in rent arrears, and this loss was compounded by the money which then had to be spent on the house.

Mr Horncastle, a schoolmaster, was rather more reliable with his rent, perhaps because the trustees had a new venue for its collection. Indeed, he and the trustees turned the occasion of his payment into a bibulous event at the trustees' expense. The accounts record, rather freely, that on 17 May 1750 2s 8d {£21} was 'Expended at the Cock & Bell when Rec'd Mr Horncastles Rent', an expenditure which rose to 3s 9d that October. However, after this such sums are entered more discretely as 'Expended in receiving Mr Horncastle's Rent'.

Chapter 8

Financial malaise and the Archbishop's intervention

1734 - 1753

Inertia and debt: the lack of management of the charity from 1735 to 1748
Any fears Simon Hillatt had about the state of the Charity's finances at the beginning of 1735 proved to be well founded. The surplus of £151 2s 6½d when he became treasurer in May 1734 was indeed wiped out in the course of the year by the cost of building the house adjoining the school. When the accounts were audited on 5 May 1735 they confirmed a deficit of 10s 10d {£70}, a small deficit but the first in the history of the school. Two months later Richard Meakins commenced his eleven years as Treasurer, a period which would prove to be financially very difficult for the school.

Two events coincided to cause these difficulties. Between 1729 and 1734 the trustees had spent all the savings they had accumulated over the previous eighteen years and all the income they could spare during these years on the building programme. It is impossible to separate the normal running costs of the school during this period from the expenditure on these works. From May 1735 the Trustees needed to balance their accounts each year, as they had done prior to 1729, and hope that once again they could start to build up a surplus. The difficulty was that the years 1729 to 1734 were also the years when public enthusiasm for charity schools began to wane, and this was reflected in the school's income. In the ten years between 1718 and 1727 annual subscriptions had averaged £66 10s and annual expenditure £70 12s; in the five years ending in July 1740 this income fell to £47 but expenditure rose to an average of just under £94 a year, so the annual deficit of £4 2s noted for the earlier period now increased to £47 {£7,000}.

Previously, the small annual deficit had easily been made up from legacies and donations of forty shillings or more, but these also declined after 1734 as the inscriptions on the church gallery showed. Leaving aside the £200 Mary Hide had left specifically for apprenticeships and the £200 which was recorded as the value of Joseph Bosworth's house, donations between 1711 and 1734 totalled £283 3s, but the average for the years from 1735 to 1740 was a third lower, £8 1s against £12 6s, with a total over these five years of £40 5s. There was also a fall in the collection at the charity sermons preached during these years, which raised only £32 7s 8d in 36/37 and £25 0s 0d in 39/40.

These financial problems were exacerbated by the apparent inertia of the trustees themselves. On 12 July 1737 it was 'Ordered at the Meeting that there be no more than four quarterly meetings in the year for the future', suggesting a lack of willingness to give any time to the Charity above the bare minimum. This was not the response James Hotchkis would have expected to his final exhortation: 'I earnestly conjure all the Trustees of the said Charity School to exert their best skill and management and application for the support and continuance of it till the final confirmation of all things . . .'

Three entries in the Accounts at this time regarding uniform are enlightening. In July 1738 it was

> Resolved whenever a child shall be entered into the Charity School the parents of the said Child and some substantial person to be approved of by the Trustees shall give a note of one pound to the Trustees as a security that the cloaths which shall be given to the said child by the Trustees shall be delivered to them upon the said Childs leaving the school provided his or her leaving the school shall be within twelve months after the child's receiving the said cloaths.

The one 'and' in this long, quasi legal sentence suggests, as we would expect, that the parents of these children could not afford the £1 deposit now being demanded for the clothes, so they have to find a wealthy patron to provide it. Perhaps this patron would be the trustee or subscriber who recommended the child, if this was how admissions were managed. The entry implies also that it was perhaps usual when children left the school to take their clothes with them; the only abuse the trustees were attempting to control was that of children leaving with their clothes within a year of their admission, perhaps cynically enrolling for the clothes rather than for the education.

The second entry, four years later, suggests either the inefficiency of the trustees or their perilous financial position - or both. On 8 May 1742 it was 'Resolved the Treasurer be desired to return the thanks of the Trustees to the person who Generously gave [money for] Clothing to the Children belonging to the Charity School', but the order then given to purchase the clothing was never actioned, as the entry for 18 October 1744 makes clear: 'Ordered that the children be cloathed against Sunday 28th September with the cloathing that was ordered to be provided the 8th May 1742'. Was this money used to balance the books for two and a half years and only spent on the clothes when there was a sufficient surplus? The accounts lack the clarity to confirm this, and the fact that the order for the children to be clothed by a date in September is noted in October suggests a retrospective entry of a decision made between meetings, the need for which perhaps being a consequence of the earlier decision to hold only four meetings a year.

Despite these problems, with the help of rents from the two houses the school somehow managed to maintain a small average surplus of just over £10 {£1,400} for the five years between May 1735 and July 1740. Over the following six years, ending in November 1746, the annual income from subscriptions fell by a further £10 to an average of £37 3s, but the trustees managed to cut expenditure by £20 to an average of £73 5s 6d a year. In 1741 there was still a surplus, just £3 5s 6d, but after that there was a deficit each year which over the six years averaged £10 12s 6d. During this period there was just one charity sermon (£39 17s 0¾d), one large donation (eight guineas), and a single legacy (£5). (This came from the estate of the Rev'd Dr John Gilman, one of the sons of the founding Trustee, Thomas Gilman.) When Mr Perkin Church took over the post of Treasurer from Richard Meakins in November 1746 the charity's finances had reached their nadir: although the deficit had been reduced to 6s 4¼d, this had been achieved by spending nothing over the previous eight months except for the payments to the Master and Mistress. Fortunately coals were not required over those summer and autumn months.

The charity's debt would have been much more serious had it not been for the income from the Mary Hide Trust. Had the school's trustees added £2 to the £10 received each year from the annuity and then allocated the £12 between three selected pupils their financial problems would have quickly escalated, but they reduced their deficit by failing to spend this income. In fact the Management of the Mary Hide Trust was also in trouble at this time, as revealed in a long entry on 12 June 1745 in the Account Book of the school trustees which explains that all the original Trustees of the Annuity which had been purchased with the £200 legacy had died except for William Hide. The Rev'ds Francis Pyle of Hornchurch and Phillip Fletcher of

Romford, Trustees by reason of their offices, then met with Hide and together appointed successor trustees: John Tyler, Thomas Hurrill, Benjamin Kennedy and Marmaduke Hornby from the Parish of Hornchurch, and Thomas Bayley, Simon Hillatt and Richard Meakins from the Parish of Romford. Except for John Tyler and Marmaduke Hornby they were all Trustees of the school. (Although John Tyler would never be associated with the school, two of his sons would be trustees and one would become treasurer.)

It is difficult to know what all these men had to do except ensure the £10 (if not £12) was paid each year and spent according to the terms of Mary's will, ensure the number of trustees was maintained, and perhaps monitor how the ex-scholars were treated and how they fared during the terms of their apprenticeships. They had failed to do these things in the past and would fail to do so in the future. The trustees of the school, so often the same people as those responsible for the Mary Hide Trust, did not learn from this episode either: on two occasions in the future difficult, expensive but avoidable problems would be created by their failure to appoint new trustees to replace those who had died or moved away.

The inertia of the Mary Hide Trustees was matched by their inertia when they met as Charity School Trustees. During this period of great financial challenge they appear to have had no ideas and no solutions; they did not even have the initiative to pay their own subscriptions, which in some cases were seriously in arrears. This lack of initiative is exemplified by the content of their meetings in 1747/48. On 16 January 1747, only the third meeting to be held in the school rather than in the usual 'Lamb' or 'Cock & Bell', nothing of significance was recorded. Eight trustees were present at the next meeting on 11 April, but the page is blank except for their signatures. On 13 October the election of Captain Thomas Johnson and John Wood as trustees was the only recorded business, although it was at that meeting that Phillip Fletcher's successor as Chaplain of Romford, the Rev'd Glocester Ridley, took his place for the first time. Ridley, a collateral descendant of Bishop Nicholas Ridley, was then aged 45. He was a renowned scholar who had been educated at Winchester and Oxford, where he became a fellow of New College. It was this appointment which had led him to the Chaplaincy of Romford. This highly cultured man wrote plays, original poems, imitations, and classical translations, and with his social connections he would prove a valuable trustee.

1748: the Captain, the Archbishop, the Nabob and the return to solvency
Eight trustees attended a meeting on the 23 January 1748 but again there was no business, so it was the presentation of the accounts on 7 April 1748 which finally provided something to record for the first time in over twelve months.

At first glance the bottom line showed a surplus of £1 9s 11½d, but attached to the figures was a memorandum which stated that on settling these accounts £13 2s {£2,100} was due to the master and mistress at Lady Day last. Fortunately a crisis was averted by an act of extreme generosity: Captain Thomas Johnson now replaced Perkin Church as treasurer, and to mark the beginning of his period in office he presented the school with part of an East India Bond, the value of which, premium and interest, was £53 17s 2d. He was treasurer for only one year, but over that time the financial situation greatly improved: £55 14s 3d was collected in subscriptions, the £28 owing from Mr Robinson for two years' rent arrears on Bosworth's property was recovered, and with expenditure having been held at £83 7s 5d Johnson handed to his successor a true and accurate balance of £11 16s 9½d. We should also note a rare entry that October which suggests a new resolve to monitor the work and progress of the boys, with those who had been attending the school for twelve months being required to personally exhibit a specimen of their writing and arithmetic to the trustees twice a year, at the meetings which followed Lady Day and Michaelmas Day. Sadly there is no later reference to these exhibitions of work and so no comments on the standards presented.

The treasurer was key to the success of the Charity, and whilst acknowledging there was a national decline in support for the movement at this time one cannot fail to attribute some of the blame for the precarious financial situation in Romford to the indolence and lack of enterprise of those who had held this office over recent years. Captain Johnson had shown the way forward both in his own generosity and in his initiative. He was succeeded on 13 May 1749 by Thomas Bayley, aged 41, a younger son of the original trustee Christopher Bayley.

Three months later the Foundation received what was probably its first mention in the national press. On 5 August 1749 the *Stamford Mercury* reported an announcement in the *Whitehall Evening Post*:

> The Collection at the Charity Sermon at Rumford on Sunday last, preached by the Archbishop of Canterbury, amounted to 72 l. and

upwards, there being a great many Persons of Quality and Distinction there on that Occasion.

In addition to the boost the Archbishop's sermon gave the finances, his presence conferred enormous prestige on the town and its school. In one of the few memoranda unrelated to a meeting of Trustees, the *Account Book* gives further details of this visit:

> Memorandum Sunday July 30th 1749. Collectd the sum of £71 17s 4¼d for the use of the Charity School at Romford after the Honour of a Sermon Preached in the Morning by his Grace the Most Rev'd Father in God Thomas Lord Archbishop of Canterbury and Ld Primate of all England, procured at the request of John Comyns Esq. a Worthy Trustee of the sd Charity School, and at this time Churchwarden of the sd Parish, And another in the afternoon by the Rev'd Mr Glocester Ridley Minister of the sd Parish, in the Room of the Revd Doctr Allen, Archdeacon of Middlesex, who had been so good to undertake it, but was suddenly & dangerously taken Ill the night before which prevented him.

Thomas Herring had been Archbishop since 1747 and was a man both of his time and for his time. He was an ardent protestant who recognised the great threat posed to Britain by Roman Catholicism. In 1743 he had been appointed Archbishop of York, and he was there on 21 September 1745 when Bonny Prince Charlie defeated the royalist army in the first significant engagement of the Jacobite rising, the Battle of Prestonpans. Two days later Herring gave a rousing sermon in support of the House of Hanover and the Protestant Succession, and the following day he delivered a great patriotic speech at York Castle in which he described France and Spain as 'our old and inveterate, (and late Experience calls upon me to add, our savage and blood-thirsty) Enemies'. He accused them of supporting 'these Commotions in the North [that] are but Part of a Great Plan concerted for our Ruin'. His friend Lord Hardwicke, the Lord Chancellor who had ruled on Joseph Bosworth's will, reported this speech to George II. The king ordered that it be printed in the Gazette, which brought the Archbishop and his words to a far wider audience. Herring, a man of action as well as words, went on to raise money and volunteers in Yorkshire to resist the Jacobites, who were finally defeated at the Battle of Culloden in April 1746. His reward from the King came the following year, when he was appointed Archbishop of Canterbury.

Portrait of Dr Thomas Herring, Archbishop of Canterbury from 1747 to 1757, who preached the Charity Sermon in aid of the school on 30 July 1749

Boosted by the money from the Archbishop's charity sermon and the East India Bond from Captain Johnson, the accounts for the year ending 2 May 1750 showed a surplus of £76 2s 3¾d {£12,000}. This was despite an expenditure of £106 10s 6d. However, the money collected through subscriptions fell to a new low of £29 7s 6d, and the only other income was the rent on Bosworth's House from Mr Horncastle.

Perhaps it was the publicity surrounding the visit of the Archbishop which brought the school to the attention of the Honourable Governor Richard Benyon, a nabob who had served with the East India Company and who sometime the following year made a gift of £50 to the charity. In 1735, at the age of 37, he had been appointed Governor of Chennai (Madras). He is regarded as one of the best Presidents of early Madras, being one of the few early governors who was not convicted of any charges.[79] Despite this, he managed to return to England in 1744 with a very great fortune. In 1745 he bought Gidea Hall, but that same year he married the heiress of Englefield House in Berkshire and spent the remaining twenty-nine years of his life there.[80] It was very good fortune for the school that it caught his attention at this time, for although Gidea Hall passed to his son and then his grandson, no subsequent contribution from the family was to match his.

This was a pivotal year for the charity. Had others, like Governor Benyon, had their attention drawn to the school? Was it briefly fashionable once again to support this local charity? Certainly the Trustees seem to have found a renewed energy and commitment and responded positively to the fall in subscriptions, raising the income from this source to £59 16s 7½d. Some of this represented payment in arrears, including twelve guineas from the London lawyer Richard Comyns who had been a trustee since October 1730 but had fallen twelve years behind with his payments. Perhaps the Archbishop's sermon, arranged by his older brother, had pricked his conscience. His was not an isolated case and is indicative of the irregularity with which some of these subscriptions were paid. When the accounts were approved on 15 June 1751 they showed expenditure of £90 12s 8d and money in hand of £80 19s 3¼d. Governor Benyon's £50 had been invested and had brought in £5 interest over the previous two years.

What is surprising about these accounts is how low the expenditure was, and the following year this was kept to just £48 10s, enough to cover the remuneration of the Master and Mistress and to provide them with coals. It seems as if the Trustees had been so badly frightened by what had happened in the 1740's that their one imperative was to re-build their savings. Although the subscriptions had fallen sharply again to 6d under £27, no doubt because they had been artificially boosted the previous year by the collection of arrears, a gift and a legacy of £10 each and £14 rent from Mr Hardcastle helped to achieve a balance of £106 16s 11¼d on 6 June 1752.

The trustees must have invested another £50 of this money in Capital Stock, because the next set of accounts seventeen months later included income of £5 from two £50 investments. £57 4s 6d had been collected in subscriptions over this period and this, with the £14 rent from John Horncastle, covered an expenditure of £74 1s 6½d on the Bosworth property and allowed another modest increase in the cash in hand which then stood at £121 9s 10¾d.

On four occasions over the previous 43 years the annual audited accounts had been delayed by a few months. but only in 1738 had they not been presented. However, these latest accounts, approved on 3 November 1753, were to be the last for six years.

Chapter 9

Stagnation

1739 - 1760

1739 to 1758: apprenticeships under the Mary Hide Charity
As the accounts moved from the red to the black after 1748, did the Trustees attempt to meet their obligations under the terms of Mary Hide's Will? Over these 18 years the school would have received £180 from the annuity and should have apprenticed 54 children. Unfortunately the records are incomplete, but an analysis of the information we have suggests that between November 1739 and June 1758 25 boys were apprenticed which, if true, means only half the Hide Trust money was actually spent on the purpose for which it was intended. Furthermore, of these 25 boys 3 were from Hornchurch and 15 from Romford. Even if the 7 whose towns were not recorded were all from Hornchurch, this would still have been a 2:1 bias in favour of Romford, whereas Mary Hide's will stipulated that it should have been the other way round. An explanation for this might be that far more of those attending the school came from Romford than from Havering or Hornchurch. This is only supposition as we have no data on this, but it is a reasonable assumption given the 2½ mile walk each way from the centre of Hornchurch to the school, and as we have already noted the trustees tolerated a six month absence from Hornchurch children but only three months from those living in Romford.

Of the 25 boys listed, we are given the trades and destinations of 18: upholsterer (Houndsditch), carpenter (Wapping), barber & perriwig maker (London, Spittlefields and Romford), blacksmith (St James and Romford), butcher (Brooksmarket), shoemaker (Romford and 2 in Hornchurch), distiller (St Giles's-in-the-Fields), velvet weaver (Spittlefields), vinegar merchant (London), mason (location not given), gardener (Romford and in a location not given), and shovelmaker (St George's in the East).[81] It is of note that apart from the four who stayed in Romford and the two (Romford boys) who went to learn shoemaking with a John Meadhurst in Hornchurch, all the rest travelled west to East London or the City.

There are many gaps and disparities in the information we have, and an example of this would be an entry from the beginning of this period when the trustees were very short of money. The *Accounts* record that on 18 November 1739 William Middleton, son of Benjamin, was apprenticed to William Hawkins of Houndsditch, 'Citizen and Upholder [upholsterer]of London'. The 'Freedom of the City Admission Papers' agree that William Middleton was the son of Benjamin, who is described as a labourer from 'Dagnham'. (It is possible that a number of those attending the school came from Dagenham, the parish adjoining Romford in the west.) However, William Hawkins is clearly entered as an 'Innholder' (or Innkeeper) and not an 'Upholder'. The document contains a printed line which confirms that Hawkins will provide his apprentice with 'Meat, Drink, ~~Apparel~~, Lodging and all other Necessaries according to the custom of London during the said Term', but a note at the bottom of the form above the signature of the clerk who witnessed the agreement states: 'the word apparell being first struck out by consent of both partys'. William is apprenticed for 7 years, and the sum entered after '. . . in consideration of' is just five shillings. Five shillings is of course an absurdly low amount; even the standard £4 was very low, and this might explain the types of apprenticeships some of these boys entered into and why we cannot find records even of some of those who were supposedly in London. And there is a final anomaly: the date of this agreement is 1 May 1736, three-and-a-half years before it is recorded by the trustees. Did the trustees belatedly provide £3 or £4 when William was half way through his apprenticeship? Or did he switch to a new master who was indeed an upholsterer?

In contrast, other apprenticeships are recorded accurately and details can be corroborated from other sources. Thomas Cranfield was baptised at St Edward's Chapel on 19 August 1744 and apprenticed to James Hammond on 7 June 1758. The 'Freedom of the City Admission Papers' inform us that he was the 'Son of Isaac Cranfield late of Rumford in the County of Essex Yeoman Deceased', and that James Hammond, a 'Citizen and Cooper of London', took him on 'in Consideration of *Four pounds given in Charity from the Free School at Rumford aforesaid* being the Money given with the said Apprentice . . .' (Words in italics inserted in ink in the space on the printed form.) The deed was signed on 6 June 1758, which for once agrees very closely with the date in the trustees *Account Book*, and the signature was of course that of Thomas Cranfield himself. He had learnt to write a very legible, unornamented hand during his time at the school.

Some of these boys left the school with a gift to help them remember their studies and uphold them in their future lives. At the back of the first volume of Accounts there are four pages which list book purchases, sometimes giving dates and occasionally who ordered them and for what purpose. Although often indecipherable, the titles which can be made out are the Common Bible, Bible with Apocrypha, Psalter, Common Prayer Book, *Whole Duty of Man* and other religious texts, and on one occasion five copies of *Advice to Parents*. Most of these books seem to be have been bought for school use, but some were bought to be given to individual children in the school or scholars who were leaving, and at least six of those named as having been awarded apprenticeships also received books to take with them: three were given *The Whole Duty of Man*, one a Bible and a Book of Common Prayer, and two received all three of these books.[82]

In May 1758 the payment of the £10 annuity from the Mary Hide Trust passed from John Merttins to Thomas White. Whereas Mertins had been a trustee since April 1733, White seems to have had no previous connection with the School.

1741 to 1759: punctuality, masters and mistresses

During the bleak decade before 1748 there are few references to the work and discipline of the children. In May 1741 concern was expressed that some of the charity children were failing to attend the Sunday service, and the trustees 'Resolved that if the Children do not keep constantly to church on Sundays they shall be dismist the school', after which was added, somewhat incongruously, 'And that the Master learn the Girls to write that are capable'. It is interesting that it is the Master who should do this, and not the Mistress. Was she too busy with her other duties, or did she lack the necessary skills at an appropriate level? In September 1744 the trustees agreed that in future the Mistress would record the girls' absences and 'faults' and give an account of these to the trustees at every meeting, 'but that the master teach them to write and sing as usual'. This entry concludes with an enigmatic sentence: 'No children shall be suffered to be absent from school except by direction or for the service of a Trustee or Subscriber.' The implication is that any Trustee or subscriber could require any child to perform any task they required during school hours, although we have no record of either the frequency with which this happened or the services the children were required to perform.

Ten months after this meeting Elizabeth Allis, the School Mistress, was dead. At the end of February she had been paid £10 for twenty-nine weeks salary, so assuming she was then fit and well her demise was sudden. She was buried in St Edward's Church on 2 June 1745, and on 6 July the trustees paid £8 14s to Ann Alliss, probably her daughter, but whether this was money owing to her mother or whether she taught the girls during her mother's final illness we do not know. Three weeks earlier, on 12 June 1745, Elizabeth Marshall had been appointed as Mistress at 7s a week. For the next seven and a half years a husband and wife team, the third, would again be running the two schools, but this arrangement ended when Daniel Marshall resigned or his annual appointment was not renewed in 1752. He does not seem to have enjoyed the confidence of the trustees as his two predecessors had done, having been passed over in favour of Mr Stracy in 1722 and then, after Stracy's death in 1732, appointed by only a majority. Then, on 15 December that year, several parents had 'insulted and abused him very grossly'. Although the trustees had supported him on that occasion and one child had been dismissed, they might have thought fault was not solely with the parents.

On 11 November fourteen trustees gathered to choose his successor but could not 'properly fix' on a new master. Twelve then met on Saturday 2 December and afterwards recorded that John Moore of Limehouse was elected by a majority, to commence from 1 January 1753 at sixteen pounds a year with the use of the School House. His terms were therefore unchanged from those of Daniel Marshall. A payment of 5s was made to a Mr Rayment, 'a Candidate for School Master', but we do not know if Daniel Marshall or any others had been candidates. Opinion was clearly divided on Mr Moore's appointment, but it would be some years before those who voted against him would find justification for their misgivings. In the meantime Mr Marshall was paid in full until Christmas. He and Elizabeth then moved out of the house, although Elizabeth would continue as School Mistress for another eighteen years.

Between the appointment of John Moore as School Master in December 1752 and the next discussion of school matters seven years later the trustees met just three times: on 3 November 1753 when the accounts were audited; on 22 May 1755 when nine trustees met and agreed that there should be Charity Sermons once every other year (although after the first of these, three days later, seven years were to elapse before the next); and in October 1757, to arrange for necessary repairs to the Bosworth property.

The meeting of 6 October 1759

When the trustees next met, two years later, six men gathered to examine the accounts. Britain had now been at war with France and Austria for three years, and the talk before the meeting began was no doubt about the danger of a French invasion of England and the fighting in Canada. The first was a real possibility. Tens of thousands of French troops were gathered in readiness at the mouth of the Loire, and the defeat of the French Mediterranean fleet at the Battle of Lagos had only delayed their transport, not prevented it. The situation in Canada would have seemed just as bad to these men in the 'King's Arms', who did not then know that the fighting there had already reached its climax with the Battle of the Plains of Abraham on 13 September. It would be another ten days before the news of this victory - and the death of General Wolfe - would reach London.

It was twenty-five years to the month since James Hotchkis had died, and with the exception of two or three years after the Archbishop's sermon in 1749 the conduct of the trustees throughout this period had been marked by a lack of energy and enterprise. However, if Thomas Bayley had achieved little else as treasurer up to this time - which, indeed, appears to have been the case - he had managed to keep the accounts in good order since the previous reconciliation six years before. Over this period the income had totalled £461 9s 6½d, which added to the sum of £121 9s 10¾d brought forward from the last reckoning gave a total of £582 19s 5¼d. £414 7s 10½d had been spent over this period, leaving a balance in hand of £168 11s 6¾d. On average, therefore, annual income had exceeded expenditure by £7 17s {£1,200}. For the first time there is reference to 'the annual subscriptions book', suggesting a greater degree of organisation in collecting these contributions. Regular income continued to come from John Horncastle's rent of £14 a year for the Bosworth property, from the interest on the two investments of £50 from Governor Benyon and 'Capital Stock', and from a recently invested donation of £40 from Frances Cornwall. There had also been the regular £10 payments each year from the Hide Trust and £76 3s 3½d from the collections at the charity sermons on 25 May 1755. Three legacies had been received over this period, including £3 from Simon Hillatt, the former treasurer, who had died in 1751, and £10 in December 1758 from Mrs Pyle following the death of her husband, Francis, who had been such a loyal supporter of the school over the thirty-three years he had served as Vicar of Hornchurch.

The expenditure over these years had been held at an average of just £69, of which £44 was paid out in salaries to the Master and Mistress. It is not surprising, therefore, that other expenditure had covered a very limited range of items such as coal and the house and window taxes on the two properties. The payment during this period of 4s to the chimney sweeper and of 5s to Tom Furniss for emptying the 'Privy' - described in earlier entries as 'the necessary House' - may be compared with the £1 17s 'Paid Mrs Hunt for Wine used in the vestry and Entertainment for the Bishop's Servants & Horses' when he visited to preach the Charity School sermon in 1755. We do not know who this bishop was, but his words raised £4 5s 11d more than those of the Archbishop six years previously, sufficient to entertain his servants and horses and then to clean out the privy twice over. A remarkable £42 5s 4½d had been spent on books and £4 13s 6d on paper. The largest expenditure was £51 on repairs to 'Mr Horncastle's House' (the Joseph Boswell property) following a survey the treasurer and other Trustees had made at the end of 1757. It must have been in very poor condition, but this expenditure of 60% of the £14 a year rent they received over this period preserved the inheritance for the future. We have already noted the failure to spend all of the income from the Mary Hide Charity on apprenticeships, and of the £60 income received over the previous six years only £12 had been spent on apprenticing 3 boys. The £8 under-spend each year from this source matches almost exactly the average increase in the Treasurer's balance, so the Trustees could have fulfilled their obligations under the trust and still balanced their books.

Having dealt with the accounts, the Trustees then addressed problems in the school which one suspects were not of recent origin. First were the perennial problems of attendance and punctuality:

> Resolved, That the parents of the Charity Children have Orders to send their Children every day at 7 o'clock in the morning in Summer & 8 in the morning in Winter & at 2 in the afternoon & to be at the School house on Sundays at 9 o'clock in the morning and not to keep them away on any pretence, (except sickness) without Leave in writing from the Treasurer, or some trustee, or Subscriber: if any wilful neglect of this kind shall hereafter happen, the Children will be deprived the Benefit of their Learning & Cloathing at the approaching Charity Sermons, by being turned out of the School.

(There is no evidence that these 'approaching Charity Sermons' ever took place as no income from such a source is recorded in the accounts.)

Second was the conduct of the School Master, which no doubt contributed to the children's failings:

> On Complaint of neglect against Mr Moore the Schoolmaster after an admonition of the Trustees, & Promise of more care for the future from the Schoolmaster.
> 'Resolved that Mr Moore be continued on trial of his good behaviour 'till next Lady day, & that he be removed from the School at that time if his conduct is not then approved of.

Evidently Mr Moore's behaviour did not improve. A meeting was arranged for 1 March 1760 to address this, but only three trustees attended and it had to be postponed. Lady Day was 25 March, and as no replacement had been appointed the Trustees no doubt re-appointed Mr Moore for another three months, but the active Trustees were determined not to extend his services again. On 8 April 2s 6d was paid for a man and horse to deliver letters to all the Trustees, the first such entry in the accounts. This letter informed them that a meeting was to be held on Saturday 12 April in the 'King's Arms' in Romford to appoint a new Master. It is a sign of the dysfunctional state of the trustees that at the appointed time only five were present, only just outnumbering the candidates. The minutes record:

> ... there appeared Four Candidates for School Master, viz Mr John Horncastle, Mr James Nash, both of the Town of Romford, Mr Martin, late of Shenfield, and Mr John Salter, Assistant Master to the Charity School at Poplar, the consideration of which was referred to the Next meeting appointed accordingly on Saturday the 3rd of May following.

John Horncastle was, of course, the leaseholder of Mr Bosworth's House, who paid his rent with some conviviality in one of the local inns. On 29 April the man and horse were again hired, and this time eight trustees were motivated to attend the meeting at which John Salter of Poplar was unanimously elected, to commence on 24 June at sixteen pounds a year and the use of the School House. The remuneration therefore remained unchanged. 24 June was midsummer and the next quarter day, and so the earliest date Mr Salter could leave his employment in Poplar. Mr Martin had the consolation of 1s 6d to cover his expenses at the inn.

John Moore's duties, and those of his successor, included that of parish clerk, and although the school records give us no evidence of the 'neglect' and poor behaviour for which he was dismissed, these are very clear when the registers of St Edward's Chapel are examined. He was appointed schoolmaster on 1 January 1753, and after a marriage on 7 February 1754 an entry appears in the register: 'This was the last marriage before the new Act to prevent Clandestine marriages took place, the subsequent marriages are to be entered in the Parliamentary Register Book.' This refers to the Hardwicke Marriage Act of 1753 which came into force on 25 March 1754 and from then the bride, groom and two witnesses had to sign the register. From 11 October 1754 'J. Moore' is more often than not one of the witnesses, and on two occasions Mary Moore is the second witness. His final signature was on 25 May 1760, a month after John Salter was appointed and a month before he took up his post. Moore was obviously in Romford on that date, but did he abscond soon afterwards? After the record of a burial on 29 April, the day Mr Salter was appointed, a note in the register reads: 'Mem. John More who officiated as clerk having absented himself the greater part of the two following months, viz. May & June, the account of Burials in those months is imperfect.' There is a similar entry in the baptismal register. Did he simply fail to keep these registers up-to-date, or did he leave his employment early, and if so we are left wondering who was running the Boys' School in the weeks before John Salter arrived.

Chapter 10

Reform

1761 - 1762

1761: a royal wedding and a hasty wedding
John Salter had been Master for four months when King George II died on 25 October 1760. He was 77. Short tempered, parsimonious, a man who was more at home in Hanover than Britain, he had not been popular. He had had a notorious falling out with his son Frederick, the Prince of Wales, who had headed a rival court of opposition politicians until his sudden death in 1751. This event deprived the country of its first King Frederick, but he left a son, George, who now ascended the throne. The people of the Royal Liberty joined those across the country in celebrating their new king who, unlike his grandfather, had been born in Britain, spoke English without a German accent, and was not George II.

George III was then 22 and unmarried, but within a year the renewed urgency to find him a bride brought 17 year old Princess Charlotte of Mecklenburg Strelitz to Harwich on 7 September 1761. She had been at sea for ten days, and spent her first night in England at Lord Abercorn's house at Witham. The Annual Register reported that:

> On the road she was extremely courteous to an incredible number of spectators on horse and foot gathered on this occasion, showing herself, and bowing to all who seemed desirous of seeing her, and ordering the coach to go extremely slow through the towns and villages as she passed, that as many as would might have a full view of her.[83]

A royal visit has always attracted crowds, and one can imagine that the following day Romford would have been packed with people, including the children from the Charity School, pressing to obtain the best view of their soon-to-be Queen as her equipage swept past the toll gate and school house, across the Market Place, and drew up at a three-storey, flat-fronted Georgian building in the High Street. The princess alighted and passed between the two pillars supporting the small portico which protected the front door. This house, where she now took coffee, belonged to a wine merchant called Richard Dutton who had been elected a trustee of the Charity School the previous year. Here the Princess 'was pleased to indulge the spectators with the sight of her person from a window' on the first floor, where she made several appearances. At one o'clock she departed in the King's Coach which had been sent to meet her, escorted by two duchesses. It was her only stop on the journey, and Mr Dutton subsequently renamed his property 'Queen's House'. At three o'clock she arrived at St James's Palace, and six hours later she married the young king. That night saw 'the greatest rejoicings at Rumford ever known in the Memory of Man, great quantities of liquor [being] given to the Populace'.[84] As the people of Romford celebrated that evening, some would have wondered how many other towns could boast of having entertained a Queen for coffee on her wedding day. Sadly, Richard Dutton's good fortune and celebrity did not last: three years later he declared bankruptcy.

Three weeks after the Princess's visit the trustees met for the first time since appointing John Salter seventeen months before. Now they were meeting to appoint his successor. Once again a man was sent round to distribute letters prior to the meeting. (There is no reference to a horse on this occasion, which appears to have saved 1s 6d.) Despite this effort to encourage attendance, just six trustees were present at the meeting on 29 September 1761, all of whom had been present when John Salter had been unanimously appointed. The number of candidates on this occasion is not recorded, but the minutes state that 'At this meeting Thomas Grove of St James Clerkenwell was unanimously Elected by the Trustees then present School Master for the Charity School in Romford, to Commence from this Day, at Sixteen pounds a year, and the use of the School House.' Having performed this task, the trustees did not meet again for another eight months.

We do not know the circumstances of Mr Salter's departure, but he was the witness at a marriage on 7 September 1761, just three weeks before this meeting. The fact that Thomas Grove was to start immediately indicates that he had no contract to work out and that John Salter was no longer in post. Why he departed is a mystery; we only know that there is no record of his burial following an accident or an attack of smallpox or one of those other maladies which suddenly carried people off in the eighteenth century.

In that year of celebrations, there is no evidence of any event that January to mark the schools' fiftieth anniversary. Looking back over the previous half century, an elderly citizen would have noted how much and how little had altered in the Liberty. The Essex toll road, an element in that first co-ordinated attempt to improve land communications since Roman times, was undoubtedly the most significant change. As with all elements of infrastructure, its importance lay not in its physical presence, often unwelcome, but in the further changes and developments which it enabled. It has been observed[85] that the continental travellers in the 18th century were more complimentary about the state of English roads than were the English themselves. In 1761 Count Frederick Kielmansegge, a Hanoverian nobleman very distantly (and illegitimately) related to the King, visited England for the coronation on 22 September. He said that the road from Harwich to London 'is always kept in good order with fine gravel and sand, and the slightest unevenness is mended at once.'[86] There can be no doubt that from 1722 onwards this road accelerated not only the journeys of those travelling to and from Romford but also the lives of those living in the Liberty. It brought fashionable shops to the town, like that of William Smithfield, the clockmaker, who arrived about 1750, and it brought new ideas and ways of thinking. Science was replacing superstition. A century earlier Thomas Gilman had obtained a certificate from Phillip Peck, the then Chaplain of Romford, allowing him to have his three year old son Samuel touched by the King because he was suffering from the King's Evil, but this traditional practice had ended fifty years ago in the reign of Queen Anne.[87]

But for all this change, the life and institutions of the Liberty had altered very little over the last half century. The ancient manors of Romford and Hornchurch were still part of the physical and the administrative landscape, and the families who owned them were those which dominated the social and economic life of the community. They still lived in their large houses, even if these had been modernised as Gidea Hall had been in about 1720 when the old mansion, dating back three hundred years, had been pulled down and a new house built. The Royal Liberty of Havering, levying taxes and administering justice, was still a reality three hundred years after it had been created, although its administrative buildings had changed. Between 1737 and 1740 the Court House which the Charity School boys had used for a year as a school room had been rebuilt by the Crown, as had the gaol.

And what of the Charity School and its new Master? It had certainly been the pride of the town in the Rev'd Mr Hotchkis's day, but there was no longer the enthusiasm which had marked its early years and the school children were now just part of the town scene. They had had five Masters in fifty years, but the trustees had now appointed a man who would still be in post forty years later, Mr Thomas Green Grove. Knowledge of his middle name and his parish of origin allow us to identify him from the many others named Thomas Grove (or Groves, we find both spellings of his name in the *Accounts*) who populated the 18th century. He was baptised at St James, Clerkenwell on 31 January 1723, and was a teacher by 1751 when he gave his occupation as 'writing master literature/education' when he subscribed to a new publication, *The Tutor's Assistant; being a Compendium of Arithmetic and a Complete Question-Book in five parts.*

This book was the work of the master of the boarding-school in Kensington, Francis Walkingame, and was an early example of a teacher compiling and publishing his own teaching notes and exercises. Many more such books by entrepreneurial teachers would follow over the next 250 years before the internet began to challenge the text book as the primary teaching resource, but few would be as successful. Walkingame's work would prove the most popular 'Arithmetic' both in England and America for ninety years, until superseded by the works on algebra (published in 1841) and arithmetic (in 1843) by John Colenso (the future Bishop of Natal). There would be at least 275 editions, the last in 1885. Thomas Grove subscribed to the very first and to each new edition of this work until 1775, so he undoubtedly used it with his students at Romford.

On 17 February 1754 the 31 year old Thomas had married Abigail Green, also of St James' Clerkenwell, in the private May Fair Chapel run by Mr Alexander Keith. The circumstances surrounding this wedding are of interest. Keith was a Church of England clergyman who had been excommunicated in 1742 and sent to prison for several years for performing clandestine marriages without banns or licence. On his release he set up his own private chapel where marriages, although still clandestine, were perfectly lawful because until the Hardwicke Marriage Act came into force on 25 March 1754 the only indispensable element of a marriage in England was a Church of England clergyman, which Alexander Keith still was. It was a profitable business which Keith promoted with frequent newspaper advertisements which gave the cost as one guinea for 'the licence on a crown stamp, minister and clerk's fees, together with the certificate'. At its height he and his curates performed six thousand marriages a year at this chapel.

But why did Thomas and Abigail choose to be married here? In brief, they were in a hurry. If they had waited 35 days the Hardwicke Marriage Act would have come into force, requiring them to be married in a church after the publication of banns or the obtaining of a license. We do not know Abigail's age, but if she was under 21 and they had waited they would also have needed her parents' consent. And why could they not wait? The register of St James' Clerkenwell gives the reason: a son, also called Thomas Green Grove, was baptised there on 28 July, having been born eighteen days before. In the ensuing seven years Thomas seems to have been joined by at least one brother and sister, the evidence for this coming, sadly, from the St Edward's Burial Registers. (Thomas himself died at the age of 10.) It seems to have been a family of at least five that the new, 38 year old schoolmaster brought to Romford in September 1761.

1762: another attempt at reform and renewal
The next trustees' meeting, held at the 'Cock and Bell' on Thursday 3 June 1762, was the first General Meeting since October 1759, but there were too few trustees present to transact any business. This problem had arisen because over the previous seventeen years only seventeen new trustees had been elected, and two of these had been clergy. These men had included Thomas Bayley in February 1745; Abraham Culver and John Comyns in June 1745; the Rev'd Glocester Ridley and Captain Thomas Johnson in October 1747; Joseph Letch in 1748 and Thomas Mashiter in 1749 (both of whom will feature later); William Dearsly, a Hornchurch carpenter who lived at Rainham Hall, in 1751; John Russell of Stubbers, the grandson of Sir William, in 1755; and in 1759 the Rev'd William Harris, who had succeeded Francis Pyle as Vicar of Hornchurch the previous year. They had each brought a guinea to the accounts and one or two performed a significant act of service to the Charity, but only the two clergy, Thomas Bayley and William Dearsly had been consistently regular in their attendance over the previous decade.

The meeting was postponed until 12 August, when seven existing trustees were joined by ten others who had agreed to be appointed and were present to sign their names in the *Accounts*. The original seven trustees were now able to approve and sign the accounts which recorded an income of £132 2s 0d and expenditure of £124 9s 8d, leaving £176 3s 10¾d in the treasurer's hand. There had been no charity sermons or legacies to boost the income of the school over these three years, and there had been no expenditure on clothes (now paid for by the £1 deposit) or buildings. Apart from just £3 3s 3d spent on books and £1 11s 6d on Copy Books, all the expenditure related to salaries and the taxes on the two houses. In 1761, for example, the trustees paid £1 5s 6d House and Window Lights tax, £1 8s Poor Rate, and 7s Chapel Wardens' Rates on Mr Horncastle's house, and on Mr Salter's house they paid 5s Chapel Wardens' Rates and 5s Poor Rate.

The ten new trustees were then formally elected. Never had so many been welcomed in one cohort, but only two of these men would show a lasting commitment: the Rev'd James Ridley, and the farmer and contractor from Dagenham who occasionally undertook bricklaying work for the trustees, Edward Sumpner. Two others will be of later interest: Thomas Debuke, who would become treasurer in name only in 1769, and John Harle Junior of Rainham Hall. Harle had had a childhood disrupted by bereavement: his father had died when he was two, his mother when he was nine, and the aunt he then went to live with when he was eleven. He then passed into the care of an uncle in London. The contents of Rainham Hall were sold and the house was rented out to William Dearsly, who co-incidentally became John's sole trustee in 1758. Now aged 20, young John joined William as a trustee of the Charity School.

With seventeen trustees now present, the meeting then addressed the terms of employment for Mr Grove, the School Master they had appointed eleven months previously.

> Thursday 12 August 1762: The Trustees of the Charity School of Hornchurch and Romford do agree to give Mr Grove a Salary of twenty five pounds per Annum two Chaldrons of coals Annually, and the Use of the House upon these Conditions that he teach the forty Boys to Read, Write, Cast Accounts and sing the plain Psalm tunes and teach the Girls two days in the week an Hour each time to Write, and provided they shall hereafter upon a Vacancy elect his Wife to be School Mistress (if she be found Capable) then Mr Grove's Salary to be Reduced to the former Income of sixteen pounds per Annum the Chaldron of Coals and the use of the House.
>
> I agree to the above Conditions
>
> (Mr Grove's signature)

It was only in October 1732 with the appointment of Daniel Marshall that the trustees had raised the combined salary of the Master and Mistress from 16s a week to 17s. When the house had been provided as part of the package in April 1737 4s had been deducted from this, reducing the figure to 13s. John Moore had been appointed December 1752 on £16 with the house, as had John Salter in May 1760 and Thomas Grove in September 1761. Now, less than a year later, his salary had been raised by over 50%, he retained the use of the house, his duties remained unchanged, and he had been promised the post of School Mistress for his wife in due course. One can assume from this that after the problems with Mr Moore and the short tenure of Mr Salter the trustees were very pleased with the manner in which Mr Grove was performing his duties, that good schoolmasters were hard to find, and that having secured such a one the trustees wished to ensure he was not tempted to move elsewhere. If this was their intention, they certainly succeeded.

There are various details to note in this record. First, the master's main teaching duties are secular, to teach the boys 'to Read, Write, Cast Accounts', with no mention of instruction in the Church Catechism which fifty years earlier the SPCK had laid down as the Master's first duty. The difference in religious philosophy is well summarised by A. R. Humphreys: 'The reign of Queen Anne cannot be understood without a knowledge of the violent winds still blowing from the storm-centres of the seventeenth century', whilst of the later period he writes:

> It interpreted religious values differently from the century before: man tended to be, as Professor Tawney observes, not primarily a spiritual being prudently acknowledging economics to keep alive, but an economic being prudently acknowledging religion as an insurance for his soul.[88]

True, he has to teach the boys to sing the plain Psalm tunes, but one senses this is to enable them to take a fuller part in the services rather than to save their souls. He also has to teach the girls to write (if only for two hours each week), a duty he has had since 1741.

Elizabeth Marshall had now been mistress for seventeen years and a widow for the last six of these, the burial of Daniel Marshall having taken place at St Edward's Church on 26 July 1756. There are no criticisms of her in the records, which makes the final part of this agreement intriguing: that if there should be a vacancy Thomas Grove's wife would become the School

Mistress 'if she be found Capable', and that his salary would then be reduced to the level from which it had just been raised: sixteen pounds per Annum, a Chaldron of Coals and the use of the House. If they were referring to Abigail one would have thought both parties would have known whether she would be 'found Capable' or not, but it seems she was no longer alive. Unfortunately no definitive record can be found of Abigail's burial, but there is a record of the marriage of Thomas Green Grove to a Rebekah Clayton in St Edward's Chapel on 7 January 1766, followed by the baptisms of Rose in July 1768, and Henrietta in 1770.

Whoever the Trustees and Thomas Grove had in mind as a possible School Mistress in August 1762, she never had the opportunity to take the job. Had she done so, he would have lost £9 a year, whilst she would have received Mrs Marshall's 7s a week, or £18 4s a year. For her work the couple would have been just £9 4s {£1,400} a year better off, and the Trustees would have saved £9. It seems a curious arrangement on both sides.

The third item of business at this important meeting was to review aspects of the schools' operation, which resulted in ten agreed resolutions to clarify procedures:

1. Trustees to meet quarterly; no child to be admitted except at these meetings; every person before admission must produce a register of their age, and that no child whatsoever be admitted before their seventh birthday.
2. If no child aged 7 or upwards belonging to the parishes of Hornchurch or Romford appears then it will be lawful to any trustee to propose a proper object of another parish.
3. No second child of the same parents be Admitted except no other proper object be offered.
4. Every Boy or Girl to be discharged at the Quarterly meeting after their 14th birthday.
5. The children at present in the school under the age of 7 be discharged but are recommended to the trust to have the preference of being readmitted when of age and eligible.
6. For the future, this charity cloth[e] 20 boys and 10 girls annually, the 20 senior boys and the 10 senior girls according to the dates of their admission, and that the treasurer be ordered to have them clothed by the next charity sermons.
7. That application be made to the Rev'd Mr Gerritt and Rev'd Mr Adams to preach two Charity Sermons on Sunday 19th September next.
8. As the necessary business to be transacted cannot be done at this meeting, and being chiefly relative to the Laws concerning the Parents and their

Children, a committee be appointed to regulate the same and to issue out orders concerning the same which shall be inforce till the next quarterly meeting. A meeting is accordingly appointed at 4pm next Thursday 19th August and whichever Trustees attend will be considered as the committee.
9. All Bills brought in be immediately paid by the treasurer.
10. School Master's additional salary [to] commence from Lady Day last.

As always, the need to agree these resolutions and commit them to paper gives a glimpse of issues of which we might not otherwise have been aware. The decision to meet quarterly had been made (and broken) before, as had that to limit the age range of the schools to between 7 and 14. However, the Trustees now show a new-found determination to manage the admission and discharge of pupils at their quarterly meetings, basing their decisions on evidence of each child's true age. One wonders how admissions had been organised up to this point, and how many children under seven were now to be discharged. The decision to ration the places available to one from each family was presumably intended to spread the advantages of schooling, and particularly the benefits of literacy, to more families than would otherwise have been the case. This seems both wise and fair.

Item 2 suggests there was no permanent waiting list for a place at the school. It assumes that children will come from the parishes of Romford or Hornchurch (treating them as separate parishes 87 years before legally they were so) but makes no mention of the children from Havering-atte-Bower. It is difficult to know from where else children might have come to fill any vacant places: the two nearest parishes were Dagenham and South Weald, neither of which had a charity school at this time, but they were respectively four miles and six and a half miles from Romford.[89]

The decision to clothe half the boys and half the girls (interestingly according to their length of time in the school rather than their age) helps to clarify the situation on uniform. After a hesitant start, by 1719 all the children were clothed and shod and this provision continued until the early 1730's, but after the trustees funds were exhausted by the building of the School and the Master's House there was little money for this. The decision in July 1738 that in future a £1 security would be required for their clothes does not indicate how many children were in fact clothed. The evidence of the account book and this decision in 1762 both suggest that few (if any) children had worn a uniform for about twenty years. In deciding to clothe just half the scholars the trustees no doubt had one eye on the budget and the other on the image of the school. Such an obvious outward change in the appearance of half the children would be noted around Romford and Hornchurch and be seen as symbolic of a new start to the school when they were first worn at the two charity sermons in September.

The agreement which Thomas Grove had signed stating that he would teach 'the forty Boys' is important. We know that by March 1714 the number of boys had risen to 50, but figures in the *Accounts* for clothing from 1723 suggest that by then the figure had dropped back to 40. An entry on 11 July 1729 is explicit: 'cloathing for the children of the school viz 40 boys and 15 girls', and on 24 March 1733 it was 'Resolved that the order for clothing of 14th April 1732 be enlarged to 43 boys and 19 girls.' One can imagine that at this meeting in June 1762 Mr Grove may well have argued that he could not be expected to teach more than 40 boys or any outside the 7 to 14 age range, and that he wished to ensure agreement on these points was recorded. He had now been Master for eleven months and must have had a considerable influence at this meeting to have increased his salary by half and to have had this backdated by twenty weeks.

Finally, resolution 8 is intriguing. It would seem that by 'Laws' the trustees meant their own 'Rules', with no legal connotations. Eight trustees met as arranged the following Thursday, but their only recorded action was to elect another trustee, Thomas Wake. However, it seems likely that they discussed what their expectations of parents and children would be in the future and that these were then confirmed at a subsequent meeting, because in October it was 'Order'd that the Rules and Orders [in] relation to the Parents and their Children and the prayers for the Children be Printed.' Presumably every parent was to be given a copy of this document.

If the Trustees had sometimes been lax in carrying out their responsibilities, for nearly thirty years the boys had lacked a strong master. Daniel Marshall appears to have been less than effective, John Moore neglected his duties and misbehaved, and John Salter, who might have been good, had stayed only a year. Thomas Grove no doubt wanted to tighten up the resulting lax attitudes of both the students and their parents and to ensure that he had the full support of the trustees.

It is the record of the appointment of Thomas Wake which concludes the first volume of the trustees' accounts. The record of the meeting of 12 August 1762 forms a natural break in the story of the school, and as though in recognition of this the Trustees ignored the remaining pages in the original *Account and Minute Book* and commenced a new volume at their next meeting. Consciously or not, it was a symbolic gesture of their new found determination to address the weaknesses in the administration of the charity which had been all too evident over the last twenty years. Would the dynamism of Mr Grove and, if implemented, the resolutions of the newly enlarged body of trustees bring about the reforms necessary to ensure progress and improvement over the coming years?

Chapter 11

The school and society during the early years of George III

1762 - 1771

The life chances of an unwanted child in the 1760's
It is easy to forget how extremely fortunate poor children were to survive babyhood, and how doubly fortunate were those who then had the opportunity to attend a charity school. In September 1742 the foundation stone had been laid for the Foundling Hospital, and an examination of its development in the twenty years since then reminds us of the state of child poverty when George III came to the throne. Although unbelievably well supported by the aristocratic and the wealthy, private funding was insufficient to meet the demands placed on it. In the six years between January 1750 and December 1755, 2,523 children were brought for admission, but only 783 were taken in. (What, one wonders, happened to the rejected two-thirds?) In response to this over-demand the House of Commons adopted an extraordinarily enlightened policy: from 1 June 1756 the Hospital was to accept all applicants and its excess costs would be paid from public funds. With the maximum age for admission then being raised from two months to one year, babies started to arrive from the workhouses across the country where they had been abandoned, and in less than four years 14,934 children had arrived. (Of these only 4,400 were to survive to become apprentices. The other two-thirds would die.)

The cost to the exchequer had now reached an alarming £500,000. (For comparison, it would be another 73 years before parliament voted its first grant for education, a sum of £20,000 for one year.) After a scheme to raise the necessary funds by taxing parishes was rejected - parishes were already burdened with the poor rates - it was decided to end the system of indiscriminate admission which had lasted less than four years. In doing so, Parliament washed its hands of responsibility for the fate of many of the successors of those 4,400 babies admitted in the previous four years who would survive to become adults. Having to rely solely on its own resources once again, between 1760 and 1763 the Hospital admitted only orphans of military fathers, many children in such circumstances being unable to receive help under the Poor Laws as they were not registered in a local area or parish.[90] It then reverted to admission by petition, and then adopted a policy of receiving only children who came with 'considerable sums (for example £100)'.[91] (This was probably not an insurmountable problem if you were an aristocratic lady trying to dispose anonymously of the bastard conceived without your husband's knowledge, but if you were poor . . .) In 1801 the policy changed again: only babies, and no money, would be received in future, but the committee of inquiry had to be satisfied that the mother had previously been of good character, was then in genuine need, had been deserted by the father of the child, and that relieved of the child she would be enabled to return to the path of virtue and pursue an honest livelihood. The nineteenth century therefore opened with all the children at the Foundling Hospital being the firstborn of unmarried women.[92]

1762: a new beginning for the Romford Charity School

If the new system the trustees had set up for admissions was to work, they had to ensure that they met every three months as they had pledged to do, and indeed the first year they met six times and made a splendid start to their programme. Nine were present at the 'Crown Inn' on 16 September 1762 for the first of these meetings, where it was resolved 'that John Hill, being next in succession, shall have the school Cloaths, instead of Ezra Wells, who is discharged.' The clothes had therefore been provided as agreed. Three days later the Charity Sermons raised £50. The next month it was agreed that the necessary repairs to the Charity School and School Master's House were to begin immediately 'and that the Workmen be ordered to set about it without loss of time and finish it with as much frugality as possible', and at the same meeting it was 'Order'd that the Rules and Orders [in] relation to the Parents and their Children and the prayers for the Children be Printed'.

In January 1763 it was 'Order'd that those children Girls as well as Boys who are at present on the list of charity children and have not the benefit of the cloathing be allowed a pair of stockings and shoes and that the Treasurer be desired to furnish them therewith immediately', and in June it was again resolved to clothe the twenty senior boys and ten senior girls before the Charity Sermons which that year were held on 14 August and raised £28 0s 5½d. The Trustees also kept to another resolution at this meeting: a boy wishing to join the school was turned away because he had not brought the certificate proving his age; he brought it to the next meeting in April and was admitted.

One notable difference between the entries in the first and second volume of the *Accounts* is the inclusion from August 1762 of the names and ages of the children admitted and details of those discharged. In the course of 1763, the first full year for which we have such records, there were 30 admissions: 2 aged 13, 2 aged 11, 4 aged 10, 3 aged 9, 6 aged 8 and 13 aged 7. It is significant both that two children were admitted aged 13 even though they would be discharged as 'over age' in less than a year, and that three quarters were under 9 and nearly a half only 7. No doubt this was a disproportionate number of seven year olds because those previously discharged as under age were now being given preferential re-admission. Thirty seems to have been a high number of admissions for one year, nearly half the school; in the twenty-eight months between May 1767 and September 1769 only 32 children obtained places, of which 3 were aged 11, 5 were 10, 5 were 9, 9 were 8, and 10 were 7. These two sets of figures suggest that having discharged the younger children and then re-admitted them at seven the Trustees were able to establish a more even spread of ages between 7 and 14.

The most common reasons given for children being discharged were that they were past the age of 14 or had been taken away by their parents. On 1 May 1766 it was 'Ordered that George Markwell be Discharged for neglect of coming to school and other misdemeanours', which is notable for being unusual. In October 1767 a boy was discharged for being absent for 6 months, and in February 1768 Thomas Manning was discharged after 4 months absence, neither having had 'leave from Treasurer'. No reason is given why parents took their children out of school until May 1767, when three boys were discharged 'being taken out by their parents to go to service'. From now on this becomes an increasingly common phrase with another fourteen children leaving for this reason over the next two years.

At a meeting on 7 September 1769 the Trustees radically changed the policy on the education of boys, cutting their education from seven years to four: 'Ordered at this Meeting that for the future no Boy under eight years of age shall be Admitted into the School And that they shall be Discharged at the Age of twelve if the Trustees think they have Received sufficient Education.' The ages of entry and discharge for the girls were unaltered. In February the following year six boys were 'superannuated . . . as appears by the order of September 7th 1769', and at the end of May a further ten boys were discharged 'being past the age of 12 years'. Predictably, there is no reference to any assessment to ascertain whether they had received 'sufficient Education', whatever that might have meant. No reason was given for this change. Were so many of the older boys being removed by their parents to go into service (or for some other reason) that few remained in school over the age of 12? If this was the case, were those who remained both frequently absent and a trouble when present? And did these problems compound the difficulties of teaching these older scholars alongside so many younger children in a useful programme of learning? One can sense the personality of Thomas Grove behind the change, rationalising the problem and then persuading the trustees that boys learnt most between the ages of 8 and 12 and a shorter, more concentrated experience would greatly improve the efficiency of the school by allowing many more boys to receive a basic education with only a little disadvantage to a very few. Such a proposal would not have been made unless there were additional boys waiting for a place, which suggests that following the reforms of August 1762, and with a strong Master in charge, the image and popularity of the school had improved.

Some parents, and possibly also their sons, must have been disappointed and perhaps resentful that their expectation of schooling to the age of fourteen had been so suddenly dashed. At a meeting on 25 October 1770, a year after the new policy had been agreed and when the third or fourth cohort of twelve year olds was about to be discharged, the embryo of another new policy emerged which would have helped both to mitigate any such resentment and to embed the learning achieved in school. Jeremiah Hill and John Wingar 'being past the age of 12 years' and Elizabeth Maidle and Lucy Chapman 'being past the age of 14 years' were all discharged, but each was to have their clothes, a Bible, a Prayer Book, and *The Whole Duty of Man*. We have seen evidence that many children appear to have retained their clothes when they left school, but the only previous records of a gift of books are jottings recording an apparently random practice between about 1737 and 1743.

In March the following year five boys and three girls were discharged, being past the ages of 12 and 14 respectively, and each was again given their clothes and received the three books, but at the same meeting it was decreed that those whose parents had taken them out of school were to be discharged and their clothes returned to the trustees. The policy was therefore being refined to encourage parents to leave their children in the school for their full term. That November of 1771 another two 14 year old girls and four 12 year old boys were discharged with their clothes and those three volumes, but after this there is no further mention of the books as a leaving gift. Did the practice cease, or was it now an embedded policy which no longer warranted a special note in the Trustees accounts?

The accounts in the 1760's

The figure carried forward into the new account book on 12 August 1762 was an impressive £176 3s 10¾d, and before the next reconciliation on 13 October the following year there had been two annual charity sermons which together brought in an additional £78 0s 5½d. Other income had included the £14 from Mr Horncastle for the year's rent on Boswell's property and donations from eight individuals totalling £7 17s 6d (or 7½ guineas). Subscriptions were generally of a guinea or half guinea, but other sums recorded as 'Rec'd of sundry Persons, in full' make it impossible to work out the exact number of subscribers.

The charity sermons were now an annual event, but the £50 collected in September 1762 was exceptional, and over the following six years the sum raised each year averaged just over £31 {£4,500}. During this decade these events seem to have become more costly to put on, so raising £50 in 1762 entailed expenses of £5 13s 6d for 'Printing the Hymns etc.', and from 1763 it cost 10s (or £1 10s if a horse was hired) for a man to 'Carry the Hymns about the Country'. The Sermons were now also being advertised in the newspapers, costing 8s {£62} in the *London Chronicle & Daily Advertiser*, 3s in the Chelmsford and Ipswich newspapers, and 2s in the *Chelmsford News Carrier*. In addition to these costs a 'supply' preacher was frequently needed to attend the clergyman's church whilst he was preaching in Romford, which cost another guinea, and between £1 and £2 was needed for refreshments and other miscellaneous expenses. In October 1765 an additional 17s was paid to the Rev'd Mr Hopkins for a Post Chaise for one day to attend the Rev'd Mr Jacob who was preaching that year. However, after these expenses were deducted the sermons always raised useful additional income and the effort required to host these public events was repaid by the prestige they brought to the schools.

The sermons also provided an incentive to ensure that representative students were newly and smartly attired. The order to provide stockings and shoes to those who did not have the benefit of clothing was repeated in

January 1764 and 1765, except that in 1765 the order continued '. . . except James Hamstead and he is to be exempted from the above Benefits as he has been guilty of theft', a rare example of clothing being withheld as a punishment. In June 1764 the twenty senior boys and ten senior girls were again given clothing prior to the two Charity Sermons, which that year raised £34 2s 8¼d. In October 1765 it was decided 'that the three Senior Boys and the two Senior Girls be forthwith cloathed that were not cloathed at the last general Cloathing, and that the Girls make up their own Cloathing', and in June 1766 the usual figures of 20 boys and 10 girls to be clothed were amended to 23 and 12. This now became the policy, and from 1770 through to 1802 there was a consistency in the provision of clothes for the 23 senior boys and 12 senior girls before the annual sermons, and of supplying those not so clothed with hose, shoes and buckles.

The house in Hornchurch Lane continued to bring in £14 a year but the arrangements for the letting altered, and the management of this exemplifies the Trustees' lack of clear policy. On 8 November 1764 they agreed to lease the premises to their fellow trustee Edward Sumpner for 61 years at six guineas a year, the lease to commence at Christmas. It would seem that some trustees had misgivings about this arrangement, because in January 1765 it was mutually dissolved and a new agreement was made with Mr John Horncastle for 61 years at £10 a year 'clear of all expenses' (such as taxes and repairs) from Lady Day next. This sum was more than the six guineas Mr Sumpner would have paid but less than the £14 John Horncastle was currently paying. Then, at a meeting in May, it was 'Ordered that the Treasurer be desired to Advertise the Estate of the late Mr Bosworth on a Building Lease for the term of sixty-one years', and it was confirmed in the record of the meeting on 7 July that 'on Wednesday the 14th of August next the House & Premises now in the Occupation of Mr John Horncastle School Master be Lett on a Lease to the best Bidder for the term of Sixty One Years from Lady Day next'. On 16 January 1767 Mr James Holland paid £7 {£1,100} for half a year's rent which had been due at Michaelmas last. Mr Horncastle had therefore left the property after 16 years, and the new lessee was paying exactly the same as he had been but the Trustees now had this payment guaranteed for 61 years. Mr Horncastle left a brewing copper, a pair of old grates, and an old brass kettle in the house, for which a Mr John Thomas paid the trustees £3 1s, a small sum but a contribution to the increasing cost of owning this property.

Payments over this period, from 12 August 1762 to 13 October 1763, included £4 11s 3d to Mrs Marshall and £6 5s 0d to Mr Grove for their quarter salaries, £23 18s 4d for clothes, £2 15s 0d for leather breeches, and £3 11s 8d for shoes. There were also the housekeeping expenses, including £6 for coals, 5s for 'Emptying the Privy', and 5s for 6 months taxes 'upon Mr Horncastle's House & Window Lights'. With all these expenses it is pleasing to note the trustees still found 5s to give 3 'Good Boys' and 2 'Good Girls' 1s each. On 13 October 1762 the treasurer 'Paid Mr Grove his additional salary which commenc'd from Lady Day last, by order of the Trustees £2 5s 0d'. However, in the course of these fourteen months there were significant exceptional expenses following the decision in October 1762 to repair the school and the adjoining school house: £ 94 3s {£14,000} was paid to William Dearsly for this with another £4 19s 3d for his mason. William Dearsly was the trustee (and carpenter) who lived in Rainham Hall who had already been paid £37 3s for 'Carpenter's Work done at the Charity School House & at Mr Horncastle's' in August 1757. (It is of interest that the project manager for this work, as for the building of the school and the adjoining house, was the carpenter rather than the mason or bricklayer.) With a further £19 7s paid to Robert Longthorp for unspecified services, these expenses reduced the balance in hand in October 1763 to just £52 4s 2¼d.

These figures, with the exception of the building expenses of course, were typical of annual expenditure through to the end of the decade. They were more than balanced by the regular income of about £120 {£18,000} a year which was boosted some years by a significant gift or legacy: in July 1764 a bequest of £20 was recorded from Robert Tyler of Hornchurch, in September 1767 another £20 was bequeathed 'by the late Benjamin Goodwin Esq, of London', and the following year's accounts record a £10 legacy from Mrs Elizabeth Gilman, the widow of Thomas Gilman Junior, who died that November. There was also a £50 donation from Richard Comyns.

Payments over the later 1760's included 12s 9d in window tax in February 1767 and £1 2s 10p to the Manor of Mawneys the following February for nine years quit rent. In 1767 the Treasurer had been instructed to insure the Charity School and the adjoining house with the Sun Fire Office for the sum of £500, and in March 1768 a premium of 19s was paid which covered these buildings and the house and premises in Hornchurch Lane. Despite the earlier heavy expenditure, there were still ongoing repairs which now focussed on the drains. On New Year's Day 1765 it was 'Ordered that a new privy be built in the most convenient part of the Garden, and what necessary repairs are wanting to the Charity School and School Masters House to be done with as much frugality as possible.' Two years later it was 'Ordered that a brick drain of one feet wide in the clear be laid from the pump in the Charity School underneath the High Road into the Loam pond.' The loam pond stood immediately opposite the school and was an important source of water for the livestock on market days, and the work was no doubt a great inconvenience to the traffic passing through the tollgate. The following November a decision that Mr Sumpner should be requested to estimate the cost of draining the school cellar indicates that all was still not well.

Sometime in 1768, for the first time, 65 pairs of buckles were purchased at a cost of £1 1s 8d, a minor but recurring expense from now on. The only books purchased over these seven years were 'Spelling Books' in 1766, which cost £1 5s 6d, and Bibles, Books of Common Prayer, Psalters, and *The Whole Duty of Man*, 24 copies of each, ordered from the SPCK in October 1767. Whether these were for school use or were the ones subsequently given to scholars when they were discharged we do not know.

1762 to 1771: a merry-go-round of clergy and treasurers
One reason why the school had survived for fifty years when so many other such foundations had closed was due to its good fortune in having a succession of competent treasurers. The treasurer was the one executive officer on the board of trustees, managing the accounts, chairing the meetings, and ensuring that decisions were executed. It was an onerous responsibility, but the treasurer had always been supported by the clergy, one of whom had been present at every trustees' meeting, as was required by the order agreed fifty years earlier. This continued to be true in the 1760's, despite more frequent changes of both clergy and treasurers.

1762 saw Robert Speed replace William Harris as Vicar of Hornchurch and Glocester Ridley's son James begin to officiate at Romford after his return from India, where he had been serving as an army chaplain. The five trustee meetings between 19 August 1762 and 7 April 1763 were attended by a Ridley and also a Rev'd Freeman, who then disappears. It is possible that the intention was that he should succeed Glocester until James returned to England and obtained the reversion (or right to succeed). Like his father, he had the important advantage of having been educated at Winchester and New College. James was gaining celebrity as a novelist, having published

The History of James Lovegrove, Esquire the previous year,[93] but the climate and the privations of his life abroad had fatally undermined his health and he died prematurely on 24 February 1765, three months before the birth of his third child. We do not know whether his father was still living and ministering in Romford during these years, but in May 1766 he was appointed to a prebendal stall in Salisbury Cathedral, and on 17 July 1766 the Rev'd John William Hopkins attended his first meeting of trustees as the new Chaplain of Romford. He was 32 years old and, yet again, had been educated at Winchester and New College.

At most meetings until 1765 both clergy were usually present, and between the death of James Ridley and the arrival of John Hopkins in Romford Robert Speed was punctilious in his attendance. However, after three meetings at which they were both present he missed four meetings, attended one on 14 July 1768, and then seems to have left the parish. On 9 May 1769 Thomas Bayley stepped down as treasurer having held the post for twenty years. He was replaced by Thomas Debuke. It was now over a year since Robert Speed had left Hornchurch, and the trustees seem to have known that he was unlikely to return. When they met on 7 September 1769 they would also have known that John Hopkins would be leaving Romford, having been appointed Rector of Upminster from 1770. They were also aware that, as the rules stood, if neither the Vicar of Hornchurch nor the Chaplain of Romford were present they could not enact any business. This explains why they agreed at this meeting to dispense with the Order of 21 April 1718 'which may frustrate the meeting', and resolved that for the future the decisions of any five trustees assembled by order of the treasurer would be 'valid full & compleat'. John Hopkins was present when this decision was made and then attended his final meeting on 22 February 1770, having missed only one meeting in his four years as a trustee. (Sadly, he was to be buried at his church in Upminster ten years later, aged just 46.) This change was absolutely necessary in the circumstances, but such small changes can be symbolic and may lead to unforeseen consequences. In this case, fifty-seven years were to pass before it brought humiliation and embarrassment to the Charity and its trustees.

There was also at this time another premonition of that distant future crisis, equally obscure in its long term import to contemporary observers. William Dearsley of Rainham Hall was a successor to those trustees of 1710 in his Church of England faith. However, in 1763 his daughter Sarah married his ex-ward and fellow Charity School trustee John Harle, and they began to take an interest in the growing Methodist movement. They became friendly with a preacher named John Valton in Purfleet, and on 12 March 1767 Rainham Hall was the venue for a gathering of Methodists to hear another, more famous preacher. William was outraged and forcefully intervened, threatening to horsewhip the preacher (who prudently ran upstairs) and then holding Valton over the fire in the kitchen (perhaps to give him a foretaste of the flames of hell which awaited all Methodists). Onlookers intervened to rescue Valton and eject him from the house, but a mob waiting outside attacked him, pulling his hair, tearing his shirt, and threatening to duck him in the pond.[94] The sectarian quietude which had followed the turmoil of the Civil War and then the Jacobite risings was coming to an end, and from the turn of the century religious zeal would increasingly divide the country and the provision of its schools along sectarian lines. John Harle, the early Methodist, would not live to see the high-tide of his faith, however. He died five years after James Ridley but at the same age of 29, Fate thus thwarting the establishment of a younger generation of trustees.

1770 - 1831: Romford, Hornchurch and the abuse of Ecclesiastical Plurality

The most notorious abuse of the Church of England in the 18th-century was pluralism, where a priest held more than one benefice, received the emolument which went with each, but could clearly be resident in only one. For sixty years the clergy in Hornchurch and Romford had lived in their parishes and been committed to their 'flock' and to the schools, but after 1770 this changed. The decision at the meeting of 7 September 1769 had ensured that their absence would not impede the transaction of business, but it certainly contributed to the unfortunate events which would unfold in the 1820's so it is necessary to examine the situation in the parishes over the intervening years.

In May 1786 the papers[95] reported the death of the Rev'd Robert Speed, describing him in the present tense as being the 'incumbent of the donative of Hornchurch, in Essex, and formerly Fellow of New College'. No additional information was given. He last attended a meeting of the trustees on 14 July 1768 and does not appear to have been resident in the parish for eighteen years. He was succeeded by William Henry Reynell, who would be Vicar of Hornchurch from 1786 to 1809. Reynell was born in Bristol in 1741 where his father, who later became Bishop of Derry, was a clergyman.

He graduated from New College in 1763, enrolled at the Middle Temple and became a barrister-at-law in 1767, and then, according to his entry in the list of Oxford Alumni, was 'vicar of Hornchurch, Essex, and of St Anthony Meneage, Cornwall, 1778, until his death 1809'. St Anthony Meneage is at the mouth of the Helford River and was in the patronage of the Lord Chancellor, so if Reynell's law studies had borne fruit, so had his studies at New College when he was presented to the living of Hornchurch. The only evidence in the *Accounts* of Reynell's association with the parish is the entry in April 1787, in the first year of his incumbency, recording that the 'Rev'd Mr Reynolds' paid the annual guinea subscription from New College, Oxford. One can assume that as the trustees did not know the man's name - calling him 'Reynolds' rather than 'Reynell' - they did not know the man. (Whether Reynell was a subscriber himself we do not know; the Rev'd Speed was, having paid the subscriptions for both himself and New College in November 1785.) It is unlikely that such a man would have voluntarily exiled himself in Cornwall, so it is quite possible he was resident in London and paying others to take the services in his two parishes out of the double income he received.

The situation in Romford after John Hopkins left the parish in 1770 is unclear. The *Victoria County History of Essex* (Volume 7) states that 'Between c. 1770 and 1848 Romford chapel seems to have been left for long periods in the care of an assistant curate, who usually served also as Sunday afternoon lecturer.'[96] From time to time there had been clergy apart from those of Romford and Hornchurch who attended trustee meetings, such as the Rev'd Samuel Bradshaw, Rector of Upminster, who attended between 1737 and 1746, and the Rev'd John Woodroffe, Vicar of Cranham between 1734 and 1786, who maintained an irregular attendance between 1736 and 1769. However, there is no obvious candidate for an 'assistant curate' from either Romford or Hornchurch until November 1779 when the Rev'd Harry Fletcher attended his first meeting of trustees.

1730 - 1834: Tylers, Comyns, Wallingers and Mashiters - continuity and social context

There would not be another resident Chaplain in Romford until 1814 or Vicar of Hornchurch until 1819, so the management of the school depended even more on the treasurer and on a constant renewal of at least a few committed trustees. Friendships and family connections over the generations would be crucial in maintaining and extending this support, and we have seen how the relationship between Gilman and Bayley was important in the setting up of the school and how each had a son who would become a trustee and then treasurer. In the century between 1730 and 1834 at least four other families produced at least two members who were more or less active supporters of the school, and it is instructive to examine the social position of these men who brought education to the Royal Liberty.

In June 1745 John Tyler of Hornchurch was appointed a trustee of the Mary Hide Charity (at the same time as John Comyns of Romford, who is introduced below). He was probably the son of Robert Tyler of Dagenham who in June 1764 would leave a legacy of £20 to the Charity School. In May the following year John and (probably) his brother Christopher were elected trustees. Until November 1779 Christopher (from Hornchurch) attended about half the meetings, after which he attended only once, in May 1784. John (from Romford) had an attendance record similar to his brother's until after his year as treasurer from 1770 to 1771. He was then absent for four years, possibly living away from Romford, but from his return in August 1775 he missed only two meetings over the next 28 years. As we shall see, he would make a most important contribution to the charity with his initiative in 1771 to inaugurate and then manage the town collections. He died in 1808 at the age of 69, and his burial on 2 October was recorded at both St Edward's and St Peter and St Paul in Dagenham, where presumably he was interred in the family vault. Three weeks later the *Account Book* records: 'By the request of the late J. Tyler Esq of Mawnes a donation of twenty Pounds.' This suggests that he held the lease on the Manor of Mawneys, placing him at the top of Romford society.

In May 1800 John Tyler Junior was elected a trustee, and in November 1801 Christopher Tyler Junior attended a meeting. They were wealthy landowners in Hornchurch, with John recorded as the owner of the Mardyke estate in 1812 and Christopher as owner of Wyebridge, now part of Elm Park, but neither would play a major role in the Charity. Finally, in August 1834 the family association with the school entered its fourth generation when John Tyler of Romford was elected. An oblique reference to this John in the report of a court case two years earlier states that he was the lessee, under New College, of the great tithes of the north side of Romford, further confirming the family's high social and economic standing.

The Comyns family had been in the area since before January 1568/9, when William, a tanner by trade, died in Barking.[97] If succeeding generations moved only a little way east, they moved a great way up the social and economic ladder by the time Richard Comyns was born in Romford in 1695, his parents then living in Hare Street. This branch of the family was now wealthy and increasingly well educated, with Esq. rather than 'tanner' after their names. Richard was a very successful lawyer who became one of the 'six clerks' of the Court of Chancery. He was elected a trustee of the school and attended his first meeting on 16 October 1730, sitting alongside James Hotchkis. Until he retired to Brakes Place in Romford Richard lived mainly in London, so his attendances at meetings were necessarily few and irregular. However, he presumably paid his subscription regularly, donated the £50 in September 1768 which we noted earlier, and supported the school over a period of 41 years.

Meanwhile the two sons of his father's cousin had also become very successful lawyers. This branch of the family had also started in the Romford/Dagenham area but had then moved out to Writtle, near Chelmsford. Sir John Comyns (1668-1740) entered Lincoln's Inn in 1683, became a serjeant-at-law in 1705, was an MP for Maldon in 1701-08, 1711-12, and again in 1726, was sworn a baron of the exchequer and knighted in 1726, and was appointed Lord Chief Baron of the Exchequer by Lord Hardwicke in 1738.[98] In 1730, to compliment his elevated position in Society, he built Hylands House in Writtle. Meanwhile his brother Richard (1675-1740) also entered Lincoln's Inn and became a Serjeant-at-Law, and if his career was eclipsed by that of his elder brother he was more successful dynastically. Both men were married three times, but Sir John had no children whereas Richard had six, and his youngest son John (1703-1760) would outlive his Uncle John and inherit Hylands House.

This John was born on 13 January 1702/3 and baptised at St Giles-in-the-Fields, presumably because his father was then working in the courts in London. He entered Queen's College Cambridge in 1720 and then became a lawyer of the Inner Temple and Lincoln's Inn. By 1747 he seems to have retired from London and the law and moved to Romford, and both children of his second marriage to Elizabeth were baptised at St Edward's Church, John Richard in 1747 and Mary in 1748. An entry in the Gentleman's Magazine of May 1756 recording Elizabeth's death suggests he was then living at 'Petits', a small estate near modern Pettits Lane lying north-east of the town centre.[99]

He was obviously a man of influence in the town and more widely. He was a churchwarden at St Edward's in 1749, and it was he who arranged for the Archbishop of Canterbury to preach one of the Charity Sermons that year. Although the note in the Accounts describes him as 'a Worthy Trustee of the Charity School' he seems to have attended only two meetings, the first in June 1745 and the second in February 1746. It could be that he began to attend when appointed churchwarden, realised the financial situation the Charity was in, and then used his influence to arrange the Archbishop's attendance. He does not seem to have attended again, so perhaps shortly after this he moved to Hylands House, 17 miles from Romford, which he had inherited in 1740. (He died in 1760 and the Hylands estate passed to his 13 year old son John Richard Comyns. Oxford University Alumni lists this John as 'son of John of Romford and of Magdalen College', again linking his father with Romford.)[100]

It was possibly Richard Comyns who brought the charity to the attention of his wealthy and well connected 'good friend' John Wallinger. Wallinger described himself in his will as 'of London Merchant' and being in 'the Stone trade', but he also had connections with Oporto, including his 'good friend' William Warre, to whose son he was godfather. (William and his son were the first two generations of what would become one of the oldest and most prestigious British port houses, and the son would become the British Consul in Oporto.) Wallinger was buried in Chelmsford on 20 August 1767, and at a meeting of the trustees of the School at 'The Dolphin' inn[101] on 8 October an extract from his will, written fifteen months earlier, was copied into the *Accounts* book. This recorded a legacy of £200 on trust, the interest to be used for the benefit of the Charity School at Chelmsford, and a further £100 for the use and benefit of the Charity school at Romford. His main beneficiary was his nephew John Arnold, who now added Wallinger to his name and at this same meeting was elected a trustee. The legacy from John Wallinger, with the £100 received in 1731 from the Will of the Honorable Mrs Ann Rider, was the third largest legacy the charity had ever received and was duly inscribed on the board in the church, for which task a Mr Hay was paid a total of £3 5s 6d over this period.

Wallinger's estate included a farm called Goodwins in Hare Street (now Gidea Park), and his nephew, who had previously taken over his uncle's partnership in the stone trade, immediately replaced this with a small Palladian mansion, Hare Hall. This was designed for him by James Paine, completed in 1769, and built of the Portland stone in which he traded. At the time Paine was building the much grander Thorndon Hall near Brentwood for Lord Petre, and the two buildings reflected the social standing of their owners. Unlike Thorndon Hall, Hare Hall was small, inconvenient, and built to an off-the-shelf design. It also faced north, rather than the conventional sun-facing south, so its frontage of white Portland stone would be visible from the toll road which was the main highway leading into and out of Romford. To the aristocratic elite there was something rather vulgar about the house and its pretentious owner, the social-climbing Portland stone merchant Wallinger,[102] but times were changing, money was changing hands, and the Charity School would increasingly rely on support from the nouveau riche and the developing middle class.

View of Hare Hall in Essex, the Seat of ___ Wallinger Esqr

Finally, we come to the Mashiter family. One of the high-status families in 16th century Romford was that of Nicholas Cotton, who died in 1570. In the 18th century his descendents lived in a grand house and estate on the London Road opposite the original 'Sun' public house, which stood where its 1937 successor now stands.[103] (Their family name lives on today in nearby Cottons Park, the closest park to Romford town centre.) For perhaps a century this estate was leased by the Mashiter family, and it was here that Thomas Mashiter died in 1778, his will having been witnessed by James Cotton and his son, another James.[104] He had been elected a trustee of the Charity School on 13 May 1749 and attended 8 of the next 12 meetings, the last in February 1755, after which he disappears from the records.

The Mashiters were a Lancashire family, and before moving to Romford Thomas had lived in Ormskirk. He had moved south by 1744, when his eldest child, Blandinah, was baptised at St Thomas of Canterbury church in Brentwood. On 10 August 1769 Blandinah married her Lancastrian first cousin, William Mashiter, in St Edward's Church. William was a very wealthy wharfinger, owning and managing wharves and warehouses in the busy port of London. He also seems to have owned other property there and in Lancashire. The couple's principal home was near St Katherine's by the Tower, where their ten children were baptised, which would explain why William was never a trustee of the school in Romford. However, he retained the lease on the Cotton estate and was to die there in 1811. His obituary in the *Gentlemen's Magazine* reads:

> *June* 16, At Cotton's, Essex, much respected, in his 68th year, William Mashiter esq. of Tower-hill, many years in the commission of the Peace for the counties of Middlesex, Essex, and the liberty of the Tower of London, also Chairman of the Court of Sewers for the Tower Hamlets and the Precinct of St Catherine.

In 1801 William had been elected Master of the Worshipful Company of Bowyers, a position another four members of the family would hold over the next century. This symbolizes the social position the family had now acquired, supported by their property and great wealth.

At least two of William's children, Thomas and Octavius, married into the cream of local society and settled in the Liberty, living on their private fortunes and dedicating themselves to public service. Thomas was born in 1780, married Miss Parker of Great Warley Hall in August 1814, and lived at Hornchurch Lodge. In March 1826 he was elected a trustee, but on 29 April 1828 there is a curious and unique entry in the trustees' *Accounts*: 'ordered that the resignation of Thomas Mashiter Esq as a Trustee be accepted'. In the past trustees may not have attended meetings, have stopped paying their guinea, or died, but a resignation had never been minuted before. The reason for his action will become clear as we explore the events of 1826, 1827 and 1828. He would accept reappointment in June 1833, but unlike his brother he would not play an active part in the affairs of the school in the very important years which were to follow.

Octavius was born in 1785 and married Maria Tyler, daughter of the Charity School trustee Christopher Tyler. They settled on an estate called 'Priests' on the Havering Road where the 1841 census was to record them and their five children enjoying the care of six servants. Octavius, like his father, was involved with the Court of Sewers, which had very important responsibilities because if the waterways and sea walls along the north bank of the Thames were not well managed there was a danger that the low lying marshlands from London to the Liberty would be inundated. (In 1707 a great breach in the sea wall protecting the Dagenham Level caused the flooding of over a thousand acres. Owing to mismanagement and corruption it took thirteen years to close the breach and recover this farmland.[105]) Octavius was elected a trustee in November 1820 and would play an important part in the events of 1833 and 1834, key years in the development of the school.

Many charity schools did not outlast the 18th century. That the school at Romford has managed to survive is in no small measure owing to the interest and financial support of representatives of these four families.

Rumford and the part of the Royal Liberty to the north of the town, from Chapman and Andre's 1777 map of Essex, showing Rumford Market Place with the Charity School and the turnpike. The toll road runs north-east past Richard Benyon's Gidea Park estate. The estates of Marshall's, East House, Pettits, and Gobians also lie in this quarter of the Liberty. Two roads run north-west to Collier-row and its Common, beyond which (and off the map) lies the village of Havering-atte-Bower.

Chapter 12

The early years of Thomas Graves, treasurer

1771 - 1786

The meeting of 28 March 1771: Thomas Graves and the Trustees in the 1770's
Our examination of the wealthy and influential families whose support ensured the Charity School's survival over its first century has taken us from the 1730's to the 1830's, but we now return to 1771. Richard Comyns attended his last trustee meeting on 28 March that year and was interred at Dagenham, after a service at St Edward's, on 1 September 1775. By now the renewed enthusiasm the trustees had shown in the 1760's was waning. If in the period since then they had not met regularly every quarter as they had pledged to do, on average they had met four times a year. Throughout the 1760's these meetings had been held in one of the many inns in the town, as had been the custom since the school's foundation. On 18 April 1770 they met in the School House, but probably the inn was just too comfortable and on 25 October they returned to the 'Cock and Bell'.

On 28 March 1771 they met at the 'Lamb' next to the church. It had been built in 1681 and is still flourishing, if in a new building, 340 years later. This would prove a very important meeting, and fifteen people, the highest number for 25 years, gathered to elect a new treasurer. Thomas Bayley had held the post for twenty years and had brought in the reforms to the charity in August 1762, and between then and September 1769 he had not missed one of the thirty meetings. Over these years attendance had rarely reached 10, and only Bayley himself, the clergy (until 1769), and (usually) Edward Sumpner could be relied on to be present. Captain Thomas Debuke had replaced Bayley as treasurer in 1769. Like Sumpner, he was one of those ten elected in August 1762, but unlike Sumpner he had attended only eight of the subsequent thirty meetings; having been elected treasurer, he never attended another, passing a balance of £126 16s 10d to his successor, John Tyler, in April 1770. John Tyler, treasurer from April 1770 to March 1771, had been and would be a very committed trustee, but for some reason was unable to serve beyond this year. Since his election as a trustee in July 1765 he had attended just over half the meetings, and over the ten years from June 1777 he would be present for all of them, but his absence over the next six years suggests he was living away from Romford. Who would succeed him? Thirteen months had now elapsed since the Rev'd Hopkins had attended his last meeting and left the parish, and the Charity now faced a crisis. It would seem an urgent message had been sent to all trustees to attend if possible, and those present at the 'Lamb' included John Arnold Wallinger (attending his third and last meeting), Richard Comyns (for the last time), John and Christopher Tyler, Edward Sumpner, James Holland, William Wankford, Thomas Graves and seven others, for two of whom this would be their only meeting.

The man they duly elected was Thomas Graves, aged about 40 and a grocer in the town, whose only previous meeting had been at the 'Cock & Bell' in October. Unusually, there is no formal record in the *Accounts* of his election as a trustee. He now received the balance of £91 6s 9½d {£12,800} and the meeting moved on to its second important item of business. Two months earlier Elizabeth Marshall had died and been buried in St Edward's churchyard. She had been Mistress for twenty-five years. Mrs Jane White was now unanimously elected Mistress from the previous Lady Day at £18 5s a year with use of the School House, probably meaning the rooms in the upper storey above the schoolrooms. There is no mention in the records of the agreement at the meeting on 12 August 1762 that if a vacancy occurred Mr Grove's wife would be elected 'if she be found Capable', nor of who had been teaching the girls between Mrs Marshall's death and Lady Day on 25 March. Perhaps it had been Jane White. Thomas Grove (Master), Jane White (Mistress), and Thomas Graves (Treasurer) would now serve together for the next twenty-three years, almost to the day, providing stability and continuity to the life of the school. Thomas Graves would be treasurer for the next thirty-six years.

Under Graves' chairmanship meetings fell from four to just two a year, and only one in 1773, 1776 and 1777. With no representation from the clergy, between his election in 1771 and 1776 attendance averaged only eight, and perhaps the small numbers and the lack of a clergyman explain the change of venue. Graves held the next two meetings in the 'White Hart' in the High Street and the 'King's Arms' in the Market Place, then in May 1772 in the School House, after which the next seven meetings (between

1774 and 1777) were held in the Church Vestry. Apart from himself and Sumpner, at this time Graves could rely on only two others: James Holland, a trustee since 1769, and Samuel Skinner, from 1771.

There were, of course, many other trustees: in the eight years between 1762 and 1770 no fewer than 39 men had attended at least one meeting and a number attended several, but few showed a regular commitment and the average attendance was only 8 or 9. However, it would be hasty to condemn all these people as apathetic. The social position of a number of the school's supporters and Romford's proximity to London meant that not a few of them might have been resident in the city, as perhaps John Tyler was from 1772 to 1775. Certainly Richard Comyns and Samuel Skinner were. Skinner attended his first meeting in July 1766 and his second in November 1771, after which he only missed two of the next ten meetings.

Despite the small attendance and infrequency of these meetings (but possibly because of the sober venue in which they were held) the school seems to have run more or less smoothly over the next five years. Graves' tenure began with an important fund raising innovation, recorded in the *Accounts* on 29 April 1771 as £11 16s 9d 'Collected in the Town'. This was probably John Tyler's initiative, because there is no reference to another such collection until 1777 when he returned and organised it. The sermons also evolved during these years, but became more expensive to arrange. In 1773 Mr Seymour at the 'Lamb' was paid £3 19s for entertaining the singers on the Charity Sermons day, and from then on singers were a regular addition to the festivities and expenses.

The sermons in 1773 incurred another novel cost, an entry that year noting: 'Lost by Light Gold Collected at the Sermon' £1 1s 10d and 'Lost by Bad Silver' 8d 6d. Whenever coins have been made out of precious metals there have been criminals prepared to risk the ultimate punishment by clipping the edges and then recycling the accumulated gold or silver. It was a very profitable enterprise which had been practised since antiquity, and in England the coinage had become so devalued by the end of the 17th century that in 1696 the Recoinage Bill set in motion a huge operation to issue new coins and redeem the old, debased ones. This became so expensive that the Government compounded its problems by introducing the notorious Window Tax to cover the cost, and yet it did not solve the problem. Why such a perennial abuse should suddenly have become an issue in the collection at the charity sermons is not clear, but for the next 43 years 'light' or 'bad' coins are as regular an annual entry as that for the payment of the singers, the abuse finally ending with the Great Recoinage of 1816.

It was at this time that the trustees made a more determined effort to collect the subscriptions, particularly from those living outside Romford. In June 1772 and again in July 1774 12s 9d was paid for a chaise to collect the subscriptions at 'Hornchurch, Raynham, etc'. In 1773 New College, as patron of the living, subscribed a guinea, which they would continue to do for many years. However, Arnold Wallinger proved very tardy in paying the interest on the £100 his uncle had left for the benefit of the schools. In April 1776 it was

> Ordered that Mr Dearsley be desired to apply to the Trustees named in ye Will of the late Mr Wallinger deced for payment of the Interest of the Sum of one Hundred pounds from the time of his Decease and also to report in what Security's the said Sum is vested for the Use of Romford Charity School.

John Tyler had recorded three sets of balanced accounts in his one year as treasurer, but Thomas Graves did not produce his first until April 1776. This showed a balance in hand of £26 8s 10d, although this figure was not countersigned and confirmed as correct by the other trustees as had always been the case in the first volume of accounts.

April 1776 was the ninth meeting since he was elected treasurer, and only twice had attendance reached ten. Sumpner had died in 1774, and the only 'regulars' Graves could now rely on were James Holland, Thomas Bishop and Samuel Skinner, but Skinner was now old and he and Bishop would attend only one more meeting. It was now, therefore, that there was another drive to attract more trustees, and at least another twelve were recruited over the next two years, of whom James Marshall, Charles Waghorn, Henry Goody, Abraham Delamare, and Isaac Palmer would prove very regular in their attendance. Three of these had businesses in Romford: James Marshall, like Thomas Graves, was a grocer; Charles Waghorn was a 'Taylor and Draper' who supplied the school clothes; and Abraham Delamare ran a Gentlemen's Boarding School. These five were joined by John Tyler, who in August 1778 had become an active trustee again, and in May 1782 by a Mr Cotton who might have been a scion of the family who leased their house to the Mashiter family or the grocer or 'Corn factor & seedsman' of that name who traded in the town at that time.[106] These seven men formed a core of loyal trustees behind Thomas Graves, ensuring that attendance at meetings would average 12 or 13 for the next eighteen years.

Two characteristics of this new team now running the school should be noted. First. in general they represented a different strata of society when compared with those who went before them. They were not Oxford educated clergy, lawyers, and local landowners. John Tyler was certainly a man of consequence in the town and we know nothing of Henry Goody, but in 1791 Isaac Palmer was landlord of the 'Cock and Bell' and Romford postmaster, and Thomas Graves and the other active trustees were middle-class shop-keepers and traders. One senses they were down-to-earth, practical, upright citizens who minded their pennies, but not men who mixed with members of the influential London society. Second, although we do not know from which community some of them came, those we do know all came from Romford. It has been calculated that in 1801 the population of Romford was 3,179 and of Hornchurch 1,300.[107] When the clergy from each community had attended meetings Hornchurch had been strongly represented, particularly because the Vicar was senior to the Chaplain of Romford; now one senses Hornchurch felt a less significant partner in 'The Charity School for Hornchurch Romford and Havering'. This feeling would eventually find expression in the desire to develop its own school.

This lay in the future, however, and for now John Tyler's imperative was to revive the town collection. On 1 May 1777 the accounts record that he collected £16 10s 6d in Romford and Mr Higgs collected £6 11s 6d in Hornchurch. In November Tyler collected a further £21 12s 3d in Romford. From then on these collections make an irregular contribution to the income of the charity, with Mr Tyler always responsible in Romford and Mr Higgs in Hornchurch until the Rev'd Harry Fletcher took over from him in October 1780. Between May 1777 and November 1781 these collections brought in £125 6s 3d, or an average of nearly £28 {£3,800} a year.

The sermons were now an even more important social event in the town, always taking place between July and September. On each occasion there were still two sermons and two preachers, some of whom appear to have charged for their eloquence: in September 1778, not for the first time, £5 {£675} was paid to one preacher, and in August 1780 a total of £3 13s 6d was paid to them both, although this payment may have well have been for their expenses. The list entered in the accounts for July 1781 gives a flavour of the other miscellaneous expenses now associated with these occasions: 17s 6d 'Paid Sundry Persons for Delivering out Hymns Tuneing the

Hapsichord &c'; 'Paid Mr Hudson for Hymns & Attendance' £5 9s; 'Paid Mr Mead for Wine' 10s; 'Paid Mr Marshall for Sweetmeats' 15s 4d. Despite the continuing annoyance of 'bad money', the trustees had reason to be pleased with the income from these sermons. In the past, when the sermons had been less regular events, the sums collected had varied. They had peaked in 1721 at over £76, and the Archbishop's visit in July 1749 had raised nearly £72, but a figure of £30 to £40 had been more frequent. They now provided a regular annual income which averaged £37 a year over the decade.

The income from subscriptions is impossible to analyse because of the irregularity with which some - perhaps many - appear to have paid. Another source of income, the payment of interest by John Arnold Wallinger on the £100 his uncle had left the Charity, also remained elusive. In January 1778 it was ordered that 'Mr Dearsely be desired to apply a second time . . .'

The decline in legacies at this time reflected the general decline in support for charity schools, and over the 1770's only two were received which together totalled just £15. Despite this lack of large donations, over these ten years income regularly exceeded expenditure because expenditure remained minimal, still confined mainly to salaries, coal, uniform and taxes. Window tax had always been paid on the Charity's residential properties, but it seems that in April 1771 the School House itself became liable for this, which cost 12s 9d. In 1781 £2 5s 6d was spent on books for the girls and £6 17s 10d on books for the boys, the first such entries for several years. This parsimony ensured there was no financial crisis such as that of the 1740's. Indeed, in 1772/3 there was even sufficient spare money to invest another £50 {£7,000} in 3% bank stock, increasing future investment income. The next big expense came In October 1780 when the treasurer was requested to put the School House and the Master's House in proper repair, but the following month, providentially, Arnold Wallinger finally paid the £41 0s 10d he owed for 12½ years' interest.

In November 1781, after ten years as treasurer, Graves reconciled his accounts for a second time. These showed a balance of £86 12s 2½d, an increase of £60 3s 4½d over the figure five years before. Once again this figure was not countersigned and confirmed as correct by the other trustees. It would be another fifteen years before the next reconciliation.

The experience of the Romford Charity School scholars in the 1780's
Studies of life expectancy in Britain in the 18th century suggest this was about 35 to 40 when measured from birth, but of course those who survived the hazards of childhood could hope to live much longer. By 1780 many children had passed through the school and died, but there were a few still living who remembered it from its earliest days. Irrespective of how long they lived, these 18th century scholars are the most important but the most invisible people in this story, invisible because few of their names have come down to us and because we can only conjecture from information in the *Accounts* what their experience of school was like. We know it was a long day, 7.00 am to 5.00 pm in the summer and 8.00 am to 4.00 pm in the winter, with a break from 12.00 to 2.00. Holidays were much shorter than today, perhaps a fortnight in the summer and a week at Christmas and Easter, and there were no half-term breaks except possibly for a day or two at Whitsun. The curriculum had not changed over these seventy years: when new books were ordered they were similar to those purchased when the school had first opened. For boys, learning was limited to reading, writing and arithmetic; for girls, reading and a little writing were augmented by the practical domestic skills of sewing and knitting; for all, the teaching of the basic tenets of the Christian faith was reinforced by the expectation of church attendance. About half the pupils enjoyed a complete set of clothing, the others being provided with shoes and buckles, hose and bands. We also know that pupil turnover could be high, particularly amongst the boys who now left at 12. Traditionally boys were apprenticed at 13 or 14, but reducing the leaving age to 12 would have made little difference to their life chances because the *Accounts* record few, if any, now benefiting from apprenticeships. The funding of such placements by the trustees of the school had ended almost as soon as it had begun, and by now the placement of three boys - of *any* boys - under the terms of the Mary Hide Charity seems to have ceased. Instead, we now hear of boys and girls leaving to go into service.

It is against this background that we can set the information and changes recorded in the late 1770's and the 1780's. Following a meeting in June 1777 an enigmatic entry appeared in the minutes: 'Ordered at this Meeting that the Children that are Discharged not to have their Cloath's till after the Charity Sermons.' As the new clothes were issued before the charity sermons so the children looked their smartest at this key fundraising and celebratory occasion, the trustees presumably wished to ensure those who were leaving did not take their new clothes and disappear before this important event. In May 1786 the trustees went further and decided that those who were within a year of leaving would no longer have new clothes: 'Order'd at this Meeting that the Girls and Boys have the cloaths 12 Kalender Months before the expiration of leaving the school, under that period to be left for the succeeding Boys & Girls.' Did this mean that those in their final year no longer received new clothes, or that they received them but then left them for younger children when before they would have kept them? (There had been an earlier requirement for children to have a sponsor who would provide £1 to cover the cost of their clothes. There is no record of this having been rescinded, but the implication is that this was no longer enforced - if it ever had been.)

The provision of these clothes and the retention of them after being discharged from the school was a valuable privilege which could be withdrawn on account of poor conduct. This happened in October 1770 when Mary Buck was denied her clothes because she had frequently absented herself from school. The trustees gave the clothes to the next senior girl and an unspoken warning to every other scholar. Such mention of absenteeism was then rare, but we can assume it was still an ongoing problem because it was addressed at a meeting on 23 April 1779 when it was ordered that 'No boy or girl admitted to the school should be absent (sickness excepted) under the penalty of being discharged there from.' The following April they repeated the threat in the context of lax church attendance,

> It having been reported at this Meeting by a Trustee thereof that several of the Charity Children belonging to the distant parts have neglected attending divine Service on the Lord's day –
> It is at this Meeting ordered that for the future all the Charity Children do attend at the School house every Sunday Morning & from thence proceed with the Master & Mistress to hear divine service at Romford Chapel & in case of their non attendance that they be Discharg'd from the School & that the Master do give proper Notice to the Parents of the Severale Children.

Such resolutions had been made before, but this time the trustees acted on their threat. Between November 1779 and November 1783 fifteen boys and five girls were discharged 'for Disobeying the Orders of the School' or 'for Absenting Themselves from School', and a further three boys were ordered to 'be Discharg'd . . . without their Fathers attend the next Meeting, to shew just cause for their Neglect'. In 1785 six boys were discharged for absenteeism, the same number as were discharged for being over age. As the number of boys had been limited to 40 since the agreement with Mr Grove in August 1762, these figures suggest that at this time perhaps ten per cent were dismissed for absenteeism, and that in 1785 the total turnover was 35 to 40%.

During the 1770's the practice since 1762 of recording the ages of those admitted was dropped, and the reasons for leaving are almost without exception because the child was past 12 (or 14 for the girls), had been 'taken out by their parents', or had 'gone to Service'. Sometimes there is a mismatch between the number of (mainly) boys discharged and the number admitted, making one wonder whether between trustee meetings some students stopped attending or obtained work and were never formally recorded as having been discharged, or if some children were admitted who were not recorded in the trustees minutes. With the trustees now meeting only once or twice a year this seems quite possible. On 11 May 1786, for example, only 4 boys were discharged but 8 were admitted, whilst in November 1795 9 boys were discharged yet only 3 admitted. Another possible explanation is that the trustees were unable to exactly match admissions with departures, so there were periods when there were unfilled places. This would suggest there was no waiting list. Looking ahead a decade, in the final years of the 1790's the evidence suggests that only a quarter of boys stayed on at school until they were 12 and 'over age', the remainder having been taken away by their parents before then to go to work. Unfortunately there is no record of the age at which they did leave nor of the work they left to do.

The information that James Read was discharged in May 1786 for 'being a cripple' makes one wonder why this made it impossible for him to continue his studies. Six months later Edward Cuffin was discharged, 'being dead'. This is the first such entry, but he is followed by Mehetable Ruffle in April 1789, William Bettis in May 1790, Seth Bumford in November 1791 and William Finch and James Panton in May 1793. There is no reason to believe this frequency was unusual, or that had the reasons for discharge been recorded previously this child mortality rate would have been any lower. Certainly burial figures in Romford between 1758 and 1760 would suggest this.

The charity schoolboy apprenticed: the rags to riches story in fiction and fact

Those children who had been admitted to charity schools in the first two decades of the century and were still living were now in their sixties or seventies. The charity school boy who had made good had become a character in popular fiction, and before this first generation pass away we will briefly examine three such men and how they lived (or were imagined to have lived) their lives.

John Cleland did not attend a charity school himself, but he included one such man in his best known novel, *Fanny Hill or Memoirs of a Woman of Pleasure*. Cleland was born in 1709, the son of an army officer who then became a civil servant. Like Carew Hervey Mildmay, his parents were acquaintances of Alexander Pope and Lord Bolingbroke. John attended Westminster school for two years before leaving (or being expelled) in 1723, after which he travelled to Turkey and then, in 1728, joined the East India Company. As a schoolboy in London he must have seen many Charity School scholars in their distinctive uniforms, and as an adventurer abroad he undoubtedly met those who had gone into foreign trade to make their fortunes. He returned to England in 1741, but unlike Governor Benyon, who had returned three years before him, Cleland had not made a fortune with 'the Company': on the contrary, after failing to make a living from writing he was arrested for a debt of £840 {£125,000} and incarcerated in the Fleet Prison. It was there that he re-wrote and in 1748 published his famous novel.

The high tide of benevolent enthusiasm for charity schools was fast ebbing, but in his book Cleland gave posterity an image of the product of such an institution in his idealised portrait of the nameless 'plain well-dressed elderly gentleman . . . of three-score' who became the heroine's final 'gallant' and benefactor before her reunion with her beloved Charles:

> his parents, honest and failed mechanics, had, by the best traces he could get of them, left him an infant orphan on the parish; so that it was from a charity school that, by honesty and industry, he made his way into a merchant's counting house; from whence, being sent to a house in CADIZ, he there, by his talents and activity, acquired not only a fortune, but an immense one, with which he returned to his native country.

Honest and industrious, he is also modest: he lived in opulence 'without the least parade of it', and studied 'the concealment [rather] than the show of a fortune.' Furthermore, it was he who taught Fanny 'that the pleasures of the mind were superior to those of the body' - an important lesson for such a heroine.

Warren Hastings was a man who in real life made a similar journey. Born in December 1732 and orphaned soon afterwards, 'Warren was brought up by his grandfather and educated in a charity school with the poorest children in the Gloucestershire village of Daylesford.'[108] He was then rescued by an uncle who sent him to be educated at Westminster School, but the uncle died when he was 16 and his guardian found him a place as a writer with the East India Company and he left for Bengal, fame, fortune and impeachment. In 1788 Hastings bought a grand country house and estate in Daylesford, where his life journey had started in poverty.

Both Cleland and Hastings started as humble clerks in the East India Company. For those with ambitions to get-rich-quick in the eighteenth century a position with 'the Company' was the equivalent of a place on a trading floor in the City of London today (but physically much more dangerous). Of course, a charitable uncle and Westminster as a finishing school helped, as it still does. Perhaps the experience of Samuel Skinner provides a more typical example of a charity school education, and how this might lead to comfortable prosperity and a position in society far above that occupied by one's parents.

Samuel was born about 1715, the son of a husbandman, and educated at the Romford Charity School. Then, with the help of the Hide Charity, he was apprenticed on 1 October 1729 to Israel Hammond, a fruiterer in London. He married a lady called Elizabeth, had a son named Francis, and prospered. In the 1768 Poll book he is listed as living in Wheeler Street, Spitalfields, and his life was spent between here and Romford. When he wrote his will in 1777 he was living in Ratcliffe, between the two, and it is this document which tells us most about him. The Church of England faith with which he had been indoctrinated at school had not diminished over the years: he was 'indisposed but of a good sound and disposing mind memory and understanding praise be given to Almighty God for the same', and he 'recommend[s] my soul into the hands of Almighty God that gave it in the hope of a joyful resurrection through the merits of my beloved Saviour Jesus Christ'. It was conventional to express such sentiments at the beginning of such a document at this time, but there is perhaps an elevated degree of fervour in his wording. He wishes to be interred in Romford 'according to the discretion of my executors', one of whom, Thomas Meakins, comes from

Hornchurch. He then turns to 'such Worldly Estate as it hath or shall please God to bless me with in this life', of which there appears to be much: he speaks of 'Estates, Messuages, Tenements, Hereditaments Lands and Premises', annuities in both the Old and New South Sea Stock, as well as the usual household furniture, plate, rings and apparel. One of his few itemised bequests is to the Romford Charity School. He left the school £10 {£1,375}, directing that this 'be placed on the board of Benefactions in the parish church or chapel'. He wanted his charity to be noted.

In his will he remembers his 'kinswoman' Mary, wife of his executor Thomas Meakins. We do not know in what degree they were related, nor whether Thomas was related to Richard Meakins, Treasurer of the Charity School from 1735 -1746, but we do know that Thomas and Mary Meakins lived in Hornchurch and that Mary's father, Abraham Vinton, was baptised (1703) and married (1728) in St Edward's Church, Romford, where in 1786 Samuel Skinner was laid to rest in the churchyard. It was a smaller and more interconnected world in the early 18th century.

Samuel Skinner did well by his master, Israel Hammond. When he was in the third year of his apprenticeship he was joined by Caleb Franklin, who had also benefitted from the Romford Charity School and the Mary Hide Charity. Caleb is recorded in the 1768 Poll Book as a Fruiterer in Bishopsgate Street in the City of London, so we can assume he also did well, possibly helped by his marriage in June 1751 to Elizabeth Hammond of 'Chinkford', Essex, at St Botolph's, Bishopsgate. Had Israel now retired to Chingford, and at the age of 33 did Caleb belatedly wed his former master's daughter?[109]

Chapter 13

Absent clergy in a time of political revolution

1786 - 1797

1787 to 1796: the Reverend Nathaniel Alsop Bliss
Between joining the trustees on 4 November 1779 and his disappearance from the records after 7 November 1786 the Rev'd Harry Fletcher was one of the seven men who could be relied on to attend (almost) every meeting of the trustees. He missed only one, and from October 1780 he took responsibility for the town collections in Hornchurch, but we do not know whether he was an unattached clergyman, connected to another parish, deputising for the absent Reynell at Hornchurch or substituting for the absentee chaplain at Romford. This last possibility is supported by the coincidence that on 16 March 1787, four months after Fletcher's final meeting, the *Essex Chronicle* reported that 'The Rev. Nathaniel Alsop Bliss A.M., Fellow of New College, is presented by that Society to the Chapelry of Romford.' Four years later the 1791 Universal Trade Directory for Romford named the Rev'd N. A. Bliss as the Vicar and the Rev'd Thomas Puddicombe as the Curate of Romford, but would Bliss have been recognised in the town, or would the town have been recognised by Bliss?

Bliss was born in Tormarton, Gloucestershire, in March 1747 and obtained his BA from New College in 1769, the same year that he was ordained deacon. Two years later he was ordained priest and in February 1773 was instituted as the Vicar of Colerne in Wiltshire, eight miles from Tormarton. However, he continued to live at New College, as we know from a brief entry in the diary of James Woodforde[110] which tells us much about the character of Bliss. From 1773 to 1776 Woodforde held a fellowship at Oxford and sometimes undertook relief duties at St Andrew's Church, Headington, where Bliss had clerical responsibilities. Woodforde records how on a Saturday in August 1774 he walked through the meadows and across a temporary bridge in a heavy thunderstorm to marry a young couple 'for Blisse'. The St Andrew's history website comments:

> The Bliss in question is his friend, the Revd Nathaniel Alsop Bliss, who may have bribed him with what appears to have been a rather higher than normal fee to brave the thunderstorms and walk up to Headington.[111]

We learn more about this man from his response to a list of questions sent by Bishop Barrington of Salisbury to the officiating clergy in all the parishes under his jurisdiction in advance of his primary visitation in July 1783. The Bishop was very interested in pluralism and the non-residency of clergy, and with good reason: of the 232 parishes which made returns only 90 were served by a resident incumbent, with 39 others having a resident curate. The most common reason for non-residency was pluralism, and of the 262 clergy 68 were incumbents holding two livings and 25 were incumbents serving a second church as curate. Of these 93, 15 did not reside at either of their parishes. There were also 31 curates serving two or more churches.[112] This contemporary evidence makes it easier to understand why it was not seen as a public scandal that William Henry Reynell, the Vicar of Hornchurch, held two livings 340 miles apart and was quite possibly resident in neither of them.

In his return for Colerne Nathaniel Alsop Bliss wrote that '[He] reside[d] constantly at Colerne but not in the vicarage house' and that he also held the curacy of Ditcheridge, 'distant about one mile and half'. How much time he was still spending at New College, the patron of the living, we do not know. However, in August 1784 his life changed when he married Mary Drewitt of Colerne and settled there. Until 1877[113] there was a ban on fellows of Oxford and Cambridge colleges being married, and the subsequent birth of (probably) four children confirms his abandonment of these rules on celibacy. Then, two-and-a-half years later, New College presented him with the Chaplaincy of Romford. But did he ever live there? There is no evidence in the Charity School Accounts of him attending a single meeting, and the statement that 'Between c. 1770 and 1848 Romford chapel seems to have been left for long periods in the care of an assistant curate' suggests that he did not. The same source says that in 1792 the chapel vestry complained that the lecturer had stirred up controversy by delivering 'heavy and pointed denunciations from the pulpit'.[114] We do not know who this lecturer was, but Bliss was far away in Wiltshire where Mary died in March 1795 and he died a year later. He was 49 and had been the nominal Curate of Romford for nine years. On 14 April 1796 the *Bath Chronicle and Weekly Gazette* advertised a five day sale of

> All the Modern and Elegant HOUSEHOLD FURNITURE, PLATE, LINEN, CHINA, GLASS, and BOOKS, of the late Rev. NATHANIEL BLISS deceased, At his late Dwelling-House, at COLERN, WILTS.

Is there more definitive evidence that he never lived in Romford?

A week in April 1794: the fall of Danton and the rise of Dorothy Cloke
The death of their absent vicar would have caused little remark in the town, unlike the sudden death of Jane White two years before. This was the most dramatic change in the life of the School for twenty-three years. Her final salary, which had remained the same throughout these years, was paid on 25 March 1794, and she was buried at St Edward's Chapel on 3 April. At a meeting seven days later the Trustees appointed

> Mrs Dorothy Cloke as Mistress . . . to teach the Girls, reading, Knitting, Sewing and all other Requisites for making them Good Servants at the Salary of Eighteen Pound five Shillings & 1½ Chaldron of Coals per Annum provided Mrs Dorothy Cloke continue that time otherwise in proportion for the time she assists in the above capacity. Mrs Dorothy Cloke to resign the Appointment whenever the Trustees . . . shall think it expedient. Mrs Dorothy Cloke appear'd & accepted the appointment upon the above conditions.

Underneath this entry is Mrs Cloke's slightly quavery signature. Perhaps she signed with some hesitation, aware that these terms gave her no job security whatsoever; perhaps her signature simply betrayed a less than confident hand, but if so it was of little concern as her principle duty was to ensure the girls became 'Good Servants', the chief requisites of which the trustees had defined as including 'reading, Knitting, Sewing' but not writing. Her conditions of service were identical with those Mrs White had accepted nearly a quarter of a century earlier, and the curriculum she was to teach was identical with that Mrs Hopkinson taught when the school opened in 1711 with one significant difference: once again there is no specific mention of having to instil 'the Knowledge and Practice of the Christian Religion, as Profess'd and Taught in the Church of England'.

The statement that Mrs Cloke's duties were to make the girls 'Good Servants' deserves further consideration, not only because the narrow aims of the programme of study the girls still followed had never been so explicitly stated but also because of the wider political context of the time. In France, King Louis XVI had been executed fifteen months earlier, and now the Terror was in full spate. On 5 April Danton and Desmoulins had been guillotined, and now four days later in Romford Mrs Cloke was charged with educating girls to be 'Good Servants'. Traditionally this meant knowing your place in society ('The rich man in his castle/The poor man at his gate'), showing proper respect, and performing the tasks assigned to you dutifully. The expectation that those who had been educated at a charity school would have had these virtues ingrained from an early age would no doubt have given them an advantage when seeking a position. Such girls had been brought up to be God fearing and to know the commandments by heart: knowing 'Thou shalt not steal' and 'Lead us not into temptation' gave their employer's silver an additional line of defence before that provided by the legal sanctions of transportation or execution.

Charity School children would also know the commandment 'Thou shalt not murder'. These were strange times and new ideas were circulating, for many people frightening ideas, ideas inspired by events across the channel. Who knew to what behaviour such ideas might lead? Who knew where education of the lower orders might lead? With hindsight, we know that extreme revolutionary violence did not spread to these islands, but news from France would have re-ignited the fears experienced just fourteen years earlier during the Gordon Riots of June 1780. These had started when a petition to Parliament against recent concessions to Catholics had been hijacked by violent and criminal elements: prisoners had been released; breweries, distilleries and taverns plundered; chapels and the houses of Catholics and of magistrates torched. Many were killed in the riots or shot by the military as they fought to regain control. Afterwards, 135 were put on trial, 59 sentenced to death, and 26 eventually hanged. If the London mob was not as flammable as the Parisian mob at present, it too was suffering the consequences of the very bad harvest in 1792, and it too had its grievances and its prejudices. As we shall see, anti-Catholic sentiments would continue to flourish in Romford (as elsewhere) sixty years later.

In these circumstances one can see why those who could afford servants might want them to be God fearing and unable to write. With agitation for political reform increasing over the coming decades, Hansard will record the arguments of reactionary politicians opposed to any proposal to spread popular education. The workingman does not need education! If you teach him to read you will only encourage his political dissent!

Meanwhile the French Revolutionary Wars were convulsing the continent, and in 1794 the French won great victories over the Austrians and the Spanish. With fighting across the channel in the Spanish Netherlands it was decided in 1795 to build cavalry barracks in Romford to protect London from a possible French invasion. These were located in the south-west corner of the town, south of the toll road to London and west of South Street. Much of the work was destroyed by an accidental fire before it was completed and so had to be built a second time. The regular, measured pace of life in the Liberty over so many years quickened, and from now on the St Edward's parish registers record the marriages of local girls to young dragoons. Had some of these young brides been educated to be 'Good Servants' in the school across the Market Place?

1797: the Will of Citizen John Redman

Of course, it was not just the English equivalent of the *sans-culottes* who embraced revolutionary ideas; they were debated and disseminated by members of the many reform societies which were now springing up in Britain. The London Corresponding Society was formed in 1792 and its membership consisted mainly of skilled artisans who circulated pamphlets to spread their ideas. They sought political reform through education rather than agitation, although this would not have reassured those who were terrified by the rapid growth in their numbers and the information that members called each other 'citizen' in the new French style. The members of the Society for Constitutional Information, founded in 1791, came from the highest echelon of society and included such celebrities as the future prime minister Charles Grey, the brewer Samuel Whitbread, the dramatist and politician Richard Brinsley Sheridan, and the painter George Romney. They recommended the publication of a cheap edition of Tom Paine's *The Rights of Man*, originally published in March 1791 and (Part 2) February 1792. One of their members might well have been John Redman.

Redman was a man who had nothing to do with the Charity School in Romford and yet unexpectedly bequeathed it £100. His generosity would deserve no more than an equally generous footnote in this history were it not that in his 'extraordinary and curious will' he was eccentrically representative of the attitude of a type of revolutionary Englishman at this time.[115] He was bibulous, irreligious, contemptuous of the prevailing social order and hierarchy, but supportive of a multitude of charities to support the poor and destitute. In 1750, at the age of twenty, he had inherited Tylers Hall from his mother's brother, Andrew Branfill. This house was part of the Upminster Hall estate which his grandfather, another Andrew Branfill, had purchased in 1686.[116] In 1771 Redman purchased Greenstead Hall in Essex, and he also owned a house at Hatton Garden. It was here that this very wealthy man wrote his will on 5 July 1797.

He opens with the proclamation: 'The last Will of John Redman Citizen of the World of Upminster in Essex now residing in Hatton Garden Holborn . . .' In what follows there are none of the conventional references to Almighty God or a hoped for resurrection, such as those we noted in Samuel Skinner's will. He wishes to be buried ten feet deep in an unadorned grave in Bunhill Fields, where his grandfather, Captain John Redman, had been interred. Having ignored his soul and disposed of his body in this way, he turns to the distribution of his considerable worldly estate. He names his executors and arranges their expenses and then continues, 'All my wine either to be drank on the premises or shared by and between my four Executors'.

If his political views are not obvious from the title 'Citizen' which he gives several of his legatees, he leaves no doubt with his legacy 'To that valuable ffriend to his country in the worst of times Charles ffox Member for Westminster 500 Guineas'. Another bequest is 'twenty pounds for mourning and a sett of Tom Paine's *Rights of Man* bound with *Common Sense* with the answers intended by the long Heads of the Law the ffat heads of the Church and the Wise heads of an insolent usurping Aristocracy'.

Having provided for his family and his estranged wife, he makes a number of charitable donations which again indicate the extent of his fortune: the London Hospital is to receive £1,000; the Girls' Charity School, Stepney, and the Small Pox Hospital, £500 each; Raine's Hospital for Girls, Wapping, £500; the Magdalen[117] and the Asylum, £100 each; and £5,000 to the Boys' School of Greenwich Hospital for their education, maintenance and apprenticeships. Finally, almost as an afterthought, 'To the Charity School in Rumford Essex the sum of one hundred pounds'. Perhaps Redman added this because Romford was the nearest local school, there being none in Upminster.

The Charity was undoubtedly very grateful for this £100, and we have noted that in comparison with many others it had been very fortunate in the legacies it had received over the century. In total these now added up to just over £1,000 (including the value of Joseph Bosworth's property, £200, and the £200 Mary Hide left for apprenticeships). But what if it had received the £5,000 {£460,000}, with the added value in interest this would have given over the coming years and centuries? Many very wealthy charities today, including some independent schools, owe their considerable present fortunes to having received a number of such donations prior to 1800.[118]

John Redman's Will ends, or nearly ends, with his wine, which he wished to be enjoyed after his death. A codicil 'desire[s] and direct[s]' his executors to keep on both his London home and his house in Essex 'for at least one year after my death' and to meet in them regularly in order to consume the contents of his cellars. However, the very final thought of this epicurean 'citizen' - or, to be correct, afterthought, and it is telling that it should be so - is for those who have looked after him: 'If Omitted in my Will I order five pounds for Mourning to each my several Servants and to my Man in Essex'.

1796: the Trustees and their accounts in a time of war

In December 1789 it was ordered that the accounts be audited at the next meeting. For the last twelve years Thomas Graves and his group of seven loyal trustees, usually augmented by four or five others, had met regularly every six months. On 29 January 1778, after five years of sobriety, temptation had eventually overcome abstinence and they had left the austerity of the vestry for the pleasures of the 'Golden Lyon'. Perhaps this is what cemented their loyalty. It would be thirty-four years before their successors would again forsake the local hostelries.

Two more years now passed and there had still been no reconciliation and the treasurer was again ordered to prepare the accounts for auditing at the following meeting, and again he did not respond. The order was repeated a third time at a meeting in June 1795 and finally, in November 1796, the balanced accounts were presented. These showed that since the previous reconciliation fifteen years earlier the total income received had amounted to £2065 4s 4d, and that the balance in hand after all expenses and investments had been accounted for was £100 6s 11½d.

The main entries in the accounts had now been the same for many years. During this period the average collection at the annual sermons had risen to £45, although there appear not to have been sermons in 1790, 1791 and 1793. The expenses on these occasions had continued to rise: in August 1783 the beadle was added to the payroll, receiving 2s 6d for his attendance, and a Mr Pearl (a loyal trustee from 1779 to 1789) was paid £6 19s 2d for some unidentified singers. Music continued to make an important (and more expensive) contribution. The following year Mr Marshall was paid £3 3s to cover 'the Expences Attending the Portland Singers from London to Romford', but in May 1786 it was ordered 'that Application be made to the Romford Singers to perform at the next Charity Sermons'. However, this cheaper, local talent does not seem to have been of the same quality, for in August 1793 the Crayford singers were paid 4 guineas (even though there is no record of a charity sermon that year).

In 1783 an entry in the accounts recorded £8 18s 6d (or 8½ guineas) having been received from sundry Trustees at the meeting on the 4th November. There had already been a number of similar entries, suggesting this was a new initiative to ensure all the annual subscriptions were paid. From 1784 onwards a single entry in the accounts includes both the Town Collections and money collected from Trustees at their meetings, confusing the amount raised from each source. However, together these contributed an average of £30 6s a year to the funds over the fifteen years from 1781, and the Trustees had good reasons to be grateful to John Tyler for the initiative he had taken back in 1771 and his organisation of the collections over nearly a quarter of a century. He had worked with the Rev'd Harry Fletcher until 1786, then with James Marshall, and after he retired in 1794 (or possibly earlier) it was James Marshall and Charles Waghorn who took over this responsibility. This raises the possibility that the town collections were now being made through their shops. Entries for money collected in this way would continue from time to time until 1804 or 1805, after which there seems to have been only one more such entry in the accounts, in 1813. It may not be a coincidence that the decline in this source of revenue coincides exactly with the financially difficult years of the Napoleonic Wars.

One theme which goes through the accounts over these fifteen years is the late payment of rent and legacies. Having waited 12½ years for the first payment from Mr Wallinger on his uncle's bequest, it was not until October 1790 that the second was paid: £37 15s 0d of accumulated interest over 11 years. In the meantime further legacies had been received from former trustees: £21 from Joseph Letch in 1786, £10 the same year from Samuel Skinner, and in 1787 £27 from James Holland, who had been a very loyal trustee from February 1769 until his death in June 1779. This last sum represented his legacy together with the added interest which had been obtained after the treasurer had applied to the executor for this.

In April 1794 another gift (or legacy) of £100 was received in most unusual circumstances. The story was reported in a book published two years later by the Rev Daniel Lysons, AM, the Chaplain to the Right Hon the Earl of Orford (as he styled himself): *The Environs of London being an Historical Account of the Towns, Villages and Hamlets within Twelve Miles of that Capital Interspersed with Biographical Anecdotes.* In his chapter on Romford Lysons writes:

> There is a school for forty boys, and another for twenty girls, in this parish, instituted about the year 1728. Benefactions to the amount of some 850l. have been given to these schools, by various donors; in addition to which fund, there is an annual voluntary subscription, and two charity sermons.

He then lists the principal benefactors, ending: 'And Mr Spurgin, a traveller, who accidentally stopping in Romford, about four years ago, approved of the establishment, 100l {£10,000}.' On the list of benefactors in the church this man appears as Mr Thomas Spurgeon of East Mersea Hall, with the date given as 1794 but no indication of whether this gift was a donation or a legacy; however, in the *Accounts* it is recorded as a legacy, received on 17 April 1794. Whichever it was, that a stranger should be incited to an act of such generosity in such a circumstance is testimony to the excellent manner in which Thomas Grove and Jane White were perceived to be running the schools.

The trustees invested this £100 and other spare money they had in interest bearing bonds. In the year ending April 1790 the total income of the charity was £127 5s 0d, of which the interest on the five Bonds they then held contributed £11 5s. {£1,350}, or just under 9% of the total. These business men (who significantly in 1791 had elected Thomas Graves to the post of Treasurer 'to this Society', rather than 'to this charity') believed that now was a good time to invest, and that by so doing they would help to safeguard the funding of the charity in the future.

Two of these investments are of particular interest. At the meeting on 7 November 1786 it was 'Order'd at this Meeting that the Sum of £150 be laid out in Bonds of £50 each granted by Act of Parliament on Security for raising a Certain Sum of Money towards Building a Workhouse for the Parish of Romford.' The original workhouse of 1723, which had possibly stood near the Market Place, was replaced in 1787 by a new workhouse to the west side of North street, behind the Roger Reede almshouses. It would have been the largest and most significant building to have been erected in the town for many years. The growing town needed a larger facility, and this could house up to 250 inmates. This additional accommodation might explain why there had never been a previous entry in the *Accounts* like that of 30 April 1789, reporting that Ann Rasbrooke was discharged from the school because she had 'gone in the Workhouse'. She was followed by Joseph Plair in June 1792, Hannah Young, John Johnson and William Johnson in November 1792, John and Thomas Perrin in November 1796, and Thomas Marsden and Thomas Carter in May 1801.

The second investment was a response to the falling price of consols as a result of the economic turbulence caused by the French Revolutionary Wars. In November 1791 the trustees bought 100 £1 3% consols for £88 5s. The previous year they would have had to pay about £77, the following year £90. However, the price then started to fall again and in November 1793 they bought another 100, paying £75 10s. With the price still falling they invested in a further 100 the following May, this time paying only £70 7s 6d. Prices were to fall much lower: in 1798 they would have had to pay between £50 and £51, but they were not to know this. They had now bought 300 3% consols which would bring them another £9 in interest each year.

Another reason why it made good sense to the Trustees to invest the money as they had done was because the war had also brought inflation: money in the bank was losing value, and the cost of wages and commodities was rising. Prices would peak in 1815, the year of Waterloo, 50% to 70% higher than they had been in 1785. In 1760 a Chaldron of Coals had cost £1 16s for each teacher, but Mr Dearsley's coal bill had now risen to 11 guineas; in 1768 the cost of fire insurance had been 19s, but by April 1785 it had risen to £1 11s 5d; Tom Furniss had emptied the privy in 1756 for 5s, but in 1787 it cost £1 11s 6d. In November 1790 the allowance for pens and Ink was raised from 18s a year to two guineas. The obverse of the policy of investment to raise income was to cut expenditure to as little as possible, which in practice meant restricting it to the payment of the Master's and

Mistress's salaries and other essentials, which significantly still included the annual provision of clothes. By 1794 these were being provided by the loyal trustee Charles Waghorn, and that year the school paid him £26 10s. He would hold this price until 1800, the year of his death. It was to the advantage of both the trustees and himself that he did so, but it was a generous gesture: the decade 1790 to 1800 saw the greatest inflation in the 18th century, causing the value of this annual payment of £26 10s to fall by almost a third, from the 2020 equivalent of £3,240 in 1790 to £2,190 in 1800.

4 November 1797: The Reverend Charles William Bathurst

The month Nathaniel Bliss died, March 1796, Thomas Graves completed his 25th year as treasurer. On 4 November 1797, a year after the reconciliation of the accounts, the Chaplain of Romford attended a meeting of the trustees for the first time since the Rev'd John Hopkins had last done so on 22 February 1770. The man New College appointed to succeed Bliss was, as usual, one of their own: 31 year-old Charles William Bathurst. If the trustees were aware of his father's record they would have had little optimism that their new curate would be a success. Bathurst Senior had represented three Parliamentary constituencies between 1713 and 1767 but never once spoken in the House, perhaps the political equivalent of holding a living but never once preaching in the church. He was not just negligent in his duties, he was corrupt. In 1764 he had written to the Prime Minister, George Grenville, to propose vacating his seat in exchange for a pension of five hundred pounds a year being settled on his wife during her life, a proposal which even at that notorious time was too audacious to be accepted.[119] Bathurst Junior made a promising start in that he arrived in Romford and attended five of nine meetings before disappearing from the record in November 1801. Whether he was a support to the schools and the trustees during these four years we do not know; where he went to we do not know, although, as we shall see, he might have moved to Sussex. We will not hear of him again until March 1807, but we should note that it was his absence, and that of Nathaniel Bliss before him, which paved the way for the crisis in the 1820's.

Chapter 14

Sectarian Strife

1796 - 1807

1796: how a finger in the sand in Madras in 1789 would write a revolution in Britain
The aim of the SPCK's 'charity school movement' at the beginning of the century had been to encourage the establishment of a school in as many parishes as possible. For a few years it had collected and published data on the success of this enterprise, but otherwise it took no further interest in the individual schools and provided no central co-ordination. Where local enthusiasm had provided endowments or where money surplus to the school's immediate needs had been wisely invested, the school had probably survived; where there were no such resources, it had not. Each surviving charity school, having been set up more or less according to the SPCK's published template, was an independent entity which had then developed in its own, unique way.

By the close of the 18th century the first ripples of two new movements to establish national systems of popular education were emanating from Aldgate, north of the Tower of London, and Southwark, just across the Thames. These differed from that of the SPCK a hundred years before in that their momentum would be sustained, and over the next century they would become two mighty, opposing waves which would sweep across the country. They would leave in their wake many new schools, they would profoundly change many existing ones, and in their passage they would swirl up the sectarian conflict which was never far below the surface at that time. The energy and inspiration for the first of these movements came once again from the Church of England, and although it emanated from Aldgate, the quiet epicentre of this new natural force was an idea conceived in far away Madras in the mind of a dominant and dominating Anglican clergyman. Whereas the individual leaders of the SPCK were more or less anonymous, self-effacing men, the formidable Reverend Doctor Andrew Bell, who had returned to England in 1796, was one of those extraordinary personalities - brilliant, fanatical, intolerant, tsunamic - who battered early nineteenth century England into becoming Victorian Britain.

Bell was born in St Andrew's, Scotland, in 1753, the son of a barber and wig-maker, and was educated at the grammar school and university in the town. In 1774 he sailed for Virginia where he lived for seven years as a private tutor to the sons of wealthy tobacco plantation owners, at the same time indulging in a little tobacco trading himself. In 1779 he was engaged to tutor the sons of Carter Braxton, who three years earlier had signed the Declaration of Independence, but with the revolutionary war becoming ever more intense Bell must have found the ambiguity of his position increasingly uncomfortable. In 1781 he returned home, bringing the two Braxton boys with him to continue their education in Britain.

Four years later he was ordained, and in 1787 he sailed for Calcutta where he intended to lecture in science. However, when the ship stopped in Madras he decided to stay and give a brief course of lectures. It was a fateful decision. First, he decided to abandon his plans to go to Calcutta when he was offered the appointment of Chaplain to four regiments; then, in 1789, he was asked to run the Male Orphan Asylum which had been set up in the city by the East India Company. This was a boarding school for the orphans and illegitimate sons of native women and British soldiers. The teaching methods Bell encountered there were appalling, but as he was pondering how to address this problem he chanced upon an open-air native school where the pupils were being taught the alphabet by writing their letters in the dry sand. This, he realised, might be the answer to his problem. Instead of books, he equipped the school with sand-trays.

Bell's inability to relate to others would be a recurring theme throughout his life. Alienated by his overbearing manner, the master and two ushers working under him would not cooperate with his plans to teach the children to write using sand, leading him to choose a bright, 11 year old boy called Johnnie Frisken to teach the younger ones. He later rationalised this decision, saying it was based on his belief that 'There is a faculty, inherent in the mind, of conveying and receiving mutual instruction.' When the master and ushers then left, he segregated the school into classes which were instructed by the most able boys - his pupil monitors - each of whom taught a younger group of children the lesson they had themselves just been taught by Dr Bell. This was the Madras system, which Bell developed from his early experiments in what we would now call 'peer led instruction'. The system worked well and standards in the school greatly improved. The children were taught reading, writing and arithmetic, and this curriculum was underpinned by a strong moral education based on admonition and praise. The curriculum sounds very similar to that of the Boys' Charity School at Romford; the revolution was in the teaching method, which would allow the number of boys under instruction to grow exponentially.

Dr Andrew Bell in later life
Mezzotint by C. Turner, 1825, after W. Owen

Bell, like East India Company chaplain James Ridley a generation earlier, found the Indian climate was not good for his health. In 1796 he returned home, wishing to marry and settle down. By then Frisken was 12 years and 8 months, and he and his assistants were in charge of 91 boys. Apart from being a successful educator Bell was also a very successful business man, and the £128 10s which he had brought to India had now increased to

£25,935 16s 5d {£2,600,000}. He was a very wealthy man. Within a year of his return he had published a report on his work in Madras and opened a few charity schools which utilised his system, funding these from his own resources and with some outside support. St Botolph's School in Aldgate had become the first school in England to be conducted under his system, closely followed by a school in Kendal. From then on his methods began to spread across the country. In 1801 he was appointed Rector of Swanage in Dorset, where he converted the teaching in the Sunday school to the Madras system.

Professor Meiklejohn, one of Bell's early biographers, explains in more detail the differences between Bell's method of teaching and that used in the existing schools:

> The children (this is in Bell's system) were to teach each other; each child was to rise or fall in his place in class according to his accuracy; or even to fall or rise from class to class. Before Dr Bell's plan, the master 'heard' all the lessons; and forty-nine children were always more or less idle while the fiftieth was occupied in 'saying' his lessons. But now the little boys were arranged in divisions; one of the boys taught; when one was reading, all the others listened; and the next boy corrected when an error was made. The lessons were always very short; and each child prepared what he had to without a single mistake. A register was kept by the monitors and 'Teachers' and even by the boys themselves; and thus the whole school became a scene of unceasing activity and constant healthy emulation.[120]

This mutual tuition was confined to the memory work and drill which formed a predominant part of the plan. Literacy began with learning one's letters by tracing them on a board strewn with sand, then learning to read by joining these letters into syllables and then the syllables into words. By using short steps pupils were rewarded and encouraged by seeing the immediate results of their efforts. The aim, in Bell's words, was to 'get everything perfect'. Careful records were kept of the work covered and of each pupil's progress, and there was also a register of misdemeanours, which the pupils called the 'black book'. Entries in this book were read to the entire school, and faults were commented on in moral terms. The system provided what the early 19th century wished for: a cheap and relatively effective means of mass education with a moral and social element. By moving pupils up or down the class according to their individual level of performance it also provided motivation and inevitably led to self-selection. It was claimed that the system also helped to train working-class children for responsible jobs in the future for, as Bell said, 'Give me twenty-four pupils today and I will give you twenty-four teachers tomorrow.'

1798: Bell v. Lancaster

And what of the second wave, rippling out of Southwark? One would have thought Bell's claim to have devised this system of peer education which obviated the need to employ additional assistant masters was unassailable, but two years after he opened his school in Aldgate this was challenged by Joseph Lancaster, the son of a Southwark shopkeeper and a man 25 years younger than Bell. In 1798 Lancaster, aged twenty, founded a free elementary school in Borough Road using the 'monitorial system'. It is difficult to accept as a coincidence that two men had the same basic idea at the same time and in almost the same place. Some claim that Lancaster had asked Bell for help and advice which had been freely given, and had then altered details of the scheme, renamed his amended version the 'monitorial system', and then claimed ownership of the original idea.

What were these differences? Lancaster said of his system that it was designed to produce a 'Christian Education' and 'train children in the practise of such moral habits as are conducive to the welfare of society'. He prescribed smaller classes than the 36 or so advocated by Bell, and was very specific in his description of the ideal classroom, which should be a hall twice as long as it was wide with windows six feet from the floor. The model classroom he and others advocated at the beginning of the century were to be found in schools a hundred years later, so the layout of the classroom described by Gladman in the 1880's would have been accurate seventy years earlier:

> The floor should be inclined, rising one foot in twenty from the master's desk to the upper end of the room, where the highest class is situated. The master's desk is on the middle of a platform two to three feet high, erected at the lower end of the room. Forms and desks, fixed firmly to the ground, occupy the middle of the room, a passage being left between the ends of the forms and the wall, five or six feet broad, where the children form semicircles for reading.[121]

Children were classified according to their ability in reading and arithmetic. Class lists and registers were kept. In order to stimulate effort and reward merit, 'Lancaster used Place Taking abundantly. He also had medals and badges of merit . . . Tickets could be earned too; these had a trifling pecuniary value.' Prizes were given 'to excess' and ceremonially. Discipline was reinforced by frequent changes of routine, exact movements in response to a code of commands, and by corporal punishment. Compared with this, Bell's Madras System was less rigid and the children were less regulated. A 'Bell' school was arranged in forms or classes, classified by reading ability only. The hall was similar to that proposed by Lancaster, but desks were placed against the walls and the Master's desk was raised. (Gladman did not like this arrangement of the teacher's desk: 'Fixing the master thus, deprived him of much of his power; he would do more good in passing from class to class, and teaching.') The similarities between the two systems were far greater than the differences, however, which is why attribution of the original idea is frequently ignored and this mode of teaching referred to as the 'Bell-Lancaster method', implying, erroneously, that they worked together harmoniously and deserve equal credit for the innovation.

In 1803 Lancaster wrote a book, *Improvements in Education*, which further promoted the method he claimed to have originated. Mrs Sarah Trimmer, a well-known contemporary writer of religious pamphlets, was sceptical of his claims, believing he had simply added a few improvements to a system he had plagiarised from Bell. Lancaster's supporters would not have been surprised that she took this view because the dispute went much deeper than the question of what we would now call 'intellectual property rights': it was a sectarian division, and Trimmer and Bell were of the Established Church and Lancaster was a Quaker. This sectarian divide between the two men and their followers, between the Church of England and the non-conformists, would dog popular education throughout the nineteenth century, although in Romford its full impact would be delayed until 1872 and the election of the first School Board.

Overleaf: Two images from *Méthode britannique d'éducation lancastérienne* (1816), a French edition of Joseph Lancaster's *Improvements in Education (1803)*.

Deux admoniteurs[122] au travail...

... ce qu'il ne faut pas faire, élèves non attentifs.

1801 to 1805: Mr Grove (retired), Mrs Cloke (deceased), and Mr and Mrs Saunders (resigned)

The incipient revolution, whether created in Aldgate or Southwark, could have been taking place in Madras for all the effect it would have on the school in Romford over the next thirty years. Here, pedagogy and the curriculum had never changed, and salaries only rarely. At the time of Mrs Cloke's appointment in 1794 Mr Grove was still receiving the £25 a year he had negotiated thirty-two years earlier, the value of which had reduced by over 20% in this time owing to infltion. However, in September 1795 it was noted that he was allowed 'half Guinea a Week for 10 Weeks agreed Last Meeting', but as there is no record of this agreement we do not know why this temporary additional payment was made. He does appear to have been augmenting his salary in others ways, however, because on 29 May 1801, with his retirement seven months away, the trustees 'Order'd that Mr Groves[123] clear the Charity School House of all Inmates and Lodgers before midsummer day'. These may have been private students he was teaching alongside the charity children - a practice which three and a half years later the trustees would accept, regulate and record - or they may simply have been lodgers.

At this same meeting in May it was 'Order'd that an advertisement for an assistant to the Charity School be inserted in the *Chelmsford Chronicle*.' This was duly done, but there is no record of an appointment being made nor a reason given why it was thought necessary to make such an appointment. Be that as it may, at a meeting held at the 'Cock and Bell' on 5 November that year:

> Mr John Saunders applied to be elected Master of the Charity School, & he was unanimously appointed to undertake the care & management of the said school, & to be paid the Sum of Twenty five Pounds per Annum, & the House & premises to live in, as the late Master occupied, & two Chaldrons & ½ of Coals to be allowed annually. Mr Saunders appear'd here & accepts the same & to commence from Christmas next.

His remuneration was just half a chaldron of coal more than that Mr Grove had negotiated in 1762, and all we subsequently learn about him is that he had been born in Essex and was aged thirty at this time. At this same meeting the Trustees agreed 'that the sum of Ten Pounds be Annually paid Mr Thos Green Groves, for his past service & good conduct, in managing the Charity School for 41 yrs.' Mr Grove had been a good and faithful servant and was the first person employed by the school to receive a pension. He enjoyed two years of retirement before being laid to rest in St Edward's Chapel on 13 November 1803. His funeral expenses came to £3 16s 4d and these were paid by the trustees. On Christmas Day they made a payment of £2 10s to Mrs Grove, the only such payment recorded.

Within a year the School Mistress was also dead, the St Edward's Church Register recording the burial of 'Dorothy Cloack' on 26 October 1804. She had been Mistress for ten and a half years. At a meeting of the Trustees on 13 November

> Susannah Saunders wife of John Saunders the present Master of the Boys school, was unanimously elected Mistress at the yearly Salary of eighteen pounds five shillings, One chaldron and a half of Coals – and the use of the school house; on condition that she take not more than six children, Day scholars; and that John Saunders the present Master elect, be limited to take not more than fifteen boys either Boarders or Day scholars. – and they are accordingly elected for one year certain; commencing from Christmas day next: and if his or her conduct be not approved, he or she shall be removed on receiving six months warning from the majority of Trustees convened for that special purpose – or if they resign they shall give six months notice – thereof.

This is the first time that the permission of the trustees to take private students had been written into the teachers' contracts, although it is possible that previously there had been an unwritten agreement that Thomas Grove could do so. By including details in Mrs Saunders' contract the trustees now formalised the situation and placed a maximum on the number of additional students which the schoolmaster and mistress could accept. If the Saunders' had exploited this to the maximum, teaching an additional twenty-one scholars to their own financial advantage alongside those admitted to the charity school, the couple would have enjoyed a not inconsiderable supplement to their income. (One must presume that any boys who boarded would have slept in the accommodation in the School House. We have no plans of the Masters House, but although pictures suggest it was commodious it would hardly have been able to accommodate a possible additional 15 boys.) We have seen how costs had risen since 1790, yet Mrs Saunders was paid not only the same as Mrs Cloke, but the same as Mrs

White when she had been appointed thirty-three years earlier, over which inflationary period the purchasing power of this salary had fallen by 45%. Perhaps it was to avoid the pressure to pay the couple more that led the trustees to compromise by allowing them to accept private students.

This agreement is significant. Although many children from the higher and lower levels of society received no education at this time, for the large band in the middle there were not even schools for them to attend. These were the sons of the emerging middle class, the more prosperous tradesmen and shop-keepers whose status and income were below those required to send their children to one of the old public schools or to educate them at home, but above that where they would have attended a charity school (if one was available). Some places had an ancient grammar school or an independent charitable foundation which might take such children, but if this was not in an advanced state of decay, then frequently the Master in charge was. The agreement that the Saunders' could take in paying students is evidence of a developing market for private education from parents able to pay for it. Additionally, the fact that some parents would wish to send their children to the Romford School perhaps suggests that under Thomas Grove it had acquired a strong reputation. As demand grew, so would the number of schools, but at this time the only 'Gentlemen's Boarding School' we know of in the town was the one run by Abraham Delamare, the loyal trustee of the Charity School.[124]

John and Susannah Saunders were entrepreneurial and could see that private education was a burgeoning and lucrative market, and if the trustees hoped that with this agreement their services would be secured they were to be disappointed. Three-and-a-half years after John's appointment the couple resigned and moved to Upminster where the records show that from 1804 to 1843 they kept a boarding school at High House, Corbets Tey. This establishment was educating 35 children in 1819 and 37 boys in 1833, considerably fewer than the numbers at the Charity School.[125] Had the Saunders' used the agreement on private students and their brief time in Romford to recruit the nucleus of their own private school, at no 'start-up' financial risk to themselves?

June 1805: Thomas Bandfield and Mary his wife, Master & Mistress with recommendations

The trustees now had to find a new Master and Mistress. The minutes of a meeting held on 11 June 1805 begin:

> Thomas Bandfield and Mary his wife of South Ockendon in Essex both of whom are of the established Church of England and by a Copy of Recommendations underwritten applied to be elected Master & Mistress of the said Charity School in the room of John and Susannah Saunders who have resigned the same . . .

They were unanimously elected on the same conditions as their predecessors. However, without leave of the trustees he is permitted to take no more than 6 boarders and 14 boys and girls as day scholars 'above the number of Charity children in the said school'. Had John and Susannah Saunders negotiated the higher figure of 15 boarders with the Trustees and then found this was just too many to manage in addition to the charity scholars, or for the accommodation they had? Or, by lowering the number of borders, did the Trustees hope to prevent the Bandfields creating their own school as the Saunders' had possibly done? Whatever the reason, the Bandfields accepted the terms and were elected for 'one year certain' from Midsummer day next, with six months' warning on either side if they wished to resign or 'if his or her conduct be not approved'. Such safeguards were now routinely written into the agreement; there was always the possibility they might unwittingly appoint another master like John Moore, whom their predecessors had had to dismiss in 1760.

Appointment procedures were gradually becoming more formalised, and beneath their signatures, for the first time, two testimonials were copied into the Accounts. The first reads:

> Understanding that a vacancy has taken place in the Mastership of the Charity School at Romford, I take the liberty of recommending to your notice Mr Bamfield of So. Ockendon who I believe should you honor him with your protection will be found every way equal to the Situation, the importance of which I am well aware of. May I hope to be excused the having intruded myself on your notice and that you will believe me to be Gentlemen with great good will
>
> Your most obedient and very humble Servant

It was signed: 'Thos Barrett Lennard'. Thomas Barrett Lennard! To have obtained a reference from the owner of the magnificent Belhus estate was a great coup. Thomas Barrett Lennard had inherited the property from his distant cousin the Honourable Dacre Barrett, whom John Locksmith had visited eighty years before in order to collect his £16 in outstanding subscriptions to the Charity School. In June 1801 the Barrett-Lennard Baronetcy of Belhus had been created for him, and as Sir Thomas Barrett-Lennard he had subsequently been elected Member of Parliament for Essex South. South Ockendon is very close to Belhus, and if Mr Bandfield wanted an impressive local name at the bottom of his reference he could not have chosen better. But how well, and in what context, did Sir Thomas know Thomas Bandfield? They obviously moved in very different social circles, and if the reference was correctly copied Sir Thomas had misremembered Bandfield's name. It seems the trustees made no further enquiries. As always, *caveat emptor*.

The second testimonial was as unspecific as the first but equally reassuring, even if the signatures of Lockhart Leith, Rector of South Ockendon, and five of his parishioners were less exalted. This stated that they 'do recommend Thomas Bandfield and Mary his wife, as persons duly qualified in abilities and character for teachers in the above mentioned seminary'. The trustees must have been pleased to have replaced Mr and Mrs Saunders so quickly with an experienced husband and wife team who came with positive references from their previous parish.

The final years of Thomas Graves, treasurer

On 11 May 1797 there are two entries in the *Accounts* which speak for themselves:

> Paid Mr Graves Bill for Shop Goods from 1779 to 1788 £12 9s 6d
> Paid Mr Graves Bill for Shop Goods from 1789 to 1794 £ 6 0s 9d

Mr Graves, Treasurer and grocer, was clearly no more prompt with his own finances than he was in reconciling the school accounts. Having finally succeeded in having the accounts balanced and inspected in September 1796, his fellow trustees wished to ensure they would not have to wait another 15 years for the next presentation. As a general rule, from December 1802 through to October 1825 they would be balanced every six months.

By 1803 the second volume of accounts was full. In September 1762 it had opened with a balance of £176 3s 10¾d carried forward from the first volume, but the figure now transferred to the third volume was £4 3s 6½d. The title page of this new book is written in beautiful calligraphy and reads: 'The Accounts and Transactions of the Trustees for the Charity Schools for Hornchurch, Romford, & Havering; Commencing June 14th 1803.'

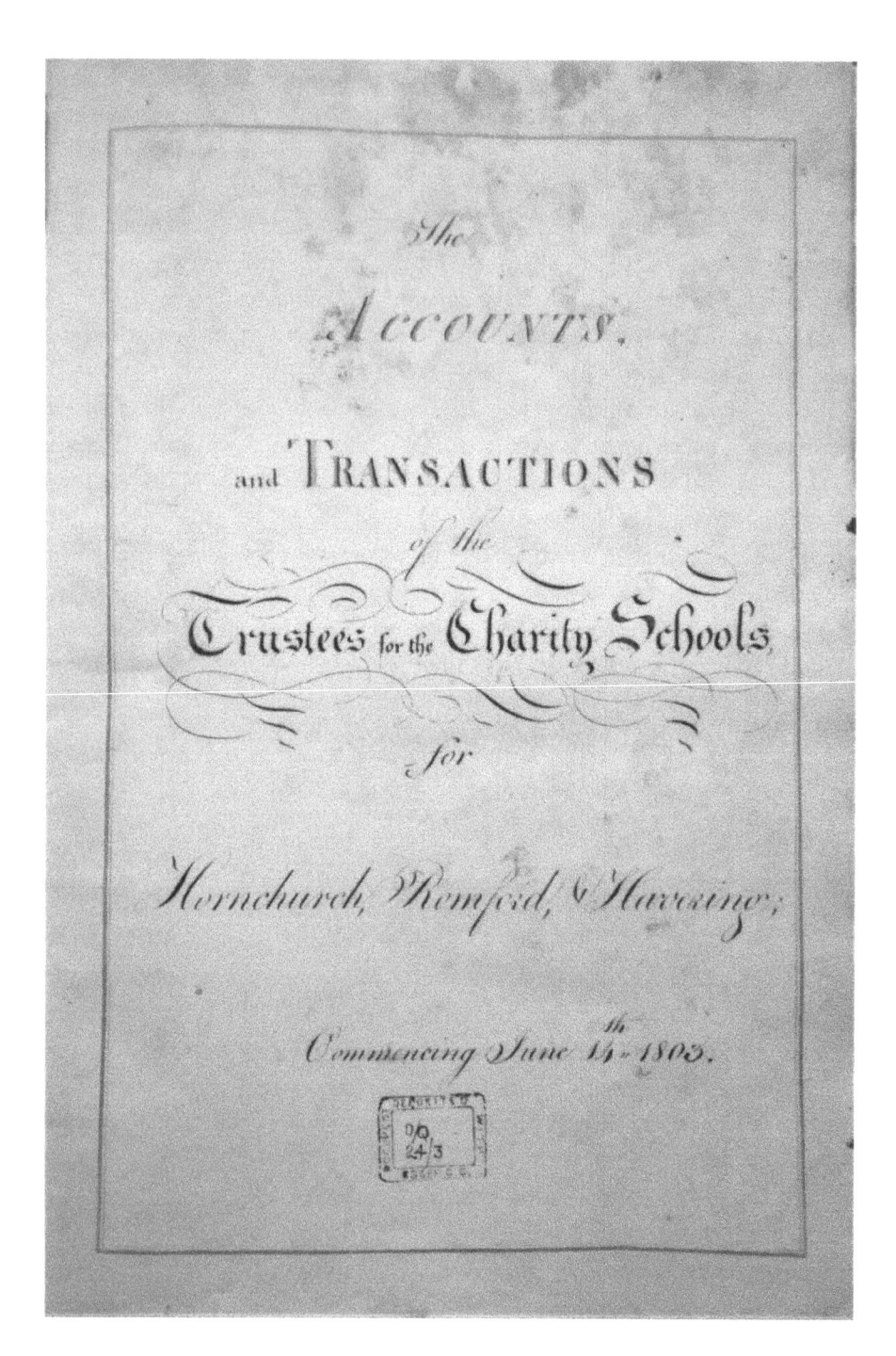

Title page of the Trustees' third volume of *Accounts and Transactions*. The calligraphy is probably that of John Saunders, then Master of the boys.

At the beginning of the second volume of accounts there is a list of the legal documents and papers belonging to the Trustees; the third volume commences with a list of the property and bonds they own showing the annual income received and, on occasions, when these assets were sold. An analysis of the income raised in the first year of the new account book, from June 1803 to May 1804, reveals just how little was now collected in subscriptions - just seven and a half guineas. This implied only seven or eight people had paid their guinea, or perhaps twice that number had paid at the new rate of 10s 6d. The town collections had also fallen from the annual average of £28 twenty-five years earlier. Only the income from the increasingly costly sermons had held up:

Rent	£ 14		[On Boswell's property]
Interest	£ 18		[On the investment bonds]
Sermons	£ 68	0s 11d	
Town colle'n/Trustees	£ 28	2s 6d	[Including subscriptions?]
Town Collection	£ 10	4s 6d	
Sundry Trustees	£ 7	17s 6d	[Subscriptions]
Donations	£ 4	16s 6d	
Total:	£151	1s 11d	

However, two legacies and a lucrative sermon bolstered the funds. First, the £100 legacy arrived following the death of John Redman, although to secure this the trustees had had to pay one of their number, the Attorney-at-Law Wasey Sterry, 17s 6d to obtain an abstract of his will. This legacy, together with other amounts they had managed to save, enabled the trustees to invest another £100 in 3% consols in November 1796, and yet another £100 in January 1799 (for which they paid just £52 7s 6d). They were fortunate again in August 1804: not only did they receive a legacy of £50 from a Miss Williams of Ilford, but the charity sermons that month raised an unprecedented £80 15s 6d.

On 29 May 1804 two new trustees were the first to sign the third volume of Accounts, Edward Ind (although he had attended the previous meeting in November) and Thomas Waghorn. We can assume that young Thomas had been running the family tailoring business since his father's death in August 1800 and was still supplying the school. In May 1805 it was noted that clothing was to be provided 'as usual' for 24 senior boys and 12 senior girls. It had been many years since every child in the school had been provided with clothes, but in June 1806 the trustees expressed the intention of doing so once again with the order 'that clothing be provided for 38 Boys and 20 Girls being all in the Institution', the last part then being altered to read 'being the whole number in the Institution', giving us rare confirmation of the size of the school at a particular time. Clothing was a good investment, not just because it provided warmth and supported the well being of the children but because it ensured future funding: in their distinctive uniform, the charity children were walking advertisements which kept the school constantly in the minds of the people of Romford and Hornchurch. It was the contributions these townsfolk made at the charity sermons and, to a much lesser extent now, their donations to the town collections which remained the principle sources of income for the school.

Throughout much of the long period Thomas Graves had been treasurer Britain had been at war, and war always brings economic uncertainties and inflation. The military campaign in India in the 1750's and 1760's, followed by the subsequent devastating famine in Bengal from 1768, had caused the East India Company (EIC) to borrow £5.5 million from the Bank of England between 1769 and 1772, causing the stagnation of public credit and raising fears of 'national bankruptcy' if the EIC failed. In June 1772, fifteen months after Graves became treasurer, thirty banks had failed across Europe in less than three weeks.[126] In 1775 the American War of Independence had broken out, and this had not ended until 1783. Six years later the French Revolution had been followed by the Revolutionary Wars from 1792, and then after the short Peace of Amiens war had again broken out. In this situation a cautious treasurer would naturally keep his spending to the minimum essentials and would no doubt economise on clothing if this was not a sensible investment. Indeed, 'sensible investment' probably best summarises Thomas Graves' policy over these thirty-six years, and future treasurers would be grateful for his financial prudence: the investment in stock would provide them with additional revenue for the present and a store of capital which could be liquidated when new buildings needed to be paid for in the future.

In August 1805 the potential crisis which had been feared since the war began seemed closer than ever as Napoleon massed his troops at Boulogne in preparation for an invasion of England. In November this imminent threat was removed when Nelson destroyed the combined French and Spanish fleets at Trafalgar, but Napoleon's great victory at Austerlitz in December proved the war was far from over. These events resulted in further price rises, a trend exacerbated after February 1806 when Napoleon forced Prussia to close its ports to British goods. In these circumstances subscriptions to the charity, many of which had remained unpaid for a number of years, could be expected to fall further. At a meeting on 18 November 1806 it was decided to confront this issue and ask the question which had long been avoided, and Mr Haws and Mr Ind were ordered 'to call upon the subscribers whose subscriptions remain unpaid, to know their determination as to continuing the same'. This was the last initiative to be taken by Treasurer Thomas Graves. Ten men were present at the 'Cock & Bell' on 12 May 1807 when he finally stepped down after 36 years. Edward Ind was then elected his successor and received the balance of £3 or £4 {£250}.

For nearly half his life Graves had served the Charity, supported by his core team of seven stalwarts. Of these, Henry Goody had died in the January and Charles Waghorn in the August of 1800, both having attended their first meeting in June 1777, and John Tyler would die in October 1807 having been a trustee for forty-two years. In January 1812 the era came to a definitive end with the death of Thomas Graves himself at the age of 80. By now this Romford grocer was a very rich man. He lived in Gothic Lodge, Romford, but also owned a number of other properties in the town, the 'Bull' public house in Dagenham, and a house in Cardiff. This property portfolio, together with the £3,000 invested in the Bank of England and other stock in the East India Company, was divided between his four children after his wife's death. Fifteen months after his death his son Joseph was elected a trustee, but he never played a significant part in the Charity. However, in 1833 Lieut-Colonel Benjamin Graves, possibly a grandson of Thomas, would be one of the eighteen trustees appointed by the Court of Chancery to run the Charity under the new Scheme imposed by the Lord Chancellor that year, and he would serve in this position until his death thirty years later.

12 May 1807: Edward Ind, a new treasurer for a new century

On 14 June 1803 three new trustees had signed the *Accounts* book, under which was an unusual entry: 'At the same time James Marshall proposed Edward Ind Esq as a Trustee, and he is desired to attend next Meeting and accept the same.' He did so, on 17 November, and on 29 May 1804 was formally elected and added his signature. Now three years later he was elected Treasurer.

Edward Ind was of a new generation and a new type of Romford grandee, and his appointment at this time is symbolic of the cultural and social differences between the pre-war 18th century and the post-war 19th century. As we have seen, earlier supporters of the school had included the local gentry living in the ancient Havering manors, men such as Richard Hide of

Nelmes or Carew Hervey *alias* Mildmay of Marks. They still had their influential representatives on the trustees. Sometime after the death of the Honourable Mrs Ann Rider in 1731 her manor of Dagnams and Cockerels had been purchased by the Neave family, and in 1795 Richard Neave was created the first baronet. His grandson, Sir Richard Digby Neave, the 3rd baronet, became Steward of the Liberty in 1821, and in the 1830's he was very much a man of his times being a director of two railway companies, an assistant poor law commissioner (in the Chester area), and, as we shall see, a trustee of the Charity School at Romford. Earlier trustees had included members of the merchant class such as Thomas Gilman and Christopher Bayley, and professional men like the lawyers Richard and John Comyns. Their successors had been successful local shopkeeper such as Thomas Graves and Charles and Thomas Waghorn. Now Edward Ind was treasurer, a man who represented the new class of entrepreneurs and men of business who would later come to dominate the Victorian age.

Ind was the son of a brewer in Baldock, Hertfordshire, who wished to follow in his father's profession. Legend has it that he arrived in Romford in 1799 and bought the Star Brewery. This was apparently a small enterprise which had been founded in 1708 behind the 'Star Inn', located by the bridge over the River Rom at the London end of the High Street. However, recent research has disproved this story, not least because there is no evidence of a 'Star Inn' before 1808.[127] Whatever the truth, by 1807 Ind was well established and well respected in the town and his enterprise was developing successfully. He would work with two different partners before he and Octavius Coope would create the business which would export beer across the world and make Ind & Coope a household name for over 150 years, blazoned on bottles and public houses. But that lay in the future. Edward Ind had now been elected Treasurer of the Charity School after only three years as a trustee and having only moved to the town some eight years earlier. It was a sign of the confidence that the other Trustees had in him that he was their choice at this difficult time, and a sign of his wish to establish himself as a citizen of Romford that he had accepted. For the schools, it would prove a very beneficial relationship.

Chapter 15

A story of two brewers and two schoolmasters

1807 - 1817

The Parochial Schools Bill of 1807
Two months before the brewer Edward Ind became Treasurer of the Charity School in Romford, the son and namesake of another famous brewer, Samuel Whitbread, was bringing the subject of the education of the masses to the attention of the wealthy and privileged in the House of Commons. This was the most important parliamentary initiative yet to be taken in this matter. Whitbread proposed a new Poor Law which would have both increased the financial help given to the poor and granted every child between the ages of seven and fourteen the right to receive two years of free education if they were unable to pay.

Samuel Whitbread MP, stipple engraving by W. Holl, c. 1815

Whitbread must have been encouraged by the new enlightenment which seemed to pervade the British Parliament at that time and which was to be most dramatically expressed five weeks later when the 'Abolition of the Slave Trade Act' entered the statute book on 25 March.

He rose to introduce his bill on 19 February 1807:

> Mr. Speaker . . . I wish to engage you in an attempt at the solution of the most difficult of all political problems; namely, how to reduce the sum of human vice and misery, and how to augment that of human happiness and virtue amongst the subjects of this realm.

It was a noble and ambitious enterprise, but Whitbread soon realised that his bill was too complex and far too ambitious for the House of Commons of that time. In an attempt to secure its passage he announced to the House on 13 April that it would be broken down into separate bills, one of which was the Parochial Schools Bill.

Since the foundation of the first charity schools, powerful voices (including that of the great economist Adam Smith) had argued that universal education was both affordable and desirable. However, others argued equally fiercely against the cause, reiterating the same arguments in 1807 which the SPCK had had to counter in the 1690's. Mr David Giddy, the MP for Bodmin, spoke for many when on the second reading on 13 June he argued that

> giving education to the labouring classes of the poor . . . would . . . be found to be prejudicial to their morals and happiness; it would teach them to despise their lot in life, instead of making them good servants in agriculture, and other laborious employments to which their rank in society had destined them; instead of teaching them subordination, it would render them factious and refractory . . . it would enable them to read seditious pamphlets, vicious books, and publications against Christianity; it would render them insolent to their superiors and, in a few years, the result would be, that the legislature would find it necessary to direct the strong arm of power towards them, and to furnish the executive magistrates with much more vigorous laws than were now in force. Besides, if the bill were to pass into a law, it would go to burthen the country with a most enormous and incalculable expence, and to load the industrious orders of society with still heavier imposts . . . he never

could admit it to be just or reasonable that the labour of the industrious man should be taxed to support the idle vagrant. This was taxing virtue for the maintenance of vice.

Despite such opposition the bill moved to the committee stage, but when the report was being considered on 4 August opposition was still strong. Sir Thomas Turton, MP for Southwark, gave a practical example of how increasing the level of education of these people would lead to sedition:

> Did the house not recollect the mutiny at the Nore? He might venture to state, from the information of an honourable admiral, that upon that occasion the mutineers had daily and nightly meetings on board of the ships; at which meetings they employed themselves in reading the newspapers and other publications; and that this tended much to the consequences which ensued.

William Smith, the MP for Norwich, had already countered this argument in an earlier speech:

> it was surely much better to counteract seditious pamphlets, by their being able to read others of a contrary tendency, than to hire men to make speeches, in order to put down the effect of seditious harangues. If the government of a country were afraid of making the people enlightened and well informed, he really did not see how they could possibly stop short of wishing that they had no understandings at all.

Many others spoke in the course of these debates, both supporters and those who did not share the belief in human dignity and perfectibility which underlay Whitbread's Bill. He was an idealist, as his words (as recorded in Hansard) illustrate: 'He would wish to have men the dignified characters for which they were formed by nature', and he believed 'that the instruction of youth tended to morality and virtue'. If he could not change the fundamental prejudices of his opponents, he tried very hard to correct their misconceptions and counter their arguments that his proposals would be too expensive and would necessitate raising the poor rates: the bill would not compel a single child to attend school because the poor would choose whether to allow their children to be instructed or not; the bill would only empower magistrates to erect schools, appoint schoolmasters and raise a shilling rate to finance these if necessary, it did not compel them to do so;

the bill would not put an end to charitable contributions because 'if in a large parish 6,000 children were educated by charitable contributions, and 10,000 were not educated at all, his bill passing over the former would apply only to the latter, whose situation was rendered at present so much more distressing by the contrast'.

It was a long, visceral debate which, intentionally or not, helped to publicise the achievement of the SPCK a century before and the many parish schools which were its legacy. Issues which in the future would become staples of political discussion were raised for the first time in parliament, including the salary of teachers, the place of religion in education, and the annual examination of schools by the clergy and/or the laity. The debate also had its lighter moments. There was general agreement that the poor in Scotland were better educated than in England, which led Sir Thomas Turton to revert to his theme that education only bred discontent with one's lot and to link this to the propensity of Scots to emigrate: as he pithily expressed it, 'The Scotch are a people that do not appear to be educated for remaining at home.' In a rather more general comment in support of the Bill Mr Henry Gratton, the MP for Dublin, declared that he did not think knowledge too general 'even among the higher orders'.

These were rare moments in a very serious and passionate debate, however. Whitbread's statement 'that it . . . would be better to exalt the character of the labourer so as to make him independent of his fellow-creatures for his livelihood' expressed his utopian belief in the dignity of the individual; his assertion that universal, basic education would ultimately reduce the poor rates was a far-sighted, practical answer to the arguments over cost. He was anxious that 'such a bill should pass . . . to shew that parliament had decided that education was a good thing to be given, a proper thing to be obtained'. Unfortunately parliament did not so decide, and his bill was comprehensively defeated.

The abolition of the slave trade is forever associated with the name of William Wiberforce, but sadly the establishment of free public education is not associated with that of Samuel Whitbread. Probably none of those who voted for his Parochial School Bill in 1807 would live to see the passing of the 1870 'Forster' Education Act which encapsulated so much of what he had argued for sixty-three years earlier. Over those years the arguments of those who supported free public education and of those who opposed it remained unchanged, but the public became more enlightened. In Britain, social and political progress is evolutionary, not revolutionary.

With Whitbread's Bill defeated, Parliament turned its attention back to the abolition of the slave trade and the continuing war with France. Twenty-six years were to pass before Parliament next gave its attention to education, and then only briefly, but it was to be the decision it then made which would fundamentally change the Charity School at Romford. For now, the pattern of life in the Market Place continued to be essentially that laid down by the SPCK a century before.

1808: new trustees and absent clergy
In 1806 Mr Haws and Mr Ind had been charged with 'call[ing] upon the subscribers whose subscriptions remain unpaid, to know their determination as to continuing the same'. Whether as a result of this initiative or of others he took as treasurer, support for the charity did now rise. In financial terms, donations and subscriptions rose from the £12 14s collected in the 1803/04 calendar year to £33 1s 6d in 1813 {from £1,000 to £2,500}. This boost was undoubtedly helped by the increase in the number of trustees: in the two years prior to Ind becoming treasurer eight were elected, and in the two years following there were nineteen. These included the first two women, Mrs Newton and Mrs Woolfe, elected together in October 1808 and setting a precedent which would not be followed for many years.

March 1808 saw the election of the Rev'd Lockhart Leith, Rector of South Ockendon. In February 1797 he had been a founder member of 'The Prestonian Lodge of Perfect Friendship' which met at the 'King's Arms', Grays, until it was formally 'erased' (permanently closed) in 1828. The relevance of this Lodge is that ten of the eighty-nine men who were members over its lifetime came from Romford or Hornchurch, of whom four were trustees of the Charity School:

Name	Trade	of	Trustee	Lodge
Thomas Macklin	Innkeeper	Romford	06/06/1797	02/11/1797
William Miles	Fellmonger	Hornchurch	18/04/1797	29/11/1820
Thomas Waghorn	Tailor	Romford	08/07/1800	29/05/1804
William Ford	Grocer	Romford	03/10/1803	29/06/1802

We glimpse in them the type of small businessman who at the turn of the century was supporting the school. These men had sufficient disposable income to afford the costs of Masonic dues, regalia and monthly dining, and also the Masonic expectation that they would give generously to charitable causes. Membership of the Lodge enabled them to network to their economic advantage, allowing them to extend their business opportunities. Freemasonry also broke through existing barriers, because although it was socially exclusive it was notably inclusive as far as religion was concerned. At a time when Roman Catholics and protestant non-conformists were denied full civil rights and debarred from holding many public offices and attending English universities, membership of a Lodge allowed such men to mix on equal terms with members of the Church of England. Furthermore, there was no social hierarchy amongst the brothers inside the Lodge, and anyone could become Master or a Warden.[128] This breaking down of religious barriers would spread more widely through society as the century advanced, and the void left by the absent incumbents at Romford and Hornchurch would, in due course, allow a non-conformist and then a Roman Catholic to become treasurer of that exemplary Church of England foundation, the Charity School at Romford.

In January 1809 William Henry Reynell finally took up permanent residence in Hornchurch when he was buried in St Andrew's churchyard; if he returned earlier, he never attended a second trustees' meeting. His successor, 50 year old William Blair of New College, who seems to have been resident in the parish until 1819, never attended a first meeting. In Romford, the Rev'd Bathurst had attended his last trustee meeting in November 1801. We next hear of him in March 1807 in the *British Press* and the *Morning Chronicle* which ran repeated advertisements for the sale by Leigh and S. Sotheby in the Strand of:

> The Entire and very Valuable LIBRARY of the Rev. CHARLES BATHURST, Vicar of Rumford, Essex, and Rector of Barcomb, Sussex; and now Chaplain to the Hon. East India Company, at Madras; being a very good collection in Divinity, History . . .

Readers were assured 'The Books, in general, are in good condition.' (How many were there? There had been 500 at the sale of Nathaniel Alsop Bliss's household goods.) One wonders why he was selling them: did he not expect to return from India? What interests us is the 'and' in his list of benefices and the use of the present tense, suggesting that he retained his two benefices in England even though he was then in India. We must hope that his congregation in Madras benefited more from his reading in divinity than did his parishioners in Romford (assuming he was not selling the books, possibly unread, because he no longer had any interest in the subject).

8 May 1809: the enigma of Thomas Bandfield and 'the person residing with [him] as his wife'

In March 1808 Thomas Waghorn, William Ford and Thomas Macklin had been trustees of the school for nearly four, six and eleven years respectively. However, Macklin had attended only two meetings (in 1797 and 1798), Waghorn - who did not have his father's commitment - only one (in 1804), and although Ford had been a more regular attendee he had been absent from the meeting in June 1805 when the Bandfields were appointed to the school. It is unlikely, therefore, that any of them knew that the new Master and Mistress had supplied a reference bearing the name of their 'brother' Mason, the Rev'd Lockhart Leith. The election of Leith as a trustee that month was probably a coincidence, therefore, although it may not have been a coincidence that the first meeting he attended was in October 1808, the one immediately before the dramatic events which followed. Did Leith learn the name of the schoolmaster at this meeting, and did this cause him to share certain information with Edward Ind which led directly to the events of the following March? Or - a more intriguing possibility - was Thomas Bandfield present to take the minutes of the meeting[129] and the two men recognised each other? Or, even more intriguingly, did they not recognise each other?

The schoolmaster's tasks certainly included maintaining the church registers and writing the school correspondence. A week or two before the second anniversary of his appointment as treasurer, in a scene charged with dramatic irony, Edward Ind instructed Thomas Bandfield to write to all the Trustees requesting them to attend at the 'Swan Inn', Romford, on Monday 8 May 1809 'to consult on particular business'. Did Ind know that Bandfield knew, or had guessed, the nature of that 'particular business'? It seems that many others knew, because at six o' clock on the appointed evening nineteen men were present, the highest number ever to attend a meeting of trustees. For three people it was the only meeting they would ever attend; for Thomas Graves it was to prove his penultimate meeting. The Rev'd Lockhart Leith was absent, but William Ford was there.

Whatever it was they all seemed to know - and this is the ultimate irony - we, posterity, are tantalisingly ignorant of, because Thomas Bandfield upstaged the 'consultation' with a letter of his own, addressed to the Treasurer, which Edward Ind read to the meeting:

> Sir As you have convened a meeting to arraign my conduct without
> giving me notice on that subject, it is impossible for me, to be

prepared, in any respect, as I could have wished, and finding my accusers have alleged the most unheard of falsities (insomuch that I am condemned by all) must therefore wish to resign the situation. Please to make this known to the Trustees as a notice from me according to agreement and that my successor may do more good for the Children and Institution, is the sincere wish of your most obedient humble servant

T. Bandfield

The record continues:

> Upon which the said Trustees unanimously accepted the resignation of the said Thomas Bandfield to quit the school and premises in 6 months from that day as agreed on 11th June 1805. And it is ordered that notice be given to the person residing with the said Thomas Bandfield as his wife to quit the said school and premises at the same time.

At this time the trustees kept duplicate log books, both probably maintained by the schoolmaster. The account of this meeting is recorded in only one of these, and is written in a different hand from any of the other entries.

Bandfield's letter had denied the meeting the opportunity to put the accusations to him in person, and his blustering tone and immediate resignation without attempting to defend himself and Mary from these 'unheard of falsities' suggest that perhaps the accusations, whatever they were, were not groundless. Alternatively, perhaps they were genuinely innocent of all charges but he had decided that resignation was better than a biased investigation and then immediate dismissal, possibly without the financial cushion of a six month period of notice. Significantly, there are no earlier suggestions that his work or conduct had been unsatisfactory, as there had been before John Moore's dismissal in 1760. By resigning in this way he has deprived us of the knowledge of the nature of the allegations he faced or the identities of his accusers. Does the phrasing 'the person residing with the said Thomas Bandfield as his wife' in preference to the simpler 'Thomas Bandfield and his wife' give a clue as to the nature of one of the accusations? Was he accused of having falsified his references? And was he guilty of this? We do not know, but he would have known and the Rev'd Lockhart Leith would have known. Maybe it was the knowledge that he might have to face this man, whose evidence would be decisive, which decided

Bandfield's course of action.

The trustees were no doubt pleased to avoid the scandal which would have attached to the school had the couple been investigated and dismissed, and there is one fact we can be sure of: relations between the Bandfields and the Trustees must have been very awkward during the six months that the couple served out their notice.

There is one final mystery concerning Thomas Bandfield. On Monday 9 October 1809 a 'Thomas Bandfield of the Parish of Romford, Essex, Bachelor', married Lucy Jeggins 'of this Parish, Spinster', by Licence, at St Botolph's-without-Bishopsgate in London. Of course this could be a coincidence, but the details lead one to wonder whether this was the same man. First, he comes from Romford, and the confident and elegant signature in the register reveals him to have been a man of education. Then there is the timing of the wedding, a month before he was due to leave Romford, and the fact that it was a marriage by licence. This was usually the case when the couple did not want the banns called and their nuptials to be advertised, or when they were getting married in haste. The statement that she was 'of this parish' was often a formality and did not prove any meaningful residency. If this was the same Thomas Bandfield, who was Lucy Jeggins? Was this the real name of 'the person [who had been] residing with [him] as his wife', calling herself Mary, but who now became his 'lawfully wedded wife'? Or was that escapade coming to an end and was Thomas Bandfield, putative adventurer, about to start a new - and this time a lawfully solemnised - union?

19 September 1809: William Adams and Jemima his wife

In the course of the debate on the Parochial Schools Bill Samuel Whitbread had contended that 'It would be easy to find schoolmasters [for the new schools that his Bill would cause to be set up], among whom there would doubtless be a competition for appointments'. This suggests that by then there had been a growth in the number of those qualified and available for such posts. Politicians frequently tread a fine line between optimism and overconfidence and often lose their footing, and two years after Whitbread's assertion the response of the trustees in Romford would, at best, have been sceptical. It was 19 September 1809, and a record twenty-three were gathered at the 'Lion' to make their third appointment of Master and Mistress in eight years. At least five very irregular attendees were again present, as was the Rev'd Lockhart Leith, attending his second (and possibly last) meeting. After the Saunders' short stay and the débâcle of the Blandfields, they must have been hoping to find another Thomas Green Grove. At the end of the meeting they recorded that 'William Adams and Jemima his wife of Great Waltham in Essex both of whom are of the established Church of England ... were unanimously elected.' The Saunders and the Blandfields had also been 'unanimously elected'.

William was appointed on the same conditions as his two predecessors, £25 pa and 2½ chaldrons of coal; however, the Mistress's salary was raised from £18 5s to £21 with the same 1½ chaldrons of coal. They enjoyed the same use of the Master's House, free of all expenses, and the same right to take up to 6 boarders and 14 boys and girls as day scholars above the number of charity children. They were elected for one year from 8 November 1809, but the amount of notice on both sides was reduced from six months to three. Were the trustees not as confident in their latest appointment as their unanimity implied? Or were they just ensuring that if the appointment were to prove a mistake they would not have to endure the prolonged farewell they had experienced with the Bandfields, who finally left the school on Tuesday 7 November, having worked out their notice?

The following day William and Jemima Adams took over their duties. On the Thursday the Trustees made an inventory in the Account Book of the property they owned in the two school rooms and in the House. In the boys' school-room there was a Master's desk and seat, two book cases and books, one cupboard and drawer, 2 double desks and stools, an ushers desk and seat, 2 single desks and seats, pegs and shelves and a stove; in the girls' school-room there was a table with drawer, a looking-glass, 2 old samplers in frames, 8 stools, and a worsted reel and stand. William Adams confirmed all this with his signature. The very randomness of this list gives us an impression of the classrooms for which they had just taken responsibility. The furnishings would seem to be very incomplete given the number of children in the school, but the two double desks probably meant two rows of double desks.

On the Friday four letters of recommendation for William Adams were copied into the Account Book. Three of these were dated 13 July 1809, over two months before his appointment. The first two were general references, one from John Morgan, Rector of Chelmsford, who described William as 'a very deserving Character, & fully qualified for the situation', and the other from William Tufnell of Langleys, near Chelmsford: 'I have known him all his life & believe him to be a Person of perfect good morals and disposition,

& am certain you will find him very competent to ye Instruction of children, in teaching English, Writing and Arithmetic.' Langleys is a large house set in its own park which overlooks the village of Great Waltham; it had been owned by the Tufnell family, who were London merchants, since 1710.

It is interesting to compare these two references and those provided for (or perhaps 'by') Thomas and Mary Bandfield only four years earlier. They all come from influential members of Essex society, but whereas Adams is obviously well known to his supporters there is little evidence that Thomas Barrett Lennard knew Thomas 'Bamfield'. Also, assuming that the references were copied verbatim into the Account Book, the two supporting Bandfield appear altogether less literate. Did the trustees now realise how little information they had had when they made their last appointment compared with what they now knew about Adams, even without the much greater detail which was provided in his additional letters of recommendation?

William was 42 years old when he moved to Romford, having been baptised in Great Waltham Parish Church on 20 May 1767. His parents were William and Susanna, and he had a younger brother, Oswald. Jemima Coote had been baptised at Shalford, Essex, on 8 April 1764, but was living in Great Waltham when she married William on 18 November 1788 in the church where he had been baptised, where soon afterwards he would become the clerk, and where in due course their three children would be baptised: another William on 20 October 1792, another Oswald on 8 October 1794, and another Susanna on 26 August 1798. Shortly before applying for the post in Romford he had relinquished that of parish clerk, however, as we learn from his third reference, written by the Rev'd G S Clarke DD, Vicar of Great Waltham.

> The Church Clerk of my parish, who has been twenty years in the place, twelve of which I have been Vicar, having expressed to me the commendable desire of making an opening in this parish for his eldest son grown up, by offering himself for the mastership of your Charity School, I have not only consented to accept his son in his stead, but now request leave to recommend the father, William Adams Senior, to you.

At the time this was written William Junior would have been three months short of his seventeenth birthday.

The fourth reference, written by J G Bramston of Chelmsford and dated 28 July 1809, informed the trustees that William had much more experience for the post in Romford than just that of a church clerk, which in any case was not a full time job. Mr Bramston had lived in Great Waltham for nine years, and this had given him the opportunity of forming an opinion of William's 'qualifications and general conduct':

> During the whole of that time Adams kept a day school of considerable credit; he also was the Church & Vestry Clerk of the parish but he was perhaps more particularly brought under my own personal observation by his acting as clerk to me as a magistrate in respect to such business as I did at home & by his having been employed to teach my children to write & cypher.

Samuel Whitbread had said that 'It would be easy to find schoolmasters among whom there would doubtless be a competition for appointments.' We do not know if there were other candidates competing for this post, but as the years passed, so the significance of 19 September 1809 grew: this was the day when the Trustees had indeed finally found an experienced and well respected teacher, their next Thomas Grove. Grove had served the school for forty years and three months; William and Jemima Adams and their son Oswald were destined to serve the school over a period of forty years and seven months.

One of those present at that meeting on 19 September 1809 to elect William and Jemima Adams was old Thomas Graves. He had been a trustee since October 1770 and this was to prove the last meeting he would attend. It is satisfying to believe that he met the new master and mistress that day, their handshake linking their two long periods of service.

1811: the church bells peal and the Charity School expands
William Adams was undoubtedly aware of the new ideas and teaching methods being promulgated by Dr Bell, but at this time the bells he was interested in were those in Romford church. They had been silent since 1795, the year before Nathaniel Alsop Bliss died in Colerne. It is unlikely that Charles Bathurst took the initiative to have them repaired, and even less likely to have been the assistant curate, Dr John Wiseman, dismissed after a dispute in 1810. He was later to act as assistant curate at Havering-atte-Bower where the Rev'd Henry Ward, vicar from 1784 to 1834, was non-

Romford Chapel looking south, with a glimpse of the Market Place behind it. This engraving was published in February 1809, the year of Thomas and Mary Bandfield's resignation and the appointment of William and Jemima Adams as Master and Mistress.

resident after 1816.[130] Professor Ged Martin's lively description of Wiseman gives a picture of both an individual and the arrangement for the care of souls in the Royal Liberty at this time:

> The vicar of Havering[-atte-Bower] was so badly paid that he didn't bother to live locally. Wiseman, the stand-in ecclesiastical odd-job man, must have been very poor indeed. John Wiseman worked until his death, aged 76 in 1835. To make ends meet, he also served as curate in Romford and at Navestock. With a large family to support, he rented a farm at Noak Hill as well. Wiseman was a typically outspoken Yorkshireman. 'He honoured not the rich on account of their riches, nor despised the poor on account of their poverty.' Splendid sentiments! Unfortunately the rich ran the Church of England, and his attitude probably explains his failure to net a well-paid job. Wiseman boasted that he could preach a sermon, plough an acre of land, and drink a bottle of wine with any man in England.[131]

The last entry in *The Romford Ringers' Book* in 1795 had been immaculately scripted, but no more so than the next entry fifteen years later. This announced that the peal of bells at St Edward the Confessor's Chapel, Romford, 'were put into Tune and compleat Repair Anno Domini 1811', and recorded that 'On Sunday Evening the 10th of February 1811 the first true Peal of 720 Changes . . . was Rung upon the six heavy Bells'. William Adams had arrived in the town on 8 November 1809, fifteen months before, and it seems certain that he was one of those who persuaded the churchwardens to carry out this restoration. The names of the six ringers were duly recorded, one from Great Waltham, two from Hornchurch, one from Barking, one from Warley, and finally William Adams from Romford. This entry, in beautiful calligraphy, is signed 'W. Adams Junr Script' either side of a plume. The inclusion of the 'Junr' suggests that this was the work of the schoolmaster's son, now the Parish Clerk in his stead at Great Waltham, because William the schoolmaster's father had been buried in Great Waltham Parish Church in October 1806. It would have been the schoolmaster who taught his son to write such beautiful script, however, so this entry undoubtedly reveals the skills of both father and son.

Eight days later, on Monday 18th, 'The Society of Cumberland Youths' rung 'at the reopening of the Bells, a true and compleat Peal of 5248 changes of Oxford Treble Bob, in 3 hours 36 minutes, being the full extent in 13 Courses, and the most of the method ever rung in this Steeple.' All eight bells were rung, and although William Adams did not ring on this occasion it was most probably he who made the entry, replete with a drawing of a swan, in the Ringers book.

His contribution as Master must have been as impressive as his contribution as campanologist, because five weeks later, on 26 March, it was 'ordered that at the next general Meeting of the Trustees the number of Boys be increased to forty five and that the Master's Salary be advanced from that time to Thirty one pounds Ten Shillings per annum' {£2,300}. This was a 28% increase in William's salary.

On the 5 November that year, 1811:

> At a meeting of the parishioners held in the vestry . . . it was unanimously agreed upon, and entered in the Parish Book, that the following Ringing days should be allowed and paid for by the present and future Church Wardens. - Viz: 29th May Restoration

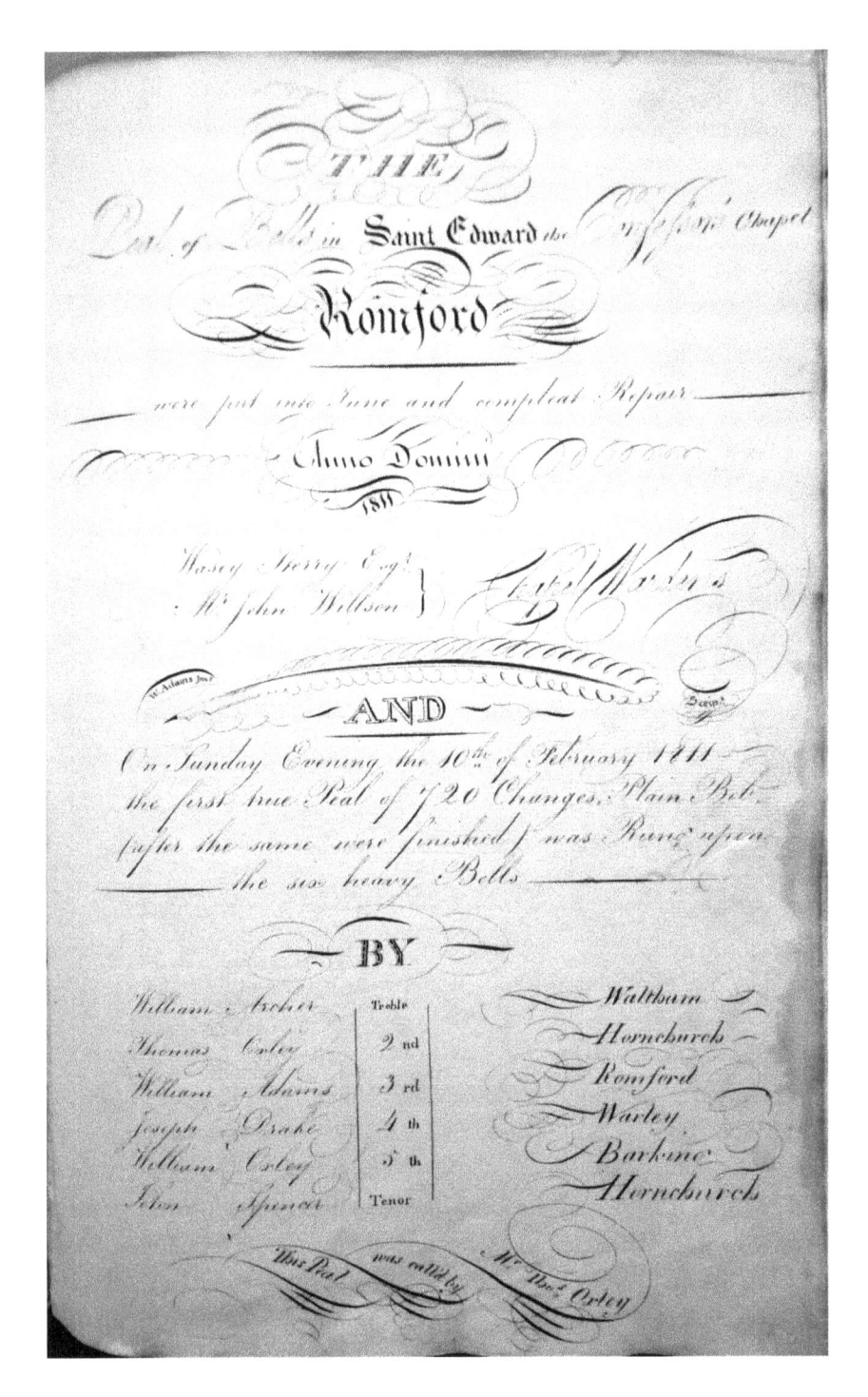

'W. Adams Junr Script': the entry in *The Romford Ringers' Book* recording the peal rung on 10 February 1811

of King Charles; 4th June being his present Majesty's birthday; August The Charity Sermon; 22nd September Coronation; 25th October Accession to the Throne; 5th November Gunpowder Treason; 25th December being Xmas Day.

It is interesting that the celebration of the school charity sermons is the only one of these seven occasions unconnected with heavenly or earthly kingship, and that although we know from a record of the payments made to the ringers on this occasion that this agreement was honoured, there is no further mention in *The Romford Ringers' Book* of ringing on any of these seven annual occasions.

On 28 May 1813 William took part in a peal using six of the bells in the tower of Romford 'which [peal] contains the greatest number of Bobs & Singles within the limits of a true six Bell Peal that ever was rung in this or any other Tower'. Three days later, on the 31st May 1813, an entry in the *Ringers' Book* records:

> We the undersigned agree to meet at the Chapel of St Edward on every Monday and Wednesday evening at 7 o'clock, for the purpose of practising the art of Ringing; and for every neglect to forfeit 3d; such forfeit to be paid into the hands of the Master, Joseph Wiggins, the next time such member attends. Witness our hands, 31st May 1813, . . .

This is followed by 24 signatures, not written in alphabetical order but headed by that of William Adams, suggesting his pre-eminence.

1811: Centenary thoughts

In February 1811, fourteen months after William and Jemima Adams had moved into the Market Place, the Regency Act was passed. This empowered George, Prince of Wales, to act in place of his father who had been declared insane. The war continued and the economic crisis worsened. Austria would go bankrupt in March and in May the government in Britain would be forced to adopt paper money as currency. If in the excitement and anxieties of those febrile times there was any celebration to mark the hundredth birthday of the Romford Charity School in January, it went unrecorded. We have no idea how many children had passed through the school in this time, but if there were forty boys in the school and each stayed on average for four years we have a total of a thousand, with half as many girls. The greatest achievement of the school was that it had survived, whereas those in Dagenham and South Ockendon, to name but two, had not. But survived to achieve what? This education of the poor had been a messy business! The children had been erratic in their attendance, they had sometimes stopped coming at all in the winter, they had been unreliable in their attendance at church on Sunday, their parents had taken them away from school if there had been an opportunity to send them to work .... and yet somehow they had managed to acquire some learning. The entries in the *Accounts* giving the reasons why scholars had left early suggest the girls were in demand as servants, implying that they were respectful and disciplined and could sew well and read and write a little, and the few signatures which exist on apprenticeship papers indicate the boys could write a fair hand.

We now have a longer perspective and more reliable evidence than contemporaries had to evaluate the achievement of the 18th century charity schools. They had many shortcomings and they accommodated very small numbers, but their impact was not inconsiderable. To take one example, writing of Wellington's campaigns it has been said:

> Thanks to increasing levels of literacy, we have accounts not only of well-educated officers but also of a number of ordinary soldiers ... One only has to compare the paucity of voices from the ranks of Marlborough's wars a century earlier to marvel at the riches available to the student of Wellington's campaigns.[132]

Perhaps some of those accounts were penned laboriously in a camp or occupied town in Portugal, Spain or France and sent to Romford in a letter home. We have just the smallest glimpse of the subsequent lives of a very few of the estimated thousand boys who had by now been educated at the school, but as a garrison town in a time of war it is extremely unlikely that some of them were not recruited and sent abroad.

The charity schools could also claim another great achievement: by contributing to the gradual increase in literacy and numeracy they helped prepare public opinion for the next great development in popular education, the National Schools.

Edward Ind, from a now missing portrait

Chapter 16

The National Society, expansion and reform

1811 - 1817

1811: National Society for Promoting the Education of the Poor in the Principles of the Established Church in England and Wales
We now return to Dr Andrew Bell and Joseph Lancaster, who for the past dozen years had been promoting their rival yet essentially similar 'Madras' and 'monitorial' systems of education. Each of these movements was now to receive impetus from the formation of a co-ordinating committee, but before examining this development we must note the rising toleration which allowed Joseph Lancaster and his followers the platform they now enjoyed.

Throughout the eighteenth century the dominance of the Church of England had been underpinned by the various Test and Corporation Acts which had been passed between 1661 and 1678. These required members of town corporations and holders of civil or military offices to subscribe to a declaration against transubstantiation and, within three months of their appointment or election, to receive the sacrament according to the rites of the Church of England. Between 1689 and 1702 these requirements were extended to beneficed clergy, members of the universities, lawyers, schoolteachers and preachers. These Acts excluded Roman Catholics, Protestant Dissenters and followers of the Jewish faith from holding public office, and the SPCK had therefore been unopposed in its promotion of Church of England charity schools.

However, this period of muzzled sectarian opposition and apparent unity was to be comparatively short lived. The agricultural and industrial revolutions over the following century led to a movement of population away from the country parishes to the expanding industrial towns and cities. Perhaps the number of hours these migrants spent in the factory was the same as those they had spent in the fields, perhaps the rural slum they had left may have been no better than the urban slum they now occupied, but the disruption to their spiritual lives had been profound. The working day, previously determined by the rising and the setting sun, was now regulated by a factory hooter, and the diversity and flexible disciplines of the agricultural seasons had now been replaced by the iron discipline of the machine, unvarying throughout the day, week, month or the change from spring to summer or autumn to winter. Because the creation of each new Church of England parish required a separate Act of Parliament, the established church could not readily respond to the needs of these people. Instead, it was the more flexible ministries of the Methodists and the dissenting groups which moved into this spiritual vacuum, creating a more complex but tolerant theology as the 18th century ran its course.

By 1800 the spirit of the age was very different from that of 1700. The Corporation and Test Acts remained on the Statute Book but were seldom enforced, and the regular passage of Acts of Indemnity ensured non-conformists were allowed to hold public office. The Methodists who assembled at Rainham Hall in 1767 had been assaulted and had had to flee for their lives, but forty years had seen an enormous growth in toleration for their beliefs and in support for other non-conformist churches. In this climate, the new schools promoted by Dr Bell and his Church of England followers would be vociferously opposed by Joseph Lancaster and the nonconformists in their rivalry to capture the souls of the young poor.

In an article published in the *Edinburgh Review* in 1805 Mrs Sarah Trimmer, the religious pamphleteer and great supporter of Bell, warned with great prescience that Lancaster's example might increase the growth of nonconformity in England. She repeatedly tried to persuade Bell to come to London to organise a campaign against Lancaster and his methods, and in 1807 he finally agreed to do so. He stayed a month, during which time he set up a charity school in Whitechapel with the assistance of two of those who had been involved in running the Swanage Sunday school,[133] but more importantly he realised that he could not both serve his parishioners in Dorset and promote his educational reforms nationally. In May 1807 he obtained two years leave of absence from his Bishop.

In 1808, no doubt again encouraged by Sarah Trimmer, Bell published a pamphlet entitled 'Sketch of a National Institution' in which he urged the Church of England to use his Madras teaching methods throughout the country. This provoked further acrimonious division between the Anglicans and the non-conformists, with speeches, sermons, magazine articles and pamphlets appearing in support of one side or the other. It also stimulated the non-conformists to organise themselves, and that same year the 'Society for Promoting the Lancasterian System for the Education of the Poor' was founded by the Quakers Joseph Fox and William Allen and the MP Samuel Whitbread, whose Parochial Schools Bill had been defeated the previous year. It was supported by William Wilberforce and several other notable evangelical and non-conformist Christians.

In 1809, at the end of his two year leave of absence, Bell resigned his Swanage living to dedicate himself full time to educational reform. On 16 October 1811 his 1808 pamphlet found its response with the establishment of the 'National Society for Promoting the Education of the Poor in the Principles of the Established Church in England and Wales', with Bell himself as its Superintendant. The principal objective of this society was that

> the National Religion should be made the foundation of National Education, and should be the first and chief thing taught to the poor, according to the excellent Liturgy and Catechism provided by our Church.

This statement could have been taken from an SPCK publication a century earlier. The ambition of the Society was to establish a National school in every English and Welsh parish, to be sited as close to the parish church as possible and named after the same patron.[134]

The foundation of the National Society at this time was a response both to the concerns expressed by many members of the Church of England about the growing influence of Lancaster and the non-conformist schools and to the realisation that as the Madras system spread across the country Bell could no longer provide the necessary support and advice on his own. The new society had the full support of the Establishment with the Archbishop of Canterbury as its president and a committee which included the Archbishop of York, the Lord High Chancellor and the Speaker of the House of Commons. Encouraged and supported by this National Committee and by such poetic luminaries as William Wordsworth, Samuel Taylor Coleridge and Robert Southey, the Madras system expanded rapidly.

The revolution Dr Bell had begun now rolled inexorably forward. In 1812, within months of its foundation, the National Society boasted 52 schools with 8,620 pupils; in 1813 this number increased more than fourfold to 230 schools with 40,484 pupils. According to one of his assistants, by 1813 Dr Bell's chief occupation was acting as the general inspector of all these schools, which would have been an impossible task even had there been railways at that time.

The very public schism between the two education societies now widened, exacerbated by the characters of the two leading protagonists. Bell was a man of enormous enterprise, energy and talent, but dogmatic, intransigent and irascible. His tendency to shout people down in argument did not make him an ideal committee member and there were moves to exclude him from the National Committee. He came to believe that he had been appointed by Providence to bring the gift of the Madras system to the nation, but it seems Providence had failed to endow him with the tact and patience needed to give positive encouragement and support to the schools he inspected. He too quickly condemned them for their weaknesses and for the smallest departures from the system he advocated. The poet Robert Southey, who was not only his biographer but a personal friend, wrote that 'his manner of condemning trifling inaccuracies in those schools which he visited in his travels was often unnecessarily harsh and violent; and, while the slightest omission called forth unlimited blame, it required a very high state of perfection to obtain his commendations'. This judgement was highly diplomatic compared with that of Meiklejohn:

> His character is faithfully mirrored in the style of his writings - cumbrous, clumsy, chaotic, dull even to heaviness, full of involutions, repetitions, misplaced limitations - it is a severe penance to be obliged to read a page.[135]

Sadly, Bell's marriage did not last: the wife he married at the age of 47 on his return from India could not live with his difficult personality.

12 October 1813: a further expansion of the Romford school
If the expansionist enthusiasm and zeal emanating from the National Society twenty miles down the toll road to London influenced the trustees of the Charity School at Romford to take in more pupils, its effect was not sufficiently strong for them to adopt the Madras system. At a meeting on 12 October 1813 they 'resolved to enlarge the present school Room according to a plan submitted this day by Mr Roger Talbot . . . [and] to increase the number of Boys to 60 and the Girls to 30, and that the Master's Salary be increased to £50 {£3,750} per annum and the Mistress's salary to £30 {£2,250} per annum from this time.' No time was wasted, for on 23

November it was noted that 15 boys and 5 girls had been admitted 'to augment the number upon the establishment Viz: from 45 to 60 Boys and from 25 to 30 girls.' It is clear from the speed with which this work was accomplished that it had been planned in advance, and the abrupt entry in the minutes only records the final approval. Roger Talbot was not a trustee, although a William Talbot, possibly a relative, had been elected in May 1805.

This work cost £112 9s 11d {£8,500}, although unfortunately we do not know in what ways the original building was altered. Where did this money come from? Since the third volume of accounts had commenced in June 1803 with a balance of £4 3s 6½d the accounts had been reconciled at least once a year and are therefore much easier to follow. Between November 1803 and October 1808 the annual balance had averaged £13 12s 10d, fluctuating between -£15 17s 7¼d and £33 0s 2¾d; in the four years which followed it was never in deficit and averaged £122 15s 2d. In the course of these four years the Charity benefited from four legacies: in October 1808 £20 from John Tyler and £20 from Henry Bevan; in June 1811 £105 9s 3d, being the principal and accumulated interest on the bequest of John Redman which had finally been received following his death in 1798; and in January 1812 £89 6s 8d was received from a Mrs Richardson. In 1813 the regular sources of income had raised the unprecedented sum of £251 15s 10½ {£19,000}, including £91 11s 10 ½d from the charity sermons, £21 9s 6d from town collections and £33 1s 6d in donations and subscriptions. Had there been a drive with attendant publicity to raise money for an expansion of the school? For comparison, fourteen years later the income would amount to only £200 4s 3d {£17,500}. This additional money allowed the trustees to invest in another £200 of consols at a cost of £127 15s in September 1811, £150 Navy 5 per cents at a cost of £112 9s 11d in February 1814 and, the same month, to pay Roger Talbot's bill of £112 9s 11d.

For a hundred years the number of boys had varied between 40 and 50 and the number of girls had remained unchanged at 20, but now both schools abruptly increased by 50%, and in less than four years the Master's salary had doubled and that of the Mistress had risen by nearly 50%. We know that there were probably other children being educated in the school, the 6 boarders and 14 day scholars whom the Adams were permitted to take in addition to the charity children, but these additional children were on the foundation, a fact emphasised in March 1814 when it was ordered that they should be provided with clothing 'as soon as convenient'.

If they were not about to adopt the Madras system, there was no obvious reason why the trustees should decide to expand the school at this time, so why did they do so? First, there must have been a demand for the additional places, indicating once again the popularity of the school. Then there was the character of William Adams. In four years he and Jemima must have proved themselves to be competent teachers who could handle the additional children. He was clearly ambitious for himself and his family, hence his move to Romford leaving his seventeen year old son William to take over his previous post. His second son Oswald had turned nineteen four days before the decision to so dramatically increase the numbers, and it is possible that he was helping his parents in their school rooms at this time. Indeed, he may have been been helping them from when the initial expansion had taken place two and a half years earlier, and that it was the success of this arrangement which persuaded the Trustees to authorise the second expansion. (We know nothing of Oswald's life before 1817 except that for a period before or after this date he was writing master at Felsted Grammar School.) Until now the school had been run by a master and mistress, but the ideas and teaching methods being promulgated by the National Society were encouraging ideas of larger schools with the teachers being supported by monitors.

Was the prime mover behind the expansion William Adams himself? Did he put forward the idea and offer the services of his son in exchange for the increases in salary? If he did so, he would have needed the support of Edward Ind, whose successful career as a brewer proves him to have been an excellent man of business. Ind would not have wanted to lose the services of William and Jemima, and even if he was not particularly knowledgeable about the National Society and its ideas he would have understood William's financial position and his arguments for expanding the school. It seems probable, therefore, that the unlikely, sudden and dramatic expansion of the school at the height of a major war happened for the reasons which usually provoke such change: new ideas, the circumstances at the time, and the personalities involved.

November 1814: Mr Jacobs' contested legacy
The expansion of the school in Romford would be followed within a decade by the expansion of the school at Havering-atte-Bower. We have noted how in 1724 Ann, Lady Tipping of Pyrgo Park, had built a free school on Havering Green for 20 poor children, and that when she died four years later

she had endowed it with an annuity of £10 to be paid by Pyrgo Park. In 1771 this school was still functioning and the schoolmaster was the curate, but by 1808 it had closed and the building was in ruins. The annuity was still being paid, however, and in 1818 sufficient funds had been accumulated to pull down the old buildings and construct a new school in North Road.[136] It is possible that over the proceeding thirty or forty years parents in the village might have exercised their right to send their children to the school in Romford for the first time since 1724, but by the 1820's their own school was flourishing once again. In 1833 there were 21 boys and 16 girls on the books and Michael Field of Pyrgo Park clothed the 20 charity children and provided their books. The population of the village was only 188 in 1801, rising over the next forty years to about 430, a figure which remained fairly constant for the next eighty years. With these numbers the school would probably have been able to cater for the needs of the village until the 1870's, so it is unlikely many of the children would have travelled to the Charity School in Romford.

Hornchurch also had its own endowed school, but this was of a very different order. In 1731 Alice Aylett of Hornchurch had died and left land in trust to pay £10 a year for a schoolmaster to teach ten poor boys. The first schoolmaster had not been appointed by the parish until 1746, when his classroom was the church vestry.[137] We do not know the subsequent history of this school, but we can be sure it had very few pupils and it certainly did not have its own, permanent accommodation. This explains why there are not infrequent references to children from Hornchurch attending the Romford school, but none to children from Havering-atte-Bower. However, this school in Hornchurch now enters our story.

On 7 November 1814 the accounts of the Charity School at Romford recorded a payment of £186 15s 0d received as a legacy from William Jacobs, 'late of Havering', who had bequeathed 'to the Trustees or Guardians of the Charity School of Hornchurch aforesaid the sum of Two Hundred pounds to be by them applied towards the purposes of that Charity or establishment'. This payment was immediately disputed by the Minister of Hornchurch, William Blair, and his two churchwardens who claimed that the legacy was not intended for the 'Hornchurch, Romford and Havering Charity School', but for Mrs Aylett's charity school in Hornchurch. On 23 December fourteen trustees met at the School in Romford to discuss the matter, and they agreed to retain the money until they had obtained Counsel's opinion. It is significant that the Rev'd William Blair, one of the three authors of this dispute and an ex-officio trustee by virtue of his being Vicar of Hornchurch, was absent. Indeed, as we have noted, he never attended a single trustee meeting during his ten years in the parish.

We can assume they had obtained this advice by 23 February 1815 when ten of them reconvened and agreed to return the money to the executor of Mr Jacobs' will, a Mr Hutchins, with notice that they would prosecute their claim. Their grounds were that there was not a charity school established at Hornchurch entitled to such a legacy and that the poor of the parish of Hornchurch were educated at the school in Romford which was 'known and identified as an Established School for the Education of the poor of the parish of Hornchurch jointly with the poor of the parishes of Romford & Havering'. The money was returned on 27 March 1815 and there, for the next few years, the matter rested. We may wonder why these good men of Hornchurch, who were represented on the Trustees of the Romford School, wished to divert this money to such a small and underfunded establishment which offered so much less to the poor children of Hornchurch. As we shall see, they had their reasons.

October 1817: the Rev'd William Everett and the post-war reform of the Charity School

1768 had been the last year when the Trustees had met on four occasions; from 1769 to 1808 the rule was twice, in the Spring and Autumn, and the four years when they met three times were balanced by those when they met only once. At several meetings there had been no business apart from noting the names of the children discharged and those admitted and balancing the number. No reason is now given for why children leave the school, and although it would be rash to assume that all those discharged were 'over age', it had been some years since truancy had been noted. It is perhaps not surprising, therefore, that apart from at special meetings attendance by trustees was falling. In November 1813 it was decided to request the Rev'd Mr Roach (presumably a 'stand-in' curate at St Edward's) 'that morning Service be performed twice every week Viz: Wednesdays and Fridays as was formerly the case'. This is one of the few entries at this time which refers to the religious life of the school, and it also provides another example of how former standards had lapsed.

At the end of October 1814 the papers had carried the announcement of the presentation of the Rev'd William Everett, BD 'to the Curacy of Rumford'. He was 40, and until then had been a Fellow of New College.

This had been the background of all the clergymen in the Liberty since the foundation of the school with the exception of James Hotchkis, so it is important to understand that this institution was then very different from what it is today. A succinct portrait of New College at this time can be found on its website:

> Many Fellows lingered after taking their degrees, until appointed to lucrative college parishes at which point they resigned and could get married.
> While not entirely a sybaritic, slothful backwater, New College was prevented by its medieval statutes from adapting to rising demand for university education. Having been the largest college by far in 1379, by 1800 it was one of the smallest, with at most 20 of the 70 fellows being undergraduates - all exclusively Wykehamist and dominated by 'Founder's Kin', real or pretended.[138]

'Slothful' and 'sybaritic' would seem to be not inappropriate adjectives to describe the absentee Rev'ds Bliss and Bathhurst, but they hardly apply to their successor, William Everett. Now, for the first time since the Rev'd John Hopkins moved to Upminster in 1770, Romford had a clergyman committed to both the parish and its Charity School. He attended his first Trustee meeting on 28 March 1815, in time to contribute to the ongoing discussions regarding Mr Jacobs' legacy and the post-war reform of the Charity School.

It had, of course, been a tumultuous period in the history of the country and the history of Europe, and it is therefore not surprising that the trustees had failed to give the school the attention it had once enjoyed. In July 1808 the war had brought another royal visitor to Romford when 'The grand old Duke of York', George III's son Frederick, came to review the 18th Dragoons and to enjoy 'a sumptuous dinner' provided by the officers. The following September the barracks had been occupied by those members of the 10th Dragoons who had survived the disaster of Corunna, where they had had to slaughter their horses before boarding the transport ships which had been sent to rescue them. Then, finally, on 18 June 1815, the Napoleonic saga had ended at Waterloo. The celebrations in Romford included the naming of a pub in the Market Place 'Blucher's Head', although a century later - a year into the First World War - it was belatedly but patriotically renamed the 'Duke of Wellington'.

Professor Martin has observed that although the battle of Waterloo is commonly said to have been won on the playing fields of Eton, 'the cavalry charge that broke the French at Waterloo was rehearsed alongside Romford's Straight Road'.[139] He is referring to Romford Common, where the Duke of York had reviewed the 18th Dragoons in 1808. For centuries this had been a large open space on the Romford side of where Straight Road now divides the town from Harold Hill, but in 1814 it had been divided into fields under the Romford Enclosure legislation. Enclosure was one of the earliest of those major changes which would progressively make nineteenth century Romford unrecognisable to the ghosts of its eighteenth century inhabitants.

With the fighting finished and the continental blockade and threat of invasion lifted, the economic and social life of the country could find a new equilibrium. On 27 October 1817 the Trustees finally took action to reform the administration of the school, the first such comprehensive review since that of 12 August 1762, fifty-five years earlier. They agreed seven orders, which once again give a glimpse we would otherwise not have of how the school then functioned and how it had changed.

1. Ordered that the Boys & Girls attend divine service regularly on the Sunday afternoon unless leave of absence be given by the master. [At the meeting on 6 October 1759 it had been ordered that the children were to be at the School house on Sundays at 9 o'clock in the morning and not to be kept away without leave in writing from the Treasurer. Sunday afternoon attendance seems less austere and rather easier for those travelling from distant parts of the parish, and responsibility for granting absence has now been delegated.]

2. Trustees and Managers of the Savings Bank be permitted to use the Private Room at the Charity house with the consent of the Master. [The significance of this is explained below.]

   Holidays in future will be 7 days at Christmas, 7 days at Easter, 2 days at Whitsontide, and 14 days in August or September at the discretion of the Master. [Permitted holiday times have never been confirmed in this way before, and pupils today would be appalled by their brevity. Responsibility has again been delegated to the Master.]

3. A writing desk to be purchased for the use of the Girls school. [The girls school had not had a writing desk before. In 1762 Mr Grove's contract included a provision to teach the girls to write for an hour twice a week, and in 1794 Mrs Cloke was appointed to teach the girls to read, knit and sew, but not to write. This provision suggests confirmation of an important change in the girls' curriculum.]

4. An account to be kept of those who absent themselves from school, and that such account be laid before the trustees at their half yearly meetings. [This is yet another attempt to improve attendance, with the Master and Mistress now being tasked with preparing figures for the Trustees.]

5. In future girls to be supplied with copy books, and boys with Cyphering Books. [This confirms that writing is to become a more important part of the girls' curriculum and they will now have appropriate books to work in, and that the boys will now have appropriate books for their arithmetic. William Adams had undoubtedly requested these, but we do not know whether it was he or Jemima who was now teaching the girls to write.]

6. A public examination of the Charity children to take place twice every year, in the week preceding each half yearly meeting, and that the treasurer and six or more trustees be required to attend in rotation. [For the first time the Trustees are assuming responsibility for monitoring the improvement in the standards of the scholars' work. The Trustees are making a commitment to involve themselves in this aspect of the school, but not to meet any more frequently.]

It was now six years since the National Society had been inaugurated, and the momentum it had generated continued to sweep the Madras system across the country. By 1816 there were 756 schools, and the ideas were soon to cross the seas to the continent and then to North America. The Charity School of Hornchurch Romford & Havering had been affected only marginally by the movement, but at a meeting on 19 November 1818 it was proposed that the school should be enlarged and conducted 'upon the principles of the National Institution'. The motion was discussed, but it was decided by a majority of the fifteen Trustees present that 'no alteration should take place in the system adopted at [the school's] origin & continued to the present time with credit, advantage & usefulness'. It was a proud vote for independence and the status quo, but a seed had been sown which further national changes would germinate with dramatic results fifteen years later. Over these intervening years the school would have other challenges to face.

October 1817: The Romford Trustee Savings' Bank
The reference to the Savings' Bank in the minutes of the meeting of 27 October needs to be explained because this institution will play an important part in the history of the school. The savings bank movement began in Scotland in May 1810 when the Rev'd Henry Duncan of Ruthwell,

Dumfriesshire, opened a bank to encourage his poor parishioners to save against ill health, unemployment, old age and the other vicissitudes of life. The idea spread, and by 1817 there were over eighty such banks across Scotland, England and Wales. They differed from commercial banks in that they were charitable, not-for-profit organisations; like the charity school movement a century before, they were run by the voluntary efforts of local worthies to encourage 'habits of industry, economy and sobriety among the poor and labouring population'.[140]

There was a difference in the regulations north and south of the border, however. In Scotland these banks could earn interest for their depositors by placing their funds with a commercial bank, but this was not possible elsewhere until the passing of Rose's Act in 1817 allowed English and Welsh savings banks to deposit their funds in an interest bearing account managed by the Commissioners for the Reduction of the National Debt at the Bank of England. This galvanised the movement, and within a year over 465 banks had opened across the country, including in Romford. The essence of the movement required costs to be minimal, and at this time these banks were accommodated in existing buildings such as inns, churches, schools, or in the dwelling house of the actuary. In Romford the schoolmaster's house in the Market Place, at the geographic and commercial centre of the town, was the obvious place. The extent of William Adam's involvement in the bank, if any, is unclear, but from the beginning his son Oswald was the actuary. We do not know who the initial trustees of the bank were, but the names reported in the press fifteen years later were the leading men in the Liberty at that time and corresponded closely with the trustees of the school, and it is reasonable to assume this was so from the start. When the Trustees of the Charity School agreed to the 'Trustees and Managers of the Savings Bank be[ing] permitted to use the Private Room at the Charity house with the consent of the Master' several of them were therefore donning an old hat to approve their own use of the school when wearing a new hat. All was now in place and the bank opened that month. When it held its first anniversary meeting on 6 October 1818 it had attracted 511 depositors from whom it had received £9,253 9s 8½d {£740,000}.

Chapter 17

A Brougham to sweep old charities clean

1818 - 1821

23 June 1819: Henry Brougham and the Charitable Foundations Bill
Individual politicians, through their pronouncements and actions, become off-stage players in the historical dramas of many individuals and institutions. The same can be true of lawyers. In the drama of the Charity School at Romford the politician Henry Brougham (pronounced 'Broom') was to play such an off-stage role, although as a lawyer he was to have a very brief walk on part.

Born on 19 November 1778, Brougham was brought up and educated in Edinburgh, where he then studied law. In 1802 he was one of the three founders of the *Edinburgh Review*, which was to become the most influential magazine of its time. In 1808 he was called to the English bar, and in 1810 he entered parliament as the Whig MP for the 'rotten borough' of Camelford in Cornwall. In 1812 the 'owner' of this constituency, the Duke of Bedford, sold it for £32,000 {£2,370,000}, and Brougham had to find a new seat as his radical politics were unacceptable to the new owner, the Earl of Darlington. He stood for Liverpool and was heavily defeated, but in 1815 he was re-elected as the Member for another 'rotten borough', Winchelsea. In 1816, aged 37, back in parliament and with a very successful career behind him, he turned his attention to education. That year the 'Parliamentary Committee on the Education of the Lower Orders' was set up with Brougham as Chairman, its original brief being to inquire into the education of the poor in the metropolis, to which was later added the utilitarian injunction 'and into the way in which the children of paupers found in the streets might be best disposed of'. However, this last clause was soon dropped and the enquiry extended to cover the whole of England and Wales and, later, Scotland. The work of this committee gives us a unique insight into the state of education at this time and the attitude of Parliament to public education.

The committee did not sit in 1817. When Brougham applied for its renewal on 5 March 1818 he told Parliament that its members were coming to the conclusion that assistance should be given by the public towards the provision of schools and accommodation for teachers where these were needed, but that schools should not receive a regular income from public money. This would be unnecessary and wasteful, as he illustrated by comparing the Irish Charter schools with the Hibernian school society in London: the government provided £40,000 to supplement the £20,000 raised from private giving to educate just 2,500 children in the 33 Irish charter schools, whereas the Hibernian Society in London educated 27,000 children in 340 schools with an income of between £5,000 and £6,000 raised by 'several praise-worthy individuals'.

He then explained how the education system the committee proposed could be funded at little public expense.

> There existed throughout the country large funds which had been bequeathed by individuals for all purposes of charity - and particularly for the education of the poor. Those funds had, in many cases, been grossly misapplied . . . schools richly endowed in many parts of the country, had fallen into entire disuse.[141]

He proposed that the second 'Parliamentary Committee on the Education of the Lower Orders', which he was now recommending be convened, should appoint commissioners to visit all parts of the country (to save the cost of bringing witnesses to London) to enquire into every charitable bequest for the education of the poor. He believed (on what evidence, if any, he did not say) that the annual income of these amounted to between £200,000 and £300,000, adding that money had also been bequeathed for various other purposes and the House ought to inquire more generally into the misapplication of all such charitable funds.

There had long been national concern over the misuse - sometimes deliberate and criminal - of legacies, endowments, and other 'charitable benefaction' given for all sorts of purposes, but frequently for education. Only rarely had action in court to correct such abuses been successful. Evidence of one such is found in the SPCK *Annual Account* for 1712, which records a new school at Low Leighton in Essex:

> A school for 14 boys, 7 of Leyton and 7 of Waltham-Stow. Founded on a charitable Benefaction given by Will some Years ago, and lately rescued, and settled by Law. Since which Time, 6 of the Boys are cloathed at the Charge of a Private Gentleman.

That same year, on 17 April, the Society received a letter from Sam Sandford of Presteign, Radnorshire, touching on the same theme. The abstract of his letter notes:

> That the abused Charitys in his neighbourhood remain yet unrecover'd, tho the violaters are to be call'd to an Acct. at ye next assizes. That he is very much pleased to find there is a Bill depending in the House of Commons for the better recovery of Charitys misapply'd, and wishes it might extend so far as to convert some of ye Grammar Schools into Charity Schools.

Samuel Sandford's optimism had been unfounded. Only now, a century later, was a proposal being made for a commission to examine the workings of all the nation's educational charities and, where necessary, to recover and redirect any funds which were being misapplied.

The commission to inquire into the abuses in educational charities was duly appointed, and then on 21 May the following year Lord Castlereagh, then Leader of the House of Commons, was given leave to bring in a Bill to extend the powers of this act to cover all Charitable Foundations. Henry Brougham seconded the motion, which he said both enlarged the powers of the commissioners and extended the objects of the commission, 'both which objects had been originally well secured in his bill of last session, though afterwards in a great measure given up'. This Bill would now achieve what he had originally proposed.

On 23 June 1819, in the course of the debate on Lord Castlereagh's bill, Brougham explained how the proposed commission would work. There were to be five boards, each consisting of two stipendiary commissioners. The boards would be empowered to call for papers and records, and there was to be no limit to the fine which might be imposed on those who resisted. To the objections that the commission would be very expensive and would have to sit for a great length of time he replied that the expense would be justified and would not be so great because once established the commission could be self-funding from the money saved from the abuses it uncovered. He said that there were about 40,000 charities of all kinds in the kingdom, and to illustrate the potential revenue some of these might yield he cited 'an estate to the value of £4,000 {£325,000} a year [which] would, through the means of [the commission's] investigation, be ultimately recovered for a charitable foundation'. To illustrate the corruption the commission was attacking he then launched a virulent attack on

> the almost universal abuse of free grammar schools, which the masters generally regarded as perfect sinecures; for whether from the decay of the places at which they were established, or the smaller importance now attached to the learned languages (the masters generally conceiving themselves bound to teach nothing else), good houses and gardens and glebe land and often ample salaries, were enjoyed by masters who taught no free scholars, but kept private boarding schools for their own profit.

Brougham was a man with a mission.

Robert Peel, the Tory MP for Oxford and future Prime Minister, then rose to attack both the bill and Brougham. He objected to the way the committee had enquired into the universities and the public schools; he believed they had exceeded their brief, and he accused Brougham of behaving unconstitutionally both in his conduct of the committee he chaired and in aspects of his enquiries. It was a long, vicious and personal attack, which elicited an equally long and scathing response from Henry Brougham, caught unprepared for this attempted assassination of his conduct and character. Peel was, of course, a political opponent, but there were no doubt many Whigs who were not unhappy to see Brougham discomforted. His contributions to the *Edinburgh Review* had shown him to be very gifted and had brought him fame when still a young man, a combination which alone was sufficient to alienate his political friends as well as his political enemies. But there was also his ebullient self-confidence and his pretentions. This was the Edinburgh man who had 'devised for himself a mighty English pedigree so that he sat under one of the largest family trees in Christendom, but, as someone cruelly said, in the rapidity of its growth it resembled the Indian mango tree'.[142]

Following this very lengthy exchange Lord Castlereagh, hinting that the mission sometimes got the better of the man, said that on this occasion Mr Brougham 'had made a very reasonable statement . . . [and] after a more deliberate consideration, he had not imputed to charities generally corruption, or to government a disposition to skreen abuse', accusations which he had made previously. The inquiry might be expected to continue for nine or ten years, he said, but the result would be a confidence that charities were properly managed. (In nine or ten years time 'Nine or ten years' would prove to have been far too optimistic an estimate.)

Supporting the bill, William Wilberforce said that '[when] he first brought in his bill for the registration of charities, he received letters from all parts of the country, containing proofs of the existence of such abuses . . .' and added his own example of the large sums which might be recovered: ' . . . A friend of his, by taking a hint from a grave-stone in a country churchyard, had been led to prosecute his inquiries till he had recovered £16,000 or £18,000 {£1,375,000} per annum, which were now applied to their original purposes.'

Brougham then proposed the striking out of a clause which exempted colleges, free schools, and certain other foundations from the operation of the bill, but this amendment was defeated. He had now achieved most of what he originally wanted, a commission empowered to examine (almost) all the charities in the country.

1820: Brougham's Education of the Poor Bill

Twelve years after Whitbread's Parochial Schools Bill had failed there was another attempt to introduce a national system of popular education. With his Charity Commissioners now having commenced their work, on 28 June 1820 Henry Brougham introduced his Education of the Poor Bill in the House of Commons. Although this was also to fail, it is of interest because of the data on the current state of education Brougham gave in his opening speech and because of his ideas on how a national system might be financed and administered.

Prior to his charity commissioners commencing their work his Education Committee had sent a questionnaire to the incumbent of every parish in England and Wales, a total of about 11,400, from whom he had received 11,200 replies. These indicated that the average number of children in each parish was about 85, and that across the country some 704,000 children were then receiving some form of instruction. However, 100,000 of these received only 'a very small modicum' of education at Sunday schools, 53,000 were educated in Dame Schools, and 50,000 at home by private tuition. This left about 501,000 children who were educated at unendowed schools and 165,432 (a remarkably precise figure) at endowed schools, together giving an average of about 1 in 15 children. This average concealed extreme regional variations, however. In the eastern counties, including Essex, the proportion was 1 in 21, and 'in the six midland counties . . . where lace-making was the ordinary occupation, and the great enemy both to education and morals, the average was one-twenty-fourth'. (Such opinions and pomposities were characteristic of both his address and his character and help explain why so many people found him such an easy man to dislike.) Interestingly, he said that the average across England for the number of poor receiving an education was one in twelve, higher than the one in fifteen overall average and perhaps reflecting the work of the charity schools over the previous century.

Regarding the distribution of schools, the returns showed that of the 12,000 parishes in England 3,000 had endowed schools, 3,500 had no school of any type, not even a dame school, and the remainder relied entirely on unendowed schools which were, he said, 'of course fleeting and casual'. The figures were this high, he added, only because of the 'new schools' introduced since 1803 and based on the systems of Dr. Bell and Mr. Lancaster: there were now 1,520 of these schools receiving about 200,000 children. (This suggests an average of 130 pupils per school, a much higher figure than in the old charity schools.) Before 1803 'England might be justly looked on as the worst-educated country of Europe. What a different picture was afforded by Scotland!' he said, where 1 in 9 children now received an education, and '[in] Switzerland . . . one in eight, and there was not above one person in sixty who could not read and write.'

Brougham, like so many opinionated men, had all the answers, as was evident in the explanation he then gave the House of the system he was proposing for the education of the poor. His plan fell under four headings: how schools were to be set up; the appointment of masters; the admission of scholars and their mode of tuition; and how the system was to be financed. The Church of England, the legal authorities, and the local tax payers were central to his scheme, and so he said it would be the diocesan authorities, the parish priest, two justices, or any five resident householders who could petition for a school to be established in the parish. A notice would be affixed to the church-door 'for the period of a month before the first day of quarter-sessions', and the quarter-sessions would then be the tribunal for determining and adjudicating on the subject. The notice should give the necessary information, including an estimate of the expense of the school-house. This should not exceed £200 {£16,300}, and the cost should be borne by the county treasurer.

Brougham's proposals for the election of the schoolmaster were similarly precise and legalistic. This was to take place at a meeting 'of inhabitant housekeepers, rated to the school rate', announced a month in advance by a notice posted on the church-door. Voters were to assemble in the church between 12 and 3 o'clock, and 'proprietors of above 100l. a year might vote by their agents, authorized in writing for that purpose'. The senior parish-officer was to preside, and he would have a casting vote in case of equal numbers. However, '[t]he parson might, upon the examination of the successful candidate, reject him, and direct the parish officers to issue notices for a new election'.

The master's salary should 'not be less than £20 or more than £30' {£1,650 - £2,450}, which Brougham admitted was a low figure, but he did not wish to attract 'sinecurists' or to remove the desire of obtaining day scholars, but not boarders: school-houses should be buildings 'where the master and his wife, with a guardian to assist him, might reside, but in which no boarders should be admitted'. However, he allowed that this low salary could be increased if two-thirds of the householders paying the school-rate concurred. He believed the cost of maintaining the schoolmaster would be a 'small additional burthen of a few shillings . . . or even of a pound a-year' on 'country gentlemen', but said that 'in a very few years' these people would benefit from a diminution in the parish poor rates as a result of the increased level of education in the community. The schoolmaster's payment should be a local matter because those with local information could best decide on an appropriate salary and because it gave them a degree of control over his conduct, but his continuance in office was to depend on the bishop, archdeacon and other senior diocesan clergy. They might visit the school at any time and remove him or direct that he be 'superannuated, with a pension not exceeding two-thirds of his salary, after a service of 15 years continuance'. This would ensure he did not become too old to perform his duties (and would have been an enlightened policy and a very generous pension). Every year the diocese was to make a return (presumably to parliament) of the names of the masters, the number of children under their care, their salaries and average emoluments, with any relevant remarks.

It was the parson who would monitor the school from day-to-day for, in Brougham's words, 'Let the House look to the alacrity, the zeal, the warm-heartedness, which the established clergy manifested for the education of the poor.' He was to have entry to the school at any time and be free to examine the children. Brougham had an equally dewy-eyed vision of his ideal schoolmaster who was 'so honourable, that none was more highly to be esteemed, if the individual were faithful in the discharge of his duty—so useful, that no man, he believed, effected more good in his generation than a good parish schoolmaster'.

Under his scheme, parents were expected to pay towards their children's schooling. He said the parish-officers should fix the rate at between 2d. and 4d. per week, limited to 2d. {66p} per week for the children of those receiving parish relief. If their parents could not pay this small sum, he was sure the parish-officers would defray the expense, since be believed most of them felt that education was the surest means to check the growth of pauperism. He then expressed what was, for the time, an unusually inclusive principal: 'Between those who were thus paid for, and those whose parents defrayed the charge, he would allow no distinction to be drawn. If there were a line chalked across the schoolroom, indicating that on one side of it there were gentlemen who paid, and, on the other, paupers who did not pay, it would be attended with the worst moral effects.' It is a distinction which is still only too evident in aspects of British society.

He next turned to the management of the school and the curriculum, his ideas for which had not advanced since those of the SPCK 120 years before. The parson, he said, should decide the course of teaching 'according to the state of the parish' and fix the vacation arrangements. These should not exceed a month, in either one or two blocks. He should also fix the passages from scriptures 'to be rehearsed'. No other religious book was to be taught, nor any book, without the consent of the parson, nor any form of worship to be allowed in the school except the Lord's Prayer and other passages from the Scriptures. He then expressed an opinion which would be echoed half a century later in a discussion by the Romford School Board on the subject of sectarian education. He believed the Bible was, 'in many parts, a much better school-book than any other', and that if the children studied only the Bible no Christian could object and no 'sectary' (or non-conformist) could refuse to send his children to one of these schools. By keeping to the Bible the schoolmaster would not be teaching any 'particular religion'. The children should attend church once every Sunday, either with their parents or with the master, and the dissenters should take their children to their own churches or chapels. At this point he did reveal a glimpse of a new understanding of child psychology: to take the children to church once on the day set apart for it he conceived to be sufficient, because it was not a good plan to keep children more than an hour and a half at religious worship; 'it was not the proper way to make them love and respect it'. However, there should be a school-meeting every Sunday evening to teach the church catechism and other portions of the Liturgy. Finally, almost as an afterthought, he added that 'Reading, writing and arithmetic to be taught in all the schools, and to all the children of fit age'.

His final section addressed the issue his charity commissioners were then investigating: how to make the existing endowments more available for the purposes of educating the poor than they now were. At this point he gave one dramatic example of how such money could be redirected where there was a failure of the objects of the trust. There were now, he said, £4,500 {£365,000} a year belonging to the Tunbridge school, but £500 a year was twice as much as was wanted for that institution. The superfluous £4,000 would, according to his plan, be sufficient to provide for the support of 200 schools, which would be quite enough to educate the poor children of the whole county of Kent.

He concluded with further remarks about the expense of his proposals. He calculated that about half a million {£40,000,000} would be sufficient, remarking that this was a smaller sum than parliament had granted for the building of six churches. There had been a time when voluntary subscription would have met this need 'without any hesitation or delay', but now the various burdens of taxes and rates had put an end to those feelings of philanthropy, and he was compelled to require the necessary aid of parliament. However, the expense of building these schools, combined with their maintenance which he estimated would be about £150,000 {£12,000,000} a year, 'was so comparatively trivial that he could not suppose parliament would refuse to assent to it; especially when the important objects in view were duly taken into consideration.'

In the course of his speech Brougham had made certain comments which are of particular interest in the context of the school at Romford. First, he said that '[t]hat ancient but now degraded body, the parish clerks' were the best calculated to fill the office of schoolmasters. This was, of course, the office William Adams had held in Great Waltham. Second, as a lawyer Brougham was careful in his plans to guard against any possible corruption, and he said that the greatest vigilance must be exercised regarding the manner in which the building of schools was contracted for and carried out. No parish officer should be employed in building a school, and where the land was purchased from such a person the county surveyor should be called in to inspect it and to report on its value. We have seen how Alexander Weller, a trustee, sold the land on which the Romford School was built to his fellow trustees, and we have seen and will see again that the trustees frequently benefited from the school's custom, providing coal, clothes, shoes, and undertaking building work. Of course, such arrangements were not necessarily corrupt - indeed, there is evidence that the school benefited from the good will of trustees like Thomas Waghorn who held the price of the clothes he provided despite the wartime inflation - but Brougham was right in pointing out the possibilities of corruption. Third, in the section of his speech on the operation of trusts, he gave five remedies for addressing the problem where the number of trustees had fallen below the quorum. These do not include going to Chancery - perhaps surprisingly for a lawyer - which, as we shall see, was the costly solution to which the trustees in Romford would have to resort when they fell into this predicament.

Two other ideas in his speech are of interest. The first was his prediction that as a result of his plans dame-schools would fall into better hands, be better conducted, and become what we now call 'child care' centres. He referred to a dame school at Westminster where none but children aged between three and five were admitted, and where they were kept off the streets and taken care of by a 'parental indulgent dame', enabling their mothers to go out to work. The expense of this establishment, he said, was quite trivial, especially compared to the good which it produced. Such establishments could be set up at little cost. Whether the children learnt less or more was of little consequence, the moral discipline being the main consideration and the freedom it gave their mothers to work. There were a hundred such children in the school at Westminster who did little more than attend the school, but this enabled their mothers to earn 3 or 4 shillings a week at the cost of just a single penny for their children's education (or, perhaps, 'education').

The second idea lay in an observation his friend M. Fellenberg had made when Brougham had visited him in Switzerland. Talking of the Bell and Lancaster system, Fellenberg had said, '[I]t teaches too fast—you make mere machines of your scholars.' Brougham told the House he had not been able to answer that objection. The answer was in fact already at hand and lay in the work of the Swiss pedagogue and educational reformer Johann Heinrich Pestalozzi. Pestalozzi would die in 1827, and it would then take another quarter of century before his ideas would be taken seriously and begin to be adopted by the British educational establishment.

At the end of the debate Brougham was given leave to bring in his bill. The first reading took place on 11 July 1820, and rising to move that it be

Henry Brougham in 1820, from an image published
in the *London Magazine* after a portrait by J R West

read a second time the next day Brougham said that he wished to allay the fears which he understood his bill had excited amongst the Protestant Dissenters and the Roman Catholics. People wrongly thought that it was intended to compel Roman Catholics to send their children to Protestant schools and Protestant worship, and certain dissenters seemed to consider this as a bill introduced for the purpose of 'rooting out the last remains of religious liberty in this country'. When he had introduced the Bill on 28 June he had said that those applying to be schoolmasters must prove their membership of the established church by taking the sacrament in the month prior to their appointment. The bill still provided that the schoolmaster should be a member of the established church, but he was now dropping this sacramental test 'as he knew persons who were averse from taking the sacrament (not from any objection to it, but, on the contrary, from a reverence for the ceremony), because they did not think it was fitting to receive it as the passport to a civil office'.

The motion was agreed and the Bill was read a second time and was ordered to be committed on 14 July, but Brougham then withdrew it in order to take into account the recent developments on education charities. He was then a very busy man. On 17 August the trial of Queen Caroline opened in the House of Lords, and on 3 October Brougham opened the case for the defence with a speech which the diarist Charles Greville described as the 'most magnificent display of argument and oratory that has been heard in years.'[143] When he reintroduced the Bill early in 1821 he had divided it into two separate bills. In the same way that Samuel Whitbread had separated his Parochial Schools Bill out of his New Poor Law Bill, Brougham now presented a Bill 'to secure to the poorer classes a useful and religious education'. His other Bill addressed the issue of the endowments: 'to regulate and improve endowments for the purposes of education'.

Whilst the alterations to remove the threat of additional taxation and the proposals to improve the administration and application of historic endowments were welcome, the Bill was lost on the religious question which from then to the present day has dogged - although, due to government compromises, not defeated - all subsequent educational legislation. It was the Church of England (and Bell) and the non-conformists (and Lancaster) who had made the greatest contribution to advancing the education of the poor since 1803, as Brougham had acknowledged when he introduced his original Bill. He needed their support, but the concessions he made to win over the Church of England alienated the Dissenters. He was forced to withdraw the Bill, later commenting: 'My Parish School Bill had been introduced, which I afterwards was prevented from carrying by the absurd and groundless prejudice of the Dissenters, when it was supported by the Church - the Dissenters opposing it because it was so supported.'[144]

Yet another opportunity to introduce a nationwide system of popular education had been lost. Forty-nine years would now pass before the Forster Act would achieve this goal.

Chapter 18

Sarah Bourne and Oswald Adams

1814 - 1823

1814: The development of mutually antipathetic sectarian schools after Bell and Lancaster
In the speech introducing his Bill on 28 June 1820, having acknowledged the contribution of the 'new schools' based on the systems of Bell and Lancaster, Brougham said of Lancaster that 'in mentioning him, although he lamented his errors, he could not but express his sense of the great service which he had rendered to society'. We have noted Bell's difficult personality; Lancaster's character failings and 'errors' were in a different league.

First, his intemperate nature overcoming his common sense, he had written an article in which he claimed that he alone had invented the Monitorial System and accusing other claimants (presumably with Bell in mind) of being imposters. He was then discovered to have been privately beating a number of the boys with whom he worked, and in 1814 he was expelled from the Society which bore his name. Founded by Quakers, in its six years it had been supported by evangelical and non-conformist Christians, Roman Catholics and Jews who wished to see public education based on non-sectarian principles. Although still dedicated to propagating Lancaster's System, the Society was now renamed the 'British and Foreign School Society for the Education of the Labouring and Manufacturing Classes of Society of Every Religious Persuasion'. This name could not have been better designed to trip up rather than to trip off the tongue, whichever sectarian persuasion the tongue confessed, and it was soon truncated to the 'British and Foreign School Society' (BFSS).

Lancaster's later career is quickly summarised. In 1816 he opened a school in Tooting which failed, leaving him bankrupt. Whereas Bell was a canny Scot who had made a fortune first in America and then in India, Lancaster's financial management was so poor that he was imprisoned for debt. Having provoked the contest with Bell, he was now forced from the field and in 1818 his Quaker friends sent him to the Americas to lecture and to promote his ideas. Although a school he opened in Baltimore failed, he continued to travel and to spread his educational theories. He would die on 23 October 1838 (from injuries sustained when he was run over by a horse carriage in New York city), by which time there were said to be between 1200 and 1500 schools using his methods in Canada, the United States, Venezuela, Colombia (where Simon Bolivar had presided at his wedding), Ecuador, Peru and Mexico.

Joseph Lancaster, from a portrait by John Hazlitt

In England and Wales Bell's victory was complete, and after Lancaster's departure the BFSS authorised him to travel the country as an inspector of their schools. This was necessary, for despite initial successes there was criticism of the Lancasterian schools for their poor standards and harsh discipline. Bell had been bullied at school, and both he and Lancaster rejected corporal punishment, but in Lancaster's schools it was not unknown for children who misbehaved to be tied up in sacks or hoisted above the classroom in cages. Their reputation was such that Robert Southey stated he would rather be beaten than subjected to Lancasterian discipline.

However, despite Lancaster's disgrace and the weaknesses in many of his schools, the Anglican establishment which supported Bell and his National schools would not have a monopoly over the development of public education. By the 1820's there was a growing and ultimately successful campaign among Unitarians, Methodists, Quakers and other dissenting groups for the repeal of the Test and Corporation Acts, with a simultaneous campaign being waged for the lifting of discriminatory laws against Catholics. In 1828 the Test Acts were repealed with little controversy, followed the next year by the passing of the Catholic Emancipation Act.[145] The formal removal of these legal restrictions re-energised the non-conformists, and over the course of the next 70 years the non-denominational British and Foreign School Society and their British Schools would make a significant contribution to this second great drive for universal elementary education.

Unfortunately the dogmatic intransigence and Anglicanism of Dr Bell made it impossible for the adherents of the two systems to agree on the best methods and to move forward together. Popular education had become, and would remain, a new field for sectarian combat. For the next sixty years the schools sponsored by these two rival organisations would engage in a contest to capture the souls of the young, a struggle which would later be joined by the Catholics. In 1847 the Catholic Poor School Committee was founded, and with the restoration of the Catholic hierarchy in England and Wales in 1850 the education of the poor became its first priority, with the building of schools often taking precedence over the building of churches.

The struggle between the Anglicans and the non-conformists would be continued after 1870 for influence on the School Boards, by when a more fundamental conflict was developing between the supporters of denominational schools and those who were viscerally and intellectually opposed to any involvement of the church in public education - a conflict which continues to this day.

1820 and 1821: a new Treasurer, a new Mistress, and further reforms

On 17 November 1820 a vote of thanks to Edward Ind was formally proposed and seconded 'for the handsome manner in which he has filled the situation of Treasurer for 13 years', the record noting 'that the Trustees accept[ed] with regret his Resignation.' John Willson was proposed, seconded and appointed in his place. The proposing and seconding suggest that during Ind's period in office a new level of formality had been introduced at these meetings. Over these thirteen years the personalities which stand out are those of William Adams and Edward Ind, and it was probably the happy conjunction of these two moving and entrepreneurial spirits which led to the two outstanding reforms of this period, the 50% increase in the size of the school and the decision to teach all the girls to write.

Two months later, on 15 January 1821, a Special Meeting was convened at which the seven trustees present unanimously appointed Sarah Bourne Mistress of the Girls' School following the resignation of Mrs Adams. We do not know why Jemima stepped down at this time, but she was nearly 57, Oswald was increasingly able to assist his father, and she still had the private scholars to attend to outside the classroom. She may also have been unwell at this time. Sarah Bourne was then aged 34. She had been born in Rainham, and in September 1811 she had married Benjamin Bourne at St James', Piccadilly, although he had been baptised at St Edward's in Romford, where he had also been buried at the age of 29 in October 1819. She had therefore been a widow for fifteen months at the time of her appointment. She was a member of 'the Established Church of England', and her application was supported by 'several recommendations' which unfortunately were not copied into the Minute Book. The fact that she was to commence on the day of her appointment suggests that she might already have been substituting for Jemima. The terms of service were unaltered: £30 a year, 1½ chaldrons of coal, and the use of the Girls School House free of all expenses, although the trustees only had to give her 3 months notice if they wished to dismiss her whereas she had to give 6 months notice of resignation. (The Girls' School House would have been where Jane White and Dorothy Cloke had lived, almost certainly the accommodation above the school rooms.) At this meeting those present now 'Ordered, That it be recommended at the next meeting of the Trustees, to take into their consideration the propriety of making a division of the Garden appropriated to the use of the Master and Mistress'.

When William and Jemima Adams had been appointed in November 1809 they had been given charge of 60 charity children, were paid £46 a year, and had the same right as the Bandfields to take up to 6 boarders and 14 boys and girls as day scholars above the number of charity children. The first mention of private pupils had been made only five years before when Susannah Saunders was appointed Mistress. Within four years of their appointment the Adams were responsible for 90 charity children and their salaries had risen to £80. We do not know the number of private scholars they took or the arrangements which were made for these additional children, but there is no evidence that the allowed number had been reduced with the expansion in the number of charity scholars. Their increase in salary was related to this increase in numbers and possibly also reflected the inflationary pressure on wages during the war years, but there is no evidence of an element of compensation for the permitted number of private scholars having been reduced. With Sarah Bourne's appointment the Trustees had to reconsider this, and decided that she should be allowed to take just two day scholars, down from the six Susannah Saunders had been allowed in November 1804.

Three months later the Trustees refined their administration of the school. Having formalised the arrangement that meetings would take place only every six months, they now decided that each year a sub-committee would be appointed consisting of the Treasurer and five trustees (and with a quorum of three) to act at quarterly meetings. In future the half yearly meetings would be held on the Tuesday next after 5 April and 10 October and the quarterly meetings of the sub-committee on the Tuesday after 5 January and 5 July, reflecting the pattern of the quarter days. The members of this first sub-committee were the Reverend William Everett, Robert Surridge Esq (of whom more, much more, later), and Messrs Peter Delamare, John Ping, and Joseph Last. Joseph Last was a hairdresser and peruke maker who had been elected a trustee in March 1815, when he was 44. His name will recur in this history because he was destined to be a loyal governor and trustee of the Charity for half a century.

At the following meeting in October of 1821 it was decided that the children would be discharged on the next meeting of the trustees after they had arrived at the age of 13 years. The decision taken in June 1762 had been that children would be admitted when aged eight, that the girls would leave when 14 and the boys when 12, but we do not know whether over the years the initial strict enforcement of this policy had been relaxed. Certainly those girls who were not withdrawn early and would have stayed until aged 14 were now deprived of a year's education, but if the previous rule had not been relaxed the boys now gained a year.

The meeting of 16 April 1822

This is the first meeting when the list of those present starts by stating that Mr Willson, the Treasurer, was 'in the Chair'. From now on this becomes routine, and it is important for two reasons: first, it shows a further development towards the procedural conventions for formal meetings which we now take for granted, and second, it formally acknowledges the pre-eminence of the treasurer. When the school had opened in 1711 the treasurer had been one of six trustees, two of whom were the ex-offico clergy, and they all influenced and agreed the decisions which were taken. Over the following century the number of trustees had grown and the number attending the meetings had varied. In these circumstances, and with the increasing legal and financial complexities of the Charity, the executive role of the Chairman became ever more important, and with fewer regular meetings successive treasurers appear to have had to make an increasing number of decisions on their own responsibility. The quality of the treasurer was more important than ever to the success of the school, and although it was still considered important that the Master and Mistress should be members of 'the Established Church of England', this rule did not apply to the trustees or the elected Treasurer.

Twelve months previously the first sub-committee had been elected which would meet quarterly, and their successors should now have been chosen. Instead, it was 'Ordered that the sub-committee appointed on the 19th April 1821 be from this day discontinued.' No reason is given for this abrupt change of policy, but perhaps it was felt that too much influence now lay with the treasurer and those on the sub-committee. Over the next five years the trustees would meet as a body on four, five or even six occasions each year rather than half yearly as they had agreed in October 1817.

This decision is followed by an even more surprising development: 'Ordered that Mr William Adams' resignation be accepted and that Oswald Adams his son be elected in his stead, and that the salary of £50 be continued, with the same privileges & exemptions from rates & taxes as his father.' Presumably the use of the family's house next to the school and the arrangement for private scholars were encapsulated in the 'same privileges' which were to be continued. What a father William Adams was! When he had moved from Great Waltham he had arranged for his elder son to fill the seat he was then vacating; now he had secured that his younger son should take over his post in Romford. (His third child, Susannah, had returned to

Great Waltham in December 1819, six weeks after her twenty-first birthday, to marry a George Eve.)

Oswald had been born on 8 October 1794 so was now 27 years old. We know that for a time he had been writing master at Felsted Grammar School,[146] and we have speculated that this may have been before his possible return to Romford in October or November 1813 to help his parents following the expansion of the school. The next certain facts we have are that in 1817 he was appointed actuary for the newly established Romford Savings Bank with its office in the Schoolmaster's House,[147] and that on Christmas Eve 1818 he married Mary Kemp at St George's Hanover Square, and on their second wedding anniversary their first child, yet another Oswald, was baptised at St Edward's. Did William now relinquish his post and his house in anticipation that Oswald and Mary needed the job security and the accommodation for a larger family?

William was a month short of his fifty-fifth birthday. We know from the manner in which he managed to position his two sons that he planned for the future with great care, and he undoubtedly had arranged another place for himself. It is possible that, working alongside Oswald, he was increasingly involved with the day-to-day work of the savings bank. He was very good with figures, as we know from the final Herculean task he had to perform before relinquishing his post to his son, detailed at the end of this minute:

> Ordered that the receipts and disbursements for the last seven years be made out by Mr William Adams before he finally quits his Office and a copy of the said account be sent to each Trustee with a letter requesting his attendance on Tuesday the 14th May next, for the purpose of considering the means of liquidating the debts, and promoting the future support and welfare of the Charity.

The debt in question, expressed as the 'Balance due to the Treasurer', was then £149 0s 9¼d {£12,500}. What had gone wrong?

1822: Financial crisis! What financial crisis?

We have already noted that between June 1803 and March 1814 the accounts were balanced at least once and sometimes twice a year. This would also be true of the period from April 1818 to May 1835, when the third Account Book closed. However, exceptionally, there was no reconciliation between 18 March 1814 and 9 April 1818.

When Edward Ind had taken over as Treasurer from Thomas Graves in May 1807 there had been a very small balance in hand of £3 or £4. For the next eleven years the balance had always been positive: indeed, on 12 October 1813, before the payment of £112 9s 11d to Roger Talbot for the necessary building work to expand the intake, it had stood at £182 3s 0d. Following this it fell to £19 13s 5d in the final reconciliation before the four year gap. However, a headline figure such as this, or the £149 0s 9¼d deficit which William Adams was now charged with investigating, can mask both the real state of the finances and some fundamental changes which had taken place during the previous, economically turbulent, twenty years.

To understand how the income of the charity had changed over ten years of war a breakdown of the income for the year from January to December 1813 can be compared with that for the year June 1803 to May 1804, examined in Chapter 7 *[and shown here in italics]*:

	January to December 1813
[June 1803 to May 1804]	
6 months interest of the directors of the poor of Romford	£ 2 5s 0d
Dividend on £718 18s 5d	£19 8s 0d
1 yrs dividend on £150 at 5 per cent	£ 6 15s 0d
2 yr interest on £800 at 3 per cent	£43 4s 0d
2 yrs on £50 at 4 per cent	£ 3 12s 0d
[Interest £18 0s 0d]	£75 4s 0d
Church collections (charity sermons)	£91 11s 10½d
[Sermons £68 0s 11d]	
Town Collections x 2	£21 9s 6d
[Town Collections x 2 & Trustees £38 7s 0d]	
Overatt's rent	£12 12s 0d
[Rent £14 0s 0d]	
Received by property tax allowances	£ 9 19s 6d
Rec'd of the Trustees at the meetings	£ 7 17s 6d
Donations and subscriptions	£33 1s 6d
[Donations & Sundry Trustees £12 14s 0d]	
Total in December 1813	£251 15s 10½d
[Total 1804 £151 1s 11d]	

247

In 1803 £151 1s 11d was approximately equivalent to £14,100 in 2020; in 1813 £251 15s 10½d was approximately equivalent to £16,800 in 2020.

Bearing in mind that there might have been an especial effort to raise money in 1813 prior to authorising the building works for the expansion of the school, these figures show the continuing importance of the charity sermons, which in the decade 1810 to 1820 usually raised between £80 and £90 each year, and that although the town collection had fallen by a third the rise in donations and subscriptions had more than compensated for this. The most noticeable change, however, is in the income from interest, which had been boosted by the trustees' policy of using any legacies and excess of income over expenditure to buy investments during the war years. This had paid off handsomely, and not only had the annual interest payments risen from £18 a year to £75 4s over these ten years, but the Trustees had £1,718 of investments together with the £150 in bonds invested in the 1787 workhouse.

The incomplete evidence we have suggests that Edward Ind had managed the finances of the charity well but had been lax in reconciling the accounts over the last five years of his period in office, hence the task given to the schoolmaster. There is no record of a meeting to approve the accounts on 14 May, suggesting that it never took place. Perhaps sorting out the receipts and expenditure over the last seven years was just too great a task, even for a man of William Adams' abilities. It was over the last two years of Edward Ind's treasurership that the balance had moved from black to red, and in November 1820 he had handed over a deficit of about £35 to John Willson. By the meeting on the 16th April 1822 this had grown to the superficially alarming £149 0s 9¼d {£12,400}, but there was no crisis as there had been in the 1740's when the Trustees had been running a much smaller deficit but had no resources, having spent all their capital on building the school and master's house. In 1822 they had higher reserves than ever before, and the only problem was one of cash flow.

22 May 1823: The three year schooling rule and ...
When the trustees received notice of the meeting scheduled for 22 May 1823 it contained notification of an intended proposition to admit children into the school between the ages of 8 and 11 only, and that those admitted should remain in the school three years and no longer. Just eighteen months earlier they had agreed to discharge all children once they had reached the age of

thirteen, but it would seem that they had now realised that under this ruling late entrants would enjoy only one or two years of education. This new proposal would mean that all children would receive three years of schooling and no more, and that a child who entered the school at the age of eight would leave at eleven but a child who entered at eleven would not leave until they were fourteen. The age range of 8 to 14 therefore remained unaltered, and all things being equal a child would be put into a mixed age first class when they arrived and stay with that group for the next three years. These new admission arrangements were confirmed at the meeting.

The reason for this change was undoubtedly to meet the increasing demand for a basic education. Across the country the ever growing number of Madras and monitorial schools was increasing the available school places, but also the demand for these places as expectations rose. In this climate the old charity schools in towns where there was no other provision must have come under increasing pressure to expand their intake. With ninety children, the Romford school could not expand further, but it could increase its 'throughput'. Fifty-four years previously, before the age range for the boys was limited to between eight and twelve years, a child could have six or seven years at the school, but no doubt much of this time was wasted. By allowing a greater number of children to pass through the school and receive a basic education the system now adopted was more efficient or, to use a word then in vogue, 'utilitarian'.

... the lost Deeds

Lost objects rarely warrant a historical footnote, but there are occasions when they are the mainspring for an ensuing drama, particularly in the case of lost legal documents. In January 1820 a 'special Meeting' of the Trustees had been called at which it was ordered that Mr Tweed, a solicitor and trustee, should be requested to compel Mr James Delamare to transfer the stock belonging to the Charity and standing in his name. It was also ordered 'That Mr John Tyler be requested to give up to Mr Tweed the Deeds belonging to this Charity.' Presumably Mr Delamere transferred the stock, because we hear no more of this, but the problem of the missing Deeds was raised again at a meeting in November 1822 when it was agreed that Mr Tweed should be instructed to apply again to Mr John Tyler to deliver up all the deeds and papers relating to the school and that Mr Tweed should cause a strict search to be made for them in any other quarter he might think fit. Had John Tyler had charge of these papers when he was treasurer from April

1770 to March 1771, and then retained them during the long treasurership of Thomas Graves? If so, when he died in 1807 they would have passed to his son, John Tyler Junior, who had been elected a trustee in May 1800, and it would have been to him that the trustees were now applying for their restitution.

On 13 May 1823 it was 'Ordered that a Meeting be held on the 22nd May instant at 12 o'clock for the purpose of investigating the loss of the Title Deeds belonging to the House in Hornchurch Lane the property of this Charity and that John Tyler Esqr be requested to attend such Meeting.' Presumably John Tyler was unable to attend, because at the meeting it was 'Ordered the investigation re the loss of the title deeds be postponed until the next half yearly meeting.' In fact, three years were to pass before the next attempt to locate the missing deeds, by when the trustees had more serious issues with which to contend.

Chapter 19

The scandal of the Methodist banker

1823 - 1826

1823: the new Treasurer of the Charity School, Robert Surridge of the Romford Agricultural Bank
In the Royal Liberty, as nationally, over the second half of the eighteenth century the issues of pluralities and non-resident clergy had brought the ministry of the Church of England into increasing disrepute. During the period of bloodshed and anarchy which had accompanied the French Revolution and the wars which had followed the attitude to religion generally and 'the Church' in particular had been ambiguous. For some they represented all that needed to be changed, whereas for others they were a reassuring symbol of the status quo, a bastion of the British constitution and of society on these islands. Seen in this light, the position of the Established Church and of other religious bodies had been strengthened. Indeed, it was a Methodist claim that it had been their influence over the working classes which had prevented the import of French apostasy.[148] However, after the Napoleonic War the reputation of the Church and the esteem in which its clergy were held fell sharply. In the words of Bishop A T P Williams, 'There is no doubt of the general unpopularity of the Church in the years between Waterloo and the Reform Act of 1832.'[149] The immediate cause of this lay in the reactionary Toryism of the administration of Lord Liverpool, which had dragged on from 1812. To bolster the position of the Established Church it granted £1,500,000 {£100,000,000} for church building, reinforced measures against dissenters, and opposed Catholic emancipation. This garnered support from a number of churchmen, but provoked furious opposition from liberals and radicals and caused the Church to be seen as an obstacle to innovation and change.

In 1820 the crown passed from the solid and dependable 'Farmer George' to his son, whose period as Prince Regent had been characterised by the irresponsibility and showy excesses which would continue during his reign as George IV. The contrast between father and son can be seen as a metaphor for the profound changes which affected the whole country during this period. At its best there was a willingness to embrace the many social and industrial challenges and opportunities which that most inventive of ages was spawning; at its worst it was a shift from reliability and substance to superficiality and extravagance. The old, staid, agricultural market town of Romford had acquired an edge over the previous thirty years: it was sharper in trade and business, as it was in fashion, but its values would eventually prove to have remained closer to those of the old king than to those of his son.

John Willson served as Treasurer of the Charity School for three and a half years, and on 15 July 1823 a special meeting was called to elect his successor. The 44 years of absentee clergy in Romford had ended nine years previously with the arrival of the Rev'd William Everett as Chaplain, and he was in the chair to receive the nomination of Robert Surridge, proposed by Joseph Last and seconded by William Bulmer. Only four others were present[150] and the motion was carried, the minute concluding: '. . . since which meeting Mr Surridge has attended at the school and accepted the same.' It was symptomatic of the general decline in hard-line Church of England orthodoxy and the religious toleration of the time (despite the Test Acts still being on the statute book) that none of those present - including the Rev'd William Everett - thought it inappropriate or of consequence to elect a Methodist to the most important post in this Church of England foundation.

The new treasurer was a greatly admired local banker, a wealthy man who was well known for his charitable deeds. His story illustrates well the changed and changing nature of Romford and the Royal Liberty at this time, and the drama which was to play out over the next three years is more than peripheral to this history because several of its key players were trustees of the school and because Robert's son, named North Surridge after his grandfather, would serve the Charity with distinction later in the century.

Robert Surridge was born in 1771 in Rainham, where his father was a successful farmer. In December 1786 he was apprenticed to a carpenter in Newgate Market in London, but he subsequently moved to a respectable banking house in the City where he worked as a clerk for sixteen or seventeen years, the end of which period coincided with the rise of the country banks. The origins of these banks in Essex and elsewhere are usually obscure but tended to follow a similar pattern. To begin with, as part of his regular business activities, a leading tradesman or merchant in the town would have to correspond with a banker or some other financial agent in London. He would then be asked by other, smaller tradesmen in the locality to negotiate their bills and drafts for them through this London agent, and his role as a middleman would gradually grow until he became a de facto country banker in addition to managing his original business. As the banking side of the enterprise grew, the original business usually declined until the one time merchant became a full time banker, the gradual change from one business to another making it impossible to state precisely when any particular enterprise became a bank. There are few records of country banks in Essex prior to the nineteenth century and certainly none relating to the Romford Agricultural Bank, but if its precise origins are a mystery the key partner behind its formation was undoubtedly Joseph Joyner, the neighbour of Robert's father, North Surridge.

Joyner was a very wealthy man with land in Rainham and Romford which he farmed with his son Joseph Sumpner Joyner.[151] Whether he had any experience as an intermediary, peripatetic banker as described above we do not know, but he seems to have realised there was money to be made in this new financial business and to have agreed with North Surridge to open a bank in Romford, funded with their money and run by their two sons. Confidence is a key to success in banking, and there was no reason for anyone to doubt the viability of this new enterprise: both men were well known in the district, and the public would have been reassured by the security offered by the senior Joyner's considerable assets. The two older men, in turn, had confidence that Robert had acquired sufficient banking experience for his new, elevated role and that he had the skills to transform the younger Joseph Sumpner Joyner from a farmer into a banker.

The new bank was certainly in business by 1811 when Joyner & Co was listed in the London and County Directory as one of the two banks in Romford.[152] As Robert Surridge had been elected a trustee of the Charity School in March 1810, to be followed a year later by his business partner Joseph Sumpner Joyner, we can assume they were respected members of the local business community by then. In 1812 old North Surridge died, leaving just three partners to enjoy the economic boom in the decade following the end of the Napoleonic Wars. Joyner, Surridge, and Joyner prospered, both corporately and individually. They traded as the Romford Agricultural Bank and had premises in the Market Place and also at Epping, Ongar and Grays.

Old Joseph Joyner enjoyed his wealth, purchasing the Hunter Hall Farm Estate in Dagenham and keeping a cellar of choice wine there. As one of his most unforgiving critics wrote later, he revelled in being

> miraculously placed at the head of a flourishing concern ... driving round the market in his Carriage, attended by a liveried lacquey, paying high flown compliments to such as he thought worthy of such condescension, and then, standing at the door of the Bank, to attract notice, in the same austentatious manner.[153]

That was one face of the Regency period, the flashy exhibitionism of the Prince Regent, Beau Brummell and the provincial Joseph Joyner. Another face was the austere philanthropy of Elizabeth Fry, William Wilberforce and the provincial Robert Surridge. A pious Methodist of 'sober and sanctified demeanour', Surridge used his wealth to support all manner of religious and charitable works. He financed the building of chapels and the pensioning of ministers, and he appeared on lists of subscribers for worthy charities such as the 'Widows' Friend and Benevolent Society'. Like Edward Ind in his brewery, he was a representative of that new type of Romford grandee, the self-made man of business, but perhaps at the age of 52, sitting in his bank in the Market Place, he appeared an even more impressive figure. When in July 1823 he was elected Treasurer of the Charity School and became its public face it must have seemed that he was the perfect man for this position.

7 December 1824: Mr Jacobs' legacy - the dispute resolved
At the meeting on 28 October 1823 Surridge took a long overdue initiative regarding Mr Jacobs' disputed legacy, which had been returned to his executor over eight years previously. On 19 November 1818 Mr Sterry had been 'requested to take a [legal] opinion on the subject of the late Mr Jacobs' Legacy and that the same be acted upon', but nothing had happened. Three years later, on 5 November 1822, the trustees resolved that they would not relinquish their claim to this £200 but that they were ready to divide it according to the opinions of Mr Trower and Mr Bell, whom we can assume were the lawyers whose opinions Mr Sterry had sought. The executors of the will and the churchwardens of Hornchurch were to be informed of this, and the offer was to be made without prejudicing the claim of the trustees to the whole of the legacy. Still

nothing happened. It was now agreed, at this meeting on 28 October 1823, that Mr Oswald Adams (in his role as clerk to the trustees) should request the Rev'd John Walker, the Vicar of Hornchurch, to draw up a case on behalf of the Trustees of the Alice Aylett School and request the Rev'd William Everett, Chaplain of Romford, to do the same on behalf of the Trustees of the Charity School at Romford. Their papers were to be submitted to the Treasurer who would call a Special Meeting 'as circumstances may require'. The writing of the letters by Mr Adams was a formality as both clergymen were trustees of the Romford School and were present at the meeting when this resolution was agreed.

Were these cases drawn up and submitted? We do not know, because six months later at a special meeting on 11 May 1824 it was ordered 'that a diligent search be made for the Case upon which Mr Trower and Mr Bell founded their opinion, and if found or a copy thereof procured the Treasurer is requested to call a Special Meeting on the receipt of such case or copy.' It seems they had cited a legal precedent which was now, belatedly, being sought. The next development is noted in the minutes of the half yearly meeting on 26 October 1824, which record that 'The Rev John Walker Vicar of Hornchurch, the Rev James Bearblock and Mr James Cove churchwardens of that Parish and Trustees of Mrs Aylett's School, declined dividing the £200 in question.' In light of this it was 'Ordered that the business of this Meeting so far as regards the question of the right to the Legacy bequeathed by William Jacobs Esq. be adjourned to the 7th of December next', on which date a Special Meeting of the Trustees of the Charity School was to be held to determine 'the question of the right to the Legacy of £200 bequeathed by the late William Jacobs Esqr.'

Who were these obstructive Hornchurch men? The Rev'd John Walker had been appointed Vicar of Hornchurch in succession to William Blair in 1819 at the age of 48, having spent twenty-three years as a Fellow of New College where he was the Dean of Canon Law. The period of absentee clergy was now over, and like William Everett at Romford he seems to have been resident in the parish. James Cove was a fellmonger and woolstapler[154] in Hornchurch, who attended his first meeting of the Trustees in November 1822. One hundred years earlier, in October 1722, a James Cove of Hornchurch, an early pupil of the school, had been apprenticed under the Mary Hide Charity to a glover and fellmonger in Dagenham.[155] The coincidence of name, town and trade is too great for us not to conclude that he was an ancestor of the present James Cove, and that his attendance at the charity school had enabled him to start a business which had passed down through several generations. In February 1830 the *Essex Herald* would report the bankruptcy of the present James Cove and the sale of his equipment and stock of skins, but later that year he seems to have paid off his debts and returned to business, and he was one of those registered to vote in the Parliamentary Election in February 1835.[156] His brother, Charles Cove, may have helped him through his financial difficulties. He was a builder and surveyor in Hornchurch who had been elected a trustee of the school in April 1824. He will reappear in this history.

The other churchwarden was the Rev'd James Bearblock who had attended his first trustee meeting on 16 October1821. He was born in West Smithfield, London, in 1766, the son of a London gentleman. He was educated at Eton and matriculated at Trinity College, Oxford in May 1784, but by Michaelmas that year he had migrated to King's College, Cambridge, where he was a Fellow from 1787. In 1788 he became the (presumably non-resident) Curate of Dunton Waylett in Essex. Then in 1803, at the age of 37, he was removed from his fellowship in the belief that he was a married man, an allegation which is examined in a thick parcel of papers still retained at the National Archives. At some point he was appointed Chaplain to the Board of Ordnance, an ironically appropriate position for a man who was by nature very disputatious, although his legal quarrels were mainly to do with the non-payment of the tithes due to him as leaseholder of the Hornchurch Hall estate.

To understand this arrangement, we must go back to 1391, the dissolution of Hornchurch priory, and the purchase of its estates by William of Wykeham as part of his endowment of New College.[157] Five hundred and fifty years later the College still held 930 acres in the parish, 280 of which belonged to Hornchurch Hall, which was in effect a rectory manor. Throughout this time the Hall had usually been leased along with the great tithes, and the litigious leaseholder in the early 19th century was the Rev'd James Bearblock.[158] Tithes were his passion, and in 1806 he had published a *Treatise upon Tithes*. It was ironically inappropriate that a man with such a personality should live in a property called Lilliput, rather than in the Hall itself, and he will play a more than lilliputian role in this history, as will his two sons, John and Peter Esdaile Bearblock.

These were the three men who by declining to divide the £200 were playing for all or nothing. All three were trustees of both schools, but if their loyalties were divided the greater loyalty clearly lay with Hornchurch. At least two other Hornchurch men were present, one of whom was Thomas Wedlake. Those attending from Romford included Richard Digby Neave, James Marson Carruthers, Octavius Mashiter, and Joseph Last.[159]

The first item on the agenda of this meeting of 7 December marked another step towards the now accepted formalities of such meetings, the confirmation of the minutes of the previous meeting on 26 October. They then addressed the main item on the agenda, and their decision is summarised in the subsequent minute:

> At the Meeting of the Hornchurch, Romford and Havering School, at which the Trustees of Mrs Aylett's Charity School at Hornchurch were present, called together by a circular letter to each Trustee for the purpose of amicably deciding the question of right to the £200 left by Mr Jacobs for charitable purposes, it was agreed by both parties that the feeling of the Meeting be fairly decided by ballot, and that the result of the same be forwarded to Mr Hutchins by the Treasurer, accompanied by the cases and opinions of Messrs Trower, Bell, and Cooper [which presumably had been found and duly considered]. The result of the Ballot was as follows:
>   In favour of Hornchurch   11
>   In favour of Romford   3
>
> Ordered that the thanks of this Meeting be given to the Treasurer for his attention to the business of the day and for his impartial conduct in the Chair.

After ten long years, this saga had finally ended. The story of this legacy is of far more interest than just another example of the convoluted workings of inheritance in the 19th century and who should benefit from this £200 {£17,500}. Why did those present decide, by a large majority, to give the money to the school in Hornchurch rather than to the one in Romford which was much larger, infinitely better endowed, properly housed, and which (to an extent) provided uniforms for its charity children? Hornchurch was in theory well represented on the trustees of the Romford Charity School and its children had no less right to attend the school than those from Romford.

Sir Richard Digby Neave of Dagnams, from a portrait by his friend John Constable. He was elected a trustee on 27 April 1824 and was present at the meeting on 7 December.

The answer is undoubtedly related to the distances the children in Hornchurch had to travel to attend the school in Romford, for although the centres of the two communities were only two and a half miles apart the parish of Hornchurch extended considerably further south than this, being two miles across but nine miles long. The Mary Hide Trust was now dormant, as we shall see, but there was no doubt a memory that in the past it had provided many more apprenticeships to Romford boys than to boys from Hornchurch. There may well have been a long held sense of discontent about this inequality in provision, and perhaps the Trustees of the Alice Aylett School hoped that with this additional £200 - twice her original endowment - they would be able to create a better school for their own community. Perhaps there had been discussion before and during that final, decisive meeting on 7 December 1824 of using this money to 'pump prime' the conversion of their existing charity school into a National school, a solution which might have appealed to the trustees of the Romford school as much as to those from Hornchurch. One only has to look at the numbers: the population of Romford in 1826 was 3,777[160], Hornchurch was perhaps half this size, and the recently enlarged school in Romford could take just 90 children. The National Society was now a major force, having opened hundreds of schools across the country. Romford had boasted a pioneering charity school a hundred years earlier, but for all its good work it was not keeping up with the new demands, and it would certainly have been beneficial to the whole Royal Liberty to have a thriving National school in Hornchurch.

At least five of those present who lived in Romford had voted for the money to go to the Hornchurch school, so these men clearly did not see this as an adversarial issue, with those from each community struggling to retain the money. Instead, they appear to have looked at the needs of the Royal Liberty as a whole and made a considered judgement as to where the money could do the most good.

We do not know how the £200 was used, but it is reported that by 1837 the school in Hornchurch had ten poor boys and several paying pupils who were being taught reading, writing, and arithmetic in the master's house. Perhaps the interest on this £200 funded these ten poor boys, because we know that Alice Aylett's Charity never owned a building.[161]

February 1826: the disgrace of Robert Surridge
Surridge had been Treasurer for eighteen months at the time the issue of Jacobs' legacy was finally resolved, if not quite to everyone's satisfaction or the benefit of the Romford school. He was to take one other important initiative. Edward Ind had passed on a deficit of £149 0s 9¼d to John Willson, which Willson had turned into a surplus of 3s 1d when he in turn passed the accounts to Surridge. Between 1803 and 1835, the period covered by the third Account Book, the balance in hand was clearly recorded on

forty-two occasions, or once every nine months on average. Between November 1819 and October 1825 the twelve reconciliations all recorded a deficit, a situation which only happened on three other isolated occasions. However, men of business and finance like Edward Ind and Robert Surridge knew that this was only a temporary problem of liquidity, and that the charity's finances were underpinned by both property and government bonds. This enabled the nine trustees present on 22 March 1825 to agree that clothing would be provided for all the 90 children. They also agreed that 'the Boys in future be provided with trowsers instead of breeches'- the newest Regency fashion! At the same meeting the Reverend William Everett was asked to procure 50 Bibles and 50 Prayer Books from the SPCK. The only issue of concern amongst all this positivity was the condition of the properties in Hornchurch Lane which the present leaseholder, a Mr Heaphy, had allowed to fall into a dilapidated state. This was noted, but no action was taken. It was then 'Resolved unanimously that the Trustees present do request Mr Surridge to continue his services as Treasurer to this School and that he will accept their thanks for the care and diligence he has evinced in discharging the duties of the situation.' All was going well.

The meeting on 25 October was inquorate, with only Robert Surridge, Thomas Townsend, William Miles and Joseph Last present. Having noted the death of a pupil, Sarah Fry, they agreed 'that in consequence of the thinness of the Meeting it is not deemed advisable to enter into the consideration of the documents lately discovered by Dr Kerrison relative to Mr Jacobs' Legacy.' It is scarcely believable that after eleven years and having taken legal advice and finally agreed the money should go to the school in Hornchurch, further documents had emerged. However, events suddenly and dramatically changed the agenda, and with no further recorded discussion of the Jacobs legacy we will never know what was in these documents.

This inconsequential meeting was to prove Robert Surridge's last. Within two months he was a disgraced man, ruined in days when the post-war economic boom which he had ridden so successfully suddenly crashed. The cause lay far from Essex, in a county in - or not in - South America, a country called Poyais. In the early 1820's many people were persuaded that Poyais offered financial returns of Brobdignagian proportions and invested all they had, and more which they borrowed. As with the Tulip Mania of the 1630's, the South Sea bubble of the 1720's and the Dotcom bubble of the 1990's, fraudsters capitalised on public credulity, cupidity and stupidity. When it was realised that Poyais had no more reality than Brobdignag the stock market crashed and people then rushed to remove their savings from the local banks. Some of these country banks could not meet the demands this panic placed on them and were forced to close their doors. In Essex, Cricket and Co of Chelmsford, the second most important banking firm in the county, became the first to succumb when it stopped payment on Christmas Eve in 1825. It was followed three days later by the smaller Searle and Co of Saffron Walden, and then by Joyner, Surridge and Joyner of Romford on 2 January.

The crisis was eventually ended by a large loan from Britain's oldest and most recent enemy, France, demonstrating how international the financial markets had become by this time. However, this injection of capital from the Banque de France came too late for the communities served by the 73 banks across the country which had failed during those few weeks in 1825 and 1826. In Romford the shock must have been considerable, even to those who did not lose any money. There must have been much discussion in the Market Place in the early months of 1826 regarding the characters and the fate of the two Joyners and Robert Surridge, particularly after they were declared bankrupt on 18 February. At this time bankruptcy was a criminal offense and brought disgrace and humiliation to the individual and his family and associates. The bankrupt could lose everything they owned and their reputation would be in ruins. Debtors could remain in jail until their debts had been cleared, and even then they needed the permission of their creditors to be released.[162]

The Trustees met for the first time since these bank failures on 7 March. Over the previous 10 years the average attendance at their meetings had been eleven, but on this occasion fourteen men gathered in the school. How did they now view the treasurer whom they had unanimously re-elected twelve months previously? The Rev'd John Walker of Hornchurch took the chair, and a curt entry records that it was 'Ordered that Mr Surridge's resignation be accepted and that the Trustees present return him thanks for his past services.' James Marson Carruthers, a thirty-five year old surgeon who lived in Romford, was voted in as the new Treasurer and the business then turned to the dilapidations of the houses in Hornchurch Lane. This discussion was continued when eleven of these men re-gathered on 21 March, at which meeting they elected three new trustees: Thomas Mashiter (who was introduced earlier with his brother Octavius),[163] James Macarthy and John Elsee. James Macarthy was well known in the Liberty both as a 'Chymists and Druggists (& soda water and ginger beer manufacturer)' in the Market Place[164] and as a popular amateur actor. He will play a very significant part in this history. John Elsee's brief appearance would be entirely overlooked were it not for his pamphlet.

Elsee epitomised the 18th century self-made man. For a number of years he lived at Hampden House, Collier Row, where his hobby was the breeding and sale of merino sheep, in addition to which he owned at least three properties in the City of London. At this time he was aged about 76. His pamphlet was entitled: *The Late Romford Bank. To the Creditors of the Estate of Messrs Joyner, Surridge, and Joyner, Bankrupts*, and was printed in Romford in 1828. By then the bankruptcy procedures had been finally wound up, but Elsee's anger and contempt had not cooled and he illuminates Surridge and his bankruptcy in a pyrotechnic display fuelled with vitriol. Allowing himself to be elected a trustee immediately following the resignation of the disgraced Surridge and Joyner seems like an act of calculated revenge, but he probably had a genuine interest in the charity children because his start in life had been very similar to many of theirs.

> When I set out in life, I was a poor and almost friendless boy, I wanted the advantage of education, even of the most humble description, for I was never put to school, but at that early age, I learned to eat the bread of industry, and by that alone, have I obtained my present independence. In the beginning of the year, 1760, I went into service with a Farmer, and from that period until 1776, I was never a month out of place. I then came to London, and got a situation, as a porter, in Cheapside where I continued until my Master died, in 1784, when I took a house near Queenhithe, and commenced business as a wholesale Stationer, (and where I continue to have connexions to this day,) and at one time I shipped more Paper and Stationary abroad than any other house in the kingdom; my almost unexampled success induced others to try the same experiment, and from that time it became the Paper Market.

He seems to have been a very different character from Robert Surridge, but until the bank collapsed these two men had been close friends for 30 years; indeed, Elsee had said Surridge was 'one of his best friends'. He now despised him. Overnight this friendship turned to a deep animosity and contempt which he vented in his pamphlet with a cold, controlled intensity.

He personally had lost £10,000 {£870,000} as a result of the collapse of the bank, but this is not the reason for his enmity:

> Had they fallen into embarrassment by the unforeseen and unavoidable casualties, which often betake men engaged in Trade, I should probably have not been the last to come forward and assist them out of their distresses; but there is a wide distinction between a man's faults and his misfortunes, the one demands censure, the other commiseration. In the former predicament, I think, Mr. Surridge is placed; I was once his friend, but that I am so no longer, I do not hesitate to avow; for I should blush to be on terms of amity or intercourse with any man who had acted as he has done.

He now believed the bank to have been flagrantly mismanaged from the start and that Robert Surridge had never kept proper accounts and had allowed the three partners to grossly overdraw on the funds for their personal expenditure. When the bank collapsed they had failed to disclose all their assets, secreting money and plate away from their creditors, and when the official enquiry into the collapse of the bank started they produced accounts which were 'ambiguous, complicated and indefinite' and which were designed to 'bewilder and mislead'. As a result of this obfuscation there were over fifty meetings of creditors and the two Commissioners took over two years attempting to understand what had happened, and then only accepted the accounts because until they did so the dividend, 15s in the £1, could not be paid to the creditors who were demanding an end to the procrastination. When Elsee obtained nine signatures demanding that the assignees call a meeting of all the creditors to explain exactly what was going on, he was attacked in the press by, among others, Robert Surridge himself. It was this that galvanized him into writing his pamphlet, 'the only object [of which] is to expose fraud and to unmask hypocrisy'.

In John Elsee's eyes, old Joyner was to be pitied: 'his pride got the better of his prudence, and to that he owes his present degradation. Though a well meaning, and so far as I ever knew, a strictly honest man . . . he was wholly unfit for the station to which he had been thus suddenly lifted up: when he became a Banker, he got out of his natural element.' Of the younger Joyner he had little to say, but on the occasion he is mentioned he is portrayed as reckless but honest, in comparison with the reckless, dishonest, and hypocritical Robert Surridge:

> We learn, indeed, that Joyner, jun. has made away with no less than £90,477 {£8,000,000}, and he has the effrontery to let his Creditors know that his property will produce £6,000 {£520,000}. The *pious Mr. Robert Surridge is only £70,000 deficient, for which he gives somewhat a* similar apology. Young Joyner makes an effort at explanation in regard to a part of his defalcation, he puts it down to " losses by Stock and Share Transactions with Mr R. Surridge " but, Mr. Surridge, thinking no doubt, that the character of a gambler would not mix well with that of a Chapel-builder, had the ill-manners to Contradict what his Partner had solemnly deposed to on oath, by asserting in a letter to the edition of a London Newspaper, (the Courier) that he never trafficked in Stocks or Shares; though, unfortunately for him, that assertion has not been borne out by subsequent discoveries that I have made. The contention between these worthies is pretty much like that between Peachum and Lockitt,[165] and just as much entitled to credit, though of the two, I should prefer taking Joyner's story to Surridge's refutation, as the latter had a most cogent reason for keeping the gambling affair in the back ground; but the truth will come out in spite of him.

Robert Surridge bears the brunt of Elsee's accusations and scorn. He is 'the religious Mr. Robert Surridge!' a member of that 'weak and selfish tribe called Methodists'. 'If a begging subscription was set on foot, whose name appeared at the top of the list? But the pious Mr. Robert Surridge!'

> Banking was Mr. Surridge's vocation, and the mendicant pastor could not have made a more eligible choice of a Patron, than one who always had money at command, no matter whether it belonged to himself or to the Public.
> Perhaps some will say, I have no right to question the purity of Mr. Surridge's principles, that I think is best left between God and his own conscience; but what I contend is, that he should not have made the Public suffer from the indulgence of those pious leanings; he should have worn two large pockets, one to hold the conventicle money, the other the Bank money, having especial care never to mistake one for the other.

The other targets of his scorn and rage were the Assignees, those three gentlemen who were appointed to manage, sell and distribute the proceeds of the bankrupts' estates on behalf of the creditors. He accuses them of 'tardy and imbecile conduct' throughout the whole Commission and condemns 'their supineness and indecision, together with a too pulpable inclination to screen the Bankrupts'. He is outraged that these men, who were meant to be acting for the creditors, used 'hole and corner' meetings attended by half a dozen friendly creditors to carry a particular measure which they then claimed represented the opinions of the hundreds of others who had not been heard. In this way the Assignees justified being unduly lenient with the Bankrupts. One example he gives is the arrangement which ensured Mr Surridge's household furniture was returned to him rather than being sold for the benefit of his creditors. The Chairman of the Assignees was reported to have said 'that the Bankrupts had assisted the Assignees so materially in the arrangement of their affairs, that Mr. Surridge had a strong claim on their sympathy.'

> Dear Sympathetic souls! So, because, indeed, a Bankrupt Banker who has contrived to make away with some thousands of the money committed to his care, in the character of a Public Trustee, his sycophant friends, must turn round, and say that he has a strong claim on Public sympathy, because indeed he had been compelled to do his duty.

So who were these Assignees, these 'sycophant friends'? The Chairman was none other than Thomas Mashiter, a man of great prestige and influence in the Royal Liberty who had been elected a trustee of the Charity School at the same time as Elsee himself, and one of the others was Edward Ind. No wonder Elsee accused the Assignees of favouring the bankrupts, their social and previous business relationships no doubt extending well beyond Charity School trustee meetings.

He was in no doubt of the punishment the two younger partners deserved:

> these three Bankrupts have fraudulently kept back and plundered the Creditors, and thrown every impediment in the way to prevent the truth being come at, and before half the Meetings were had, if justice had been done, two of them ought to have been committed.

For the sake of balance, it should be noted that in their report on the 'Final Examination of the Bankrupts' on 11 November 1826 the *Suffolk Chronicle* noted that 'the general feeling was, that the partners had acted with very great honour' - but this was after the creditors had heard that they would be receiving fifteen shillings in the pound and perhaps more later. Earlier in the meeting the disclosure that Surridge owed £26,000 lost in stock jobbing transactions and that Joseph Joyner junior had lost £3,500 in this way had caused much angry discussion: 'Some creditors [had] expressed their reprobation of the bankrupts' conduct in embarking property belonging to the public in such a dangerous sort of speculation'. The paper reported one of those present as having observed that 'want of caution was one of the most dangerous vices that a banker could inherit, because he should be considered as a public trustee.'

It was in February 1824, only two years before the bankruptcy of Surridge and the two Joyners, that Charles Dickens's father was arrested for insolvency and taken to the Marshalsea Prison. His son was to fictionalise this experience in *Little Dorritt*, giving the world a grim and claustrophobic image of the treatment of bankrupts at this time. However, despite Elsee's view that he ought to have been committed, Robert Surridge, no doubt protected by his friends and his recent position in society, escaped this trauma and degradation. On 3 June 1828 he was appointed as the British Postal Service Deputy in Romford, to gain which position a third party must have underwritten the required £400 penalty. (His application gave his occupation as Banker's Clerk.) But if he believed justice had been done and the bankruptcy was now behind him, John Elsee did not. This was the year he wrote his damning pamphlet, and until Elsee's death early in 1833 these two men would be estranged.[166]

Robert's mother, sixteen years younger than her late husband, was still alive to witness her son's disgrace. Perhaps it brought on her death, because she was buried on 2 December 1827 at the age of 56. The partner who suffered most from the Bank's collapse, as the *Suffolk Chronicle* pointed out, was old Joseph Joyner, whose Hunter Hall Farm Estate in Dagenham was sold on 3 May 1826. Not only had he not lost other people's money by gambling on the stock exchange, he did not even know that his other two partners were taking money out of the bank for this purpose. He had invested his share of the profits in property, wine, and other assets which could be forfeited and sold for the benefit of the creditors. These raised about £45,000, without which the dividend would have been comparatively trifling. He, however, was reduced 'almost to beggary'. The speed and suddenness of his ruin is encapsulated with pathetic brevity in the opening of the revised will which he wrote on 31 August 1827. It begins:

> Whereas about Nov 1825 I Joseph Joyner made a will providing therein for the whole of my children Joseph Sumpner Joyner [and another four children] and my dear wife . . . . but by unfortunate and imperfect management of the Romford Bank the above named Will is become nugatory and useless . . .

He was buried in Aveley parish church on 3 March 1834.

And what of his eldest son, partner in the bank and onetime trustee of the Charity School? Perhaps he immediately sought refuge and anonymity on the west coast of Ireland, and there built a new reputation. Was it a coincidence of name and profession, or was it the same Joseph Sumpner Joyner who was the subject of a letter in the *Connaught Watchman* on 16 November 1853 paying tribute to his management of the Ballina branch of the Provincial Bank of Ireland since its opening 26 years before? The letter lamented his retirement owing to ill health and begged his acceptance of 'the accompanying piece of plate', stating that 'it is almost superfluous to say that you have always enjoyed the respect and esteem of the residents in this town and in the surrounding district'. Beneath were 95 names, beginning with 'A. Knox Gore, Lieut. and Custos County Sligo', and including the High Sheriff, the High Constable, 15 JP's, at least 4 clergy of different denominations, and representatives of the military, the police and the Bar.[167]

Chapter 20

A case in Chancery

1826 - 1832

1826: The property in Hornchurch Lane
At Michaelmas 1766 Joseph Bosworth's estate in Hornchurch Lane had been let to Mr James Holland on a 61 year building lease, which in 1778 had passed to a Mr Hambleton, a carpenter in the town. (Fifty years earlier Clement Hambleton, probably his father, had been the bricklayer who had worked with his two carpenter colleagues to build the school.) In 1796 Mr Roberts took over the lease and by 1805 it was held by Mr Overett. Over these years the rent of £14 had been paid, but in August 1812 the trustees agreed to drop it to £12. By the end of 1815 Overett was dead, the rent returned to £14, and the lease was with Mr Heaphy, who still held it in March 1826 when it had only eighteen months to run. There were now four houses on the site and the trustees were anxious to receive the property back in a good state of repair, and that is why at the meeting on 7 March, having accepted Mr Surridge's resignation, they turned their attention to this issue.

    A Mr Higgins was employed to survey and value the property, and they then wrote to Mr Heaphy to ask him what offer he intended to make respecting the dilapidations, which seem to have been extensive. Within three weeks Mr Heaphy had replied offering to surrender the lease forthwith, an offer which the trustees accepted, putting the legal formalities in the hands of Mr Townsend, a solicitor and a Trustee since October 1825. By October 1826, with the property back in their possession, they requested Mr Higgins to produce a plan and specification showing how the Estate could be made more profitable and so increase the funds available to the charity. We can assume this was produced, but the Trustees then encountered a possible and a definite problem in taking the project forward. The possible problem was the loss of the deeds, as we do not know whether they had obtained the necessary copies by then; the definite problem was that those who had been Trustees of the property in Hornchurch Lane when it was bequeathed to the Charity, those named in the deed of 16 August 1728 which legalised the purchase of the land on which the school was built, were now all dead, and there was no scheme in place giving the present 'trustees' the necessary legal authority to act (with the exception of the two ex officio clergy). Faced with this, at a special meeting in March 1827 it was resolved that Mr Townsend should prepare a case to be submitted to an Equity Barrister for his Advice respecting the future appointment of trustees and the power of the present ones over the property of the Charity. Three months later a Mr Shadwell gave the advice they sought: in his opinion the only course was to make an application to the Court of Chancery.

This was not the advice the trustees wished to hear. Charles Dickens' great satire on the Court of Chancery, *Bleak House*, would not be published for another quarter of a century, but they knew that such a course would be very expensive and so they decided to let the houses under the authority of the present Trustees on Lease, as they had done in the past. A Mr Butler had applied to become the tenant of one of the houses, and Mr Townsend was ordered to prepare a Draft Lease. However, that September (of 1827) it was decided to pull down the two properties to the north and to repair the two to the south. One can deduce from this that the houses were indeed very dilapidated. A pump was to be provided for the use of these two houses, and in March 1828 £3 was paid for digging a well. Walls were constructed to divide the gardens and to divide these properties from the remainder of the estate. At this time there was certainly one tenant in residence, a Mrs Jacobs, although the Treasurer was ordered not to renew her tenancy.

The trustees were certainly economical. Stephen Collier, an auctioneer and appraiser and one of their number, sold the building materials from the demolished houses for £64 14s 6d, but charged them £11 4s for doing so. The bricks were kept to build a wall on the west side of the Charity School Garden, replacing a fence which was then used to repair the fence on another part of the garden. It was at this point, in March 1828, that there was a discussion in the House of Commons which, as we shall see, possibly made them pause and reconsider their decision not to follow Mr Shadwell's advice and make the application to the Court of Chancery. The repair of the two houses was now complete, and the following month they sold £200 of stock from the £1500 in the 3% consols to raise the £170 10s they needed to pay for this work, but what authority did they have to sell or develop the land where the other two houses had stood?

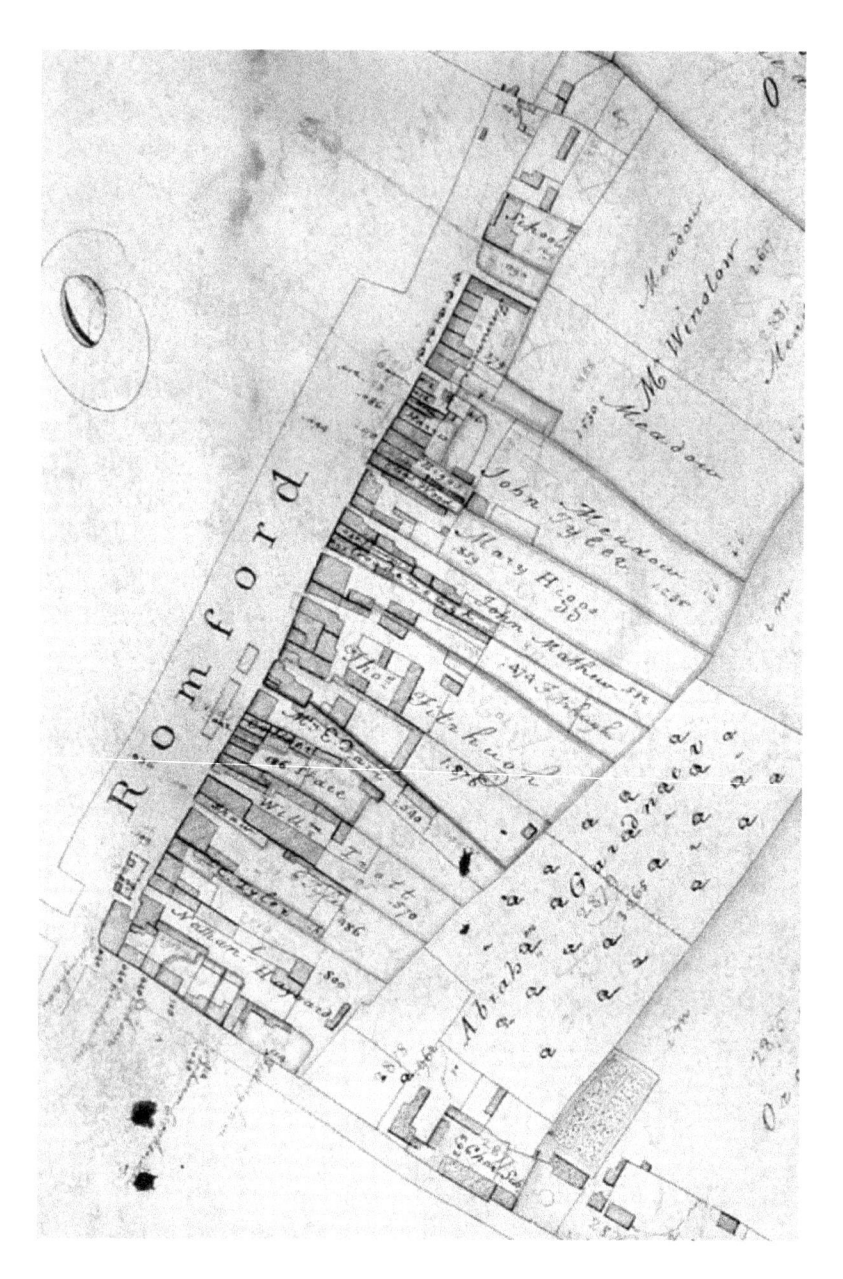

An extract from Hornchurch Parish Map, 1812. The word 'Romford' is in the Market Place, and right of centre at the top of the map a plot is marked as 'School'. The words 'Charity Sch' at bottom centre show the position of the Joseph Bosworth property on Hornchurch Lane (later renamed South Street).

1826 and 1827: lost deeds, yet another change in the years of schooling, and a new Chaplain

Three years had now passed with apparently no action having been taken to recover the lost Deeds and with no evidence that Mr Tweed had contacted Mr Tyler or that the 'strict search' for them had been carried out. The next reference to them is at a meeting in November 1826, by when the trustee Wasey Sterry had become solicitor for the Charity:

> Ordered . . . that the thanks of this Meeting be given to Mr Sterry Senior for his gratuitous services rendered to this Charity, and that Messrs Sterry and Co be requested to seek for the deeds which regulate the Trust of the Charity and the investment of the property and to procure official copies of the different wills under which bequests have arisen, and also if the original Deeds which have been enrolled cannot be found, to procure official copies of the Enrolments of those several Documents in order that the same may be deposited among the Charity's muniments at the School, taking no more than a copy of one Enrolment where the same have been enrolled in more than one Court, and to communicate to the Treasurer the result of their searches as soon as they have been made.

It is clear from this entry that many of these important documents were missing and had been missing for at least seven years. However, at another meeting two weeks later it was reported that Messrs Sterry and Co had declined to act as Solicitors to the Charity and that it had been resolved to appoint Mr Townsend as Solicitor in their stead. Mr Townsend was present at this meeting and immediately accepted the appointment. It was hoped the problem would now be resolved: either the missing papers would be found or - a costly but necessary alternative - copies would be obtained.

At a meeting in October 1826 six boys and four girls were the first to 'Go out under the new rule having had 3 yrs schooling', along with a further 6 boys and 1 girl who just 'left school', 1 girl who was 'over age', and 2 boys who went into service. At the same meeting, in yet another attempt to tackle absenteeism, it was 'Ordered that the Children do not absent themselves from School under any pretence whatever except illness and then certificates must be produced from their medical attendants'. This is the first record we have of medical evidence being required to explain absence. Those ten children who were discharged after three years of schooling were unfortunate, because the following October, in 1827, there was yet another change of policy, and after four years it was 'Resolved that the minute of 2nd of May 1823 limiting the children's schooling to 3 years [be] rescinded, and that in future, the term of their continuance be extended to 4 years; and that no child be allowed to remain in the School after it shall have attained its 13th year.' Maybe 14 year-old boys were just too large and awkward in the classroom, but if you started at the school when you 8 or 9 you could complete your four years of education.

On 24 November 1827 the *Bristol Mirror* reported the death of William Everett, Chaplain of Romford since 1814. He died in Clifton, 'where he had gone for the recovery of his health'. The paper commented that he was 'deservedly lamented by his parishioners, to whom he had endeared himself by his constant residence amongst them, and by his zealous discharge of his clerical duties'. It says much about the prevalence of non-residency in the late eighteenth and early nineteenth century that 'his constant residence' was a matter to comment on. Practices were now changing, however. His successor was John Egerton Rathbone. At the age of 49 and after 33 years at New College he had to forsake Oxford for Romford in order to marry Arabella, which he did in November 1828. At a meeting later that month he was thanked 'for his handsome present of 50 Prayer Books to the Children', and three years later it was 'Ordered unanimously that the thanks of the Meeting be given to the Rev J E Rathbone for the 3rd handsome gift of 50 Prayer books for the use of the School.' He was to play an important role in the challenges and changes of the coming decade.

5 March 1828: The slow, expensive journey of the Charity Commissioners to a town near Romford

It had been on 5 March 1818 that Henry Brougham had first outlined to the House of Commons his proposal for commissioners to carry out an audit of the nation's charities and redirect the misapplied funds to the 'Education of the Lower Orders'. Ten years later, on 5 March 1828, Daniel Harvey, the Member for Colchester, rose in the House of Commons to request a full breakdown of the costs of this work. He wished for this information because he believed that 'of all the commissions which had ever been issued at the desire of parliament, no[t] one had ever been attended with such costly results, and with such slight beneficial consequences as [this one] . . . and . . . it had also been, with a single exception, the most lavish and extravagant in its expenditure'. Its single achievement, he opined, seemed to have been the production of seventeen huge folio volumes of reports, containing, on average, eight hundred pages each. How much had all this cost?

To illustrate the failings of the Commission he cited just one example, only six uncomfortable miles from Romford. The Commissioners had reported that many years ago a charity had been very generously endowed in Brentwood, Essex, for the purpose of giving the boys of that town moral, virtuous, and religious instruction, and a classical education. Over time, and from several accidental causes, the funds had increased from £100 to £2,000 a year:

> and yet, strange to say, on that foundation not more than three children were at present educated, while the whole of the funds were in the Receipt of the patron of the school, who applied them chiefly to the benefit of his own family. Now, he would ask, had any remedy been applied to this case of evil? If none had been applied, of what use had been the appointment of the commission?

He went on to say that it appeared the commissioners had thought at one time to divert a part of the £2,000 {£180,000} to some object of county importance 'but they had subsequently displayed an anxious desire to ... stifle all inquiry into it' and were now, 'for the benefit of cunning lawyers', placing the charity under the revision of the Court of Chancery, which would certainly be expensive and might, in the long run, consume all the funds of each charity treated in this way. This was why he wished to know both the total cost and details of each case of abuse the Commissioners had challenged: the names of defendants, the outcome, the costs, and who had paid and received reparation when an abuse had been uncovered. His motion was agreed to.

The Trustees in Romford had been embarrassed by the revelation that their recent Treasurer, Robert Surridge, had been buying stocks with money deposited in good faith by his bank's clients, but there was no evidence that he had misused the charity's money. Nor had they reason to fear prosecution for such gross misuse of charitable funds as had apparently happened in Brentwood. However, the Commissioners might decide that they should have followed Mr Shadwell's advice and made an application to the Court of Chancery. What if the Commissioners placed the Charity under the revision of the Court of Chancery? Would their funds then be at more risk from these 'cunning lawyers' than if they took the initiative and went to the

Court themselves to legalise their position before the Commissioners made their slow and expensive way to Romford?

If these were their thoughts when they heard about the case in Brentwood, they took no immediate action. That October (of 1828) a committee was set up to negotiate with a prospective leaseholder for the land freed by the demolition of the two houses, but it was not until April 1830 that Mr Wedlake's offer to take this land at an annual rent of £20 was accepted. A further seven months passed, and then on 16 November a special meeting was called 'to consult and devise the best means of disposing of the piece of ground in Hornchurch Lane belonging to the Charity'. This is confusing, but it seems the problem was not *whom* to dispose of it to, but *how* to legally dispose of it to Mr Wedlake, because at this meeting 'It was resolved . . . that Mr Townsend be directed to take such steps in the Court of Chancery as are necessary to carry into effect the recommendation of Mr Shadwell contained in his opinion of the second of June 1827.' Thomas Wedlake was from Hornchurch and had been a trustee since May 1824. He was a manufacturer of machines for agriculture and other purposes whose business interests extended far beyond Essex. He had a London Warehouse at 118 Fenchurch Street, and a hay-making machine he had invented some years earlier had been awarded a prize at the Royal Agricultural Show at Liverpool. Perhaps his fellow trustees were now concerned that when the Charity Commissioners arrived in Romford they might scent corruption in the land having been leased to one of their own without a public advertisement, and that if they looked further into this they might discover that only the two ex officio clergy trustees had the legal authority to lease the land to anyone.

It is unfortunate that we do not have a record of the discussion leading up to this decision to refer their legal status to the Court of Chancery. Were they unanimous? Were there additional reasons why they now felt it necessary to take this step? Were they hearing rumours that there were Members of Parliament who now believed that a little government money ought to be made available for school buildings, an idea which had been floated in Parliament by Henry Brougham twelve years earlier? Any such talk now would have been speculative, but if money was to become available and if the Trustees were to secure some of it for the school at Romford then their legal standing would need to be beyond reproach.

1831: the case in Chancery

Lord Liverpool's administration had finally fallen on 9 April 1827 over the issue of Catholic Emancipation. In 1828 the Test and Corporation Acts had been abolished in the face of opposition from the Church of England clergy, who had argued that great dangers would follow. Once again they were behind the times: by then the Acts had been suspended annually for over a century and abolition only formalised an existing reality. Catholic Emancipation was finally achieved in 1829. In 1826 the Methodist Robert Surridge had resigned as treasurer of the Charity School, to be replaced by James Marson Carruthers. Carruthers held the post for five years and had overseen the meeting on 16 November and its immediate follow-up, but on 3 May 1831 he resigned and James Macarthy was elected in his place. James Macarthy was a Catholic, and was soon to discover that emancipation had not diminished the strong prejudice many still held against upholders of his faith.

Mr Townsend must have acted quickly, because on 18 January 1831 information was filed by the Attorney-general on behalf of nine men, the 'Relators' in the case: the Reverend John Walker of Hornchurch, the Reverend John Egerton Rathbone of Romford, and seven others.[168] They were described as 'Gentlemen' of Romford, although this might have been used generically and included some from Hornchurch, like the Rev'd John Walker. In due course this information was brought before the Lord Chancellor.

Under the deed of 16th August 1728 which legalised the purchase of the land on which the school was built 18 trustees had been named: the Vicar of Hornchurch, the Curate of Romford, and 16 others of whom 8 were to come from Romford and 8 from Hornchurch. These trustees had to appoint new trustees as occasion required. The complaint of the nine Relators in the present case was that because they had omitted to do this those who were now managing the Charity had no legal authority to do so, with the exceptions of the Vicar of Hornchurch and the Chaplain of Romford as ex-officio trustees. In their information they stated that 'the present Trustees or Persons who have been named or solicited to take the management of the said charity were the Relators' (that is, the nine of them), and that the Reverend James Bearblock and twenty-nine others, all of whom were named,[169] were the Defendants. Thirty-eight names are therefore mentioned in total, a figure which presumably included all those who at that time were recognised as 'trustees' of the charity. Because his name was placed at the head of the list of Defendants, the case is recorded as 'Attorney General at the relation of Walker and others v. Bearblock, 1833', a title which masks the fact that the subject of the case was in fact the Charity School at Romford.[170]

This is confusing, but it would appear that the logic and strategy were as follows: 38 people had been acting as trustees; 36 had no legal authority to do so, so in law there were now only two Trustees, the Vicar of Hornchurch and the Chaplain of Romford; because there were less than 7 Trustees there was no authority to take any action, including the authority to appoint new trustees; those who had been acting illegally as trustees could not take action in the courts against themselves, therefore it had been arranged that the two clergy (being 'the present Trustees') and seven stooges (being the 'Persons who had been named or solicited to take the management of the said charity') would bring the action against the 29 'illegal' trustees. The words 'Persons who have been named or solicited' is confusing legal-speak because the seven lay 'relators' had exactly the same (lack of) legal standing as trustees as the 29 defendants. The terms 'relators' and 'defendants' suggests an adversarial relationship, but this is misleading: they signify a random division of the existing trustees as a means to an end.

What the nine Relators requested, through the Attorney General, was that the Court should decide on a scheme for the future regulation of the Charity, that the funds applicable for its support and maintenance should be ascertained, that new Trustees should be appointed to administer these funds, that the land and property of the charity should be conveyed to them, and that an enquiry should be made as to the most beneficial course to pursue with regard to the land which had been left to the charity by Joseph Bosworth.

The record of the Chancery Case states that the information given by these nine men confirmed the establishment of the school in 1710 and that it had been supported by voluntary contributions from the neighbourhood and 'managed by the persons who supported it without any written regulations'. This is significant: these so-called 'trustees' were now having to attend court because from the beginning the Charity had departed from the arrangements laid down by the SPCK in their *Accounts of the Charity Schools*: 'Subscribers' had never elected 'Trustees', and the Trustees appointed when the land was bought for the school house 'on trust' under the Scheme of 16 August 1728 had ignored the injunction to elect replacements when their numbers fell below the stipulated eighteen.

The Relators then detailed the early history of the school: the accumulation of gifts and legacies, the purchase of land by William Hide, the transfer of this land to the original trustees by the Indenture of Bargain and Sale dated 16 August 1728, the subsequent building of the school, and the issues surrounding the will of Joseph Bosworth. This recital ended by stating that 'the persons acting as Trustees of the Charity by Indenture bearing date 24th March 1766' let the property left to the school by Joseph Bosworth to James Holland for the term of sixty-one years, that several houses had been built on this ground, and that the other part of the ground would be of considerable value as building land if a building lease could be granted for this purpose. This lease, they said, could be obtained only with the sanction of 'this Honorable Court' of Chancery, especially because the Conveyance of the Estate directed to be made by the decree of the 27 February 1738 had now been lost.[171] In saying this, they confirmed that the lost documents had never been found. They also confirmed that at present there was £1,300 belonging to the charity in the Bank of England, as well as £50 bequeathed by William Higgs for the purpose of providing a Dinner for the Charity Children on the day on which the Charity Sermons were preached. This money was now standing in the names of James Marson Carruthers and Edward Ind in a joint account with the Reverend William Everett and John Willson.

The Attorney General then requested the Lord Chancellor to grant a writ of Subpoena ordering the twenty-nine defendants 'to appear before your Lordship in this Honorable Court' to answer the premises and to abide by the rulings of the Court.

One month later, on Tuesday 22 February, there was a Special Meeting of the Defendants. At this meeting only two of those present had been at the Special Meeting which originated the suit the previous 16 November: the Treasurer, James Carruthers, and the trustee and solicitor Thomas Townsend who was managing the case and was the only one of the nine Relators present. Ten of the Defendants were present, and they approved the Draft Answer to the Information and requested that it be engrossed after it had been submitted to the remaining Defendants in the suit. This process took nine months to complete, the enscribed 'Answer' bearing the date 22 November and noting that the statement of the Defendants had been taken 'Without Oath' on 2nd November. In this statement the Defendants agreed with all the Information that has been laid before the Court by the nine informants, that it was desirable that a scheme should be settled for the future regulation of the Charity, and that trustees should be regularly appointed by and under the direction of the Court for the management of its funds. Finally, the Defendants made the legal and symbolic statement that they denied all manner of unlawful combination and Confederacy with which they were charged and said that if there was any matter in the Information to which they had not made sufficient answer they were ready and willing to do so, and they asked to be dismissed with their reasonable costs and charges, 'most wrongfully sustained'. Once he had ascertained that it was not possible to discover who had been the last surviving trustee the Master in Chancery was ordered to appoint a proper person to convey the lands to the new trustees who would be appointed by the court.

1832: the Romford Trustee Savings Bank

A fifteen month period now passed which included the whole of 1832. This was a year of transition for the nation and for the school. In Romford the trustees awaited the hearing in the Court of Chancery and discussed whether or not it would be advantageous to adapt the school to the National School system; in the town and across the country people followed the passage of the Great Reform Act which was to change Parliament forever.

Six years had now passed since the collapse of the Romford Agricultural Bank, but the Romford Savings Bank continued to flourish. There had certainly been panic across the county as one commercial bank after another collapsed in 1826 and 1827, but those with money in the Savings Bank were soon reassured that this was safe. Indeed, to reassure their depositors some of these institutions even paid an additional dividend out of their surplus funds at this time.

These surplus funds were an unforeseen and therefore unintended consequence of the difference between the return paid to the bank trustees by the Commissioners at the Bank of England, fixed by statute at £4 11s 2d per cent per annum, and the rate paid by the trustees to depositors, which varied from one bank to another. It was fortuitous that in 1824 an Act had been passed enabling banks to share out half of their surplus fund among depositors, retaining the other half to 'answer deficiencies'. What else could banks do with this surplus money? As early as December 1824 the Savings Bank in Redruth, Cornwall, had asked the Commissioners if they could use part of their surplus to build accommodation, but these grand personages[172] were reluctant to make a decision. The answer came four years later when, by an Act of 1828, a full time barrister was appointed to ensure the rules of the new saving banks were framed according to the law, and he decided that it was legitimate for the trustees of savings' banks to withdraw surplus funds for this purpose. However, the bank in Romford did not avail itself of this provision and its deposits continued to accumulate.

We know few details of the Romford Bank until October 1832, when the *Chelmsford Chronicle* published a report of the Fifteenth Anniversary Meeting. Those present included Colonel Graves, Major Anderson and Octavius Mashiter, all trustees of the bank, the Secretary William Andrews, and the Manager Joseph Last. All of these men were also trustees of the Charity School, as were two men who were added to the Committee of Management for the following year: the Rev'd Daniel Stacey (who in 1831 had replaced John Walker as Vicar of Hornchurch) and John Tyler of Romford. We also learn from this report that the bank was now operating in Barstable, Chafford and Ongar as well as within the Royal Liberty, and that it paid interest at £3 6s 8d per cent [3⅓%] per annum, as did thirteen of the other fourteen Savings Banks in Essex.

The following year the Savings Bank Trustees present at the Sixteenth Anniversary Meeting included the Charity School Trustees Edward Ind and William Truston, and for the first time we are given figures. There were then three branches at Romford, Ongar and Billericay, and the total receipts from all three over the previous year amounted to £130,914 {£12,000,000}, with expenses of £1,621 {£148,000}. The surplus held in the Bank of England was £38,871. At that time there were 3,132 depositors who included '695 male and female servants, 1,077 persons under age, 337 labourers, 123 widows' and so on, proving the bank was indeed serving the humbler members of the community. We also know, although it was not mentioned in the report, that all the actuarial work involved with this great enterprise was still being conducted by Oswald Adams in his house next to the Charity School.

1827 - 1832: the ongoing life of the school

1833 and 1834 would prove two of the most important years in the history of the school, and the minutes in the *Account* book at this time and in the years immediately preceding them are dominated by business. However, we should pause here to look at the ongoing, day-to-day life of the school as it is reflected in the finances.

In Chapter 18 we compared the breakdown of income in 1813 (£215 15s 10½d) with that for 1804 (£151 1s 11d). We can now compare 1813 with 1827 *shown here in italics:*

	Income for 1827	Income for 1813		
6 months interest of the directors of the poor of Romford		£ 2	5s	0d
Dividend on £718 18s 5d		£19	8s	0d
1 yrs dividend on £150 at 5 per cent		£ 6	15s	0d
2 yr interest on £800 at 3 per cent		£43	4s	0d
2 yrs on £50 at 4 per cent		£ 3	12s	0d
Interest on 3% consols for the year:£25	*5*	*3*		
Dividend on £50 3 ½ percents	*£ 1*	*15*	*0*	
Dividend on 3%consols ½ yr	*£25*	*5*	*3*	
(Value £1684 3s 8d)				
Dividend on 3%consols ½ yr	*£22*	*10*	*0*	
(Value £1500 0s 0d)				
Church collections (charity sermons)		£91	11s	10½d
Charity Sermons	*£69*	*0*	*0*	
Town Collections x 2		£21	9s	6d
Overatts rent		£12	12s	0d
Rent from Mrs Chambers	*£10*	*4*	*9*	
Received by property tax allowances		£ 9	19s	6d
Rec'd of the Trustees at the meetings		£ 7	17s	6d
Donations and subscriptions		£33	1s	6d
Total:		£251	15s	10½d
Subscriptions (+ a dontation)	*£46*	*4*	*0*	
Total:	*£200*	*4s*	*3d*	

In 1813 £251 15s 10½d was approximately equivalent to £16,800 in 2020; *in 1827 £200 4s 3d was approximately equivalent to £17,720 in 2020.*

In 1827 dividends and interest amounted to almost the same sum as in 1813 and subscriptions and donations were higher, but every other category had fallen and the town collections had now ceased. This had resulted in a nearly 20% fall in income. However, the effect of inflation was to give this lower sum a marginally higher purchasing value.

In addition to this regular income, the charity still received the occasional legacy, although these now attracted a 1% tax. In 1827 £30 was received from a Mr Grafton, and it was ordered that this be 'written on the Tablet in the Church in the usual manner', and in November 1832 £30 was bequeathed by a Mrs Carver and £100 by a Mrs Wood of Havering-well, Hornchurch. As we have seen, in September 1827, with the Hornchurch Lane property back in their hands, the trustees had decided to pull down two of the four houses and repair the remaining two, but these accounts suggest that at this time only one of these houses was let.

Throughout the 1820's the collections at the annual charity sermons had averaged £69 {£6,000}. In October 1815 the Ipswich Journal had reported that the Rev'd William Everett had preached a sermon for the London Hospital which had raised £75 from his Romford congregation, a figure in line with that raised for the schools each year. The trustees were clearly anxious to maximise this and to reduce the accompanying expenses, and in December 1826 they decided to discontinue their usual payment of two guineas to Mr Tipper for teaching the Children to sing in preparation for the Charity Sermons on the grounds that he was already paid ten pounds from the Parish 'for that purpose' - presumably teaching the children more generally to sing in church. In October 1827 it was decided it would be beneficial to move the Anniversary Sermons from August to June in future, but in 1828 this made no difference to the collection so they reverted to August. In another attempt to ensure subscriptions did not fall into arrears it was decided in October 1831 that 'the Master apply personally or by letter for the subscriptions due to the School, previously to the next half yearly meeting'.

We can balance this income in 1827 with a snapshot of expenditure for the year, some of which would have been similar each year at this time. These expenses include:

	£	s	d
Master's salary	50	0	0
Mistress's salary	30	0	0
Mr White for carpentry	7	9	3
½ year's stationery	5	8	6
Paving rate	1	0	0
Having chimney swept		4	0
60 suits and 60 caps	40	8	6
[Balance; £50 had already been paid on account]			
Drapery	33	6	1 ½
[Presumably for the girls to make their uniforms]			
Bibles and Prayer Books	15	15	3

Sundry for Sermons	7	7	6	
[Children's dinner, ringers, postage, etc]				
Printing	3	2	6	
Mr Higgins for surveying	6	6	0	
Mr Townsend, Solicitor	32	4	0	
Insurance	1	6	1 ½	
Coals (Mr C Tyler)	8	13	3	
Legacy duty	3	0	0	[1% of £300]

The arrangement for clothing varied. The suits and caps provided in 1827 indicates that every boy received new clothes that year, and the high figure for drapery suggests the girls were then making their own clothes. In April 1828 new clothes were ordered from a Mr Forrest and it was also 'ordered that 75 yrds of course cloth be provided and made into 90 bags by the girls to contain the new clothing', implying that again every child had new clothes. However, in May 1831 clothing was ordered for only 40 senior boys and 20 senior girls. The amount now spent on stationary is of note, and this is for only half a year. This figure reflects the enlargement of the school and the girls now being taught to write. We should also note the cost of the sermons (and the celebratory dinner the children enjoyed), to which should probably be added a share of the printing expenditure. From July 1823 to October 1825 the reconciliations always showed a budget deficit, but they were now again showing a surplus and would do so for the next ten years. However, this figure would swing between a high of £116 15s 0½d {£10,800} (October 1828) to a low of £7 7s 7d {£685} (October 1831).

Other entries in the *Accounts* hint at the domestic life of the Master and Mistress. In October 1829 £10 was given to Oswald Adams towards the expense of converting the cellar of the School House into a kitchen. By now he and Mary had at least six children under 10, including another William and his twin, another Susannah. His father had died in August the previous year, aged 61, and the following March his mother, Jemima, would die at the age of 66. They were both buried at St Edward's, the Romford Ringers Book recording that a Muffled Peal had been rung to commemorate the passing of that pioneering and esteemed former member of their society, William Adams.

In May 1832 it was 'Ordered that the piece of ground belonging to the Mistress on the east of the garden be partitioned off in such way as to leave the present path for the girls, the fence to form an angle up to the two privies; with an understanding that the Mistress is to have half the produce of the walnut-tree as heretofore.' We also learn that the children had a half holiday on Wednesday each week, which in October 1828 was changed to Thursday. Wednesday was the main Market Day, and we can imagine many children would have spent the afternoon working, helping, or just loitering in the Market Place. It would have been an exciting place with the animals, the vendors, the shouting, the carts and horses, and the traffic into and out of the many inns. It would have provided an opportunity to earn a penny or two, or to cause a little mischief. As so often, there is a story behind a simple record such as the change of half holiday from Wednesday to Thursday.

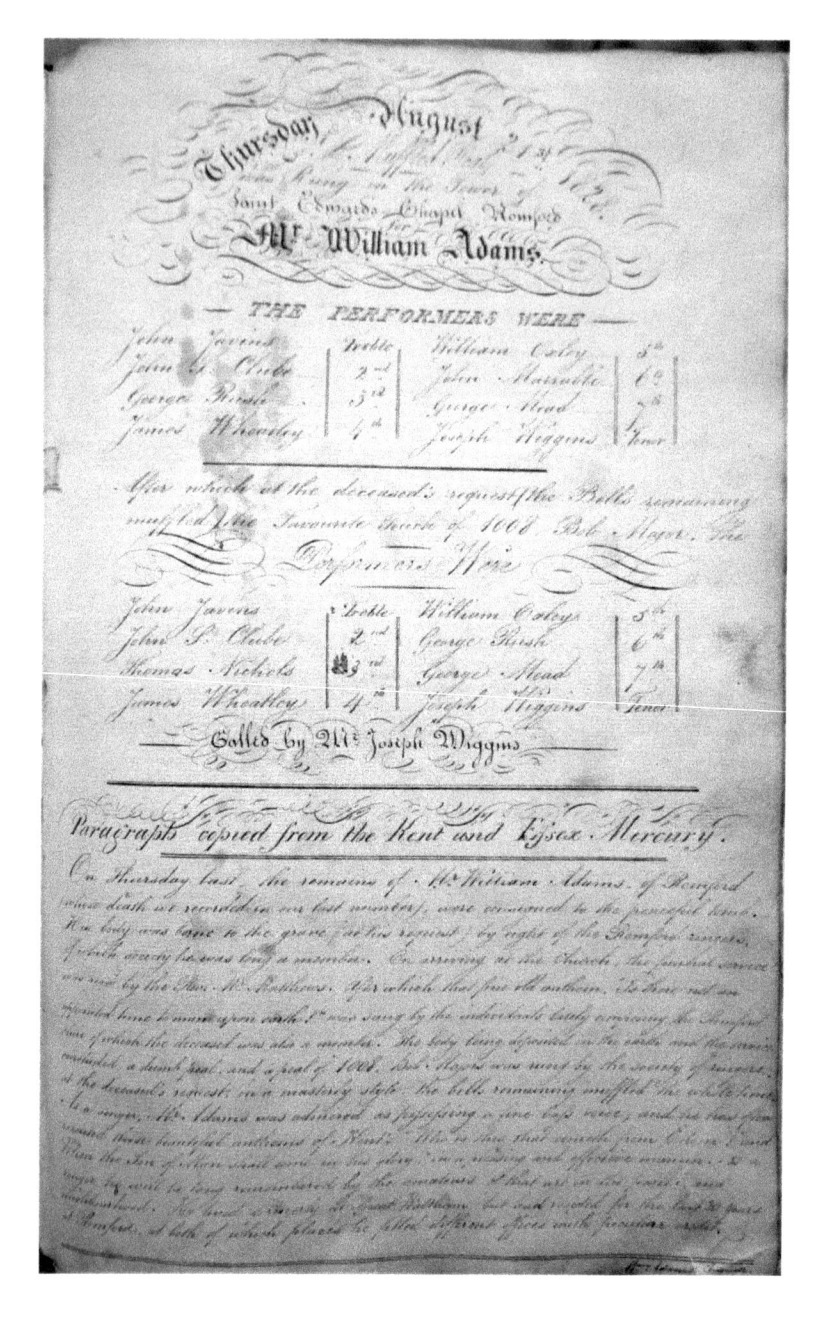

The record in *The Romford Ringers Book* of the muffled peal rung for William Adams on Thursday 21 August 1828. Underneath this is a paragraph about Mr Adams copied from the *Kent and Essex Mercury*

Chapter 21

Acrimony and a finely balanced decision

1833

February 1833: letters to the 'Chelmsford Chronicle'
The Trustees' Account Books record the decisions made, but we need imagination to conjure feeling into these desiccated records. Occasionally, however, another source briefly breathes human passion into distant events, and three letters published in successive editions of the *Chelmsford Chronicle* in February 1833 do just this. They illustrate the religious prejudices of the time, they reveal an important division within the trustees, they give us details of the state of the school building, and they confirm the high regard in which the school was then held. They also give us evidence that the decision made on 19 November 1818 not to enlarge the school and conduct it 'upon the principles of the National Institution' was now being reviewed.

When the scandal of the Romford Agricultural Bank broke in January 1826 it may have surprised some to learn that the treasurer of the Romford Charity School, an institution inseparable from St Edward's Church in the Market Place, was, in the words of John Elsee, a member of that 'weak and selfish tribe called Methodists'. Seven years later readers of the *Chelmsford Chronicle* might have been equally surprised to learn that the treasurer was now a Catholic.

This information was contained in a letter dated 2 February 1833 and printed in that week's edition.[173] It was headed 'Romford, Hornchurch, and Havering Charity School' and signed 'One of the Trustees and a true friend to the Charity'. The anonymous writer said that he hoped his letter would be read by some of his Co-Trustees before the next Quarterly Meeting in April, when he hoped there would be a full attendance 'as several things want revision'. He began by expressing his regret that this Church of England school 'has for its treasurer a CATHOLIC, one who seldom if ever enters the church where the children are twice every sabbath assembled to worship'. He then moved on to his main theme: opposition to any proposal there might be to enlarge the school and turn it into a National school. He was convinced 'that a certain party, who shall be nameless, are disposed to alter the foundation of the school, and put it upon the national principle', adding that he was old enough to recollect that this had been attempted in 1818 when it was overruled by a great majority, which he had no doubt would be the same result if it were again attempted, 'which I shrewdly suspect there is some idea of trying'. Such change, he said, would be unaffordable because even now the funds were insufficient to support the present number of boys and girls, 'as proof of which the last clothing year 30 children out of the 90 had to be provided with clothes by their poor parents and friends. The school house and premises have been upwards of a century, and during my last visit to the school I observed the woodwork was beginning to decay, and therefore the amount for repairs annually must be expected to be considerable.' Despite this, he had observed for some time that some of the trustees wished to expend the greater part of the stock in hand in enlarging the school-rooms for the reception and education of children of all denominations. 'Should this plan unfortunately succeed, I have no doubt the school itself, and that at no distant period, will go to decay for want of sufficient funds to uphold it.'

He recommended that before the meeting in April every trustee should look at the title deeds of the school, held by Mr. Wadeson of Romford, a solicitor who acted as Secretary to the Charity, and he hoped that as soon as the Lord Chancellor gave his decision in 'the suite now before him relative to the Charity' a new deed would be granted and new Trustees appointed. He further hoped that at the same time 'some gentleman professing the principles of the Establishment will be found to act as Treasurer, which I am sure the present Catholic Treasurer will not for one moment hesitate to in resigning in his favour'. He concluded by expressing his hope 'that every Trustee will take the trouble to attend at every meeting to prevent any alteration being made that may prove injurious to this Institution, which has been conducted with credit and usefulness for more than a century, and is an honour and ornament to the Liberty.'

The following week the paper published a reply from Mr Macarthy, stinging with irony and sarcasm. He had read the anonymous letter printed the previous week 'with much surprise'.

> Its writer *professes* Charity, but I "*shrewdly suspect*," to use his own phrase, that his soul is deeply imbued with uncharitableness towards the humble Treasurer to whom he alludes. An anonymous is, to say the least of it, a cowardly mode of attack, and I regret to find myself compelled, lest the Charity be marred, to notice the work of one whose benighted and evil mind "seeketh the works of darkness." The interest of the School did not demand that a public Newspaper should be the vehicle of communication to his co-subscribers. A more direct - a *gentlemanly* one, might have been adopted, as they are but few, and live in the immediate neighbourhood of, and are well known to each other.

He explained how he had come to be appointed:

> About two years since, at a numerous meeting of the Trustees, I was unanimously chosen treasurer (Catholicism was then known to be the sin of my inheritance), and after receiving some compliments from the mouth of the Rev. Mr. Bearblock, I accepted the office, which is one, not of lucre, but of cost and toil.

Following his appointment he had published the accounts with an appeal which had been answered: 'The number of Subscribers has been considerably augmented, and by various means the funds improved'.

He then challenged the accusation at the heart of his adversary's letter. What is this party 'he dares not name' through whose agency he fears the school shall put on a 'National form'?

> I am not aware of the existence of any such party, unless it be the King and the Archbishop of Canterbury, by whose command a Sermon in aid of the *National* Schools was preached in Romford Church last Sunday week, but I am proud in having Dr Croly, the learned Curate of our parish, and others of sound Christian principle and *practice*, associated with me in the opinion that admission ought to be given to a larger number of children.

There will be no departure from the original foundation, which with the schooling includes the clothing of 40 boys and 20 girls, which he hoped would never be discontinued, but the school need no longer be closed 'against the many crying out at our half yearly meetings, "Enlighten our darkness, we beseech thee."' The number was now limited to 90, the last census recorded a population of 6,812, and there were ample funds to promote the object for which Subscribers pay their money, 'the schooling of poor children from the age of eight to twelve'.

> Your liberal and Christian correspondent would exclude from the benefit of a *Parish* Charity School "children of all denominations" save one. Since its establishment no exclusive principle has ever been acted upon, - infants have never been questioned as to their own or their parents' creed, - and shall Bigotry here date its birth from 1833? God forbid!' The children are instructed in the Church of England Catechism, are taught to read in the Church of England Bible, by a Master of the same Church, and surely that is ample security against the Catholicism of a Treasurer, whose *only office* is, to promote the pecuniary means of their obtaining that wholesome knowledge.

In answer to the correspondent's invitation to resign he concludes his letter:

> I inform him that his letter has already added to the number of Subscribers, who, when he and I meet at Phillipi in April, will probably diminish the "overwhelming" majority with which he threatens me; and I assure him that my resignation shall be contemporaneous with the moment when the spirit of bigotry and malevolence which suggested his epistle shall diffuse itself into the minds of my co-trustees; for humble as my name is, I should then feel too much pride to have it so associated.
>
>   I am, Sir, yours very obediently,
>   *Romford*   J. MACARTHY
> TREASURER TO THE ABOVE SCHOOLS, AND A SINCERE FRIEND TO CHARITY SCHOOLS GENERALLY.

The final instalment of this correspondence was published in the edition of 22 February. It was dated 15 February and written by a clergyman who signed himself 'One of the Preachers of the last Anniversary Sermons', so he would have been readily identified. (He was the Rev'd John Thomas, Vicar of Great Burstead, Essex, and Chaplain to HRH the Duke of Sussex.) In the light of the recent correspondence, he begins, 'I cannot, in fairness, withhold a few observations on the subject of the Romford Charity Schools'. In his attempts to be conciliatory and to counteract any possible criticism that he is a friend of Mr Macarthy he writes a very convoluted letter, in the course of which we learn that he has twice delivered sermons for the benefit of the Charity School in Romford, but has also done so for the benefit of other Charity Schools in and outside London. He says of his visits to Romford: 'On such occasions, the collections are always particularly liberal [generous], exceeding even those at Chelmsford and other places, both in and out of the metropolis . . . & the good conduct, neat appearance, and excellent order of the children, could not fail to excite admiration.' It is customary, he continues, for the preacher on these occasions to dine with the Treasurer after the second service, and on the two occasions he has preached he received 'great kindness and hospitality', first from Mr Carruthers and then from Mr Macarthy. He is at pains to stress that this has been the only occasion on which he has ever met or communicated with Mr McCarthy, 'but, be he Catholic, or be he Protestant, it was impossible for any one to evince greater interest in the Charity, or to express himself more decidedly in favour of the Established Church.' He finishes his letter: 'In conclusion, I cannot but think it an extraordinary charge to allege against the Treasurer of any Institution, as a matter of reprehension, that he should manifest a desire to enlarge the sphere of its usefulness; although, from the zeal displayed by the anonymous author of that charge, I am convinced that he is a sincere, but, as I cannot help inferring, a mistaken friend to the charity in question.'

15 February 1833: a petition in Parliament

On 15 February 1833, whilst this parochial and denominational argument was taking place in Romford, Richard Potter, the MP for Wigan, presented a Petition in Parliament from the Unitarian Congregation of Green-gate, Salford, praying the House to take measures to promote a National System of Education. The petitioners believed that education enlightened the mind and formed the character, and thus tended to prevent poverty and crime. '[They] expressed their conviction that ample funds might be provided for this purpose from the numerous charitable bequests which had been left for the promotion of education, many of which were much mismanaged.'[174] To exemplify this, Mr Potter cited Manchester Free Grammar School which had an income of over £4,400 {£426,900} and educated only 150 boys, many of whom were not even on the foundation but paid for their tuition. If the bequest were properly managed, he said, instead of 150 boys receiving education at least 3,000 might be taught. The bequest deed, he added, provided that education should not be confined to Latin and Greek. Henry Brougham had said as much in March 1818.

John Wilks, the MP for Boston, spoke next. He noted that the petitioners 'sought for national education on those tolerant principles which could alone render the experiment comprehensive, and beneficial', and then turned to the work which had already been done, seemingly without any outcome.

> In 1816, 1817, and 1818, Select Committees were appointed to inquire into the state of the education of the lower classes. These Committees sat for three years; much labour was devoted to that object—great evils were discovered—and great hopes excited—but what public benefit had been yet the result? In the year 1818, a bill passed for the appointment of Commissioners to inquire into education and charity estates. The Commissioners had made twenty-one voluminous Reports, but half the kingdom was yet unexplored. A great expense had been incurred, mountains of materials had been collected and piled up, but no advantage had yet been produced. Ample funds existed for national education, without imposing any additional charge upon the people; and they ought to petition till the object be attained.

Daniel Harvey had said as much in March 1828.

Joseph Brotherton, MP for Salford, was the third and final speaker. He agreed that education reduced crime, but in addition it was necessary to reduce the burdens on the people and reduce their poverty, for poverty produced crime. 'If the burthens on the labouring classes were lightened, if the hours of labour were reduced in our manufactories, and a national system of education promoted, the country might expect to enjoy peace, if not great prosperity.' He then turned to the cost of this.

> According to returns made to Parliament, the revenue of endowed schools in England amounted to upwards of three millions annually; and he had little doubt, if the funds of the different charities, which had been left for the purpose of educating the people, were judiciously appropriated, ample means of instruction might be provided without additional taxation.

The Hansard entry ends: 'Petition to lie on the Table.' This brief interruption of parliamentary business came twenty-five years after Samuel Whitbread had failed to win support for the national system of education he proposed in his Parochial Schools Bill of 1807, and thirty-seven years before such a proposal would win the support of Parliament. However, the petition was not unimportant: it was the forerunner of a Parliamentary debate on the subject which would be held six months later; the reference to 'tolerant principles' as a foundation for education touched on the debate about the role of the church in education which would become increasingly divisive; the excessive burdens on the labouring poor would begin to be addressed the following year; and the reference to the Commissioners for Charities reminded the House that fifteen years after their appointment these officials were still labouring on the inquiry which Lord Castlereagh had said might take 'nine or ten years' – and they had still not reached Romford.

23 April 1833: A finely balanced decision

Two weeks later, on 28 February, a new record was set when twenty-four trustees gathered at the School House for a Special Meeting. They were attracted by the importance of the agenda and, no doubt, the recent dispute in the *Chelmsford Chronicle*.

They met 'to consider and decide upon the Heads of a Scheme for the future Conduct and Management of the Charity Estates and Funds and the other Purposes for which the Charity was established'- or, in brief, to discuss the proposed Scheme which had been drawn up for their consideration by the 'proper person' who had been appointed by the Master in Chancery. This was accepted in principle, subject to some suggested alterations, and would now be laid before the Master in Chancery for his approval. We shall examine this in the next chapter.

The Meeting then turned its attention to another issue: the enlargement of the school. Since the rejection in November 1818 of the proposal that the school 'should be enlarged & conducted upon the principles of the National Institution' the situation had changed markedly, and the petition in Parliament thirteen days earlier was symptomatic of the greatly increased national awareness of the importance of educating the poor and the need for schools. If the National Society had not yet achieved its goal of having a school in every parish, since its foundation in 1811 it had gone a long way towards achieving this. The founder and indefatigable apostle of the National School system, Dr Andrew Bell, had travelled and lectured on the continent for some years until forced by ill-health to return to England. He had retired to Cheltenham, where he had died on 27 January the previous year at the age of 78, much honoured and very rich. He now lay with the great and the good under a suitable memorial in Westminster Abbey. Over 12,000 schools in England and Wales now followed his principles, many communities offering far more places than were available in Romford. The census in 1831 had recorded 6,812 people living in the Royal Liberty, with school provision for perhaps 120. Even the neighbouring parish, Dagenham, with a population of 2,118, had relatively more school places since 1828 when Mr William Ford had endowed a free school there for 30 boys and 20 girls. And there was another consideration for the trustees in Romford: if the school did not expand and become a National School, would the British and Foreign Schools Society set up a rival school for those without a place and capture their souls for the non-conformists?

This was the background - together with their unrecorded response to the recent correspondence in the *Chelmsford Chronicle* - to the decision the trustees now made to appoint a Committee of twelve 'to inquire into the means and expediency of educating a larger number of poor boys and girls than are at present educated'. It would report to the next half yearly meeting. The importance attached to this matter is indicated by the size of the committee and the influential men appointed to it: the Rev'ds Daniel Stacy, Dr George Croly and James Bearblock, and Messrs James Macarthy, Edward Ind, Wasey Sterry, and Octavius Mashiter.[175]

The first two names take us back to the period before 1770 when the Vicar of Hornchurch and the Chaplain of Romford had both been resident in the parish and attended trustee meetings together, as they were now doing once again. Daniel George Stacey was 47 and had been appointed Vicar of Hornchurch in 1831 following the death of John Walker. Previously he had had a distinguished career as a fellow of New College, the Dean of Canon Law, and subsequently sub-warden and librarian. The Rev'd Dr George Croly had arrived in Romford in 1832 because John Egerton Rathbone had become too ill to carry out his duties. He had been born in Dublin in 1780 and graduated from Trinity College, and he was already a distinguished writer, having published poetry, plays, the novel *Salathiel* (1828), and having contributed numerous articles to the *Literary Gazette* and *Blackwood's Magazine*. In 1835 he would both publish his edition of the works of Alexander Pope and leave Romford to become Rector of St Stephen Walbrook in the City of London, a living in the gift of the Lord Chancellor, Lord Brougham. His son would write of St Stephen's: 'This parish being very small, and most of the parishioners non-resident, the new rector could still devote a large portion of his time to general literature.' The

Charity School was very fortunate that the brief sojourn in Romford of this influential and energetic man coincided with such important years in its history.

Rev'd Dr George Croly

On 23 April twenty-three men gathered to receive the report of this committee, with the Rev'd Stacey in the chair. Anticipating the distinction between Trustees and Governors to be enshrined in the new Scheme for the Charity, it was agreed 'that in future every gentleman who commences a subscription to the Charity of one guinea, and continues to pay such sum annually, be a Governor'. It was also 'Ordered that the Children's Clothes be repaired against the Charity Sermon ~~the funds being insufficient this year to clothe the 45 boys and 30 girls~~.' Why the crossing out? Was this not true? Perhaps they had the funds but wished to conserve them, knowing that the cost of the case in Chancery had to be met and anticipating a major building programme.

They then turned their attention to the enlargement of the school. The committee had met on several occasions and were now able to report that 'They [felt] convinced that an Extension of Education, would materially benefit all Classes in the Liberty' and that 'They [thought] it possible to accomplish the Building of Rooms sufficient to receive 300 additional Children, without the least Interference with, or Encroachment upon the original Establishment, and still to continue the clothing of 65 Children as at present.' The financial calculations which underpinned this assertion were simple, so simple that they would be met with derision if presented to a bank today as a serious business plan. Looking at the revenue costs, they stated that the present Income of the Charity was £190 {£18,430} per annum and the present expenditure £155 {£15,000} per annum. They proposed an increase of salary to the Master of £20 {£1,940} and to the Mistress of £10, leaving a surplus of £5 on the present income which could be augmented by £30 per annum if each scholar paid one penny a week. The Committee believed that a building capable of containing 300 boys might be erected in the school garden for about £350 {£34,000}, and that the present Boys' School Room, capable of containing 100 Girls, could then be appropriated to their use.

After the report had been read it was moved by the Rev' Dr Croly and seconded by Octavius Mashiter. One might have thought that the influence of these two men would have been decisive, but the writer of the anonymous letter of 8 February clearly had his supporters, and the 23 members present were divided: ten voted for, nine voted against, and four remained undecided. The motion was therefore carried, and with this slimmest of margins the most important development since the foundation of the school was approved.

Chapter 22

A debate in Parliament and a new Scheme to regulate the Charity

1833

4 June 1833: towards a new Scheme
In response to the alterations to the draft Scheme which had been suggested at their meeting on 23 April, the Master in Chancery drafted a report which was read by Mr Wadeson and then examined at a special meeting of trustees on 4 June. The school had proposed 12 trustees, but the Master required the original number of 18, 9 from each of the two towns. Those present agreed eighteen names, but were perhaps initially (and perhaps tellingly) short of a ninth eligible candidate from Hornchurch because one of those selected was 'Mr John Bearblock of Hornchurch [who] was admitted a Governor of the said Charity on payment of his subscription of one guinea.' His was the first name to be entered in the *Accounts* as a 'governor' rather than a 'trustee', although he was then immediately nominated a trustee under the new Scheme. John was the son of the Rev'd James Bearblock, and would play a controversial role as a trustee in the 1850's. Another of those eighteen names was Thomas Mashiter. He had been Chairman of the Assignees appointed to manage the liquidation and distribution of the assets of the Surridges and the Joyners following the collapse of the Romford Agricultural Bank, and it was he who had borne the brunt of John Elsee's scorn. He had resigned as a trustee in April 1828, the year Elsee published his pamphlet, but that had been five years ago: Elsee had died that January of 1833, and Thomas Mashiter was now High Steward of the Liberty. In August he would be appointed Deputy Lieutenant of Essex.

Having examined the report, the meeting proposed that the draft be returned to the Master seeking his agreement and permission for four changes. First, they wished to omit part of a clause which imposed on them the duty of apprenticing students or putting them out to service. Apprenticeship was a system born in the middle-ages and was now too restrictive to meet the needs of an increasingly industrialised society. Many of the industries and trades which had developed in the 18th century were outside the jurisdiction of the Statute of Apprentices because they did not exist when this had been passed in 1563, and in 1814 compulsory apprenticeship by indenture had been abolished. As for domestic service, this would become the second largest category of employment in England and Wales after agricultural work as the Victorian age developed, and many of those in the Charity School, particularly the girls, would no doubt continue to find employment as servants. That being said, the trustees did not wish to be tied to promoting any particular form of employment.

The next two requested changes were linked to their recent decision to expand the school: they sought more extensive powers for building, and they requested an alteration in the wording of a clause respecting the education of the additional children in the Principles of the Established Church. If they saw every boy and most of the girls in the Liberty as prospective students, such restrictive wording would debar those from non-conformists families.

The final change related to the election of the treasurer. As we have noted, the clear cut distinction between 'subscribers' and 'trustees' envisioned in the early 18th century guidance from the SPCK had always remained blurred in Romford. The Master in Chancery now proposed to impose this distinction, with 'governors' (the previous 'subscribers') electing 'trustees' who would elect the treasurer. However, the meeting requested that the treasurer be elected by the governors, and not the more limited number of trustees. They were aware that of the thirty-eight current 'trustees' named as either Relators or Defendants in the Court of Chancery papers, only the twelve of them present at this meeting had selected the eighteen men who would be the new trustees. Reflecting the spirit of the times which had led to the passing of the Great Reform Act the year before, they wanted the most inclusive constitution. Perhaps they were also mindful of the controversy surrounding the Catholicism of their present treasurer: it was better that he was re-elected or deposed by as wide a franchise as possible.

30 July 1833: the debate in the House of Commons on a system of National Education.

On 30 July Mr John Roebuck, the MP for Bath, moved a Resolution that in the coming session [beginning in February 1834] the House would earnestly endeavour to frame a plan for the universal education of the people, which was a matter of national concern. He said he recognised the political barriers he faced when introducing this neglected subject: it was a long term project when political interest was invariably focussed on the immediate; its results would be distant, and the benefits to be expected from it could only be attained by the slow operation of time, patience, and industry; no party or individual interests were served by promoting it. He said that he could not hope for more than a very brief hearing for so unpopular a cause, but then launched into a long, detailed and rhetorical speech outlining the benefits of education and explaining why the Government should, and how the Government could, supply this.

He was perhaps naively optimistic about the consequences of what he proposed: rather than making people discontented with their situation and unfitted for the common duties of life, as some had claimed, education would create 'industrious, honest, tolerant and happy' people who would 'learn what a government could, and what a government could not, do to relieve their distresses . . . [W]e shall have no more unmeaning discontents - no wild and futile schemes of Reform'. He said that great social and political changes were already arising from the Great Reform Act, and that however unwilling people might be to contemplate it, the fact was that power was shifting from the traditional ruling classes to 'the hitherto subject many [who] are about to become paramount in the State'. '[T]he people will never be well governed until they govern themselves', he said, but at present they were far too ignorant to do this wisely and this ignorance was fostered and perpetuated by the Government. Education should be the business of Government because 'the most enlightened nations of the earth have taken upon themselves that task', including France, Prussia and Saxony where, he said, 'a more complete system of public instruction is now in operation than has ever yet had place in any nation of the world.' He quoted the Frenchman Professor Cousin, who had written that he considered 'France and Prussia the two most enlightened countries in Europe - the most advanced in letters and in science - the two most truly civilized, without excepting England herself.'

State provision of education made economic sense: there was an irony, he implied, in the government spending great sums of money on poor relief and on justice, the costs of which would be greatly reduced if all men were educated. 'We allow crime and misery to spring up, and then attempt, by a vast and cumbrous machinery, to obviate the mischief. We punish, we do not prevent, we try to put down effects, without caring for the cause.'

Government had powers and should use its powers, and he disagreed with those who believed that a good Government was one that chose not to do so.

Private efforts to promote popular education had achieved only imperfect success, and Government intervention was necessary. However, he did not believe that this would either put an end to these private efforts or destroy this means of connecting the different classes of society, the poor and the rich. Indeed, the efforts of all would be more systematic, more sustained, and less guided by caprice. Private efforts depending on random contributions produced haphazard provision, and this system also had a demeaning effect on recipients reliant on private charity; with a Government scheme there would be no patronage, no charity-schools 'of this or that individual', no ostentatious display of aid on the one hand and abject subservience on the other. The children of the poor would receive instruction and incur obligation only to the State, so no stigma or painful feeling of degradation would attach to it as is now affixed to everyone who receives gratuitous instruction.

He ended on a high, rhetorical note. It would be 'criminal as well as absurd' not to pursue the course which was now open. 'Shall it be said, that . . . we were content to suffer the mass of our population to be educated as chance might direct . . . Shall it be said, that because simply the benefit of the whole community was concerned in the matter, and no selfish interest could be promoted by it, we were careless regarding it?' He appealed to the House 'in their high character of legislators, to determine on the future destinies of many millions yet unborn; and to say whether their happiness [should] be left to the caprices of chance, or be fostered, guarded, and directed, by the paternal care of a wise and benevolent Government.'

His plan, 'by which every inhabitant of this empire might receive the instruction requisite for the well-being of society', appears to have been largely taken from a book written by the Frenchman he had quoted, Professor Cousin, which he recommended MP's to read. France had very recently passed a law to establish a system of Normal [secular] schools which would be managed in each village by a committee consisting of the maire [mayor], the curé [priest], and three inhabitants, but Roebuck's suggestion that this was a model to be followed in this country raised the various prejudices of those who now rose to oppose his scheme.

There was no disagreement that general education was a public benefit, as there had been twenty-six years earlier in response to Samuel Whitbread's proposal. There was also agreement that education went beyond learning to read, write 'and sometimes, by a stretch of liberality . . . to include arithmetic. [It] means also the training [of] the intellectual and moral qualities of the individual . . . that he may become a useful and virtuous member of society . . a good citizen [and] a good man.' This definition did not differ markedly from that of the SPCK 120 years earlier. There was also general agreement that much progress towards a national system had been made by the voluntary societies over the previous twenty years, although this had been patchy. Beyond this, however, the responses of the seven MP's who contributed to the debate showed no unanimity, as a brief summary of the arguments of five of these will illustrate. They convey strongly the opinions and prejudices of the time, as well as underlining the belief held by the majority that the church should continue to have the central role in the provision of education.

The support of Lord Althorp, the Chancellor of the Exchequer, was vital if the motion was to succeed, but he was unsupportive and complacent. He was unwilling to embark on such an enormous, Government led project, which 'he was not sure . . . would not rather do harm than good' by fatally weakening the voluntary provision. He referred back to the speech of the present Lord Chancellor [Henry Brougham] on 5 March 1818 when he presented the Charitable Foundations Bill and argued education should be funded by the existing charities.[176] He was for limited government, and said that Roebuck's suggestion that a man should be punished for not having his child properly educated would be 'going further than they ought'.

Mr O'Connell, the Member for Dublin, also believed that they should govern as little as possible and should do nothing more than providing the facilities for education, which was then best left to the clergy. He dismissed the examples of Prussia, a military state, and France, where it was of little importance to the liberal party whether a man was 'a Deist or an Atheist' and where the Government was endeavouring to enforce Normal (secular) schools. In fact 'the people preferred to have the assistance of the brothers of the Church in their education', and attitudes were the same here. Nothing, he concluded, could be more destructive than to imitate the example of France in respect to her system of national education.

Mr Joseph Hume, the Member for Middlesex, supported the motion and regretted the remarks of the member for Dublin regarding the French system, the object of which was to give instruction whilst avoiding that proselytism to which he had alluded. In this country there had sometimes been difficulties in attempting to establish Lancasterian schools because they were not under the direction of the clergy of the Church of England, and he hoped that if any schools were established they would not be placed under the domination of any Church. He saw no reason why the State, which felt itself bound to compel its subjects to provide food for its poor, should not also provide mental food and instruction for them.

Sir Robert Inglis, the Member for Oxford University, also agreed 'that it was the duty of a Government to provide for the people, as it was the duty of a father to provide for his children, the means of education', but said he didn't agree with much else which Mr Roebuck had said. Sir Robert Peel, the MP for Tamworth, was complacent. He did not believe that education in this empire was so very imperfect or that the care of the State was necessary. A compulsory system of education appeared to him to tread upon religious toleration for it must, almost of necessity, interfere with religious opinion. 'He thought that the diffusion of education would produce great benefit; but, in a country like our own, which was justly proud of its freedom, he doubted whether it ought not to be left free from control.'

Mr Roebuck closed the debate with an attack on the MP for Dublin for his unfounded attacks on the French government and his assertion that they wished to put down religion. In his book Monsieur Cousin had distinctly said that nothing could be done for the education of the poorer classes without the aid of the clergy. The sentiments expressed by Mr O'Connell were closely allied with that of the priesthood of Rome, whereas the people of France had another Church, the Gallican Church, which was preferred to that of Rome by the French government, the French people, and the Normal School. He then withdrew the Motion.

That this final, rancorous and hysterical outburst should focus on the relative roles which should be played by the church and state in the education system should not surprise us, but that it referred to the system in France and the esoteric distinction between two strands of Catholicism only confirms how far England lagged behind France, Prussia, Saxony and Scotland in its determination to establish a national system of education.

The fact that only eight people spoke is perhaps indicative of the level of interest in the subject, and those who did speak brought up old themes, contentious themes, which would continue to be debated throughout the nineteenth century: should there be a system of public education? If so, should every child be forced to attend school? Should that public education be provided solely by the church and private philanthropy, solely by the state, or do they both have a role to play? And does state intervention destroy private and voluntary enterprise? By 1902 these questions had been answered by parliament, but with strong opinions on each side of every question the answers were inevitably divisive at the time and have remained divisive. They gave us a system with a mixed provision of private, public, secular and religious schools, to which a later generation added another divisive element: academic selection. Over the intervening 120 years society has changed, raising additional divisive questions to those we inherited from our Victorian forefathers. How does a system which supports these various types of school unify a country with different faith communities and a wide socio-economic spectrum? What should be the role of parents and interest groups such as business, industry, the churches and charities in determing national provision? How can the state education system in a multi-cultural country accommodate different faith groups with fundamentally different beliefs about religion, society, and the role of the state, and different interpretations of science and other 'secular' elements of the curriculum? To what extent should citizens be permitted to educate their children outside the state system, either at home or in an independent school, and to determine the nature and content of the curriculum they receive?

John Roebuck had cited the French system as a model to be emulated. The French state would be much more proactive in answering the early, fundamental questions than Britain would be. It was eight years later, in 1841, that Jules Ferry, Minister of Public Instruction, created the modern French education system by requiring all children between the ages of 6 and 12 to attend school. This public instruction was mandatory, free of charge, and secular. In contrast, in England and Wales education became mandatory in 1880, free of charge in 1891, and - for good and ill - it is still a mixture of the religious and the secular.

1 August 1833: an Order of the Court confirms the Scheme to regulate the Charity

Two days after this debate in Parliament an order of the court confirmed the final report which the Master in Chancery had prepared on 15 June. This incorporated three of the four changes which the existing 'trustees' had requested. Because this Scheme of 1 August 1833 summarises the state of the charity at that time and would regulate the charity from then on, it is important to understand its provision.

The report confirmed the financial holdings of the charity as at the half-yearly meeting on 25 October 1831 as £1,300 {£126,000} invested in 3%

Consols, £50 {£4,850} in New 3½% bonds, and £7 7s 7d {£716} sterling in the hands of the then treasurer. In addition, the two cottages left by James Bosworth were let at £12 {£1,160} a year each for the benefit of the charity. The Master certified his opinion that these tenements on Bosworth's land should continue to be let to tenants at will, and that the trustees should have power to grant building leases on the remaining portion of the land upon such terms and conditions as they thought fit.

The Scheme approved and appointed as the new trustees the eighteen people agreed at the meeting on 4 June. The list began with the two clergy, Rev'd Daniel George Stacey (of Hornchurch) and Rev'd John Egerton Rathbone (a sick man, but still the nominal Chaplain of Romford); there were 7 who had been on the list of Defendants: John Cooper (H), Thomas Wedlake (H), William Colls (H), Richard Digby Neave (R), Edward Ind (R), Octavius Mashiter (R), and Major James Anderson (Havering); there were 2 who had been on the list of Relators: James Macarthy (R) and Charles Butler (R); and there were 7 who had not been on either list: Thomas Mashiter (H), Richard Harding Newman (H), Charles Cove (H), Samuel Francis (H), John Bearblock (H), Lieut Colonel Benjamin Graves (R), and Peter Frederick de Jersey MD (R). Some of these men have already featured in this history, and others will do so.

There were fourteen clauses in the scheme laid down by the Master under which these eighteen men were to regulate the charity in future. These can be summarised as follows:

i   The vicar of Hornchurch and Chaplain of Romford should always be two of the governors of the charity, and every annual subscriber to the charity of one guinea {£102} or more should be a governor.

ii   The exclusive management of the charity and its property and revenues should be vested in the governors, who should act in all respects in conformity with the proposed regulations.

iii   The number of trustees should not exceed 18, they should be chosen from the governors, and should they cease to be a governor (by failing to subscribe their one guinea) then they should cease to be a trustee.

iv   The 18 above named persons were to be trustees, and property belonging to the charity was to be conveyed and transferred to them forthwith.

v   The stock in the public funds should be transferred into the names of four of the trustees, and the present four should be the Reverend Daniel George Stacey, Octavius Mashiter, Edward Ind and James Macarthy.

vi   The schoolhouse and the revenues should be used for the 'reception and education of 45 poor boys and 20 poor girls, resident in and belonging to the parishes of Hornchurch, Romford and Havering'. These children were to be 'educated in the principles of the Christian religion as taught and professed by the Church of England by law established; the boys to be taught reading, writing, and arithmetic, and the girls to be taught to read, write, sew and knit', and when the majority of the governors present at a meeting convened for the purpose think it appropriate, the children should be 'placed forth apprentices or put out to service'.

vii   The schoolmaster and schoolmistress should always 'be conformable' to the Church of England, and they, as well as the charity-children, 'should and might be chosen and displaced from time to time' by the majority of the governors present at a meeting convened for that purpose, providing at least five governors are present.

viii   The governors should have power to admit an additional number of children 'resident in or belonging to' the three parishes for the purpose of education in the Christian religion, as specified above.

ix   The schoolmaster and schoolmistress should be allowed such salaries as the majority of governors think appropriate.

x   The governors should choose one of the trustees or governors to be treasurer of the funds of the charity and should have the power to displace that person and appoint another in his place. The treasurer should, at a half-yearly meeting of the governors to be held in the school-house, tender for examination the accounts of the charity for the preceding half-year.

xi   The governors should, out of the income arising from the charity, keep the school-house and dwelling-house in good repair.

xii   The trustees should have power to grant building leases for any term not exceeding 61 years upon such conditions as they should determine.

xiii   The surplus revenues of the charity should and might, with any other contribution and subscriptions made for the purpose, be applied by the governors to improve and enlarge the school-house, or to erect, enlarge or improve any building whatsoever for the purposes of the charity in any way they think fit.

xiv When the number of trustees should be reduced by death or for any other reason to seven or less, it should be imperative upon the governors to elect new trustees to join those still serving to make the number up to the full 18, and the estates of the charity should then be conveyed to the new and continuing trustees. Similarly, when the trustees of the stock should be reduced to two, it should be imperative upon the governors to appoint two other trustees so that the full number of four trustees of the stock might always be kept up.

Three of the four suggested changes to the draft report had been accepted, but not the omission of the clause enjoining the apprenticing or putting out to service of the children, although this only applied to the 65 boys and girls 'on the Foundation'. It is not clear how this requirement that children were to be 'placed forth apprentices' was to be financed, but the 'or put out to service' remained an alternative, cost free option. The word 'apprentice' may have been intended by the court to be interpreted loosely, and may have been dictated by the use of the word in the Mary Hide Trust. At this time judges were unwilling to alter the original terms and conditions of a charitable endowment, however anachronistic they might have become. As late as 1805 'the Lord Chancellor, Lord Eldon, settled a dispute among the trustees of Leeds Grammar School by declaring that arithmetic, writing and modern languages should not be added to the curriculum. In his view, only the grammar of ancient languages should be taught.'[177]

We have seen that the original charity schools offered their children clothing, education, and, if affordable, an apprenticeship afterwards. There is no specific mention of a requirement to clothe the children in the above Scheme, but it may be suggested in the word 'reception' in the injunction in clause vi that the schoolhouse and the revenues were to be used for the 'reception and education' of the 65 poor children. What is clear from this clause is that nothing had changed in the expectation of the education to be offered to these children, and the curriculum is essentially the same as that specified by the SPCK and repeated in the foundation document 123 years previously: 'the Education of poor Children and teaching them to Read & Write and Instructing them in the knowledge and practice of the Christian Religion as professed and Taught in the Church of England'. Time, and most probably custom and practice from the earliest days of the school, has added arithmetic for the boys and sewing and knitting for the girls, but that is all.

Clause viii allows the governors to admit an additional number of children, a freedom they had already exercised. True to its founding principles, these additional children were to live in the three communities of the Royal Liberty and were to be educated in the Christian religion. However, there is a subtle distinction between the 65 poor children of the original foundation who were to be 'resident in <u>and</u> belonging to' the three parishes, and the additional children who were to be 'resident in <u>or</u> belonging to' them. The first is presumably a safeguard to prevent the benefits of the charity being enjoyed by vagrant children who happened to be living in one of the parishes but, as far as the operation of the Poor Law was concerned, belonged to another parish. However, the additional children might have to pay for their education, and as long as they lived locally and could pay their 1d a week it was not important if theoretically they belonged elsewhere.

Finally, it is important to note the distinction between the responsibilities of the governors, and there could be as many of these as were willing to pay their guinea each year, and the eighteen trustees. In clause xiv it is stated very clearly that it is ' imperative' that the governors elect new trustees when the number of these falls to seven or less. The Master in Chancery did not want a repetition of the neglect of this duty which had necessitated this costly case. However, as we shall see, in this he was to be disappointed.

Subsequently, by an indenture of lease and release dated 2 and 3 October 1833, the school-house and premises and the lands and premises left by Joseph Bosworth were conveyed to the new trustees.

When the Trustees met on 22 October 1833 the final Deed was read to the meeting and it was ordered that it be transcribed into the Minute Book and that 300 copies be printed. (In fact it was not transcribed into this Minute Book.) The Trustees then had to pay Mr Wadeson's bill of £327 14s 2d {£31,800}, the expense incurred in the Chancery suit and in drawing up the Deed. To realise this sum, for the second time in five years they had to sell stock, in this case stock with a face value of £372 18s 6d. This brought their investments down to just over £900 {£87,300}. They then turned their attention to the matter which had necessitated this whole, costly case, the development of the land in Hornchurch Lane. This issue was not to be resolved until the very end of 1834, a year which was to prove as busy and exciting as 1833, partly owing to the outcome of a vote which had taken place in Parliament two months earlier.

Chapter 23

'An honour and ornament to the Liberty'

1833 - 1834

17 August 1833: Report of the Committee of Supply - Education
The reading of the Report of the Committee of Supply on 17 August 1833 caught Parliament unawares, and there were immediate complaints at its timing: Parliament would be prorogued in two weeks, not to meet again until the following February; few Members were in town; it was late at night. Mr Hume, the Member for Middlesex, 'expressed his determination not to let one shilling be voted, during the next Session, after twelve o'clock at night.' However, those who were there then proceeded to discuss the proposal by Lord Althorp, the Chancellor of the Exchequer,

> That a sum, not exceeding twenty thousand pounds, be granted to His Majesty, to be issued in aid of Private Subscriptions for the Erection of School Houses, for the Education of the Children of the Poorer Classes in Great Britain.

This grant was to be administered by the Treasury and would be distributed through the National Society and the British and Foreign School Society, with preference being given to large towns and cities.

There had now been three initiatives in parliament to establish a national system of education, promoted by Samuel Whitbread in 1807, Henry Brougham in 1820, and John Roebuck just eighteen days earlier. If none had achieved its objective, it seemed the government had come to realise that whilst the day to day costs of education might be left to the chances of historic local charity and present day benevolence, the provision of school buildings required a more systematic financial input.

Mr Hume, clearly not in the best of humours at that hour, attacked the proposal on three grounds: the sum was too small to establish a system of national education, and without such a system no grant at all ought to be made; the Report of the Commissioners on Charities showed that a sum of £500,000 was applicable for education, and he therefore saw no reason for granting further money for this purpose; and 'this miserable pittance would only dry up the sources of private bounty'.

Lord Althorp, who earlier had opposed John Roebuck's motion, explained how this money would help to achieve the system of national education they wished for without the ill-effects suggested. The Report of the Charity Commissioners in 1818 cited parishes which would have supported schools with their own funds had they been assisted with the initial expense of building the school-house. This was still the case, he said, and the purpose of this vote was to fund the building of schools in places where there were funds available from private giving to cover the running costs.

Three members then argued that a mature plan of national education ought to be proposed before the House voted any money for this purpose, one repeating yet again the old argument that public money might well reduce private charity. Sir Robert Inglis, Member for Oxford University, said he could not support any plan of education that was not based on the principles of the English Established Church, whereupon Lord Morpeth said that for him a recommendation of the plan was that 'the money was to be advanced to assist both systems of education; one exclusively on the principles of the Established Church, and the other admitting children of all creeds and of all nations'. Mr Thomas Estcourt thought that 'this was an experiment' and '[t]here was no proof of any applications having been made for this money'.

Until this point there was, perhaps, a consensus underlying these disagreements that a national system of education would be beneficial to society. William Cobbett then rose to challenge this assumption. This agriculturalist and journalist, whose *Rural Rides* had been published three years earlier, had been elected the previous year as MP for Oldham in the reformed Parliament for which he had long campaigned in the *Political Register*, the weekly newspaper he had been publishing since 1802. He was a man of strong opinions, and now said that he could not consent to tax the people 'one single farthing' in order to teach the working classes reading and writing. 'Education,' he said, 'was the knowledge necessary for the situation of life in which a man was placed.' He invited the Members to go into the agricultural districts and to compare fathers with their sons: they would find, he opined, that in almost every instance the father was the better man, being more able to do his work and more willing to do it. According to the reports received from time to time by the House, Cobbett continued, men became more and more immoral every year, so what were the benefits of this increasingly widespread education? All it achieved was to increase the number of schoolmasters and school-mistresses - 'that new race of idlers'. This proposal was a 'French' plan, a 'Doctrinaire' plan, and he should always be opposed to it.

This voice of reaction was immediately followed by a more liberal view. Mr Murray believed this grant to be very necessary, and he was pleased with the proposal to apply it to aid the education of Dissenters as well as those of the Church Establishment. In answer to Cobbett's assertion that the increase in crime was the consequence of the increase in education, he said that this opinion had once been commonly held in Edinburgh until it was disproved by an experiment. Some masters had kept a list of their workmen with columns to record their conduct over the year, and they had invariably found that those men who had received the benefits of education and employed themselves as often as they could in reading and writing were the most sober, the most industrious, the most regular at their work, and the best conducted in their families. Even the obstinate and the prejudiced masters (and here he assured the House that he did not of course mean to say that the honourable member for Oldham was prejudiced) had been obliged to confess that the result was decidedly in favour of education.

The reference to this experiment in Edinburgh stands out as the only piece of empirical evidence amongst the mass of uninformed prejudice which had so far been voiced. The next speaker, a Colonel Evans, agreed with all that had been said by Mr. Murray but thought that the House ought not to be called on to vote money for the purposes of education while there were still funds in private charities. He, too, took an ironic swipe at William Cobbett, saying that although he did not agree with his opinions they must certainly be disinterested, for if his principle were fully carried out who would there be to read the *Political Register*?

At this time there were 658 MP's in the House of Commons, of whom only 76 were present; thirteen people had spoken, four in favour of the report and nine against. Yet when it came to the vote, 50 were in favour and 26 against. In this way - at around midnight, in a nearly empty chamber, by a majority of 24 - parliament voted its first tranche of funding - just £20,000 {£1,940,000} - for public education.

A fortnight later two landmark Acts received the Royal Assent. On the 28th the Slavery Abolition Act ended slavery in most of the British Empire.

This is marginal to our story, but a reminder of the historic presence of black people within the community of the Royal Liberty, quite possibly as slaves. Their presence is indicated by entries in the Romford Church Registers: 'Charles Francis Malabar a negroe was baptised about 19 years old' in October 1702; 'Arch Angel a Black Moor' from Harold Wood was buried in November 1738; and Bridget Africa, a Foundling child, was buried in July 1754. In the 18th and 19th centuries many children left the Charity School to become domestic servants and until 1833 they may well have worked in grand houses alongside a domestic slave, many of these Africans working as butlers or other household attendants in aristocratic families.[178] Despite twenty million pounds being spent after 1833 to ensure the emancipation of the slaves in British Colonies in accordance with the Act, in many of these places slavery continued under the guise of 'apprenticeships'. In 1838 the government would propose setting up a committee of enquiry into such abuse, in response to which petitions signed by 'the Curate, Churchwardens, Magistrates, High Bailiff, and about 200 of the inhabitants of Romford' were forwarded for presentation to the Lords and Commons. These petitioners saw such a committee as wholly unnecessary, a cause for delaying the putting right of a manifest injustice. '[We] earnestly pray your Right Honourable House to put an end to the system of apprenticeship, and to confer entire freedom on such of the negroes and their children as are subject to it, on or before the 1st August, 1838.' Signing his name would be the last notable act of the Curate, John Egerton Rathbone, the *Essex Herald* of 20 February 1838 reporting both the forwarding of the petition and his death, which had taken place twelve days earlier. But this lay in the future.

Returning to August 1833, on the 29th it was the Factory Act which received the Royal Assent, and in reviewing the provisions of this we are reminded that it was a very small percentage of poor children who had the good fortune to attend a charity school and that many of those who did not have this opportunity led appalling lives. From this time forward it would be illegal to employ children in textile factories if they were less than 9 years old; children aged between 9 and 13 were no longer permitted to work for more than 8 hours a day, they had to have a break of an hour for lunch, and they had to be given two hours of education each day; children aged between 14 and 18 were now restricted to no more than 12 hours a day, again with an hour for lunch, and were forbidden from working at night. Despite the opposition to the Act from some employers, life would in future be much better for these children in the textile factories; for those children labouring in other occupations, their working conditions remained unreformed.

22 October 1833: the first meeting 'under the power of the new deed'

The meeting on Tuesday 22 October, held at the School House under the Chairmanship of the Rev'd Daniel Stacy, was sufficiently significant to be reported in the local press. It also set a new attendance record, with twenty-nine subscribers present. This was the first meeting under the provisions of 1 August for the future management of the charity, and the minutes begin 'At a Meeting of the ~~Trustees~~ Governors . . .' It would take until June the following year for the distinction between meetings, special meetings, meetings of trustees and governors, and half-yearly meetings to become routine. The new trust deed was read to the assembled company, after which James Macarthy, Oswald Adams and Mrs Bourne were re-elected as Treasurer, Master and Mistress respectively by the 'governors and managers', being those who had subscribed their annual guinea. Then the present buildings were re-evaluated and the insurances raised to £1000 for the school house and premises and £300 for the cottages in Hornchurch Lane, and it was 'Ordered that at each half-yearly meeting the Master furnish a list of the dates of the admission of the children accompanied with remarks as to their conduct.'

After this it was necessary to fill the vacancies occasioned by eight boys and seven girls having left the school, but when this had been done there were still ten children aged nine who had strong claims on the charity. The governors wished these to have the benefit of the education without being clothed by the charity, and so the parents were called in to be told by the Rev'd Stacy that if their children were punctual and conducted themselves properly they would be admitted on the foundation as vacancies occurred, when they would be clothed.

How many children were there in the school at this time? According to the report of the meeting in the *Chelmsford Chronicle*, 'This excellent institution clothes and educates forty-five boys and twenty girls', adding that

> [w]e hope to learn of additions by donations or annual subscriptions, so as to enable the governors to receive into the school an additional number of the poor applicants who appear before them at every half-yearly meeting.

However, the *Essex Standard* gives a different (and undoubtedly accurate) number and is more definite in its prediction of future expansion:

> The institution has of late years furnished education to ninety children between the age of eight and twelve years; and sixty of that number have received a suit of Sunday clothes. It is confidently anticipated, that under the present vigorous management a new school-room will be built, and instruction given to all the poor resident children of an age to be received into the institution.

This 'vigorous management', according to the paper, is owing to the Treasurer.

> The re-appointment of Mr. Macarthy to the treasurer-ship cannot fail to give great satisfaction to every friend of the institution, as it is chiefly owing to that gentleman's zeal and perseverance that the charity has been placed in its present state of efficiency.

The *Chelmsford Chronicle* ends with a reflection of the school's long contribution to the Liberty and its people.

> We are glad to learn that this school, (which has long been of so much benefit to the Liberty of Havering, and to which many of its present inhabitants, as well as others, who have moved to London and more distant places, are solely indebted - from the education and moral instruction they there received - for their advancement in the world) has within the last year received a considerable increase of new subscribers.
> Several persons educated at this charity . . . have risen to considerable prosperity in London and elsewhere, and have gratefully acknowledged that but for its aid they might have been now working in a menial capacity. From these, in particular, the charity has a right to expect some evidence of their gratitude.

4 February 1834: affiliation with the National Society
On 25 April 1833 the Trustees had narrowly voted in favour of expanding the school; on 1 August the new Scheme regulating the charity had been confirmed by the order of the Court of Chancery, empowering the Trustees 'to admit an additional number of children'; then, on 17 August, Parliament

had voted £20,000 to aid new school building work. The Trustees now needed to access a share of this money to fund the proposed expansion.

James Macarthy wrote directly to the Lords of the Treasury requesting a grant and was directed by them to apply to the National Society. The trustees had not previously engaged with this organisation because there had been no need to do so, but they now understood this would be necessary if they were to obtain a small share of this £20,000. They must also have been aware that the National Society had always attracted benefactions which it dispensed as grants to schools, grants which were additional to and independent of this new Government money. By joining the Society, the Charity would therefore be eligible to apply for two sources of funding. Macarthy therefore wrote to the Revd J C Wigram, Secretary to the National School Society, to clarify the necessary conditions which the trustees would have to fulfil in order to ally the schools with the Society and to request a grant for the proposed building work.

4 February 1834 would prove to be a key date in the long history of the school. On that day the Trustees and annual subscribers (the 'Governors') held a meeting to consider the answer which had now been received. The Rev'd Daniel Stacey was again in the chair. Wigram had offered the Trustees £150 from the share of the government's £20,000 which the Society had been delegated to distribute, plus £80 from the Society's own funds if the School joined in alliance. Mr Macarthy - 'The worthy Treasurer', in the words of the *Chelmsford Chronicle* in their report of the meeting ten days later - and several others then stated that the annual subscriptions now received were

> amply sufficient not only to clothe and educate the number of children as at present, but a much larger number, and all that was wanted was an additional building, to enable them to do so. The Trustees were unanimously of opinion, that no part of the funds belonging to the Charity should be taken to erect the building in question - in fact, it is distinctly stated, as one part of the conditions on which the public grant is made, that a sum equal to that asked for shall be raised by private subscription, and expended on the building, before any public money can be advanced, and therefore the first thing to be done was to endeavour to raise the sum named, from amongst those connected with the Charity, and from other benevolent individuals. Several of the gentlemen present put their names down for sums varying from £1 to £5.[179]

The decision to join the National Society was then 'cordially agreed upon', the offer of £80 was accepted with thanks, and the Treasurer was requested to renew his application to the Lords of the Treasury for a building grant[180] and to raise the additional sum required by public subscriptions.

The *Chronicle* closed its report with a summary of the trustees' plans:

> Should there be a sufficient amount raised, (£250, it is calculated, will be wanted in the whole,) it is intended that the building shall be erected on a vacant space of ground belonging to the Charity, immediately behind the present school-house, and that at least 300 children, of all ages, belonging to the Liberty, (in addition to the present number now clothed and educated,) shall receive a plain useful education, at the charge of one penny each per week, to be taught on the national School System, with which Society they will be connected, on the principles of the Church of England, and which Church the children will be required to attend every Sunday. The meeting, after a vote of thanks to the worthy Vicar for his conduct in the chair, adjourned to see what effect an appeal to the charitably-disposed would have.

James Macarthy returned home and that same day completed the National Society 'Application for Aid' form and sent it to Wigram with a covering letter and a plan of the proposed new building. His letter emphasised the competition between the various religious groupings which then existed for the souls of the Romford children:

> Permit me earnestly to urge our request – the population of our Town alone is upwards of 3000, the neighbourhood is poor, and an Emissary from the Foreign and British School Society has lately visited us and publicly lectured upon their system of education, inviting the Townspeople to cooperate with him in the Establishment of a School - We have at present a freehold house for the Master & Mistress and a school room capacious enough for the Girls, a Garden, part of The Freehold is attached to the house and on this we wish to erect a School Room for 200 or more boys – the cost will be between two and three hundred pounds and without your aid we shall never be able to accomplish our very desirable object – I have incurred a good deal of expense and trouble in endeavouring to better the condition of the poor here, and [as] my appointment to the honorary office of Treasurer to this

Charity School has not a little added to them, I shall esteem it no little reward if any exertions are in this instance crowned with success, and trust our application will not be marred by any informality in its execution.

The handwritten insertions (indicated below in ***bold italics***) to the 14 statements on the printed application form provide further detail to the picture his letter gives of the school and the town as it was in 1834. By reproducing the whole form, rather than summarising the answers, one can also see the questions asked of each applicant seeking financial assistance from the National Society.

1. Pop'n of district in 1831 was ***upwards of 6,000[181]*** and is now about ***the same or rather increased – children of three parishes of Romford, Havering and Hornchurch to be instructed in it.***
2. The supposed number of children therein, between 7 & 13, requiring cheap or gratuitous instruction is not less than ***300*** Boys and ***200*** Girls.
3. Provision exists therein at present for the Education (gratuitously or at very small charge) Exclusive of the school for which aid is now requested of not more than ***100*** boys and ***50*** girls, Sundays only, ***by Dissenters, and 60 boys and 30 girls daily in the established religion, for this latter school we seek aid.*** The instruction of these children is paid for by ***voluntary contributions.***
4. The school is intended to receive at least ***300*** Boys ***the present boys room to be appropriated to the girls*** [The school] is to be a Sunday and ***day*** School, and to be supported by ***a fund we have of £40 annually and voluntary contributions.***
5. The accommodation provided for the Children in the Parish Church is ***a gallery for that purpose.***
6. The instruction in the school is to be afforded by ***the weekly payment of one penny and in part gratuitously***
7. The estimated annual charge for Master and Mistress, Books, etc etc **about 100£**
8. [The paper is missing at the fold here, but the information requested relates to the dimensions of the school room which James Macarthy said were ***according to the inclosed plan*** and was 11 feet at the eves. Two calculations beside question 8 - on the

front of the form {(53 x42)/7 = 300}; on the back of the form {(55 x 32)/6 = 293} - suggest that each child was to be allocated 6 or 7 square feet.]

9. The building is to be of ***brick and slate*** and is held on the following tenure viz. being secured for the purposes of Education by ***under the Trustees.***
10. The entire estimated first Cost of the undertaking is ***£300*** viz. the ground £ ***is our own*** building ***£250*** fittings-up ***£50***
11. The present means to meet the first Cost, are ***a trifling subscription, but our neighbourhood is so poor and our applications for contributions so varyous*** [sic] ***and multiplied as to inspire little or no hope of success***
12. The exertions that have been already made to provide the means, are ***as stated above***
13. The only further exertions that can be made, are ***none. Means local £70 N.S.***
    £80
    150
14. And the utmost, that can be expected from them, is ***20£***

The form is dated 4 February 1834 and signed by George Croly, Curate of Romford, and James Macarthy, Treasurer.

The plan for the proposed school room which he sent shows a square building with each side measuring 52 feet. Two rows of four pillars, 17 feet 4 inches apart, run across the room to support the roof. There are three doors, each 3'6" wide: one in the middle of the front wall, one immediately opposite this in the middle of the back wall, and a third at the back of the right side wall. There are only four windows, all on the front wall, two equally spaced each side of the door. These windows, which are tight up to the eaves, are 3 feet high and 6 feet 6 inches long. There is a fire place 3 feet wide in the centre of each side wall. The walls are to be 6 inches thick and built of brick, and the roof is to be of slate. The effect is of a very utilitarian, barn-like hall, which in winter would have afforded neither heat nor light to aid the studies of those sitting along the back wall, furthest from the windows and the fires.

Three facts emerge from this application. First, Macarthy's reference to the 'Emissary from the Foreign and British School Society' who had recently visited Romford and the information that the Dissenters' Sunday School already attracted 150 children indicate that he wished to present the non-conformists as a serious challenge to the Church of England's hegemony over the children in the town; he wished this perception to be uppermost in the minds of those at the National Society who decided which grant applications to support. Next, Macarthy pleads the poverty of the locality and the lack of resources to fund the school. The proposed National School was to be financially independent of the Charity School, so the £900 in investments held by the trustees and the income from the Bosworth property were irrelevant to this application. Even so, whilst not wishing to err on the side of financial optimism, was this admirable man being somewhat disingenuous in his lack of expectation of further financial support? And did he and the other trustees really believe there would be no cross-subsidy, that the Charity School resources would not help fund the additional pupils? There would be one Master teaching all the boys in one room and one Mistress teaching all the girls in another, their salaries being paid as they always had been from the resources of the Charity. The Charity School children would be educated for free and at least sixty of them would be given clothing, as before, whereas the National School children would pay a penny for their education and not be clothed. It would be one school or two schools, depending on the aspect from which it was examined.

Finally, the committee which had looked into the feasibility of expanding the school had reported that they believed they could erect a building for 300 boys and that the existing building would hold 100 girls, and the return to the National Society stated that there were not less than 300 boys and 200 girls aged between 7 and 13 in the district. The Trustees therefore hoped to make provision in their National School for almost all the boys and half the girls in the Liberty.

Only eight days were to pass before Macarthy wrote again to Wigram, this time to thank him for his prompt attention to their application and for the promised grant. His letter was addressed to the Central School, Westminster, the office and teacher-training school for the National Society at this time. His letter continued optimistically and enthusiastically:

> I have according to your instructions forwarded the necessary Memorial to the Lords signed by such of the Governors as were in the little time allowed, accessible. We can, and do guarantee the collection of 70£ which with your 80£ will make 150£ one half of

the requisite 300£ the other half we hope will be supplied by the Treasury. Our expenditure in the opinion of the builders of [this] Town will exceed 300£ in consequence of the Garden requiring a wall, and the old premises also requiring repairs, but the feeling of the neighbourhood is at present so warmly excited in favour of this very desirable object that the funds will I have no doubt be readily contributed, in a few hours I have received 30£.

His application had been successful, and these last five words blatantly contradict his financial pessimism of the previous week! He goes on to describe the building 'we purpose erecting immediately', which is now to measure 53 feet long but only 42 feet wide, 10 feet narrower than his plan had indicated. He continues, clearly needing to clarify a point raised in Wigram's letter:

The Hornchurch Memorial to which your letter alludes is our memorial. Hornchurch is the Mother Church and that parish as well as the parish of Havering comprise the Liberty of Havering ate Bower, and have always had the privilege of sending their Children to the School at Romford which is therefore designated the Hornchurch Romford & Havering Schools.

Finally, his letter contains the earliest reference we have to an infant school: 'We shall besides, I think, be enabled to open an infant school in the same premises.'

Spring and Summer 1834

On 14 April 1834 the House of Commons debated a further £20,000 being made available

to enable his Majesty to issue money for the erection of school-houses, in aid of private subscriptions for that purpose, for the education of the poorer classes in England.

Those who spoke were all in agreement that the distribution of the first such sum had been a great success. Despite convictions expressed earlier by many that public money would discourage private giving, Benjamin Hawes (Lambeth) claimed that the grant of £20,000 'had had the effect of inducing private individuals to subscribe, and no less an amount than £60,000 had been raised in that way'. Lord Morpeth, who in the debate on 17 August

1833 had applauded the fact that the money was to be advanced to support both schools of the Established Church and those of the non-conformists, 'believed, that no public grant of so limited an amount had ever been productive of so much good'. The exact outcomes of this experiment and how these had been achieved was explained with scarcely believable precision by Thomas Spring Rice (Cambridge):

> The Government had been told . . . that if they did not give away the money unconditionally, the object they had in view would fail. They had not, however, so acted, for they required all parties applying to Government for the establishment of schools first to put down some of their own money for that purpose. They also paid over the fund to the two societies to whose care its distribution was intrusted in such a manner as to excite competition and rivalry between them. The result was, as might be seen from the returns on the Table, that by the grant of £20,000 of the public money an expenditure of £48,111 had been insured, and permanent means of instruction provided for 30,366 children.

Perhaps it is not surprising that within eighteen months a man capable of such attention to detail and so attracted by the pursuit of 'maximum output for minimum input' would become Chancellor of the Exchequer.

Other speakers called for an extension of the grant to include Scotland and for an increase in the grant, and William Ewart (Liverpool) 'suggested the propriety of instituting normal [secular] schools, after the plan adopted by the Prussian Government'. In contrast with the first debate on this subject, the second grant of £20,000 was agreed with no voices speaking in opposition. What a change of sentiment in just eight months!

Treasurer Macarthy had not reported on the Charity's accounts for a very long time, but fifteen days later, at the half-yearly meeting of the 'Trustees and Governors' on 29 April, he confirmed a balance of £87 18s 8½d. Perhaps now feeling financially secure, it was then agreed to admit 7 additional boys and 6 additional girls and to reward the Master and Mistress with an additional £2 {£194} each every six months for teaching these 'supernumeries'. These children would have taken the roll to 103, and their inclusion emphasises the pressure the trustees must have felt themselves to be under from the number of parents seeking a place.

The trustees now wished the existing school to be seen at its very best. In May they were extravagant in their clothing order: 'Forest & Worth to furnish the boys clothing according to the best samples of cloth and corduroy produced at the rate of 1 guinea each. Bonnets to be furnished by Miss Langham for 20 girls.' Forest & Worth, both of whom appear to have become 'trustees' (in the old sense) in 1832, would later be paid £53. On 14 August, 10 days before the annual sermons, five cobblers were paid £2 4s and one £4 13s to provide shoes for the children. It seems to have been a last minute, rushed order. That year the sermons raised £59 14s 0d, compared with £59 4s 6d in 1832 and £63 14s 9 ½d in 1833, down from the £69 they had averaged in the 1820's. On 3 January 1835 there was another payment recorded for the first time: 10s to Mr March for cutting hair.

On 3 June 1834, following a debate in the House of Commons which had ended with the setting up of a Select Committee 'to inquire into the causes of the increase of habitual drunkenness among the labouring population of the United Kingdom, and to devise legislative means to prevent the further spread of this great national evil', Mr. Roebuck rose to move the appointment of a Select Committee to inquire into the means of establishing a system of National Education. In the short debate which followed there was support but also the usual opposition, notably from Mr Cobbell, alias Mr Cobbett,[182] who

> expressed himself satisfied, that the scheme suggested by the hon. and learned member for Bath would not be productive of any good, and this he thought he could show to the House. On the subject of education in this country, it was not philosophy or reasoning that could guide, but recourse ought rather to be had to experience. Everybody knew that, within the last thirty-five years, Lancasterian and other schools had been founded, and education had increased twenty-fold; but experience showed, that the morals of the people had not mended with the increase of education. It had even been admitted that night, that drunkenness had increased wonderfully within latter years, so that education did not even prevent drunkenness. He repeated, that all this increase of education had not been productive of any good; and he ventured to say, that there was not a single country gentleman who would not say, that the fathers of the last generation made better labourers, better servants, and better men, than their sons of the present generation.

After a short debate in which various amendments were proposed, a Motion of Lord Althorp was agreed to: a Select Committee would be appointed to inquire into the state of the education of the people in England and Wales, and into the application and effect of the grant made last Session for the erection of school-houses, and to consider the expediency of further grants in aid of education. This was not the positive, potentially transformative brief Roebuck had called for, but at least discussion would continue.

Of more immediate benefit was the announcement that month of the second grant of money for school buildings which parliament had agreed on 14 April. This unsettled Mr Macarthy, who wrote again to the Rev'd J C Wigram at the National Society:

> I hope we are not forgotten. I see by Advertisement in the *Morning Herald* that another 20000£ has been granted. The money guaranteed in my last letter has been raised and we await performance of your promise to proceed to action. On Tuesday next a meeting of the subscribers will be holden, and [I] should feel delighted if by that day you could communicate to me the good tidings we have so long been anticipating.

All was well, and at a Special Meeting on 25 August Macarthy was able to announce that two grants had been promised for the erection of the New School Room, the £80 from the National Society and £150 from the Lords of the Treasury, and that donations of £58 2s had been raised towards their target of £70. At some date prior to this meeting Mr Hancock, a governor, had written to the National Society requesting plans and specifications for the erection of School Rooms. A note on the back of his letter reads: 'The Society has not any plans or designs. He had better visit a few schools in the neighbourhood such as Ilford Plaistow Barking Westham Walthamstow Leyton', indicating just how many National Schools had already been established in the surrounding area. At this meeting on 25 August, therefore, a committee consisting of Messrs Macarthy, Hancock, Charles Cove, Ashton and Last was appointed to inspect these neighbouring schools, and volunteers undertook to collect donations for this project from the three parishes: Major Anderson in Havering; Mr Macarthy, Mr Last and Col Graves in Romford; and Mr Truston and the Rev'd Daniel Stacy in Hornchurch.

Autumn 1834: the building of the National School and the lease of the land in Hornchurch Lane

Within five days the National Schools at Ilford, Leytonstone, Barking, Blackwall and Poplar had been visited (at a cost of just £3 {£291}), enabling the visiting committee to deliver their report on 30 August. In the light of what they had seen Charles Cove, the builder, had sketched a plan for a building which they now recommended for consideration. This was similar but not identical with that which Mr Macarthy had submitted to the National Society in February, the origin of which is unknown. The size of the proposed building had shrunk further, being 55 feet long but now only 32 feet wide, with the walls remaining 11 feet high. The lighting has been improved, with five windows measuring nearly 7 feet by 3 feet on the North and South sides, and one large window at the East and West ends. It was also specified that the roof was to be of slates on battens and that the floor was to be boarded. The meeting resolved that a London architect, Mr Savage at 31 Essex St, Strand, should furnish plans and specifications for a school room as close as possible to this outline, and that an advertisement should be placed in the county papers seeking tenders with a deadline of 12.00 noon on Monday 15 September. They were not losing any time.

By 15 September seven tenders had been received ranging from £396 to £468 10s. Notwithstanding that the previous estimate had been only £300, it was resolved to proceed and to accept the lowest tender. This had been submitted by Messrs J Bartlett of Romford and his partner, none other than trustee Charles Cove of Hornchurch, and it was remarkably just £1 lower than the tender received from a Mr Binder of Orsett. (One is reminded of Brougham's warning when introducing his Education of the Poor Bill in 1820 of the danger of corruption when the building of schools was contracted for,[183] although in this instance the 'inside job', if it was such and not just a coincidence, saved the Charity £1.) A committee of seven men, including Messrs Ind, Macarthy, Hancock and Last, was then appointed to monitor the progress of the work.

On 26 September the *Chelmsford Chronicle* reported in a brief paragraph headed 'Romford National & Infant Schools' that work on the building had started the previous week. We know little of the Infant School which was now being set up and advertised until 1870, when it would move into a new building, enlarge, and acquire a distinct, separate identity.[184]   On 1 November James Macarthy was able to write to the National Society to say that 'I have according to the instructions given, forwarded through the

Romford Bank an order for 80£ and beg to transmit to you the annexed Certificate'. This certificate, handwritten, begins: 'We the undersigned Governors of the National School certify that the Site of the School is their own freehold, that the building is considerably advanced towards completion, Mr Savage the Architect having certified to the outlay of two hundred pounds having been made, that after the payment of the grant there will not remain any debt, charge or claim of any kind . . . excepting only the charges which will be liquidated by the grant voted by the Lords of His Majesty's Treasury to be claimed hereafter on the proper form of certificate.' It was signed on 28 October by D Stacy, Vicar of Hornchurch, J. Macarthy, Edward Ind, Octavius Mashiter and eight others.

At a Special Meeting on 23 December a report was received from Mr Savage, the architect, in which he confirmed that Messrs Cove and Bartlett had completed the contract for building the school entirely to his satisfaction, that they had had £200 on account, and that he now recommended payment of the balance of £196. This report was unanimously approved.

Six days later the long saga of the land in Hornchurch Lane also came to a satisfactory conclusion. The new Scheme agreed by the Court of Chancery empowered the trustees to act, and at their meeting on 22 October 1833, the first under the new deed, they had agreed 'that Bosworth's Land be let on a building lease by tender to be communicated to the Governors at their next meeting'. This meeting was not held until 27 May the following year, but no tenders for the land had been received by this date. Another Special Meeting was called for 10 June when consideration was given as to whether the land should be built upon at the expense of the Charity. Octavius Mashiter objected to such a plan, arguing that the Trustees did not have the power to sell the stock to finance such a scheme. The meeting was then adjourned for a week for the purpose of obtaining information on the terms of the several Bequests. On 17 June it was moved at the reconvened meeting that the Deed be submitted to Counsel to ascertain whether the Trustees were empowered to sell the stock for the purpose of erecting buildings on Bosworth's land or not: 8 voted for doing so and 8 against, with the Chairman's casting vote deciding against the motion. We have noted in the past how some appointments had been made by a majority decision, but rarely (if ever) had the Trustees minutes recorded a division of opinion so starkly or named a trustee who raised an objection.

In an attempt to resolve this impasse, Mr Wedlake resigned his office as a Trustee and offered to take the land at £12 per annum and to bind himself to spend £500 {£48,500} in building on the land within 3 years in exchange for a 61 year lease beginning Midsummer 1834, the lease to be prepared and executed as soon as the £500 had been laid out. This was discussed at another special meeting held the following week, the offer was accepted and it was ordered that Mr Wadeson should prepare a contract to this effect. This land had been under discussion since Mr Heaphy had surrendered his lease in 1826, but there was to be one final twist before its future was settled. At yet another Special Meeting held on 11 August the agreement with Mr Wedlake was withdrawn on the grounds that it was illegal. Mr Wedlake, understandably less than happy with this reversal of the agreement, declared his intention to renounce his annual subscription of 1 guinea. It was decided that the land would be advertised to be let by tender in the *Essex and Herts Mercury* and the *Chelmsford Chronicle*, with tenders to be left at the Charity School on or before Saturday 23rd. The meeting was then adjourned until midday on 25 August.

When they reconvened, the only tender which had been received was from the long-suffering Mr Wedlake, signed 23 August, proposing identical terms to his first offer with the commencement date deferred to Lady Day 1835. Mr Sterry then informed the meeting that he had taken Counsel's Opinion on behalf of Mr Wedlake and had been informed that if the Sanction of a Court of Equity was obtained the transaction would be perfectly legal. Mr Wadeson was ordered to procure that sanction, and it was resolved that Mr Wedlake's offer be accepted. On 29 December the lease was read to the assembled Trustees and Governors and then signed, bringing to an end the long and expensive sequence of events which had begun when Mr Heaphy surrendered his lease eight years earlier.

Epilogue: Christmas 1834

Many of the good people of Romford crossing the Market Place to the church on Christmas morning that December of 1834 would have walked past the Charity School at the end of the Market and noted the recently completed but still to be used new boys' schoolroom behind the old building. Entering the church, they would have seen the Charity School boys in their uniforms and the girls in their bonnets sitting with Oswald Adams and Sarah Bourne in the gallery. Mary Adams and her eight children - the youngest, two-year-old Jemima, named after her late grandmother - would also have been at the service. Undoubtedly there would have been parents there who had been unable to secure places at the Charity School but hoped that in the new year their children would be able to receive an education at the new National School.

Exactly a hundred years before the congregation celebrating Christmas in the church had been mourning their vicar, James Hotchkis, who had died two months earlier. Simon Hillatt, the then Treasurer of the school, had been one of that congregation, and we imagined him sitting in his pew reflecting that the house adjoining the school had to be paid for and that there was little surplus money in the accounts after the purchase of the land and the building of the school. A century later the thoughts of his successor, James Macarthy, would have been far more sanguine. The last three years had been a worrying time, particularly with the involvement of the Court of Chancery, but it had worked out well. It had been expensive, of course, but now the Charity was properly set up once again. Without going through the Court, they would not have been able to expand the school or lease the land in Hornchurch Lane. Just two days ago they had had confirmation that the new school building was satisfactorily completed, and in four days time they would be signing the lease with Thomas Wedlake. Everything had worked out well.

Macarthy was not in St Edward's Chapel in the Market Place, of course. Perhaps he was at the old Roman Catholic mission at Ingatestone, run by the personal chaplains to the Petre family for over a hundred years. The passing of the Roman Catholic Relief Act two years before was another cause of satisfaction to him. Finally there was Catholic emancipation in England! Of course, he knew that sectarian prejudice was still alive and well, not least from that letter published in the *Chelmsford Recorder*. It was ironic that he, a Catholic, had written to the National Society to warn them of the risk of increased non-conformity in Romford: 'an Emissary from the Foreign and British School Society has lately visited us and publicly lectured upon their system of education, inviting the Townspeople to cooperate with him in the Establishment of a School'. Had that helped persuade them to give the new National School such a generous building grant? Oh yes, sectarian prejudice was still very much alive and well!

Reflecting on the great change which was to take place next year with the opening of the National School, did he also look back and remember some of those Masters and Mistresses, clergy, treasurers and trustees who had served the Charity School over the previous 124 years? Did he think of the congregations at St Andrew's in Hornchurch and St Edward's in Romford and wonder how many gathered there had learnt to read and write and - perhaps - cipher at the old Charity School? How many others were there in the Liberty or London, or scattered across Essex, England, or even overseas who had gained their modicum of schooling there? And, as the *Chelmsford Chronicle* had reminded its readers the previous October, several of those educated by the Charity had risen to considerable prosperity and remembered their school. Could he, as treasurer, trace other such men and test their gratitude?

Not all those associated with the school were in favour of the change, of course, but he was confident it would work out. How could they leave things as they were, forever, in a world where more and more people were demanding an education and where, two years ago, so many more men had finally been given the right to vote? It was progress. Of course, he had more than a shrewd idea who the man was who had written that reactionary and offensive letter to the *Chronicle*. He had tried to remain anonymous, but had given himself away by saying that he was old enough to remember the discussion in 1818 about whether the school should be conducted on 'the national principle'! Attempting to hide his identity had been cowardly. If there was one thing he, James Macarthy, was not, it was a coward: how could he be as a proud man and an open Catholic in the midst of this religious bigotry? And if he was viewed with suspicion for embracing what so many saw as an antique - and, for some, hostile - religious orthodoxy, when it came to education he was more in tune with the modern age than were his critics. Yes, the old Charity School had a proud history, but why were those who had voted against the enlargement of the school incapable of imagining the even more exciting and useful future it would now have? The Charity School was not closing or being replaced, it would continue to exist alongside and within the structure of the new National School: two in one; a duality.

Much had happened since the offensive letter had appeared in the *Chelmsford Recorder* nearly two years before. He regretted that the transformation which was to take place in the New Year had provoked the hostility of some, but behind this discord he knew they were all united in agreement with the sentiment - with the indubitable fact - with which the 'anonymous' correspondent had ended his diatribe: the Charity School had indeed 'been conducted with credit and usefulness for more than a century, and is an honour and ornament to the Liberty'.

An engraving of Romford Market Place in 1831
This shows the 'Swan Inn' on the left and the Court House at the end of the Market with the smoke from the brewery chimney rising behind it. On the right, next to the church, is the 'Chequers Inn', renamed the 'Cock and Bell' in 1811 and now Church House.

Appendices

Appendix I

Treasurers of the Charity School, Chaplains of Romford, Vicars of Hornchurch and Masters and Mistresses of the Charity School

Treasurers	Chaplains of Romford	Vicars of Hornchurch
William Sandford 1710 - 1718	James Hotchkis 1704 - 1734	Thomas Roberts 1696 - 1721
Alexander Weller 1718 - 1723		Henry Levett 1721 - 1725
Thomas Gilman Jnr 1723 - 1727		Francis Pyle 1725 - 1758
Thomas Pratt 1727 - 1734		
Simon Hillatt 1734 - 1735	Phillip Fletcher 1734 - 1747	
Richard Meakins 1735 - 1746		
Perkin Church 1746 - 1748	Glocester Ridley 1747 - 1763	
Thomas Johnson 1748 - 1749		
Thomas Bayley 1749 - 1769	James Ridley 1763 - 1765	William Harris 1758 - 1762

Treasurers	Chaplains of Romford	Vicars of Hornchurch
Thomas Debuke 1769 - 1770	John Hopkins 1766 - 1770	Robert Speed 1762 - 1786 (Absent from July 1768)
John Tyler 1770 - 1771	Interregnum 1770 - 1786	
Thomas Graves 1771 - 1807	Nathaniel Alsop Bliss (1786 - 1796) (Absentee)	William Reynell 1786 - 1809 (Absentee)
Edward Ind 1807 - 1820	Charles William Bathurst 1796 - 1814 (Absent from 1801)	William Blair 1809 - 1819
John Willson 1820 - 1821	William Everett 1814 - 1827	John Walker 1819 - 1831
Robert Surridge 1821 - 1826		
John Marson Carruthers 1826 - 1831	John Egerton Rathbone 1828 - 1838 supported by	
James Macarthy 1831 - 1850	(Dr George Croly) (1832 - 1835)	Daniel George Stacey 1831 - 1863

Masters and Mistresses of the Charity Schools

The Boys' Charity School

Samuel Hopkinson
1710 - 1722

William Stracy
1722 - 1732

Daniel Marshall
1732 - 1753

John Moore
1753 - 1760

John Salter
1760 - 1761

Thomas Green Groves
1761 - 1801

John Saunders
1801 - 1805

Thomas Bandfield
1805 - 1809

William Adams
1809 - 1822

Oswald Adams
1822 - 1834

The Girls' Charity School

Mary Hopkinson
1710 - 1726

Mary Stracy
1726 - 1730

Elizabeth Allis
1730 - 1745

Elizabeth Marshall
1745 - 1771

Jane White
1771 - 1794

Dorothy Cloke
1794 - 1804

Susannah Saunders
1804 - 1805

Mary Bandfield
1805 - 1809

Jemima Adams
1809 - 1821

Sarah Bourne
1821 - 1834

Appendix II

Early supporters of the School and the first trustees

The social standing of the first trustees and early supporters of the school

Those men who were present at the Vestry meeting on 5 September 1710, together with John Milligan who was not present, were amongst the wealthiest and most influential Romford citizens at that time. Those from 'Rumford' and 'Hare Street' included in the 1702 Poll Book include Thomas Gilman Senior, Thomas Gilman Junior, John Milligan, John Jermin, and John Pricklove (from whom the charity would rent the first schoolhouse). Christopher Bayley of Rumford was included in the 1715 Poll Book.

Further evidence of the social standing of these men, and of others who would later become supporters of the school, is found in the records of the Roger Reed Charity which managed the ancient almshouses in Romford. An entry for 9 July 1714[185] mentions Carew Harvey *alias* Mildmay, Thomas Gilman, Christopher Bayley, Alexander Weller, John Jermin, Thomas Gilman Junior, Christopher Bayley Junior, John Evererd and John Comyns[186] of Dagenham.

Of the first trustees, all that we know about Thomas Roberts, William Sandford and John Milligan is included in Chapter 3. However, we have a little more information about James Hotchkis, Thomas Gilman and Christopher Bayley.

James Hotchkis

The little we know about James Hotchkis raises intriguing questions, but a search for definite answers produces only tantalising clues.

The first reference in the parish registers of North Ockendon to his father, John Hotchkis, and his first wife, Elizabeth, records the baptism of their daughter Anne in May 1655. Anne was followed by Richard and William before Elizabeth died in early November 1660, a fortnight after giving birth to a daughter, another Elizabeth, who died four weeks later. There is no mention of their marriage, and we do not know how long they had been living in North Ockendon prior to Anne's birth.

Almost exactly a year after his first wife's death John married Mary Staploo (or Staplow) of East Horndon in North Ockendon Church. She was aged 25 and he was then 33, meaning he was probably born in 1628. Over the next 12 years they had eight children, of whom James was the fifth, born on 20 November 1669. Their final child, Thomas, was baptised in April 1676, and three years later Mary died. On 7 September 1691 Thomas would be apprenticed to a London weaver, and the Freedom of the City Admission Papers would describe his father as a Yeoman of 'Northockendon'. This is all we know of John Hotchkis except that they kept servants, more than one of whom was buried alongside the family in the parish churchyard, and the family were on good terms with Sir Thomas and Lady Anne Littleton, their neighbours in North Ockendon Hall.

We know nothing of James until he went up to All Souls', matriculating on 26 March 1686 at the age of 16 and gaining his B.A. in 1689. This was the same year that 32-year-old William Derham became Rector of Upminster, just over 3 miles from North Ockendon, so if James then returned home he would undoubtedly have met and associated with this great scientist. In 1693 his father died, and three years later Thomas Roberts was appointed Vicar of Hornchurch. Perhaps James stayed on in North Ockendon and it was then that he began his close friendship with Roberts.

The next definite date we have for him is 10 May 1704 when he married Elizabeth Thickness at the London City church of St Antholin Budge Row. Their marriage licence stated that he was of North Ockendon and she was of Kelvedon. Elizabeth's family were undoubtedly more affluent than his own. The inclusion of Elizabeth's father, Ralph, in the 1715 'List of the Names of the Gentleman and other Free-Holders that Voted for the Knights of the Shire for the County of Essex' testifies to his wealth and social standing: indeed, of the twenty-nine men listed who held freeholds in Kelvedon his name stands second, following that of a baronet, and he is one of only two men to be distinguished with the appendage 'Esq'. He owned land in Essex and Middlesex, including Hockley Hall which had been settled on him on his marriage to Mary Pulley in 1675. Mary was the only daughter and heir of the wealthy John Pulley of Roxwell, a village four miles west of Chelmsford, and was to bear Ralph four daughters in addition to Elizabeth. She owned land in her own right which on her death passed in equal shares to her five daughters, as we learn later from Elizabeth's own will. The income from this property no doubt allowed James and Elizabeth to live more comfortably than would otherwise have been possible.

Their marriage at St Antholin was conducted by the then rector, Robert Lasinby, but from 1 September 1679 to May 1696 Lasinby's predecessor had been Joshua Hotchkis, who had been buried in the church on 11 October 1696. Joshua's entry in the list of Oxford University Alumni indicates that he was 21 years older than James, having been born at Whitchurch in Shropshire in 1648. The relationship between James and Joshua is not clear, but in January 1687/8 Joshua appears to have officiated at the marriage of James's sister Mary in St Antholin, and in May 1716 James's younger brother Thomas was married at this same church.

Two years after his marriage James was appointed Chaplain of the Chapel in Romford. We know that 'By the 17th century, if not earlier, the inhabitants of Romford were choosing, or helping to choose, their own chaplain, though the legal right of appointment still lay with the vicar of Hornchurch as the agent of New College.'[187] Undoubtedly Hotchkis's friendship with Thomas Roberts and other local worthies helped to ensure that he obtained this position, which he would then hold for the rest of his life.

Thomas Gilman and Christopher Bayley

The Freedom of the City of London Apprenticeship Records contains a document (420/1910) recording that Christopher Bayley, son of George Bayley of Mountnessing, was apprenticed to Thomas Gilman, Citizen and Founder of London, on 14 January 1675.

Thomas Gilman's Will, written in July 1715, refers to his wife Elizabeth and to his in-laws as his brothers Richard and Christopher Bayley and his sister Sarah Bayley, which should easily identify the family. However, the Mountnessing Parish Register at this time was an ill-kept volume which records a number of families called Bayley including at least one block entry for a family containing all these common names. However, with the help of the 'Bayley Family Tree' [188] it has been possible to identify the correct family.

George Bayley and his wife Joan had six children of whom the eldest was Richard, the second was Elizabeth, born soon after 1640, and the fifth was Christopher, born in 1650. Elizabeth married Thomas Gilman, who was to become Christopher's apprentice master, business partner and fellow founder trustee of the Charity School at Romford. On 19 January 1716/17 a Codicil was added to Christopher's will, one of the witnesses of which was John Brock. Brock is recorded in the Freedom of the City of London Apprenticeship Records as coming from Bocking, Essex, and as having been apprenticed to Christopher Bayley, Citizen and Founder of London, on 10 November 1715. This reinforces the connection of both Bayley and Gilman with the Founders Company.

But to what extent were they 'Founders', making brass and bronze objects from bells to pots, pans and other utensils? Since the beginning of the 16th century there were (and remain) three methods of admission to the Livery: by patrimony, if you were the son of a free Founder at the time of your birth; by serving an apprenticeship to a member; and by redemption, or purchase. As with many City Companies, its membership was divided into two main classes, namely those admitted to the Livery in one of these three ways and a much larger number known as the 'Yeomanry' or 'Commonalty' who remained outside the Livery. As both Gilman and Bayley were at times referred to as 'mercers' - perhaps used as a generic name for merchant - and Bayley is referred to on one occasion as a grocer, it is probably correct to assume that they had little if any involvement with founding. However, being members of a City Livery Company gave them the privileges which went with the Freedom of the City of London.

By 1710, when the Charity School opened, Thomas Gilman was probably 71 and Christopher Bayley 60. They were both very wealthy, as we discover from their estates. When Bayley wrote his will in April 1714 he left £600 and all his plate and household goods to his wife, Mary; £200 and a tenanted farm near Rochford to his elder son Christopher; and £200, £750 in bonds, and a tenanted house in Brentwood to his younger son Thomas. Each of his five daughters received a legacy of £500.

Gilman's will, written in July 1715, includes bequests of 'parcel[s] of land' in Romford, Collier Row, and both the 'south end' and 'north end' of Hornchurch; three tenements in Romford, a tenement with land in Collier Row, a farm in Writtle, and a house, tenement, outbuildings and 34 acres in Wickford; and, of course, silver, plate, and household goods. He also left at least £1,100 in money and £400 which he had invested in the South Sea company, an investment he describes with prescience as a 'lottery'. (Christopher Bayley Junior, writing his will in March 1725, three years after the bubble had burst, makes only a passing reference to his South Sea stock almost at the end and as an afterthought, advising his executors to take advice from his trustees and do what they think best with his holding.)

Those charity schools which were to survive after the initial enthusiasm for the project had waned did so because of the continuing interest and financial support of a few individuals, sometimes from the same few families. The Gilmans and the Bayleys were the first of these in the Royal Liberty. Thomas Gilman Junior was the first trustee to be elected, replacing his recently deceased father. He would be the third treasurer of the Charity. Although none of his three siblings (John, Samuel and Elizabeth) were trustees, they each left a legacy to the school. Christopher Bayley Junior was elected a trustee in June 1726. He died in 1744, and in February 1745 his only brother, Thomas, twenty years younger than him, was elected. Thomas would serve as Treasurer between 1749 and 1769, after which the involvement of these two families ended, but by then two or three other extended families were supporting the school.[189]

Appendix III

Pre-decimal coinage and the changing value of money

Pre-decimal coinage
Until 'Decimal Day' on 15 February 1971 British currency consisted of pounds, shillings and pence. The symbols for these were £ for pound, s. for shillings, and d. for pence. The s. and d. always came after the figure and the £ usually came in front, but sometime the £ came after the figure when it was sometimes replaced by an l. £250, 250£ and 250l all express the same value, and all of these variations will be encountered in quotations from contemporary sources.

A penny could be divided in half (a halfpenny or ha'penny) or a quarter (a farthing). Twelve pennies made one shilling and twenty shillings made one pound, so there were 240 pennies in a pound. If 2d was added to £2 19s 11½d the amount would become £3 0s 1½d.

The guinea, £1 1s., was a frequently used unit of currency, as was the half guinea, 10s. 6d.

Currency Conversion and the changing value of money
This text contains a great many monetary figures for items such as salaries, the cost of everyday items, building work, and investments. Calculating the value of these sums in today's money is very difficult because relative worth can be looked at in a variety of ways.

We will take as an example the salary of Samuel Hopkinson, the first schoolmaster, which included payment for his wife as mistress. In 1710 he was paid 13s 6d a week, or £2 14s a month. The currency converter on the National Archives website[190] suggests that this would have been equivalent to about £283.31 in 2017. This, it suggests, would have been 30 days wages for a skilled craftsman, which perhaps indicates Samuel's social position. The Bank of England Inflation Calculator[191] gives a figure of about £370, based on annual inflation at 1.7% between 1710 and 2020. This is similar to the £361.10p on the MeasuringWorth website, covering the same period and measuring what it calls real wage or real wealth[192]. However, in April

2017 the National Living Wage (for those over 25) for the coming year was set at £7.50p an hour, equivalent to £300 for a 40 hour week and £1,200 for a month's work, suggesting Samuel and his wife had to live on the equivalent of 30% of today's Living Wage.

These figures illustrate the danger of making a simple conversion based on, for example, annual inflation figures. The real value of money at any period depends on its purchasing power, as we discover during periods of inflation when salaries may rise significantly but fall behind the rise in costs. In these circumstances we may find our salaries double over a given period but we can no longer afford the same quantity of goods.

The MeasuringWorth website takes this complexity into account and gives 'Five [different] Ways to Compute the Relative Value of a UK Pound Amount, 1270 to Present', reminding us that 'There is no single "correct" measure, and economic historians use one or more different indices depending on the context of the question.' Three of the simpler figures they give for the relative value in 2020 of £2 14s in 1710 are of interest:

- using the percentage increase in the Retail Price Index (RPI) over these years the purchasing power of £2 14s in 1710 would be equivalent to £361.10p in 2020, as noted above;
- more realistically, a figure of £6,291 is obtained if one compares the purchasing power in 2020 for a bundle of goods and services equivalent to those which could have been purchased for £2 14s in 1710;
- using a measure of GDP per capita, we obtain a figure for relative income of £7,672, suggesting Hopkinson ranked relatively high on the scale of income distribution.

How does this compare with what a teacher would earn today? Multiplying the average of £6,291 and £7,672 by 12 suggests Hopkinson earned roughly the equivalent of £83,778 in 2020. However, this was only his starting salary. In October 1713 his salary was raised to 16s a week, or £3 4s a month. Re-working these figures suggests that when he died in November 1722 he was earning the equivalent of £98,850 for running what was for the time a large and very successful school.

In 2019/20 the salary of classroom teachers ranged between £24,373 and £40,490, and in 2018 the average for those in school leadership teams in Outer London was £60,250.[193] This would suggest that Samuel was very well paid - except, of course, his putative £98,850 also covered payment for his wife's work. On the basis that he taught two-thirds of the pupils (and assuming equal pay and other concepts foreign to a time when a man owned his wife's earnings) his salary would drop to £65,900. This is remarkably close to the average of a school leader in a similar geographic location in 2020. However, we should note the bleaker description of the social and economic status of schoolmasters in the early 18th century which Peter Earle gives in *The Making of the English Middle Class* and which is quoted at the beginning of Chapter 5.

The cost of individual items
The above exercise has served to illustrate the complexities of making comparisons of value over time. The simplest method of assessing the relative cost of other items in the trustees' accounts is probably to relate them to the then salary of the schoolmaster, so the 16s a week Samuel Hopkinson was paid would have purchased at that time about 8 pairs of children's shoes *or* the uniform for one boy *or* 3 Bibles and 3 copies of the *Whole Duty of Man*.

Such comparisons remind us that the values of different items do not all change at the same rate over time. Books were relatively much more expensive in 1720, but even in 2021 an undiscounted hardback might cost £35, six therefore totalling £210. Children's leather shoes were comparatively cheaper in a leather producing town such as Romford, however: 2 shillings in 1720 would be worth about £15.28p in 2020, and yet that year a pair of children's leather shoes cost between £30 and £50.[194] To buy either six such books or eight pairs of shoes today would take the greater part of the £300 weekly pay of someone on the National Living Wage, but in 1720 it would have taken all of Samuel Hopkinson's salary and yet he seems to have been paid comparatively much more than this. Perhaps we should conclude that prices for all goods were relatively much higher then, which was why so few ordinary people owned a book and why parents had to rely on the Charity School to provide their children with clothes and shoes.

The cost of building work
The changing values of land, labour, and the other costs of construction make any attempt at giving a modern equivalent for an historic building cost highly speculative. However, for what it is worth, using the RPI and Average Earnings figures from the year in question to 2020 to obtain a simple 'purchasing power' equivalent, the relative value of the four major constructions undertaken by the trustees over this period are:[195]

Original Cost		**2020 equivalence**
1727 Cost of the land	£150	£22,810
1728 Cost of building the school	£420 4s 9d	£58,110
1728 Amount raised by subscription	£148 3s 6d	£20,490
1734 Cost of the Master's House	£183	£30,210
1813 Alterations to take 90 children	£112 9s 11d	£ 7,504
1835 Cost of National School[196]	£446	£44,900

(The surprising figure for 1813 reflects the effect of inflation during the period of the Napoleonic wars.)

Appendix IV

Ready Reckoner: the changing value of money, 1700 - 1840

As an aid to computing the changing values of expenditure and savings over the period covered by this book, the chart below indicates the relative 'purchasing power' equivalent in 2020 of a sum from an earlier decade using the Retail Price Index (RPI) figure.

Amount:	1d	1s	£1	£10	£50
1700	0.61p	£7.39	£153.50	£1,535	£7,675
1710	0.54p	£6.69	£133.80	£1,338	£6,688
1720	0.61p	£7.64	£152.80	£1,528	£7,639
1730	0.63p	£7.83	£156.50	£1,565	£7,830
1740	0.59p	£7.41	£148.10	£1,481	£7,406
1750	0.64p	£8.04	£160.80	£1,608	£8,042
1760	0.62p	£7.73	£154.60	£1,546	£7,729
1770	0.57p	£7.09	£141.70	£1,417	£7,086
1780	0.54p	£6.79	£135.70	£1,357	£6,785
1790	0.49p	£6.11	£122.20	£1,222	£6,108
1800	0.33p	£4.13	£ 82.55	£ 825.50	£4,127
1810	0.29p	£3.63	£ 72.54	£ 725.40	£3,627
1820	0.33p	£4.09	£ 81.72	£ 817.20	£4,086
1830	0.37p	£4.58	£ 91.54	£ 915.40	£4,577
1840	0.39p	£4.62	£ 92.31	£ 923.10	£4.616

The equivalent value of a guinea is obtained by adding the second and third columns, so in 1740 a guinea, £1 1s, was equivalent to £155.51p in 2020

Please note that multiplying 1d by 12 to give the value of 1s, or 1s by 20 to give the value of a £1, does not give exactly the same figure as in the next column. e.g. Using these figures, in 1790 6s 8d (a third of an old pound) was equivalent to between £40.58p and £40.73p in 2020 depending on the method of calculation.

Labour and income values of money, 1700 - 1840

One should always be wary of statements about the modern value of sums from the past. The RPI figure is widely used as a measure of price inflation, but this masks the fact that the relative cost of the items which this composite figure includes are themselves highly variable. In February 2022 general inflation was about 5% per year, but the cost of gas was rising much faster than this suggests. If £100 then bought either 20 instant meals or two weeks of winter heating, what would it buy in 2023? Possibly 19 instant meals, 5% fewer, but only one week of heating, 50% less.

The relative values given above have been calculated using 'Five Ways to Compute the Relative Value of a UK Pound Amount, 1270 to Present,' MeasuringWorth, 2021 . However, as the Tutorials on this website explain, 'The best measure of the relative value over time depends on if you are interested in comparing the cost or value of a *Commodity* , *Income or Wealth* , or a *Project* '. To supplement the figures given above, based on the RPI, the chart below gives two further (and in many circumstances more accurate) equivalent values in 2020 of sums in the past:

- 'Labour Earnings' uses an index of wages to measure 'the amount of income or wealth relative to the wage of the average worker';
- 'Income Value' measures 'the multiple of average income that would be needed to buy a commodity'. This uses the index of Gross Domestic Product (GDP) per capita.

Ready Reckoner: labour and income values of money, 1700 - 1840: equivalent values in 2020

Labour Earnings is on the left, *Income Value on the right.*

Amount:	1d	1s	£10
1700	£9.19/*£10.18*	£114.90/*£127.30*	£22,980/*£25,450*
1710	£9.32/*£11.37*	£116.50/*£142.10*	£23,300/*£28,420*
1720	£8.49/*£ 9.36*	£106.20/*£117.00*	£21,230/*£23,390*
1730	£8.19/*£10.51*	£102.40/*£131.40*	£20,470/*£26,280*
1740	£8.58/*£10.12*	£107.30/*£126.50*	£21,460/*£25,310*
1750	£8.11/*£ 9.63*	£101.40/*£120.40*	£20,280/*£24,070*
1760	£7.53/*£ 8.74*	£ 94.11 /*£109.20*	£18,820/*£21,850*
1770	£7.29/*£ 8.30*	£ 91.16 /*£103.70*	£18,230/*£20,740*
1780	£6.59/*£ 7.50*	£ 82.41 /*£ 93.76*	£16,480/*£18,750*
1790	£5.94/*£ 6.83*	£ 74.29 /*£ 85.42*	£14,860/*£17,080*
1800	£4.83/*£ 4.24*	£ 60.42 /*£ 52.99*	£12,080/*£10,600*
1810	£3.59/*£ 3.56*	£ 44.88 /*£ 44.53*	£ 8,975 /*£ 8,907*
1820	£3.44/*£ 4.44*	£ 43.03 /*£ 55.47*	£ 8,606 /*£11,090*
1830	£3.49/*£ 4.94*	£ 43.64 /*£ 63.74*	£ 8,728 /*£12,350*
1840	£3.54/*£ 4.64*	£ 44.25 /*£ 58.03*	£ 8,850 /*£11,610*

The figures in these tables are taken from 'Five Ways to Compute the Relative Value of a UK Pound Amount, 1270 to Present', MeasuringWorth, 2022 . www.measuringworth.com/ukcompare.

Appendix V

Index to places of interest marked on Chapman and Andre's Map of Essex, 1777

On the following page there is a list of the main places mentioned in the text, with a key indicating their location on the extract from Chapman and Andre's 1777 map of Essex reproduced on the facing page.

Key:
- words without brackets are as printed on the map
- (words or letters in round brackets clarify the map entry)
- *names in italics are as printed on the map beneath the name of their property*
- [names in square brackets are of those mentioned in the text associated with these places].

Marks Manor House, the seat of Carew Harvey *alias* Mildmay, is just off the map due west of Rumford. 'The Whalebone' is about twice this distance along the road to London leading west out of Rumford.

Until his death in 1710 Sir Thomas Littleton held the Manor of North Ockendon and lived in North Ockendon Hall. The Hotchkis family may have lived in North Ockendon Manor House.

Brakes Place	B2	Manor of Nelmes	B2
[Richard Comyns]		[Richard Hide]	
Brentwood	D1	Noak Hill	B1
Brook Street	D1	North O(c)kendon	D4
Charity School	A2	(North O(c)kendon)	D3
Cockerell(s)	C1	Manor House	
[Hon. Anne Rider]		North O(c)kendon Hall	D4
Collier Row	A2	[Sir Thomas &	
[John Elsee]		Lady Anne Littleton]	
Collier Row Common	A1	Pettits (Estate)	A2
Corbets Tey	C3	[John Comyns]	
Cranham	C3	Pergo (Pyrgo Park)	B1
Cranham Hall	C3	[Anne, Lady Tipping]	
General Oglethorpe		Rainham Hall	A4
Cranham Parsonage	C3	[Captain Harle; Wlliam	
(Dagen)ham (off map)	A4	Dearsley; John Harle]	
Dagnam Park (Estate of)	C1	Rainham Parsonage	B4
Richard Neave Esq		Rumford	A2
[Hon. Anne Rider]		Rumford Common	B1
Gidea Hall (Estate of)	A2	South O(c)kendon	D4
Richard Benyon Esq		South Weald	C1
(Manor of) Goos(hays)	B1	Squirrels Heath	B2
Great Warley	D2	Stubbers (Estate of)	C4
(and) New Hall		*John Russell Esq*	
Hare Street	B2	Turnpike	A2
Hare Hall (Estate of)	B2	Tylers Common	C2
John Wallinger Esq		Tylers Hall (Estate of)	C2
Havering-atte-Bower	A1	*John Redman Esq*	
Havering Hall	A1	Upminster Common	C2
Havering Well	A3	(Upminster) Parsonage	C3
Hornchurch	B3	[Rev'd William Derham]	
Hornchurch Hall	B3	Upminster	C3
[John Bearblock]		Upminster Hall	C3
(Hornch'ch) Parsonage	B3	(Upminster) New Place	C3
Lily-Put	C2	(Estate of) *James Esdail*	
[Rev'd James Bearblock]		Warley Place	D2
Marshalls (Estate)	A2	Warley Street	D2

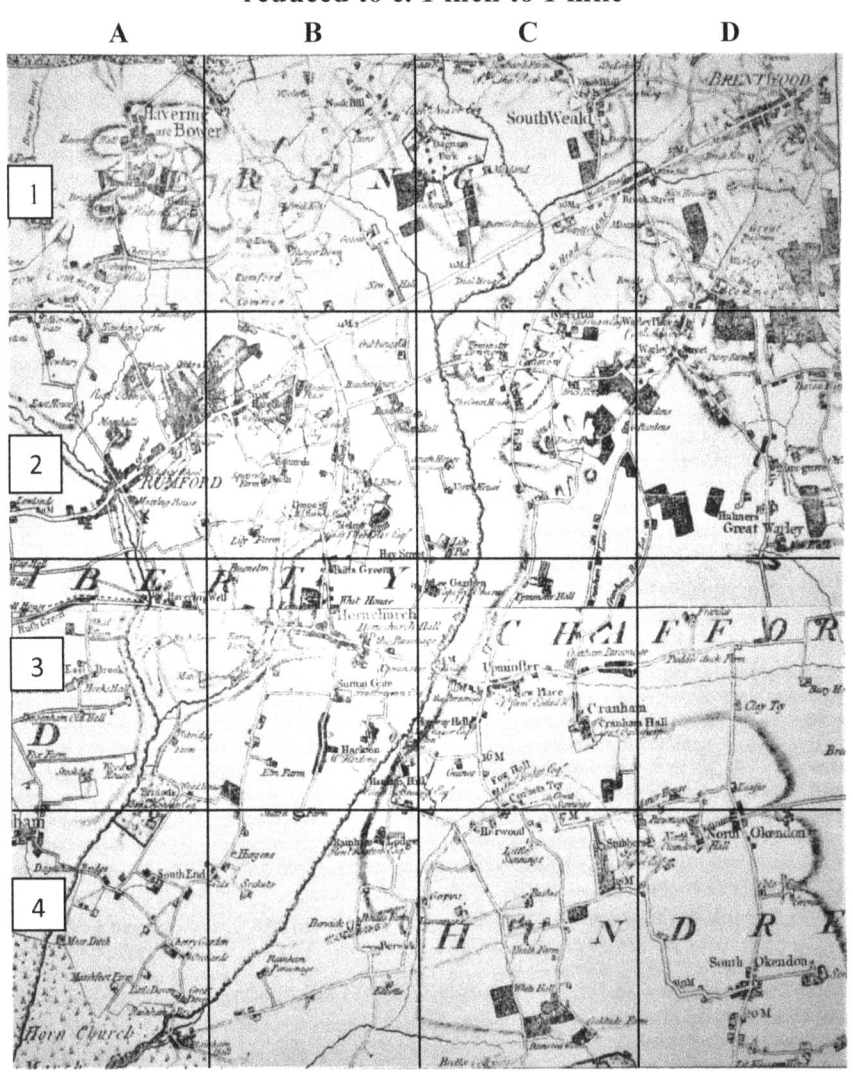

The Royal Liberty of Havering (left) and part of Chafford Hundred (right)

From Chapman and Andre's *Map of Essex* of 1777
reduced to c. 1 inch to 1 mile

The Royal Liberty of Havering (left) and part of Chafford Hundred (right)

From Chapman and Andre's *Map of Essex* of 1777
reduced to c. 1 inch to 1 mile

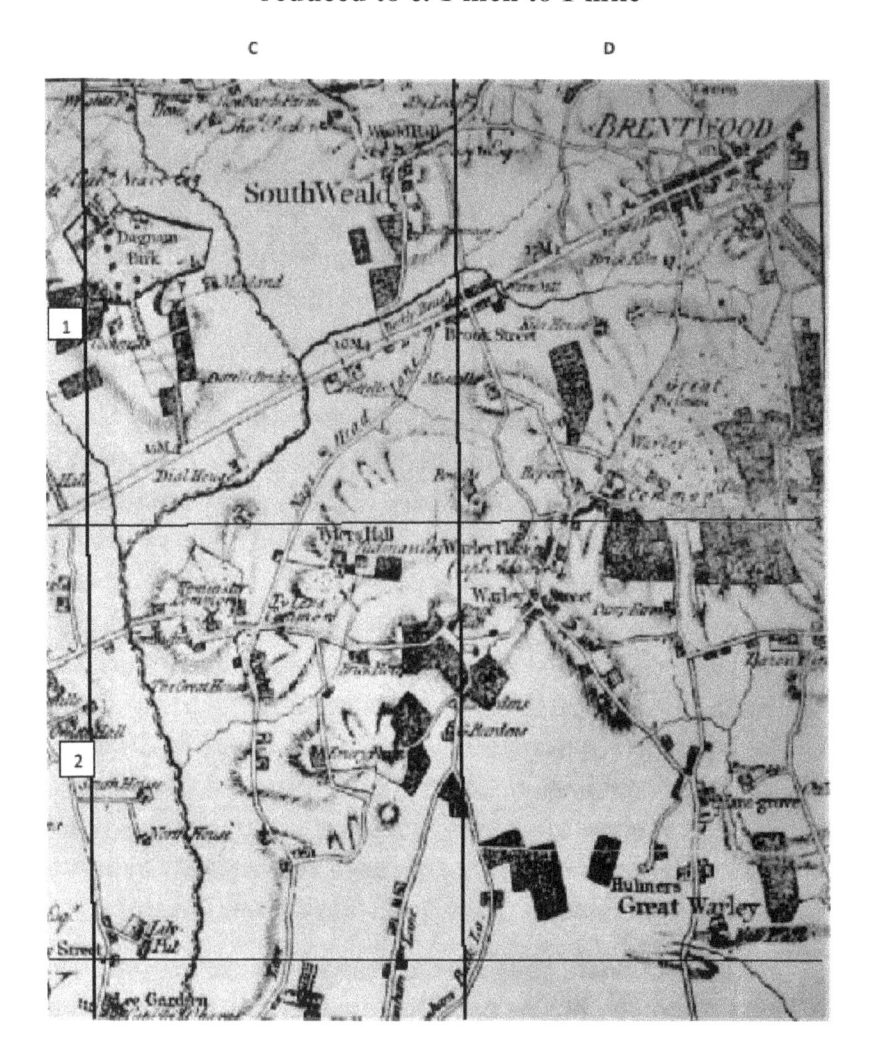

The Royal Liberty of Havering (left) and part of Chafford Hundred (right)

From Chapman and Andre's *Map of Essex* of 1777
reduced to c. 1 inch to 1 mile

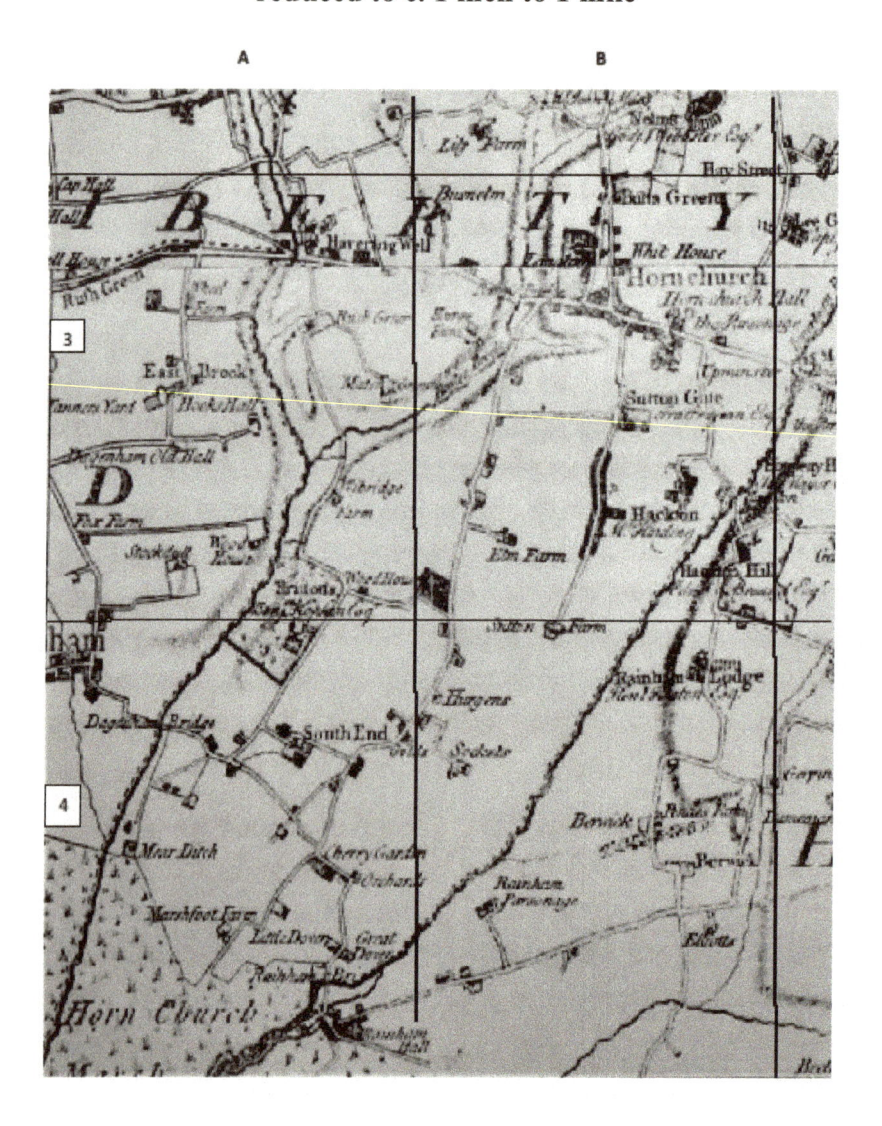

The Royal Liberty of Havering (left) and part of Chafford Hundred (right)

From Chapman and Andre's *Map of Essex* of 1777
reduced to c. 1 inch to 1 mile

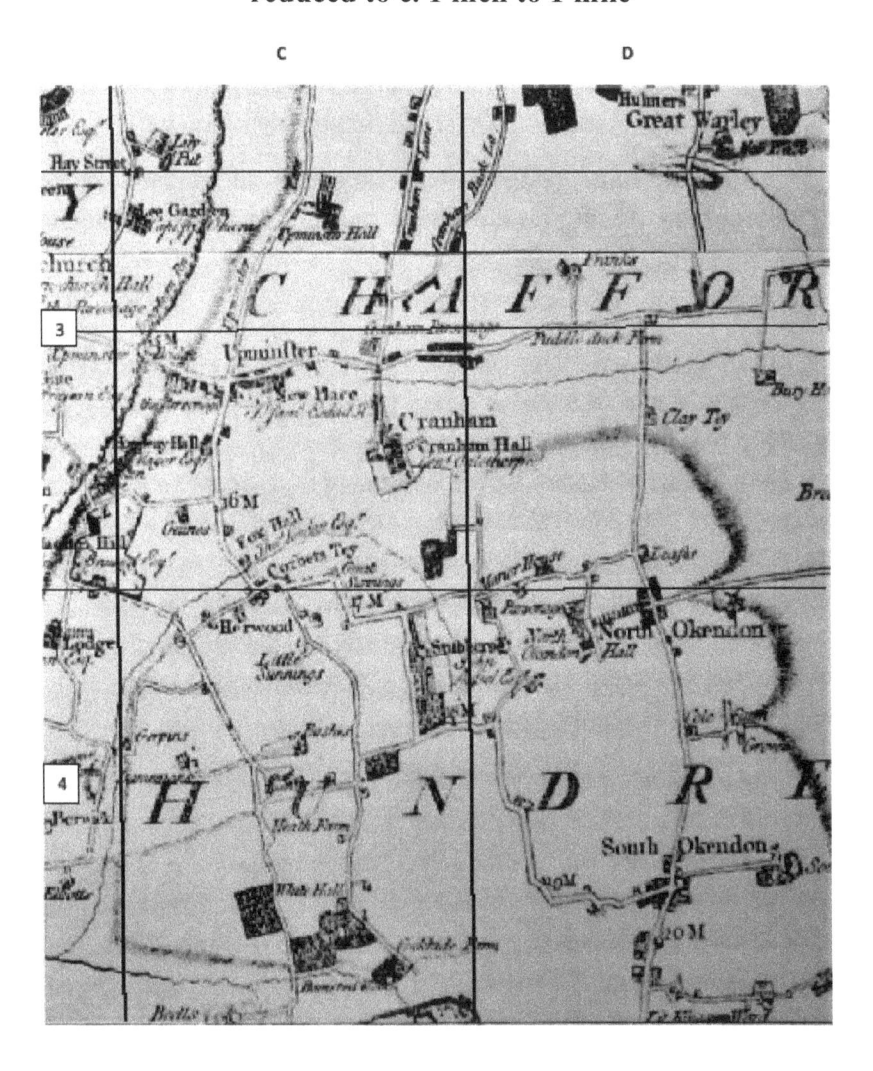

The Royal Liberty of Havering (left) and part of Chafford Hundred (right)

From Chapman and Andre's *Map of Essex* of 1777
reduced to c. 1 inch to 1 mile

Part of the 1805 Ordinance Survey map of Essex which includes the Royal Liberty and the areas to the immediate west, east and south.

Acknowledgements

Time and place: with each step one takes from the present into the deeper past, even the most familiar landscapes become infinitely confusing. Perspectives, both literal and metaphorical, change. This book is the first product of many lonely hours - occasionally exhilarating, more frequently tedious - spent searching for the significant events which took place in one such historical landscape, discovering the waymarkers between them, and seeking to identify those whose journeys along these now largely overgrown paths were to shape the present.

My first debt of gratitude, then, is to the guardians of this terrain, the staff at the four main archives I used in this research: Cambridge University Library, the National Archives, the National Society (accessed through Lambeth Palace Library), and the Essex Record Office in Chelmsford. If, like so many of us, their working lives are 'occasionally exhilarating, more frequently tedious', one brief anecdote will highlight their tenacity and skill. To my extreme consternation, on one visit to the National Archives I was told the document I requested was unavailable. When I explained that it was important to my research and that I had been working on it the previous week, an investigation was initiated. Later that day it was once again available to me: having been misfiled after my previous visit, it had been successfully discovered amongst the millions of documents held in the repository at Kew.

It was fortunate that I had finished my notes on all but the most marginally relevant of the records in these archives when the pandemic struck. Enforced isolation accelerated my earlier, tentative attempts to shape the mass of material I had accumulated into a structured narrative, and eventually I had a draft which I was not embarrassed to share with Jane, my wife. It is she who receives my second (and largest) bouquet of thanks, not only for her comments and corrections, but also for her reading and re-reading (often multiple times) of those sections which her candid criticisms demanded undergo further revision.

In September 2021 I passed a greatly amended draft to Bishop David Jennings. Bishop David retains a deep interest and affection for the two St Edward's C of E Schools from his period as Vicar of Romford between 1980 and 1992, during which time he was Chair of Governors of both schools. He had been instrumental in my appointment as Head Teacher of the Comprehensive School, and although we worked together for less than a year our friendship has endured. Early in November he sent me a list of corrections and suggestions which further refined the manuscript, and subsequently I sent him the second part of the narrative which covers the years from 1835 to 1903. This follows the fortunes of the Charity School at Romford after its change to a National School, the development of further voluntary schools in the Royal Liberty, and the development of the School Board and the board schools in Romford after 1872. These developments took place in a national context which saw the increasing involvement of the government in elementary education and its public funding, and the passing of the landmark education acts of 1870, 1880 and 1902. In 1903 the prehistory of our modern system of state education ended with the creation of Local Education Authorities with responsibility for all the schools in their area.

I am very grateful to Bishop David not just for his textual corrections and suggestions and for his encouragement and support, but also for introducing me to two influential contacts. (Sadly the introduction remains 'virtual', our interactions confined to e-mails.) Chris Paterson had held a senior executive position in a major publishing company, and his comments and advice following a necessarily very brief examination of the first part of the narrative were both encouraging and practical. The Rev'd Professor Kenneth Newport (of Liverpool Hope University, an exceptionally important institution in its historic and present commitment to teacher training) looked in greater depth at both the first and second parts of the book, covering the whole period from 1710 to 1903. Although, as he said, time constraints allowed him to only sample the text rather than read it in detail, I am extremely grateful that he was able to give it as much attention as he did at a time when he was very busy prior to his own retirement. His positive comments on the quality and originality of the research and how I might develop these in an academic context were again very helpful and encouraging.

Having decided that the 1710 to 1903 narrative was too long for a single book, I submitted the first part (1710 - 1834) to the scrutiny of my daughter Eleanor. Coming from a younger generation than those who had previously read the manuscript, her comments were particularly valuable. They highlighted the difficulties of providing necessary explanations (without being condescending) to a generation whose 'general knowledge' is both better and worse than their parents. If historical periods and religious terminology are more obscure to them, I must hope their far more highly developed 'information retrieval' skills will provide them with any explanations they might need.

Finally, having arranged the publication of this first volume and been told that I could include illustrations, I turned for help to Simon Donoghue of Havering Libraries Local Studies and Family History Centre. In January 2022 I had attended a talk Simon gave in St Edward's Church, Romford, on the development of the town in the 19th century, and I knew him to be very knowledgeable on the history of the Royal Liberty and the surrounding area. He not only produced a large selection of maps, drawings, engravings and photographs and guided my selection, but also read the manuscript and both corrected and augmented certain of my local history references. He was very generous in his summary comments, and I can only hope others will find the book as readable, interesting and occasionally humorous as he did.

Tom Chalmers and David Walshaw of New Generation Publishing have been generous and helpful in arranging publication, and I now look forward to working with other members of their team to make '*so great a Work*' available, finally, to a wider readership.

I express my sincere thanks to all these people for their support and encouragement and for correcting so many factual, grammatical and typographical errors. I apologise and accept culpability for those which remain.

Bibliography

Chapters 1 and 2: background information
The information in Chapter 1 on the early history of Romford has come mainly from the Victoria County History of Essex, Volume 7 (https://www.british-history.ac.uk/vch/essex/vol7). This source has been used widely throughout the book.

The information on or from the SPCK in Chapters 2 and 3 has come from *The Accounts of Charity Schools* and various other SPCK records, in particular:

A5/1	Standing Committee Minutes 1705-13
A30/1	Minutes of General Meeting 1717-18 (No 2)
D1/W/27-32	Robert Watts' letters to the SPCK
D2/5	Abstract Letter Book 1709-11
D2/6	Abstract Letter Book 1711-12
D2/9	Abstract Letter Book 1713-15
D4/2	Henry Newman's drafts and copy letters 1711-12

These are not available online but can be accessed at Cambridge University Library where the SPCK papers are held.

The Trustees' Account Books
The main source of information for the development of the Charity School and National School at Romford at this time comes from the Trustees' Accounts and Minute Books held in the Essex Record Office in Chelmsford:
ERO DQ 24 1A Christmas 1710 to August 1762
ERO DQ 24 2 16 September 1762 to June 1803
ERO DQ 24 3 14 June 1803 to October 1835

National Society Records
The National Society holds two files on the Romford National School and its successors, NS 7/1/10522 Primary and NS 7/1/10522 Secondary. The first of these contains the correspondence between the school managers and the National Society from February 1834 to 1981.

These files need to be ordered in advance and are then made available at the Lambeth Palace Library.

Government papers held at the National Archives, Kew
The main sources accessed at the National Archives for this early period in the school's history were the files on Building Grants (ED 103) and on the 1833 Case in Chancery.

>ED 103/136/99   School Building Application for Hornchurch, Romford and Havering National School, Essex.
>ED 103/113/2   School Building Application for Romford National School, Essex.
>ED 103/17/17   School Building Application for Romford National School, Essex.
>C 13/1002/6   'Attorney General at the relation of Walker and others v. Bearblock'. This is the record of the 1833 Case in Chancery which resulted in the 1833 Scheme to regulate the Charity.

Local people and events
A principle source of information about individual people is www.ancestry.co.uk. This has frequently yielded dates for births and deaths, and has sometimes allowed access to family trees which have clarified relationships with others of the same name. Much other information has been accessed through this site, amongst the most important being the lists of Oxford and Cambridge Alumni with dates, the various editions of Crockford's Clerical Directory, and the Prerogative Court of Canterbury Wills. (In the course of 2019 the Church of England Births, Marriages and Deaths for Essex was published on this site. Most of my research was done before this date, laboriously working through microfiche at the Essex Record Office and sometimes failing to find a result which is now quickly available online. Such research becomes ever easier.)

The British Newspaper Archive (www.britishnewspaperarchive.co.uk) is another online resource which has provided a wealth of information on individual people and events. Not infrequently one entry has led to others which have yielded even more valuable background or explanatory material. Until 1782 news about the Royal Liberty was confined to rare references in papers published in places as distant as Ipswich, Stamford and Derby - and, of course, London. However, after the publication of the first available issue of the *Chelmsford Chronicle* on 3 January 1783 this became the main source of information.

Histories of Education

I am aware of only one book covering the history of the Charity School Movement: M.G. Jones: *The Charity School Movement: A Study of 18th Century Puritanism in Action* (1938). This has been invaluable in providing the information on the SPCK and the general history of these schools which I have used in Chapters 1 and 2.

The Public Record Office Readers' Guide No 18, *Education and the State from 1833,* written by Ann Morton, is a mine of information on the development of state education from the date of the first Parliamentary Grant.

Another invaluable resource on the history of education is Derek Gillard's monumental online work: Gillard D (2018) Education in England: a history www.educationengland.org.uk/history.

The history of the Royal Liberty of Havering, Romford, and Essex

Apart from the Victoria County History of Essex, Volume 7 (https://www.british-history.ac.uk/vch/essex/vol7) and the *Chelmsford Chronicle*, both noted above, two other sources of local history have been important in my research.

Romford, A History (2006) by Brian Evans. This is an excellent introduction to the history of the town by its best known local historian.

Havering History Cameos by Professor Ged Murray. Professor Murray spent his early life in Havering, before leaving for Cambridge in 1967. His historical interests, like his academic postings, range from Australia to Canada to Ireland. In 2012 he was invited to contribute to a local history 'Heritage' column in the *Romford Recorder*, and between then and 2021 he wrote around 350 columns. These are collected in five files on his website https://www.gedmartin.net/martinalia-mainmenu-3: Havering History Cameos; More Havering History Cameos; Havering History Cameos Third Series; Havering History Cameos - The Fourth and Final Series; and Havering History Cameos, Exploring Essex (which examines places just over the Havering border). These provide fascinating and sometimes quirky glimpses of aspects of the local history of the area, and have added pleasure to my research even when they have been irrelevant to this book.

Other books I have used include Nikolaus Pevsner's *Essex* (1954) in his *Buildings of England* series, and Jenny Collett's *National Trust Guide to Rainham Hall*.

Previous Histories of the School

There have been two previous histories of the school.

The Story of the St. Edward's Schools Romford by Frederick Davis. Dr Davis was Head Teacher of the Secondary School from 1946 to 1958. In 1950 he published this monograph to assist St Edward's Church Restoration Fund. (There was an accompanying volume on the history of St Edward's Church.) It is a scholarly work which runs to thirty pages, with a Preface by the Bishop of Chelmsford. However, as Dr Davis says in his Foreword, 'this abbreviated account of St Edward's Schools omits, with great regret, much of the story'. He then lists eleven names of trustees and Masters and Mistresses whose 'personal service and contribution . . . cannot fail to arouse admiration and appreciation' and whom he would have liked to honour, had space allowed. It is clear that he had a very great knowledge of the school's history from its earliest days, and I hope he would have approved of this attempt to resurrect those people he mentioned (and a number of others) and to re-tell the St Edward's story within the wider context he was denied.

The St Edward's Schools by Philip Lloyd. (My copy of this work has no cover, but I imagine this was its title.) Philip Lloyd was a teacher at the Primary School who wrote this ten page booklet in 1960, a copy of which was given to every pupil as part of the 250th anniversary celebrations. It complements Dr Davis's work and has five illustrations, one of which is a remarkably prescient drawing of what a future secondary school might look like five years before it was built.

In the context of these previous histories and the 250th anniversary in 1960, a centrepiece of the celebrations that year was a specially commissioned play, *St Edward's Schools: 250 Years*, written by Rosemary Anne Sisson. Over the next two decades she would write countless film and television scripts, including four Disney films and the 1970s television series *Upstairs Downstairs*, for which she was the lead writer.

Other sources

In writing this book I have gathered information from other resources held in the Essex Record Office (such as *The Romford Ringers' Book*), on many occasions from articles on Wikipedia, and not infrequently from Hansard. I refer on several occasions to *The Making of the English Middle Class (Business, Society and Family Life in London 1660-1730)* by Peter Earle (London, 1989), and I am grateful to Simon Donoghue of Romford Local History Library for introducing me to Matthew Abel's work on the history of the Ind & Coope Brewery and the former inns of Romford. I have also used various 18th and 19th century publications, ranging from contemporary novels to Romford Trade Directories. These, and the many other books and websites referenced in the text, are acknowledged in the endnotes. I apologise if through oversight I have overlooked or incorrectly attributed any such references.

Notes

Chapter 1: Place and time: the Royal Liberty of Havering in 1710

1. 237,232 in the 2011 census.
2. www.british-history.ac.uk/vch/essex/vol7/pp72-76
3. www.closedpubs.co.uk/essex/romford_cockbell.html, but this information is updated by more recent research by Matthew Abel which is summarised here. From at least the the 1680's, and maybe much earlier, 'Church House' was an inn called the 'Chequers' and there was an inn in the High Street called the 'Cock and Bell'. The 'Cock and Bell' closed in 1808/9, and in 1811 the 'Chequers' changed its name to the 'Cock and Bell'. All the references to the inn of this name in this text refer to the original inn in the High Street, not to the renamed 'Chequers' next to the church.
4. This information is taken from https://www.havering.gov.uk/info/20037/parks/723/havering_country_park. Henry II was born in 1133 and reigned from 1150 to 1189. Unfortunately this source mistakenly places all these 12th century events in the 1200's. I have assumed the information included here is correct if the dates are taken back a century, and I have ignored the suggestion which this then leads to that he started to visit the palace in Havering eight years before his birth in Le Mans, Anjou, France.
5. An important source for much of the information in this section is the *Victoria County History of Essex, Volume 7*, ed. W R Powell (London, 1978), *British History Online* http://www.british-istory.ac.uk/vch/essex/vol7.
6. The river is now known as the Rom from the name of the town, an example of back-formation.
7. www.british-history.ac.uk/vch/essex/vol7/pp82-91
8. A hundred is 'a subdivision of a county or shire, having its own court'. (Concise Oxford Dictionary)
9. Daniel Defoe, *A Journal of the Plague Year* 1722
10. Browsing in a second-hand bookshop in Devonport, Auckland, New Zealand in February 2020 I found a history of Essex published in 1818 with this information. Unfortunately I failed to note the exact title and the author. It may well not be true: Professor Ged Martin (see below) quotes a source which reported the jaw of a Greenland whale had been 'lately placed' there in 1641, 17 years before Cromwell died.
11. See https://www.gedmartin.net/martinalia-mainmenu-3/323-whatever-happened-to-chadwell-street
12. Searching for 'Rumford' in the British Newspaper Archive gives 3 results between 1710 and 1719, 21 between 1720 and 1729, 33 between 1730 and 1739, and 34 between 1740 and 1749. 'Local' news over this period is

provided by the Stamford Mercury from May 1717, the Ipswich Journal from June 1725, and the Derby Mercury from October 1728.

[13] https://en.wikipedia.org/wiki/Great_Frost_of_1709 with citations.

[14] https://en.wikipedia.org/wiki/Vestry, citing Webb, Sidney and Potter, Beatrice *English Local Government from the Revolution to the Municipal Corporations* (London 1906)

Chapter 2: Religious belief and the 18th century Charity School Movement

[15] www.british-history.ac.uk/vch/essex/vol7

[16] Mentioned in Philip Lloyd's brief history of the schools in the Souvenir Booklet he wrote for the 250th anniversary celebrations in 1960.

[17] S T Coleridge, *Literary Remains*

[18] One notable exception was the Royal Mathematical School at Christ's Hospital, founded in 1673 to teach 40 of its nearly 1,000 pupils mathematics and the principles of navigation for the benefit of the navy and merchant marine. Sir Robert Clayton, an Alderman and later Lord Mayor in the City of London, was the moving spirit behind this innovation, having read how Louis XIV had supported the founding of schools in certain French coastal towns to give free tuition in the art and science of navigation to selected children. The King's aim was to make France a great maritime power, and Sir Robert had a vested interest in promoting a similar scheme in England, being a director (to use the modern term) of the Royal African Company. In the history of the Atlantic slave trade, this institution was unsurpassed in the number of African slaves it shipped to the Americas.
Information from https://www.christs-hospital.org.uk/about-christs-hospital/the-royal-mathematical-school; https://en.wikipedia.org/wiki/Robert_Clayton_(City_of_London_MP); Peter Earle, *The Making of the English Middle Class* (1989)

[19] Extract from the Church of England Catechism in *The Book of Common Prayer*

[20] See, for example, Daniel Defoe: *Giving Alms no Charity*.

[21] Peter Earle, *The Making of the English Middle Class* (1989)

[22] Discussed, for example, in http://www.jlg.org.uk/Projects/Hymns/Hymns-Politics.pdf and https://indefenceofyouthwork.com/2013/04/16/thatcherism-and-youth-work-privatising-the-public-marketising-the-practice

[23] All these quotations are from the New English Bible (1961 and 1970).

[24] M G Jones, *The Charity School Movement: A Study of Eighteenth Century Puritanism in Action* (1989)

[25] The summary which follows is based on the 1711 edition of 'The Account of Charity-Schools', published in May. This was four months after the school in Romford had opened.

[26] This stipulation appears to have been followed in Romford for almost a century. As we shall see, in 1804, perhaps earlier, the trustees would permit the Master in Romford to augment his income by teaching a limited number of private pupils alongside those on the foundation.

27 These 'Orders' are in essence not dissimilar to the home-school partnership agreements the law required schools to publish and promulgate at the beginning of the 21st century. One important difference, however, is that the 18th century charity schools had a sanction for parents who did not co-operate with them. Three hundred years later the requirement that all schools have such an agreement came to be derided as yet another example of meaningless, government-imposed bureaucracy, because whilst it had to be signed by both the parents and the school there was no penalty for non-compliant parents.

28 Bands: the neck bands still worn by barristers, some clergy, and those bluecoat schools which have retained their original uniform.

29 The allowance of three breaks a year has lasted to this day, although children now enjoy longer holidays at these times and also the benefits of half-term breaks. The Bartholomew Fair was one of London's pre-eminent summer fairs, which in addition to trade featured sideshows and such entertainments as prize-fighters, acrobats, puppets, freaks and wild animals. It started on 24 August and lasted for two weeks, but in 1691 it was shortened to four days. The moral dangers it posed to the young were well summarised in the comment in *The Newgate Calendar* that it was a 'school of vice which has initiated more youth into the habits of villainy than Newgate itself'.

30 '[T]his fair, which is not only the greatest in the whole nation, but in the world; nor, if I may believe those who have seen them all, is the fair at Leipzig in Saxony, the mart at Frankfort-on-the-Main, or the fairs at Nuremberg, or Augsburg, any way to compare to this fair at Stourbridge.' Daniel Defoe, *Tour through the whole Island of Great Britain* (1722).

31 A village between Chelmsford and Maldon, now 'Woodham Water'.

32 *The Spectator* Number 294 Wednesday, February 6, 1712.

Chapter 3: 'so excellent a Work': the founding of the Charity School at Romford

33 SPCK records.

34 The list of Cambridge University Alumni records a student named Thomas Roberts, born about 1652, who graduated from Sidney Sussex with his BA in 1673-4 and was ordained deacon in the Diocese of London 24 December 1676. The entry notes that his late father was a gentleman of Templecombe in Somerset and concludes: 'One of these names of Hornchurch, Essex, Clerk.' However, it seems more likely that the Thomas Roberts in whom we are interested is the one listed in the Oxford University Alumni who gained his BA in 1679, despite this entry ending with the similarly inconclusive suggestion that 'one of these names rector of Caundle Marsh, Dorset, 1690'. The reasons for preferring this candidate is that he attended New College, Oxford, the patron of the living and the college of his predecessor, Francis Shaw, his successor, Henry Levitt, and a number of later incumbents of the parish. He was a bachelor, and when he died he left his estate largely to relatives in Montgomery (and not Somerset).

35 In the record of the meeting on 5 September 1710 the Vestry Book is signed by Thomas Gillman, but here his name is spelt Gilman. For the sake of

consistency we will use Gilman in this text, although there is no consistency in the records. Similarly, Bayley is spelt in more than one way.

[36] This equivalence is based on the figures in Appendix IV, using the RPI figures.

[37] Please see Appendix III for information on monetary values in the past and Appendix IV for a Ready Reckoner of the changing value of money over time. From time to time, as a reminder of these changing values, a modern equivalent will be given after a figure in the text. These will be in {brackets}, will be taken from the first (RPI) table in Appendix IV, and will always refer to the value in 2020. They will also, inevitably, be an inexact approximation.

[38] Technically he was 'Chaplain and Vicar Temporal', a title emanating from the unique foundation and history of the parish. (See Chapter 1.) A list of the Hornchurch incumbents I found on the internet accorded them the title of Chaplain, not Vicar, until 1902, although it noted the designation 'Chaplain and Vicar Temporal' applied to them all. For simplicity the Hornchurch incumbent will be referred to as Vicar. His subordinate in Romford was referred to as either Curate or Chaplain until 1849, when Romford became a separate parish and the incumbent became Vicar. In practice the subservience was nominal and financial, and both men carried out the duties of parish priest independently in their own communities. The term 'curate' should not be confused with the 19th and 20th century assistant curates of Romford who will feature later in this history, who were very much junior to the Vicar.

[39] The North Ockendon parish registers record the burial of at least one of the family servants.

[40] North Ockendon Church contains an impressive monument to Sir Thomas Littleton.

[41] This medieval city church was rebuilt following its destruction in the Great Fire and finally destroyed in 1829.

[42] Information on the churchwardens and their professions comes from *Havering & Romford Essex* by Thomas Bird. In the late 19th century Bird was an important member of the local community, a Governor of the National School and a member of Romford School Board. He will be introduced later.

[43] See Appendix III for further information on James Hotchkis, Thomas Gilman and Christopher Bayley.

[44] *The Whole Duty of Man:* see the section in the next chapter on 'Book purchases' for information on this text.

Chapter 4: A new treasurer and the first substantial legacy

[45] The 2020 equivalent figures in {brackets} are included in this section to give a sense of the sums being spent. Such comparisons will not always be given but can be calculateed from the figures given in Appendix IV.

[46] James Boswell, *The Life of Samuel Johnson* (1791)

[47] The records frequently use the variant spelling Hyde, but for uniformity these references have been changed to Hide.

[48] Nelmes Manor was in the area now known as Emerson Park. The information in this section comes from Richard Hide's will. The very detailed study of the changing ownership of Nelmes Manor https://www.british-

history.ac.uk/vch/essex/vol7 makes no mention of him, but says of the relevant period: 'William Witherings was holding Nelmes in 1659, and was living at Hornchurch in 1662 and 1670. Sir Godfrey Webster (d. 1720) left Nelmes to his son Sir Thomas Webster, Bt., of Copped Hall, Epping.' Richard Hide would therefore seem to have held the Manor between the Witherings family and the Websters.

49 The fate of this beautiful old house is symbolic of the destruction of the valuable heritage of the Royal Liberty after World War II. A Tudor listed building with three acres, it was wantonly destroyed in the autumn of 1967 by the owner who had recently inherited it from his uncle. He paid a £100 fine, but this was small change compared to the maintenance and repair costs he avoided and the profit he was then able to make by selling the land for upmarket housing development. See the *Romford Recorder* 14 October 2017, which also has a picture of the house.

50 Mary was baptised on 9 January 1690, her father being named, interestingly, as Major Hide. Another Mary Hide, daughter of Richard Hide, was baptised in Hornchurch on 8 May 1677 but was buried on 22 March 1678. This was possibly an elder sister, her siblings having been born between 1667 and 1691.

51 https://www.british-history.ac.uk/vch/essex/vol7/pp51-55

52 Marks Hall was demolished in 1808 and its land is now part of Warren Hill Farm. It is remembered in the name Marks Gate, the site of a 1950's Dagenham council estate.

53 Isaac Barrow (1630 – 1677) was a mathematician and Christian theologian who was described by Charles II as the best scholar in England. Although he held important academic posts at Cambridge (where he was a mentor of Isaac Newton) he was perhaps more widely esteemed for his sermons, two of which would certainly have been read sympathetically by the Reverends Thomas and Hotchkis: 'Duty and reward of bounty to the poor' and 'The nature and property of acts of charity'.

54 https://www.british-history.ac.uk/vch/essex/vol7/pp117-126

55 I am grateful to Bishop David Jennings for the suggestion that this reference might not be to Eton College, as I had assumed, but to the 'College of Canons of the Chapel of St George within Windsor Castle', of which Derham would have been a member.

Chapter 5: Building the School House

56 The first reference to William Stracy in the Accounts Book spells his name in this way, and this spelling has been standardised (except when a different spelling is included in a quoted source), although it also occurs as Stracey, Strace and Stracie.

57 Peter Earle, *The Making of the English Middle Class* (1989). Note that Earle's description of the status of schoolmasters at this time suggests a less financially secure position than we arrive at in Appendix III, when attempting to calculate the relative worth of Samuel Hopkinson's income in 1710/13 with that of a teacher today. We should always be mindful of the hazards in making such comparisons.

58 This was the remarkable Thomas Wilson who holds the record for the longest serving Church of England Bishop. He was consecrated Bishop of Sodor and Man on 16 Jan 1698 and died in office on 7 Mar 1755.
59 As reported in the *Newcastle Courant* of 7 April 1722.
60 Except for those occasions in the second half of the 19th century when the whole school was listed in the log book prior to the annual inspection, very rarely is an individual child named.
61 Peter Earle, *The Making of the English Middle Class* (1989).
62 See British History Online: https://www.british-history.ac.uk/vch/essex/vol7/pp1-8
63 'In croachin': I assume this was a fine because some aspect of the neighbouring property, belonging to Sir Nathaniel Mead, was 'encroaching' on the property now belonging to the trustees. Until his death in 1760 Sir Nathaniel Mead was a leading citizen of the Liberty. In 1713 he inherited the Manor of Gooshays in the Harold Hill area of Romford which his father, a London linen-draper and a leading Quaker, had purchased in about 1684. Sir Nathaniel was a lawyer who in 1715 became a Serjeant-at-law and was knighted, by when he was under-steward of the Liberty. That year he was also elected MP for Aylesbury, but did not contest the seat in 1722.
64 Itemised costs for the building included: £1 to labourers for digging the cellar; £26 16s to Daniel Pain for Bricks; £31 10s to the Widow Skingly for Bricks and tiles; £37 8s 6d to Clement Hambleton for brickwork, £7 9s 5d for plastering, and £5 17s 'for Dayes work Lime Bricks and Mortar'; £3 2s 6d to Mr Hills for laths; £4 2s 8d for 'Step Stones and other charges'; £1 11s 'to Kiln Stocks'; 17s for 17 Bushells of Hair; 17s 'To ye several men that brought ye bricks to ye turnpike'; £3 4s to John Tracey, Surveyor; 14s 6d to labourers; £1 11s 6d for a millstone; £154 4s to James Hills and Thomas Molton; the £20 13s noted above to Humphrey Brent, Attorney, following the purchase of the site; £4 19s to Captain Harle; and £97 17s 8d to various people for unspecified services. There was also a payment of £16 10s to William Hide, with no accompanying explanation, but perhaps it was a balancing sum to cover a shortfall there might have been between his buying the land and then selling it on to the Trustees.

Chapter 6: The Mary Hide Charity and the death of James Hotchkis

65 These are the colours they are now painted, but there is no reason to believe this varies from the original.
66 It is possible Thomas Moulton' payment included that for Thomas Green. Looking at the proportions of the building compared with those of the School, which cost £420, one cannot imagine the house cost much more than £183.
67 The Hyde Charity file in the National Archives may throw light on this.
68 See earlier list of Apprentices in Chapter 5..

Chapter 7: Joseph Bosworth, the unintentional benefactor

69 Figures from Peter Earle, *The Making of the English Middle Class* (1989).

[70] Jerry White, *London in the Eighteenth Century* (2012) p.473
[71] https://janeausten.co.uk/blogs/landscape-and-property/foundling-hospital
[72] The celebrity endorsement and publicity the worthy Thomas Coram successfully exploited to promote the Hospital was the prototype for the razzmatazz around the annual Children in Need Appeal today, a very worthy enterprise which in its success overshadows and possibly reduces the financial support for many other needy causes.
[73] For information on the company, house and gardens see: http://villardallenwines.com/family; http://villardallenwines.com/villar-dallen; and the Tripadvisor website: Reviews-Quinta_De_Villar_d_Allen-Porto.
[74] See Henry Jeffreys *Empire of Booze* (2016) Chapter 2 for an entertaining and very informative history of port.
[75] Land Tax records for the Bishopsgate Without Ward in 1706 lists the property on which he is being assessed: 'Mr Joseph Bosworth for the next three houses, And for Two old Timber houses at ye Corner beyond the Brackett houses & for George Trotters house And the next 4 houses after his for Mr Joseph Bosworth LandLord'. The following year and in 1708 he had an additional house at Aldgate on which to pay Land Tax, but by 1709 this seems to be his only property and the records suggest he lived here until 1718.
[76] This is held by the London Metropolitan Archives at the Guildhall under the heading: ACCOUNT BOOK RECORDING SHIPMENTS OF WINE FROM MESSRS. STEVENSON AND ALLEN OF OPORTO, AND OF CORK FROM ROBERT DODD (ALSO OF PORTUGAL), TO JOSEPH BOSWORTH OF LONDON, 1715/16-1722, WITH A NOTE OF SETTLEMENT OF ACCOUNT (1733) Reference Code: CLC/B/227/MS05626 (Former Reference MS 05626)
[77] During the 1720's we can identify two men who might have been Boswell's kinsman Stephen Monteage. One was a Merchant Taylor living in Winchester Street, and he is a possibility because Susannah, Boswell's niece, subsequently married Benjamin Lewis, a tailor in Dukes Place St James. The other is of more interest. Born 5 July 1681, this Stephen was an accountant connected with 'The Governor and Company for raising the Thames Water at York Buildings'. Until 1719 this enterprise made modest profits supplying water to householders in London, but after 1719 it diversified into various unscrupulous and often unprofitable ventures which resulted, as so often, in both a number of scandals and a number of men becoming very rich. By 1735 Stephen was stock accountant to this company and also a 'proprietor.' In 1738 he was (also) employed on the accounts of the South Sea Company, whose bubble had burst sixteen years earlier, so perhaps his role in these notorious enterprises was not as an early, unscrupulous speculator but later in their history to bring order and honesty to their accounts. Whether or not Bosworth's kinsman was either of these two men we do not know, but the enterprise and speculation so typical of that period which we see in the second of them reflects Joseph's own life of enterprise and speculation. (See Dictionary of National Biography, 1885-1900.)
[78] Perhaps Benjamin and Susannah Lewis did not accept this judgement. In 1737 they were to bring a case against a certain Edward Sanderson (alias Edward Saunders) and Stephen Monteage and Abraham Culver, the executors of Joseph Bosworth's will and two of their fellow defendants in this case.

Chapter 8: Financial malaise and the Archbishop's intervention

[79] https://en.wikipedia.org/wiki/Richard_Benyon_of_Madras, citing Love, H. D. (1913). Vestiges of Old Madras pp. 271–335.

[80] Richard Benyon was also the Lord of the Manor of North Ockendon, which he bought in 1758, and Lord of the Manor of Newbury, in Ilford. There is a monument to him in St Margaret's Church, Margaretting, Essex.

Chapter 9: Stagnation

[81] An Act of Parliament of 1711 set up the 'Commission for Building Fifty New Churches in and around London' to meet the needs of the growing city. The target of fifty was not reached, but those which were built became known as the Queen Anne Churches. One of these was St George's in the East, designed by Hawksmoor and completed in 1729, and this name was adopted by the new community which developed around the church. The name St George's-in-the-East for this part of north Wapping is still found on some modern maps but is rarely used now.

[82] For information on these books see Chapter 4.

Chapter 10: Reform

[83] Quoted in John Brooke, *King George III* (1972)

[84] Some of the details in this paragraph are taken from https://www.gedmartin.net/martinalia-mainmenu-more-havering-history-cameos

[85] Rosamond Bayne-Powell, *Travellers in Eighteenth-Century England*

[86] Count Frederick Kielmansegge, *Diary of a Journey to England, 1761-1762* translated by his great-granddaughter-in-law Philippa, then Countess Kielmansegg.

[87] This certificate is tucked into the front of the Vestry Book recording the meeting on 5 September 1710.

[88] A. R. Humphreys, *The Augustan World* (1954)

[89] British History Online suggests that between 1690 and 1700 there might have been a boys school and a girls school in Dagenham, but by 1756 they were long closed. That year Thomas Waters died and left £100 to educate poor children in the parish, but this was equally ineffective. South Weald did not have a church school before 1807.

Chapter 11: The school and society during the early years of George III

[90] https://coramstory.org.uk/explore/content/blog/admissions-to-the-foundling-hospital

[91] https://en.wikipedia.org/wiki/Foundling_Hospital. The citation for this information is not clear.

[92] See above and also *Childcare, Health and Mortality at the London foundling Hospital, 1741-1800: 'Left to the mercy of the world'* Alysa Levene, (2007) and *Coram's Children: The London Foundling Hospital in the Eighteenth Century* Ruth Mcclure, (1981).

[93] His best known work is *The Tales of the Genii*, based on those in the Arabian Nights, published in 1764.

[94] See the National Trust guide to Rainham Hall, researched and written by Jenny Collett

[95] The same notice went in the *Reading Mercury* of 8 May 1786, the *Bath Chronicle and Weekly Gazette* of 11 May and the *Stamford Mercury* of 12 May.

[96] https://www.british-history.ac.uk/vch/essex/vol7/pp82-91. The *Shorter Oxford English Dictionary* defines a 'lecturer' as 'An assistant preacher in the Church of England, who delivers afternoon or evening lectures'.

[97] I have borrowed heavily from the Comyns family tree compiled by djacobs115 and available on www.ancestry.co.uk. These published family trees are often notoriously inaccurate, but this is well supported by documentary evidence and seems to be as accurate as the available sources permit.

[98] See Dictionary of National Biography Vol. 04.

[99] Today the local government and administrative area of Pettits Ward covers the Gidea Park, Marshalls Park, east Collier Row and Rise Park areas of Romford and cuts across two or three of the ancient Havering manors.

[100] See https://hylandsestate.co.uk/explore/hylands-house/history. John Richard Comyns had four daughters but no son to succeed him, and with his death Hylands House passed out of the family. Hylands House and its extensive park are now owned and run by Chelmsford City Council and are therefore open for public access.

[101] 'The Dolphin' was an old coaching inn on the north side of the Market Place. Built in 1630, it had a galleried yard with extensive stabling. It was demolished in 1900, but its name was reused for the much shorter-lived leisure centre built on the same spot which opened in 1982, closed in 1995, and was demolished in 2004. See: https://www.closedpubs.co.uk/essex/romford_dolphin

[102] Nikolous Pevsner describes Hare Hall as 'the most ambitious surviving mansion of Romford.' *The Buildings of England: Essex* (1954) In 1921 the Royal Liberty school opened in Hare Hall, where it remains today, so the house has now played an important part in the provision of education in the town for over a century. See also: https://www.romfordrecorder.co.uk/lifestyle/heritage-a-bumpy-250-years-for-hare-hall-gidea-park-3149498, written by Professor Ged Martin.

[103] See Brian Evans, *Romford, A History* (2006) p. xi

[104] The information on this family is taken from the family tree published by 'Stewmash' on Ancestry.uk. It appears to be well researched.

[105] https://www.british-history.ac.uk/vch/essex/vol5/pp281-294

Chapter 12: The early years of Thomas Graves, treasurer

[106] Romford 1791 Universal Trade Directory
[107] Figures from www.romford.org and *A Brief History of Hornchurch* by Tim Lambert
[108] William Dalrymple, *The Anarchy* (2019)
[109] In *The Making of the English Middle Class,* Peter Earle says of apprentices marrying their master's daughters that this was 'a common scenario, though not quite as common as the story books would tell us'.

Chapter 13: Absent clergy in a time of revolution

[110] See James Woodforde, *The Diary of a Country Parson*
[111] www.headington.org.uk/history/famous_people
[112] www.wiltshirerecordsociety.org.uk/pdfs/wrs_v27.pdf
[113] www.ox.ac.uk/local-community/engagement/part-of-oxford/history, although I have found other dates for this reform.
[114] www.british-history.ac.uk/vch/essex/vol7/pp82-91
[115] The phrase 'extraordinary and curious' to describe this will is from Tony Benton's Upminster History Site, which has some very helpful information on John Redman's association with Upminster. See: https://upminsterhistory.net/2018/10/06/upminster-common-revealed-part-1-bird-lane-and-around-tylers-common
[116] The importance of the Branfill family in the area is remembered today in the name of Branfil Primary School in Upminster.
[117] The Magdalen Hospital for the Reception of Penitent Prostitutes was established in 1758. See: www.childrenshomes.org.uk/LondonMagdalen
[118] The 26 June 2021 edition of the magazine *The Week* provides another possible example of this phenomenon. It reported the opposition of ecologists and wildlife campaigners to the plans of a developer to build 3,000 homes on a 500 acre site at East Chiltington, East Sussex. It was reported that Eton College, the owner of this farmland, could make £120 million pounds from the project. We do not know when or how the College acquired this land, but it is possible it was an ancient legacy or gift. When Romford was 'enclosed' in 1811 one of the beneficiaries was Christ's Hospital, which had acquired land in the area in this way.
[119] www.historyofparliamentonline.org/volume/1754-1790/member/bathurst-benjamin-1691-1767

Chapter 14: Sectarian Strife

[120] John Miller Dow Meiklejohn, *An Old Educational Reformer, Dr Andrew Bell* (1881)
[121] J F Gladman, *School Work Control and Teaching Organisation and Principles of Education* (1886)
[122] I am grateful to Simone Carling, a native French speaker, for her translation of 'admoniteur'. This is an old French word, not used nowadays, with overtones

of 'admonish' rather than simply 'monitor'. The message is clear: the two monitors in the top pictures have the attention of their pupils; the one in the bottom picture does not, and this must not be allowed.

[123] This confusing variant spelling of his name is found in the log from time-to-time.
[124] Romford 1791 Universal Trade Directory
[125] www.british-history.ac.uk/vch/essex/vol7/pp161-163
[126] See William Dalrymple, *The Anarchy* (2019) pp 228-231
[127] See the article by Matthew Abel, 'Calling Time on the Star Inn: a reassessment of the origins of the Romford Brewery', published in the *Journal of the Brewery History Society*, Number 167, 2016.

Chapter 15: A story of two brewers and two school masters

[128] See: Chase, M orcid.org/0000-0002-6997-4888 (2017) Thurrock's earliest freemasons. Panorama: The Journal of the Thurrock Local History Society, 56. pp. 28-48. ISSN 1465-1440
[129] We know that the school master was performing this task later in the 19th century.
[130] https://www.british-history.ac.uk/vch/essex/vol7
[131] https://www.gedmartin.net/martinalia-mainmenu-3/239-more-havering-history-cameos
[132] Gary Sheffield, Professor of War Studies at the University of Birmingham, in a review of *To War with Wellington: From the Peninsular to Waterloo* by Peter Snow. BBC History Magazine, December 2010.

Chapter 16: The National Society, expansion and reform

[133] One of these, Lewis Warren, was only a teenager, but in due course he would organise the opening of further schools in the West Midlands.
[134] The author began his education in such a school, St Giles's Church of England Primary School, Ashtead, Surrey, founded in 1852. It stands at the bottom of the road leading to the 11th C. Parish Church dedicated to St Giles.
[135] John Miller Dow Meiklejohn, *An Old Educational Reformer: Dr. Andrew Bell* (1881)
[136] https://www.british-history.ac.uk/vch/essex/vol7/pp22-25
[137] https://www.british-history.ac.uk/vch/essex/vol7/pp51-55
[138] https://www.new.ox.ac.uk/history-new-college
[139] https://www.gedmartin.net/martinalia-mainmenu-3/235-havering-history-cameos
[140] These words are quoted without attribution in Grace's Guide to British Industrial History. https://www.gracesguide.co.uk/Trustee_Savings_Bank

Chapter 17: A Brougham to sweep old charities clean

[141] All the quotations in this section are from Hansard.
[142] Roger Fulford, *The Trial of Queen Caroline* (1967)

[143] Roger Fulford, *The Trial of Queen Caroline* (1967)
[144] The information on the fate of the Bill in 1821 is taken from *Pressure Groups and Government Poliçy on Education, 1800 - 1839* by Michael Washington, his PhD thesis submitted in the Faculty of Education, the University of Sheffield, December 1988.
https://etheses.whiterose.ac.uk/1784/1/DX183137.pdf

Chapter 18: Sarah Bourne and Oswald Adams

[145] Restrictions continued on men attending or teaching at Oxford and Cambridge Universities until the Universities Test Act was passed in 1871, and Jewish emancipation was not fully achieved until 1890.
[146] See *Essex Newsman* 1st June 1878
[147] As above, and *Chelmsford Chronicle* 24 January 1868

Chapter 19: The scandal of the Methodist banker

[148] See *The Church of England* E W Watson 1944 Chapter VIII
[149] *The Anglican Tradition* A T P Williams (Bishop of Durham) 1947 Chapter VI
[150] These four men were all long serving trustees: Thomas Townsend since 1805, John Matthew since 1807, and John Turnstall since 1808. Peter Delamare was more recent, but his family support for the school started with his father Abraham in 1778 and included his brothers John and James.
[151] Earlier in this history there have been references to Edward Sumpner, a farmer in Dagenham who had been an active trustee, elected in August 1762. The coincidence of name and place suggests a relationship with Joseph Sumpner Joyner which I have been unable to prove.
[152] The bank was opened on the site of the original 'Cock and Bell' inn in the High Street which had closed in 1808/9. (See endnote 3.)
[153] John Elsee: *The Late Romford Bank* (1828). This source is quoted on several occasions in the chapter.
[154] A fellmonger dealt in hides and skins, particularly sheepskins, and sometimes prepared them for tanning. A wool stapler bought wool from the producers which he then sorted and graded prior to selling it on to the manufacturers.
[155] See list of apprentices in Chapter 5.
[156] See *Essex Herald* of 05/05/1829; 19/01/1830; 09/02/1830; 02/03/1830; 18/05/1830; 17/02/1835.
[157] See Chapter 1.
[158] https://www.british-history.ac.uk/vch/essex/vol7/pp31-39
[159] Those present from Hornchurch were the Rev'ds John Walker and James Bearblock, James Cove, Thomas Wedlake and William Miles; those from Romford were Robert Surridge (Chair), Richard Digby Neave, James Marson Carruthers, William Bulwer, John Laypoldt, Octavius Mashiter, Peter Delamare and Joseph Last. John Matthew was also present, but we do not know where he lived.
[160] Pigot's Directory
[161] www.british-history.ac.uk/vch/essex/vol7/pp51-55

[162] https://valmcbeath.com/victorian-era-bankruptcy
[163] See Chapter 11
[164] Pigots Directory for Romford, 1839
[165] These are two characters in John Gay's *The Beggar's Opera*, first produced in 1728. Peachum runs a criminal gang but has no loyalty to his subordinates, whom he is quite capable of incriminating in exchange for reward money. Lockit is a corrupt jailer at Newgate Prison who is Peachum's business partner. Elsee compares Surridge and Joyner to these two villains who are quite capable of betraying each other.
[166] Robert Surridge, banker and pious Methodist, was in some respects a living embodiment of the fictional banker and religious zealot Nicholas Bulstrode in *Middlemarch*. George Eliot wrote her novel between 1869 and 1872, but the action takes place between the years 1829 and 1831, and the eponymous provincial market town in which it is set is not unlike Romford at this time. The actions and true character of both men are eventually exposed, leading to disgrace and ruin.
[167] The building occupied by the Romford Agricultural Bank (Joyner, Surridge and Joyner) occupied the site of the original 'Cock and Bell' inn. (See endnotes 3 and 152.) It was taken over by another bank, Johnson, Johnson and Mann, which failed in June 1844. The site was then used for the new Corn Exchange which opened for business on 5 November 1845.

Chapter 20: A case in Chancery

[168] Thomas Townsend, Alfred Ward, Peter Delamare, Joseph Last, James Macarthy, Charles Butler and Robert Simmonds
[169] James Bearblock, James Marson Carruthers, Burchell Whennell, John Cooper, William Turston, Digby Neave, Edward Ind, Octavius Mashiter, John Elsee, John Smith, William Miles, James Anderson, Matthew Dodd, John Delamare, James Cove, Thomas Wedlake, William Colls, Richard Reynolds, John Ping, Joseph Biggs Martin, William Bulwer, William Alfred Warwick, Stephen Collier, John Forrest, William Ellis, Lewis Langham, Charles Gillham, William Johnson, Thomas Cook (the Defendants to the Information)
[170] National Archives Reference: C 13/1002/6
[171] This refers to the Case in Chancery brought by the Coopers Company to resolve the issues which arose on account of the ambiguities in Joseph Bosworth's will. See Chapter 7.
[172] By an Act of 1786 the Commissioners were to be the Speaker of the House of Commons, the Chancellor of his Majesty's Exchequer, the Master of the Rolls, the Accountant-General of the Court of Chancery and the Governor and Deputy Governor of the Bank of England.

Chapter 21: Acrimony and a finely balanced decision

[173] Published on 8 February 1833.
[174] All quotes in this section are from Hansard.

[175] The others were Messrs Hancock, Miles, W H Tolbutt, M Tyler Junior, and Simmonds.

Chapter 22: A debate in Parliament and a new Scheme to regulate the Charity

[176] See Chapter 17
[177] See the article 'Good for Nothing' by John Picton in History Today Volume 7 Issue 7, July 2023.

Chapter 23: 'An honour and ornament to the Liberty'

[178] See, for example, http://www.bbc.co.uk/history/british/empire_seapower/black_britons_01.shtml
[179] The *Chelmsford Chronicle*, 14 February 1834. There is an ambiguity in this report: it was never the intention to clothe any of the children admitted to the National School.
[180] Presumably the application was made to the Treasury and they would release this money if the school was on a list of approved beneficiaries which would have been furnished by the National Society. If £150 was typical of the sums requested, this initiative would have funded 60 to 70 National schools and an equal number of British schools (assuming the the £20,000 Treasury grant was divided equally between the National Society and the BFSS).
[181] His letter gives a figure of 3,000, so presumably this figure refers to Romford and the 6,000 to the whole Royal Liberty.
[182] www.parliament.uk/business/publications/hansard/commons Historic Hansard gives the names of speakers in blue or black. By clicking on a blue name you can then access further information such as the constituencies he served and his record of contributions to debates, with dates. No such information is available if the speaker's name is in black, as is the case with Mr Cobbell. However, as a search of Hansard gives no result for Cobbell this is almost certainly William Cobbett. The views expressed are remarkably similar to those he voiced in the Supply debate on 17 August 1833, quoted above, and he was present that evening as he had made a short but notable contribution to the previous debate on Drunkenness: 'he had published twelve sermons, one of which was upon the subject of drunkenness. Now, if the noble Lord and the Government were desirous to put an effectual stop to this degrading vice, the best thing they could do would be to purchase one or two million copies of this sermon, and circulate them throughout the country.'
[183] Chapter 17
[184] On 1 April 1936 this Infant School mutated into today's 'St Edward's Church of England Primary School'.

Appendix II

[185] Essex Record Office, reference T/B 262/14/23

[186] We do not know whether this John Comyns supported the school, but his son Richard and a later John from another branch of the family were to play a significant part in its history. See the section in Chapter 11 headed '1730 - 1834: Tylers, Comyns, Wallingers and Mashiters - continuity and social context'.

[187] https://www.british-history.ac.uk/vch/essex/vol7/pp82-91, citing E.R.O. T/A 521/1 (agreement, 1662, between vicar of Hornchurch and Romford inhabitants on appointment of chaplain).

[188] I am grateful to '8crossfields' for posting this very clear and seemingly accurate and well documented family tree on www.ancestry.co.uk

[189] See the section in Chapter 11 headed '1730 - 1834: Tylers, Comyns, Wallingers and Mashiters - continuity and social context'.

Appendix III

[190] https://www.nationalarchives.gov.uk/currency-converter

[191] https://www.bankofengland.co.uk/monetary-policy/inflation/inflation-calculator

[192] https://www.measuringworth.co

[193] These figures have been taken from the Department for Education evidence to the School Teachers' Review Body (STRB), January 2020. The figure for leadership teachers is an average of the figures for primary and secondary schools and, in each case, for Local Authority Schools and Academies.

[194] These prices for books and shoes are taken from Amazon website.

[195] Five Ways to Compute the Relative Value of a UK Pound Amount, 1270 to Present, MeasuringWorth, 2021

[196] This figure includes the building of the Boys' School, the alterations to the original Charity School building to increase the number of girls, and other necessary works.

Index

This is a general index of people, places and themes. For information specific to the school, please look under 'Charity School at Romford' and its sub-entries.

Adams, Jemima (Mistress), 234, 253, 274
  appointment and salary, 231
  background, 232
  competency, 248
  death, 317
  resignation, 273
Adams, Oswald (Master), 233, 234, 248, 273, 286, 347, 363
  actuary for Romford Savings Bank (see separate index entry for the bank), 255, 314
  and Felsted Grammar School, 248
  appointment, salary and conditions of service, 276
  background and marriage, 276
  growing family, 317
Adams, William (Master), 233, 234, 239, 253, 265, 273, 278, 279, 319
  1811, increase in salary, 236
  and expansion of the school, 248
  appointment and salary, 231
  background, 232
  competency, 247
  death and muffled peal, 317
  final task, 277
  revives campanology at Romford, 236
  surprise resignation, 276
  takes part in bell ringing record, 239
  testimonials, 232
Addison, Joseph, 72
Alexander, Mrs Cecil Frances
  and 'All things bright and beautiful', 26, 27
Allis, Elizabeth (Mistress), 96, 97, 98, 107, 136
Althorp, Lord, Chancellor of the Exchequer, 335, 343, 344, 358
Anderson, Major James, 313, 339, 359, 412
Anne, Lady Tipping of Pyrgo Park, 112
Anne, Queen of England, 12, 72, 144, 149, 406
  and political situation in 1710, 13
  letter to the Archbishops, 35
anti-Catholic sentiments, 192
Apprentices, Statute of 1563
  out of date by 19thC, 332
apprenticeships
  cost of, 83
  decline of system, 83
Aveley, 80, 300
Aylett, Mrs Alice,
  her school in Hornchurch, 286, 289, 291
  its beginnings, 249
  pupil numbers in 1837, 291
Bacon, Francis, 71

Bandfield, Mary (Mistress),
  appointment, 211
Bandfield, Thomas (Master),
  213, 228, 229, 230
  appointment, 211
  dramatic resignation and final
    mystery, 230
  testimonials, 212
Barrett, the Honourable Dacre of
  Belhus, 80
Bartholomew Fair, 33, 401
Bathurst (Senior),
  his scandalous parliamentary
    career, 199
Bathurst, Rev'd Charles William
  (of Romford), 199, 227
  appointment, 199
Bayley, Christopher (Junior), 105
  elected trustee, 86
Bayley, Christopher (Senior), 18,
  40, 49, 54, 59, 70, 75, 219,
  402
  death, 58
  relationship with Thomas
    Gilman, 15, 166
Bayley, Elizabeth,
  marriage to Thomas, 48
Bayley, Thomas (Treasurer),
  126, 128, 137, 147, 174, 175
  perfect record of attendance,
    174
  resigns as treasurer, 163
Bearblock, John, 288, 331, 339
Bearblock, Peter Esdaile, 288
Bearblock, Rev'd James, 287,
  328, 331, 411, 412
  and 1833 case in Chancery,
    310
  and tithes, 288
  background, 288
Bell and Lancaster
  differences between their two
    systems, 206
  their dispute, and the resulting
    secular divide, 206
Bell, Rev'd Dr Andrew, 242, 272,
  409, 410
  1796, ill health in India and
    return home, 204
  abrasive personality, 202, 245
  and Swanage, 243, 244
  belief in his divine mission,
    245
  death, 327
  early life, 202
  end of his marriage, 245
  his 'Madras' method of
    instruction, 203
  his school in Madras, 202
  opens first schools in UK
    using his method, 204
  Portrait, 203
  Rector of Swanage, 204
Benyon, Governor Richard, 131,
  138, 173, 184, 406
BFSS. *See* British and Foreign
  School Society
Blair, Rev'd William (of
  Hornchurch), 227, 250
Bliss, Rev'd Nathaniel Alsop (of
  Romford, absentee), 188, 189,
  199, 200, 227, 234
  death and sale of goods in
    Colerne, 190
  early life and James
    Woodforde incident, 188
Bolingbroke, Lord, 72, 184
Bolivar, Simon, 271
Booth, Charles, 27
Bosworth, Joseph, 109, 124, 129,
  405, 406, 412
  and Stevenson & Allen and the
    Portuguese wine trade, 115
  early life and career, 115–16
  his account with Stevenson &
    Allen, 118

his executors, 117
his will, 116–18, 311
mysteries about him, 117
relationship with Abraham Culver, 117
the case in Chancery over his will, 118–21
Bosworth's property, 120, 127, 131, 137, 138, 140, 194, 311, 338, 342, 354, 361, 363
1734-1750, tenants and rents, 122
1760's, tenants and lettings, 159
1766-1826, tenants and rent, 301
1827/28, works, 302
1834, discussions leading up to Thomas Wedlake's tenancy, 361
Bourne, Sarah (Mistress), 363
allowed only two private day scholars, 274
her background and conditions of service, 273
Boyle, Robert, 22
Branfill, Andrew, 193
Braxton, Carter, 202
Brentwood School, Essex, endowments, 307
Brett, Rev'd John (of Dagenham), 40, 43, 60, 61
from Romford family, 39
letters to SPCK, 39, 62
British and Foreign School Society, 270, 272, 343, 351, 354, 364, 413
creation, 270
influence of in 19thC, 272
British Schools, 272
Brotherton, Joseph MP, 326
Brougham, Henry, 256, 259, 260, 265, 266, 267, 268, 269, 270, 306, 309, 325, 328, 335, 343, 360
1818 proposals to parliament on the funding of public education, 257
and *Edinburgh Review*, 256
his background, 256
his character, 261
his plans for public education as outlined to Parliament, 1820, 262–66
on the defeat of his Education of the Poor Bill, 269
Brummell, Beau, 285
Butler, Charles, 339, 412
Carruthers, James Marson (Treasurer), 288, 309, 311, 324, 411, 412
background and election as Treasurer, 294
Catholic Emancipation Act 1829, 272
Chadwell Heath, 11
Charity Commissioners
survey of every parish in England and Wales, 261
Charity School at Romford
1710/11, opening, 39
1811, centenary thoughts, 239
1818, proposal it become a National School, 254
accounts
1710-1713, 53
1710-1718, 41–46
1718-1727, 78
1727-1734, 107
1729, for building the School House, 93
1734-1759 (summary), 137
1735 (deficit), 124
1735-1746, 125
1750 (return to surplus), 130
1751-1753, 131

1759-1762, 147
1760's, 158–62
1771-1776, collection of subscriptions, 177
1776, Graves' 1st reconciliation, 178
1781, Graves' 2nd reconciliation, 180
1796, Graves 3rd reconciliation, 195
1803-1804 (analysis), 216
1803-1813, 246
1803-1813, changes in income, 278
1803-1835, reconciliations, 292
1807-1822, 277–79
1820, income from investments, 279
1827, income, 247
1827, income and expenditure, 316
1827, income compared with that of 1813, 314
1831, financial holdings of trustees, 338
1833, case in Chancery, cost of, 342
1833, projected finances of National School, 330
1833, revenue and expenditure, 330
investment in consols, etc., 247
late payments of rents and legacies, 196
legacies and donations recorded in the church, 80
legacies, tax on, 315
purchase of consols during French wars, 198
admission and discharge
1733, ages of children attending, 104
1760's, ages of children admitted, 156
1760's, reasons for discharge of children, 156
1762, revision of policy and procedures, 150
1769, boys' education reduced by three years, 157
1770-1800, ages and reasons for pupils leaving, 183
1780's, pupils discharged for absenteeism, etc, 183
1811, increase in number of boys to 45, 236
1813, reasons for admitting additional pupils, 247
1820's, response of trustees to demand for places, 280
1821, age of discharge unified at 13, 275
1823, three year schooling rule, 280
1827, change to four year rule, 306
1833, demand for places, 323
1833, pupil numbers, 348
attendance
1730-1733, 102
1817, regulations, 253
1824, perennial issue of distance for Hornchurch children, 290
book purchases
1711-1726, 62–63
1766, 1767, 162
1825, Bibles and Prayer Books, 292

books given to leavers and
  apprentices, 135, 157
changes of clergy and
  treasurers, 1765-1770, 163
charity sermons
  1718, 59
  1721, 1724, 78
  1729 and 1730, 107
  1755, 138
  1762-1768, 158
  1778, 1780, and 1781,
    expenses, 179
  1804, 216, 217
  1810-1820, 279
  1820's, 316
church attendance
  1780's, expectations, 182
  1817, expectations, 252
clothes
  1711, provision and costs,
    59
  1738-1742, policy, 125
  1762, policy revision, 151
  1763, changes in provision,
    155
  1764-1802, policy and
    provision, 159
  1768 onwards, purchase of
    buckles, 161
  1770's and 1780's, policy,
    181
  1806, policy, 217
  1814, for additional pupils,
    247
  1825, provided for every
    child, 292
  1825, trowsers replace
    breeches, 292
  1827 and 1831, 317
  1832, 321
  1833, insufficient funds to
    repair, 330
curriculum

  1794, for girls, to make
    them 'Good Servants',
    190
  1817, girls writing and boys
    cyphering, 253
infants' school, 360, 413
  first mention of, 355
masters and mistresses
  changes of, 1741-1759,
    135–37
  masters' duties as parish
    clerk, 140
  one year contracts, 212
  private students, 208, 210,
    212, 231, 274
myth of School's foundation in
  1728, 93
National Society
  1834 affiliation, 349
pupils
  1740's, work and discipline,
    135
  1780's & 1790's, experience
    of school, 184
  1780's & 1790's, mortality
    of, 183
  1817, holiday entitlement,
    253
  1825, mortality, 292
  and Romford Market, 318
Scheme of 1833, 333–38
  commentary on provisions,
    341–42
  first meeting under new
    Scheme, 347–49
  the 14 clauses, 339
  the 18 appointed trustees,
    338
  trustees proposed changes
    to, 333
school land and buildings
  1728, building the School
    House, 91

1728, purchase of land for the School House, 88
1734, building the Master's House, 98
1813, building work to enable expansion in pupil numbers, 246
1829, provision of kitchen in master's house, 317
1832, mistress's garden, 317
1834, plan of proposed Boys' National Schoolroom, 353
statues on the school facade, 97

Spurgin, Thomas, and his £100 legacy, 197

subscribers
1710/11, estimate of number, 45
1833, great increase in new, 347

subscriptions
1710, size of, 44
1800, decline in by, 216
1806, action on unpaid, 218
1833, decision on, 329

town collections
1771, John Tyler inaugurates, 166
1771-1794, summary, and possibly shop based in 1790's, 196
1777, revival of, 179
1780, and Rev'd Harry Fletcher, 188
1803, decline by, 216
1810-1820, 279
1813, 247
1827, had ceased by, 315

treasurer
1769-1771, changes of, 174
1826-1831, changes of, 309

development of role, 275
election of, 332

trustees
1710, how management differed from SPCK model, 42
1710, the first trustees, 46
1718, resolution on apprenticeships, 68
1726-1734, election of, 86
1730-1834, support from four important families, 172
1740's, inertia, 126
1742-1759, 17 appointed, 147
1759, 6 October meeting, 137–39
1762, election of 10, 147
1762, reforms, 153
1762-1771, reforms implemented, 158
1769, resolution to dispense with requirement for clergy presence at meetings, 163
1769-1808, meetings, 250
1770's, change in social class of, 179
1770's, meetings under Thomas Graves, 176
1776, major recruitment of, 179
1776-1778, 12 or more recruited, 178
1817, reforms, 252
1817, resolution to publicly examine scholars, 253
1820-1823, lost deeds, 280
1821, administrative changes, 274
1822-1827, administration and meetings, 276

1826, lost deeds, 305
1831, case in Chancery, 312
1833, record attendance at meeting, 327
secretary Mr Wadeson, 321, 331, 342, 361, 362
Charity School Movement
and religious belief, 26
decline after 1730, 111
decline after 1730, SPCK figures, 112–13
German influence on, 28
charity schoolboy in 18thC fact and fiction, 187
charity schools, 25
as bulwark against Catholicism, 25
clothing, 32
costs in 1700, 25
costs of running (SPCK figures), 33
evidence of contribution to increased national literacy, 240
growth in numbers 1692 to 1700, 29
in Essex 1707 - 1711, 34
in Essex 1711-1726, 111
types of children to be admitted, 31
Charles I, 8
Charlotte, Princess
arrival in England, 142
visits Romford on wedding day, 142
Chelmsford Chronicle, 8, 9, 158, 188, 190, 209, 227, 299, 313, 320, 327, 328, 348, 350, 360, 362, 364, 407, 410, 413
1833 correspondence on Charity School at Romford and James Macarthy, 324
on plans for new Romford National School, 350
Christ's Hospital
and teaching of mathematics, 400
Church of England
pluralities and non-resident clergy, 282
reputation in years before and after Waterloo, 282
Church Vestry
evolution of secular powers, 14
Civil War of 1640's
and the growth of literacy, 21
clandestine marriages, 140
Cleland, John and *Fanny Hill*, 184, 185
Cloke, Dorothy (Mistress), 190, 191, 208, 253
death, 209
Cobbett, William MP, 344, 345, 357, 413
Speech in Parliament, *Rural Rides and Political Register*, 344
Colenso, John (Bishop of Natal)
text books on algebra (1841) and arithmetic (1843), 145
Coleridge, Samuel Taylor, 245
Collier, Stephen, 9, 69, 99, 173, 302, 407, 412
Colls, William, 338, 412
Commissioners for Charities, 326
Comyns, John, 126, 128, 147, 166, 167, 219
Comyns, Richard, 131, 161, 167, 168, 174, 175, 176, 408
Connaught Watchman, 300
Coope, Octavius, 220
Cooper, John, 338, 412

Coram, Thomas. *See* Foundling Hospital
Corbets Tey, 211
Corporation and Test Acts, 243
Cotton family, 170
Court of Chancery, 89, 90, 119, 167, 219, 302, 303, 307, 308, 312, 332, 349, 361, 363, 412
and *Bleak House*, 302
Cousin, Professor, 333, 335, 336
Cove, Charles, 287, 339, 359, 360
Cove, James, 82, 287, 411, 412
background, 287
Cranham, 2, 90, 165
Croly, Rev'd Dr George (of Romford), 328, 329, 353
background, 328
Cromwell, Oliver
Lord Protector, 12, 399
Culver, Abraham, 117, 118, 119, 147, 406
currency debasement in the 18thC, 177
curriculum
in the 17thC, 21
in the charity schools, 27
Dagenham, 11, 39, 44, 71, 82, 134, 148, 151, 166, 167, 172, 174, 218, 240, 285, 299, 327, 403, 407
Dame Schools, 20, 24, 261, 265, 266
Dame Tipping School
foundation, 112
history 1724-1833, 248
Danton and Desmoulins
guillotined, 191
de Jersey MD, Peter Frederick, 339
Dearsly, William, 147, 148, 160
Debuke, Thomas (Treasurer), 148, 174
elected Treasurer, 163
Defoe, Daniel, 10, 399, 400, 401
Delamare, Abraham, 178, 211
Delamare, Peter, 275, 411, 412
Derham, Rev'd William, 13, 60, 73, 74, 75, 76, 404
Dissenting academies, 22
Domesday Book, 4
Dutton, Richard
entertains Princess Charlotte, 143
East India Bond, 91, 127, 130
East India Company, 131, 184, 185, 202, 204, 217, 218, 227
Edinburgh Review, 243, 256, 259
Education Acts in the 1640's, 21
education of middle class boys
and Gentlemen's Boarding Schools, 178, 211
Edward the Confessor, 1, 2, 4, 7, 16
elementary schools
in the 17thC, 22
Elsee, John, 299, 320, 331, 411, 412
background, 294, 295
end of friendship with Robert Surridge, 295
his pamphlet, *'The Late Romford Bank'* on the collapse of the Romford Agricultural Bank, 294–99
pity for old Joyner, 296
Essex Road
1710, from Romford to London, 10
1760's, excellent condition of Essex toll road, 144
Established Church. *See* Church of England
Estcourt, Thomas MP, 344
Evans, Colonel MP, 345

Everett, Rev'd William (of Romford), 250, 251, 275, 283, 286, 287, 292, 312, 316
  his death, 306
Ewart, William MP, 356
Fellenberg, M
  criticism of Bell and Lancaster's methods, 266
Felsted Grammar School, 248, 276
Ferry, Jules
  and the French education system, 337
Fletcher, Rev'd Harry, 166, 179, 188, 196
Fletcher, Rev'd Phillip (of Romford), 106, 118, 119, 121, 126, 127, 188
Ford, William (of Dagenham), 327
Ford, William (trustee), 226, 228
Forster Education Act 1870, 225
Founders, Worshipful Company of, 49
Foundling Hospital, 113–14
  and fostering of children in Romford and Hornchurch, 113
  changing admission policies and the life chances of an unwanted child in the 1760's, 154
Fox, Charles James, 194
Fox, Joseph, 244
France, 4, 13, 115, 129, 137, 191, 192, 225, 240, 293, 333, 335, 336, 337, 399, 400
Francis, Samuel, 339
Franklin, Caleb, 100, 101, 187
Freckleton, Thomas, 44
Frederick Barbarossa, 4
Freemasonry, 226
Freemasons
  'The Prestonian Lodge of Perfect Friendship', 226
French Revolutionary Wars, 192, 198
Frisken, Johnnie, 202, 204
Fry, Elizabeth, 285
George II, 113, 129, 142
George III, 142, 154, 252, 407
George IV, 239, 283, 285
  1820 accession, 283
Giddy, David MP, 223
Gilman, Elizabeth, 161
Gilman, Rev'd Dr John, 125
Gilman, Thomas (Junior) (Treasurer), 49, 58, 80, 81, 82, 84, 85, 87, 89, 107, 161
  his death, 105
  resigns as Treasurer, 85
Gilman, Thomas (Senior), 15, 18, 40, 44, 48, 49, 54, 70, 75, 105, 125, 144, 166, 219, 402
Glorious Revolution, 25
Graves, Lieutenant-Colonel Benjamin, 218, 339, 359
Graves, Thomas (Treasurer), 174, 175, 176, 178, 179, 195, 197, 199, 213, 219, 228, 234, 277, 281
  financial policy in time of war, 217
  resigns, 218
Great Freeze of 1709 and its consequences, 13
Great Reform Act of 1832, 282, 332, 333
Great Waltham, 231, 232, 233, 236, 265, 276
Greenwich Observatory, 22
Grenville, George (Prime Minister), 199
Grove, Thomas Green (Master), 143, 144, 146, 148, 149, 150,

152, 153, 157, 160, 175, 176, 183, 197, 210, 211, 234, 253
appointment and background, 145
first master to receive a pension, 209
his salary, 208
marriage to Abigail, 146
marriage to Rebekah, 150
revised terms of service and salary, August 1762, 148–50
Hall, Very Rev'd Dr John, 1
Hambleton, Clement (bricklayer), 91, 301, 404
Hammond, Israel, 99, 100, 101, 186, 187
Hancock, Mr, 359, 360, 412
Handel, George Frederick and 'The Messiah'. *See* Foundling Hospital
Hardwicke, Lord Chancellor, 129, 140, 146, 168
judgement in case over Bosworth's will, 120
Hare Hall, 169, 408
Harle, Captain John, 94, 118, 404
Harle, John (Junior), 164
early life, 148
Harold Hill, 75, 252, 404
Harris, Rev'd William (of Hornchurch), 69, 82, 83, 100, 147, 162
Harvey, Daniel MP, 306, 326
Hastings, Warren, 185
Havering, London Borough of, 2
Havering-atte-Bower, 2, 8, 9, 11, 111, 112, 151, 173, 234, 249
Havering-atte-Bower School. *See* Dame Tipping School
Hawes, Benjamin MP, 356
Haynes, Richard, 55, 60, 87

Heaphy, Mr (tenant of Bosworth's), 301, 361, 362
allows property to become dilapidated 1825, 292
Herring, Archbishop Thomas background, 129
portrait, 130
record in the *Account Book* of his sermon, 128
Hibernian Society in London, 257
Hide, Frisweed, 64, 65, 69
her will, 65
Hide, Mary, 65, 67, 68, 69, 70, 81, 102, 123, 126, 194, 403
death, 66
her will, 64
Hide, Richard, 64, 219, 403
Hide, William, 69, 88, 89, 90, 99, 126, 311, 405
Hillatt, Simon (Treasurer), 103, 107, 109, 118, 119, 123, 126, 138, 363
Hills, James (carpenter), 86, 91, 404
Hogarth, William. *See* Foundling Hospital
Holland, James, 160, 175, 176, 178, 196, 301, 311
Hopkins, Rev'd John (of Romford), 163, 165, 199, 251
Hopkinson, Mary (Mistress), 76, 77, 85, 96, 191
Hopkinson, Samuel (Master), 40, 41, 50, 54, 55, 56, 60, 61, 77, 97
death of, 75
Horncastle, Mr (tenant of Bosworth's), 122, 131, 132, 138, 140, 147, 158, 159, 160, 161
Hotchkis, Elizabeth, 72, 106

Hotchkis, Rev'd James (of Romford), 10, 15, 18, 40, 44, 45, 46, 47, 48, 49, 60, 70, 71, 72, 73, 78, 81, 85, 89, 93, 103, 107, 137, 145, 167, 251, 363, 402, 403
death, burial and will, 105
house in Hornchurch Lane. See Bosworth's property
Hume, Joseph MP, 336, 343, 344
Hunter Hall Farm Estate, Dagenham, 285, 299
Hylands House, Chelmsford, 168, 408
Ind & Coope, 220
Ind, Edward (Treasurer), 218, 219, 220, 221, 225, 228, 229, 248, 277, 279, 285, 292, 311, 314, 328, 338, 339, 360, 412
appointment as Treasurer and his background, 219
appointment as trustee, 216
assignee in Romford Agricultural Bank bankruptcy, 298
resignation as Treasurer, 273
Inglis, Sir Robert MP, 336, 344
Irish Charter schools, 257
Jacobs, William, his legacy, 249
belated discovery of documents, 293
dispute resolved, 286–90
possible reasons for decision over, 291
Johnson, Captain Thomas (Treasurer), 127, 128, 130, 147
Jones, M G
and the 18th Century Charity Schools, 400
her book *The Charity School Movement*, 27, 69
Joyner, Joseph, 284, 285, 299

his bankruptcy and will, 299
lifestyle as successful banker, 285
Joyner, Joseph Sumpner, 284, 285, 300
his career after bankruptcy, 300
Keith, Rev'd Alexander
and marriages in the Mayfair Chapel, 146
Kielmansegge, Count Frederick, 144
Lancaster, Joseph, 242, 243
background, 205
expelled from the Society which bore his name, 270
his book *Improvements in Education*, 206
his difficult personality, 270
his later career and death, 271
Last, Joseph, 275, 283, 289, 292, 313, 359, 360, 411, 412
his background, 275
Leith, Rev'd Lockhart (of South Ockendon), 213, 226, 228, 230, 231
Lennard, Thomas Barrett, 213, 232
Letch, Joseph, 147, 196
Levett, Rev'd Henry, 72, 81, 89
Liverpool, Lord (Prime Minister)
support for Church of England, 282
Locke, John, 22, 23
Locksmith, John, 43, 213
collecting overdue subscriptions, 80
paid for advertising Charity Sermons 1724, 79
London
Aldgate, 201, 204, 205, 208, 405

Freedom of the City
  Admission Papers, 101, 134
Freemen of the City, 49
Gordon Riots, 192
Ratcliffe, 117, 120, 186
Southwark, 201, 205, 208, 223
Spitalfields, 186
St Stephen Walbrook church, 328
the city in 1710, 10
Whitechapel, 11, 12, 13, 79, 243
London Corresponding Society 1792, 193
London Workhouse of 1698, 23
Macarthy, James (Treasurer), 309, 324, 328, 339, 347, 348, 349, 350, 352, 353, 358, 359, 360, 363, 364, 412
  1833 reply to anonnymous correspondent in *Chelmsford Chronicle*, 322
  application form and letter to National Society re-funding for National School, with commentary, 351
  background, 294
Macklin, Thomas, 226, 228
Madras city, 131, 201, 202, 204, 208, 227, 406
'Madras system', 203, 206, 242, 244, 245, 246, 254, 280
Manchester Free Grammar School endowments, 325
Manors of Havering, 7
  Dagnams and Cockerels, 75, 219
  Gidea Hall, 131, 145
  Marks, 11, 71, 72, 219, 403
  Mawneys, 161, 167
  Nelmes, 64, 219, 403
  Pyrgo Park, 112, 249

Married Women's Property Act 1870, 55
Marshall, Daniel (Master), 76, 77, 97, 98, 104, 107, 121, 136, 148, 149, 153
Marshall, Elizabeth (Mistress), 136, 137, 149, 150, 160
  death, 175
Marshall, James, 178, 180, 196, 219
Martin, Professor Ged, 235, 252, 399, 408
Mary Hide Charity, 68, 69, 82, 84, 99, 102, 139, 166, 181
  apprenticeships 1720 - 1726, 82
  apprenticeships 1727-1735, 99
  apprenticeships 1739-1758, 133–35
  background of recipient apprentices, 100
  inertia of trustees in 1740's, 125
Mary Hide Trust. See Mary Hide Charity
Mashiter, Octavius, 171, 289, 313, 328, 330, 338, 339, 360, 361, 411, 412
Mashiter, Thomas, 147, 170, 171, 294, 331, 339
  assignee in Romford Agricultural Bank bankruptcy, 298
Mashiter, William, 171
Meakins, Richard (Treasurer), 62, 103, 118, 119, 123, 125, 126, 186
Meiklejohn, Professor
  on Bell's personality, 246
  on difference between Bell's system and existing practice, 204
Methodists, 164, 243, 272, 297, 320

influence of Methodism on working classes, 282
meeting at Rainham Hall, 164
Mildmay, Carew Harvey, 44, 59, 71, 77, 79, 80, 81, 184, 219
Miles, William, 226, 292, 411, 412
Milligan, John, 40, 48, 49, 54, 79, 84, 85, 87, 105
Milton, John
 and educational reform in 1640's, 21
monitorial system, 205
Moore, John (Master), 136, 137, 139, 140, 149, 153, 212, 229
 attitude, behaviour and dismissal, 141
Moore, Mary, 141
Morning Herald, 358
Morpeth, Lord MP, 344, 356
Moulton, Thomas, 91, 98, 404, 405
Mountjoux, 4
Mountnessing, 11, 49
Murray, Mr MP, 345
National Schools, 241, 322
 examples in East London in 1834, 359
 growth of movement by 1816, 254
 numbers in 1833, 327
National Society, 244, 246, 248, 254, 291, 327, 343, 349, 350, 351, 352, 354, 355, 358, 359, 360, 364, 413
 1811, foundation and aims, 244
 1834 financial offer to school, 350
 Central School, Westminster, 354
 influential supporters, 245
 rapid growth in first year, 245

Wigram, Rev'd J C (Secretary), 349, 350, 351, 355, 358
 correspondence with James Macarthy, 354
Neave, Sir Richard Digby, 76, 288, 290, 338, 411
Neave, Sir Thomas, 76
New College, Oxford, 7, 9, 38, 48, 72, 127, 162, 165, 167, 177, 188, 189, 199, 227, 251, 287, 306, 328, 402
 condition of the College in early 19thC, 251
 land ownership in Hornchurch parish in 19thC and 20thC, 288
Newman, Richard Harding, 339
Newton, Sir Isaac, 22, 403
nonconformists and nonconformity, 25, 243
 and industrialisation, 242
North Ockendon, 47, 48, 71, 73, 402, 406
O'Connell, Mr MP, 335, 336
Oglethorpe, General James, 90
Oporto and the Quinta De Villar d'Allen, 114
Paine, James, 169
Paine, Tom, 193, 194
parish clerk, 15, 43, 233, 265
Parliament
 1803, Parochial Schools Bill, 221
 1807, 'Abolition of the Slave Trade Act', 222
 1807, Parochial Schools Bill, 225
 1816, 'Parliamentry Committee on the Education of the Lower Orders', 256
 1818, 1819

Charitable Foundations Bill, 258
1818, Motion for a Committee on the Education of the Lower Orders, 257
1819, debate on Charitable Foundations Bill, 259–60
1820, Brougham's Education of the Poor Bill, 260–69
1833, debate on report of Committee of Supply, Education, 343–47
1833, debates on introducing a national system of education, 326, 333–38
1834, debate on report of Committee of Supply, Education, 355–58
pauperism in England in 1700, 23
Peel, Sir Robert, 336
Pestalozzi, Johann Heinrich, 266
Petits estate, Romford, 168
Petre, Lord, 169, 364
Ping, John, 275, 412
Poor Law Acts
  1552, 1601 and 1834, 14
Pope Alexander III, 4
Pope Boniface IX, 7
Pope, Alexander (poet), 71, 184, 328
population numbers
  1670, the Royal Liberty, 8
  1700-1800, the Royal Liberty, 3
  1722, Stratford, 12
  1801, Romford and Hornchurch, 179
  1801-1920, Havering-atte-Bower, 249
  1826, Romford and Hornchurch, 291
  1831, the Royal Liberty, 323
  2011, London Borough of Havering, 2, 399
Potter, Richard MP, 325
Pratt, Thomas (Treasurer), 86, 88, 89, 107, 119
Prayer Book
  and Catechism, 24
Pricklove, John, 56, 60, 85
  death, 84
Prior, James, 1
property in Hornchurch Lane. *See* Bosworth's property
Prussia, 218, 333, 336, 337
public education
  1820, estimate of extent of by, 261
  1820, extent and distribution of schools, 261
  and 19thC sectarian competition, 272
Pyle, Rev'd Francis (of Hornchurch), 89, 103, 106, 119, 126, 138, 147
Quakers, 207, 244, 270, 271, 272, 404
Queen Anne's Bounty, 54, 55
Queen Caroline
  Henry Brougham and her trial, 268
Rainham, 2, 94, 147, 148, 160, 163, 243, 273, 284, 407
Rainham Hall, 94, 148, 164
Rathbone, Rev'd John Egerton (of Romford), 309, 328, 338, 346
  his backgound, 306
Redman, 'Citizen' John, 193, 194, 195, 216, 247, 409
  personality, background, wealth and will, 193
Reynell, Rev'd William (of Hornchurch, absentee), 165, 188, 189, 227

Reynolds, Sir Joshua. *See* Foundling Hospital
Rider, Honourable Mrs Anne, 75, 76, 108
Ridley, Rev'd Glocester, 127, 128, 147, 162
Ridley, Rev'd James, 148, 163, 164, 204
Roberts, Rev'd Thomas (of Hornchurch), 10, 38, 40, 41, 45, 46, 47, 48, 54, 70, 72, 73, 75, 81, 105, 106, 401
Robinson, Edward, 121, 122, 127
Roebuck, John MP, 333, 337, 343, 344
Roman Catholic Relief Act, 364
Roman Catholics, 226, 242, 268, 270
Romford
  1177-1710, history, 4
  1710, appearance, 11
  1760's, the life of the town, 145
  1787, building of the new workhouse, 198
  1795, building of the Barracks, 192
  1814, Enclosure legislation, 252
  1834, condition of town, 352
  Court House, 11, 86, 87, 145
  Regency period and change in town's character, 283
  Romford Common and battle of Waterloo, 252
  visit of Frederick, Duke of York in 1808, 252
Romford Agricultural Bank, 313, 320, 331
  early success, 285
  its collapse, 292–94
  similar origins of country banks, 284

  the Poyais bubble, 293
Romford inns
  'Blucher's Head', 252, 404
  'Cock and Bell', 11, 88, 122, 127, 146, 174, 175, 178, 209, 218
  'Dolphin', 169, 408
  'Duke of Wellington', 252
  'Golden Lyon', 195
  'King's Arms', 137, 140, 176
  'King's Head', 58
  'Lamb', 126, 174, 175, 177
  'Lion', 231
  'Star Inn', 220
  'Swan', 11, 70, 228
  'White Hart', 93, 176
Romford National School, 364
Romford Ringers' Book, The, 236
  ringing for Charity Sermons to be paid for, 239
Romford Savings Bank, 253, 255, 277, 313, 314
  1818, depositors and investments, 255
  1828, Act and its effect on, 313
  1832 and 1833, trustees and affairs, 313
  1833, socio-economic profile of depositors, 314
  Oswald Adams, actuary, 255
'rotten boroughs', 256
Royal Liberty
  and ecclesiastical plurality, 164–66, 188–90
  early history, 3
  High Steward, 331
  long standing parochial dispute, 8
Royal Society, 13, 22
Russell, William, 71, 147

Salter, John (Master), 140, 141, 142, 143, 149, 153
  sudden and mysterious departure, 143
Sandford, William (Treasurer), 15, 18, 43, 45, 48, 58, 105, 108
  accounting methods, 41, 43
Saunders, John & Susannah (Master & Mistress)
  and private boarders, 212
  resignations, 212
Saunders, John (Master), 209, 215
  appointment and salary, 209
Saunders, Susannah (Mistress), 211, 274
  appointment and salary, 210
savings bank movement
  differences between Scotland and England, 255
  its early history, 254
  Rose's Act and growth of movement, 255
Saxony, 333, 337, 401
School Boards, 273
schoolmasters
  and the sacremental test, 268
Schools in the Liberty and England before 1700, 20
Scotland, 202, 224, 254, 255, 257, 261, 337, 356
Shadwell, Mr, 302, 303, 308
Skeate, Mr, 39, 40, 60
Skinner, Samuel, 82, 83, 92, 99, 100, 101, 176, 178, 186, 187, 194, 196
  his life experience and his will, 186
Smith, Adam, 222
Smith, William MP, 224
Social inequality
  and 'All things bright and beautiful', 26
  and Biblical teaching, 26
Society for Constitutional Information 1791, 193
'Society for Promoting the Lancasterian System for the Education of the Poor', 244
South Ockendon, 73, 75, 211, 213, 226, 240
Southey, Robert, 245, 272
  on Bell's personality, 245
SPCK, 29, 30, 34, 38, 39, 40, 42, 44, 45, 50, 52, 53, 54, 55, 57, 59, 60, 62, 63, 66, 73, 86, 100, 111, 112, 149, 162, 201, 223, 224, 225, 242, 244, 263, 292, 311, 332, 335, 341, 401
  1712 *Annual Account* and evidence of abuse of educational charities, 258
  An Account of the Charity Schools, 29
  and blueprint for charity schools, 30
  and parish clergy, 28
  argues for children doing useful work, 52
  charity school children to be aged 7-12, 104
  curriculum and how it should be delivered, 50
  formation and early work, 28
  on management of charity schools, 42
  qualities expected in a charity school Master, 50
  Samuel Hopkinson as model Master, 49
  the role of Corresponding Members, 37
Speed, Rev'd Robert (of Hornchurch), 162, 163, 164
Spring Rice, Thomas MP, 356
St Bernard, 4

St Paul's Cathedral, 1, 11
Stacey, Rev'd Daniel (of
    Hornchurch), 313, 328, 338,
    339, 347, 348, 350, 359
    background, 328
Stanniland, Mary, 116, 117, 118
Staynor, Thomas, 97
Steele, Sir Richard
    on Charity Schools, in *The
    Spectator'*, 36
Sterry, Wasey, 216, 286, 305,
    328, 362
Stourbridge Fair, 33
Stracy, Mary (Mistress), 85, 96
Stracy, William (Master), 77, 85,
    86, 97, 404
Suffolk Chronicle
    and bankruptcy of Joyner,
    Surridge and Joyner, 298
Sumpner, Edward, 148, 159, 174,
    175
Surridge, North (Junior), 283,
    284
Surridge, North (Senior), 284
    his death in 1812, 285
Surridge, Robert (Treasurer),
    275, 285, 291, 292, 295, 296,
    307, 309, 411
    and bankruptcy in early 19thC,
    294
    career after his bankruptcy,
    299
    the pious methodist, 285
    elected Treasurer and his
    Methodism, 283
    final meeting as Treasurer and
    his disgrace, 293
    his background and early
    career, 284
    subject of John Elsee's
    sarcasm and scorn, 296, 297
Talbot, Roger, 246, 247, 277

Test and Corporation Acts, 242,
    309
    1828 repeal of Test Acts, 272
Thomas, Rev'd John (of Great
    Burstead), 324
    responds to attacks on James
    Macarthy in *Chelmsford
    Chronicle*, 1833, 324
Thorndon Hall, Brentwood, 169
Trimmer, Mrs Sarah, 207, 243,
    244
Truston, Mr, 314, 359
Turton, Thomas MP, 223, 224
Tyler, John (Senior), 126
Tyler, John (Treasurer), 126,
    161, 166, 167, 171, 175, 176,
    178, 179, 196, 218, 247, 281,
    305, 314, 317, 412
Unitarians, 272
Upminster, 2, 3, 13, 48, 60, 73,
    80, 163, 165, 193, 194, 211,
    251, 409
Vestry Book, 2, 15, 16, 28, 39,
    402
vestry meeting
    of 5th September 1710, 16
Wadeson, Mr. See Charity
    School at Romford:trustees
    secretary
Waghorn, Charles, 178, 199, 218
Waghorn, Thomas, 217, 226, 228,
    265
    appointment as trustee and
    clothing provider, 216
Waine, Rev'd Stephen (of
    Romford), 2
Walker, Rev'd John (of
    Hornchurch), 119, 286, 287,
    294, 309, 313, 328, 411
    background, 287
Walkingame, Francis, and *The
    Tutor's Assistant*, 145
Wallinger, John, 168, 169

Wallinger, John Arnold, 169, 175, 180
Wankford, William, 175
Watts, Robert, 38
Wedlake, Thomas, 288, 308, 338, 361, 362, 363, 411, 412
background, 308
Weller, Alexander (Treasurer 1718-1723), 58, 77, 78, 80, 81, 82, 88, 89, 90, 94, 265
Westminster Abbey, 1
Westminster School, 184, 185
Whalebone and highway robbery, 12
Whetham, Rev'd Thomas (of North Ockendon), 71
Whitbread, Samuel, 193, 221, 222, 225, 230, 233, 244, 268, 326, 335, 343
proposed new Poor Law, 221
White, Jane (Mistress), 197
her appointment, 175
sudden death, 190
Whole Duty of Man, The, 51, 62, 63, 135, 158, 162, 402
Wilberforce, William, 244, 260, 285
Wilks, John MP, 325
William of Wykeham, 7, 288
Willson, John (Treasurer), 104, 273, 275, 279, 283, 292, 312
window tax, 56, 161, 177, 180
Wiseman, Rev'd Dr John, 234, 235
Wolfe, General James
victory and death at Quebec, 137
Woodforde, Rev'd James, 189, 408
Wordsworth, William, 245
workhouses, 24, 25, 198, 279

Milton Keynes UK
Ingram Content Group UK Ltd.
UKHW011858231223
434905UK00002B/18